The Cross Tarot

Owen Knight

LeftHandPress
New Orleans, Louisiana USA

Contents Copyright © 2016 T.H. Owen Knight

Format Copyright © 2016 Left Hand Press
A subsidiary of Black Moon Publishing, LLC

LeftHandPress.com

Design and layout by
Jo Bounds of Left Hand Press

Tarot Paintings © 2016 Tracey Buchwald

Star Illustration on Dedication page by
April Foster

ISBN: 978-0692623374

United States • United Kingdom • Europe • Australia • India

Contents

VOLUME I

From Piscean Tarot Into Changes	11
Tarot Trump Cards	12
Cause and Effect	14
Thoughts on Prediction	15
The Cross Tarot: The Symbol	29
Making Changes	31
Elements	32
Elemental Cards	33
Environmental Cards	48
Flags	50
Vegetation Influence Along the Path	51
Numbers Related to Trees	52
The Trees	53
Assigning Value	54

THE TRUMP CARDS

0 - Fool	56
I - Warrior	60
II - Flower	62
III - Juggler	66
IV - Crystal	70
V - Lion	72
VI - Reaper	75
VII - Scale	77
VIII - Demon	80

IX - Archer 83
X - Horned Piper 85
XI - Cup Bearer 88
XII - Wave 90
XIII - Death 92
XIV - Craftsman 94
XV - Tower 96
XVI - Gaoler 99
XVII - Star 101
XVIII - Sun 104
XIX - Moon 106
XX - Teacher 108
XXI - Hanged Man 110
XXII - Strong 112
XXIII - Love 114
XXIV - Megalith 116
XXV - Magician 119

Path Finding Cards 126
Paths of Awareness 129
The Reading 131
Looking at the Path 135
The Winding Path of Progress 136
The Solar Wheel Spread 137
Three Octave Spread 138
Questions 139
The Big Picture 140
Trump Cards and Associated Plants 141

VOLUME II - THE FINER POINTS OF THE 26 TAROT TRUMP CARDS
I - Warrior 151
II - Flower 167
III - Juggler 184

IV - Crystal	251
V - Lion	265
VI - Reaper	280
VII - Scale	298
VIII - Demon	308
IX - Archer	323
X - Horned Piper	335
XI - Cup Bearer	351
XII - Wave	359
XIV - Craftsman	369
XV - Tower	373
XVI - Gaoler	383
XVII - Star	389
XVIII - Sun	396
XIX - Moon	403
XX - Teacher	418
XXI - Hanged Man	424
XXII - Strong	431
XXIII - Love	444
XXIV - Megalith	452
Bibliography	470

Dedicated to my personal Goddess
Ariadne

Tarot

"...To open windows to a world which is never quite what it seems."

—— Ussher

The Cross Tarot

Volume I

From Piscean Tarot Into Changes

For the most knowledgeable look at the path ahead, if one is using cards, the cards used would best be ones which would have the most keys into knowledge. As the meanings of symbols, and the feelings for them change; the symbols on the cards, in order to gain the most profound look at the path, might best be changed. As the symbol representing Satan might change from one which sends forth terror, to one which gives a feeling of amusement. Satan might have gained some humourous name, and this would have tended to lessen his power. And going into an age in which man relies more on reason, the flash of intuition might tend to be less strong, so the more accurate symbols might find their demand increasing as one advances into the coming age.

As a symbol which gives shock, Hades might now replace Satan.

Tarot Trump Cards

	Cards	Deities	Corresponding Trees
0	Fool		Birch
I	Warrior	Mars–Aurora–Aphrodite	Alder
II	Flower	Maia–Flora–Belinus	Hawthorn
III	Juggler	Mercury–Aeolus–Iaso	Oak
			Ash
IV	Crystal	Juno–Hera–Epona	Willow
V	Lion	Jupiter–Lamasthu–Lugus	Ash
			Oak
VI	Reaper	Ceres–Ops–Consus	Hazel
VII	Scale	Europa–Nemesis–Minos	Apple
			Plane tree
VIII	Demon	Hecate–Styx–Semele	Blackthorn
IX	Archer	Hyperion–Helios–Cheiron	Yew
X	Horned Piper	Pan–Gaea–Sylvanus	Holly
			Ivy
XI	Cup bearer	Uranus–Latona–Phaenon	Rowan
XII	Wave	Neptune–Tethys–Doris	Elder
XIII	Death		
XIV	Craftsman	Vulcan	Chestnut
XV	Tower	Athene–Rhea–Pallas	Plane tree
			Olive
			Apple
XVI	Gaoler	Hades–Hyacenthos–Minthe	Walnut
			Elder
XVII	Star	Ariadne–Astraea–Sirona	Fir
XVIII	Sun	Apollo	Laurel
XIX	Moon	Selene–Diana–Artemis	Elm
XX	Teacher	Minerva–Bellona–Brigantia	Beech

XXI	Hanged man	Eurydice	Linden
XXII	Strong	Hercules–Donar–Omphale	Poplar
			Oak
XXIII	Love	Venus–Eros–Cupid	Maple
			Vine
XXIV	Megalith	Saturn–Ophiuchus–Proserpine	Pine
			Juniper
XXV	Magician		

Cause and Effect

If it is going to rain, good chance you'd be programmed to pray for rain.

If it is not going to rain, it is more likely, you would not.

If rain is coming, you might need to pray for it.

Thoughts on Prediction

Predicting is made possible because all matter, great and small, is connected so that it forms a network of cause and effect relationships. The movement of one particle of matter would cause a ripple effect throughout the network. The whole Universe: units within units, the boundaries between them, arbitrary: is one united whole.

Sir William Temple has said: "Unless all existence is a medium of revelation, no particular revelation is possible."

One comes to understand the character of the powers which legislate and so, one might predict what events are to come.

Many systems of prediction do not take the total system of cause and effect relationships into consideration when predicting. It has only been in recent times that there has been much of a connection made between the need for an events occurrence and its being bound into the network of cause and effect. Not under Aries was this need much recognized. In place of complex physical connections, people would search for a connection of meanings. There was thought to be a need for a spiritual rightness of things. Spiritually needed events were believed to be announced, but not announced how they were to take place. It was thought, every road a person might take would lead to the needed event. These systems which rely heavily on insight depend on the help of a special kind of person in order to make them work.

As it comes to be realized that all matter is bound together in the cause and effect network, that the spiritual laws which provide insights are completely integrated with all other laws, it is more likely that the tools needed for solving a question about a coming event will be found. The more is understood about the wonderful and mysterious network, the more detailed and accurate forecasts are likely to be. It is a complex network, so insight and intuition would be needed if much benefit were to be gained from the use of other tools.

In predicting, some useful tools would be an understanding of the place and of the time, an understanding of the physical aspects of the environment, an understanding of what the spiritual needs would be, an understanding of the meanings and influences of shape, colour and number. One might get unexpected helps: insights, perhaps triggered by some odd thing, might seem to fall out of the blue.

With place and time, in predicting, it might help to have an understanding that all matter has a continuous cyclic movement and that the circle is a basic structure of the Universe. It has been said that the Universe is constructed of circles and triangles. Time plotted as circles can, with triangles, be formed to reveal past and present and future.

Circles of time range in size from smallest, to those which extend to the farthest reaches of matter, to time without end, and each object and action has a place in many circles. Prediction would be the discovery of where or when an event involving object and action is to take place. It could be aided by knowledge of circles.

Circles are driven by energies which conflict, so that circles move so as to gain a balance of energies. The striving for balance cause the objects and energies of a circle to change, change so that they meet a need. Often after the need is met, the energies evolve to where they harm more than they aid evolved needs; so, the striving for balance brings a counter change. Cyclic evolution of many objects and systems directly involved in human development move from archaic, to classic, to decadent. The Zodiacal cycles would fit this description as they rise to peak strength, decline. A cycle might begin with crude underdeveloped or undeveloped qualities, reach its top power and beauty; then, become encumbered with frivolous embellishment, elaboration and over development, so that it loses strength and declines. The trend, toward the end of a cycle, would be to less utility in decoration and to over statement of the classic strength. More and more features would become obsolescent and held to through habit and sentiment. Philosophers, as T.E. Hulme, have studied cycles of maturation and have used the knowledge gained in predicting futures.

There are many types of forces which affect the development of systems, cause births, maturations and dissolutions. Some of these are those associated with spirit; those related to form or shape; those connected to number; those related to colour; those related to physical motion, as the rotations causing night and day and the ones causing seasonal change; those associated with the struggle to live, to hold off death; those associated with pleasure or the desire to create; and those associated with the basic properties of matter.

The properties of matter are a major driving force of cycles. Each particle of matter is constructed of one or more of the four basic elements: earth, water, air and fire. According to alchemist Rulandus, each particle contains, in varying percentages, all the basic elements, and the percentages are in constant change. With the spiritual aspects of the elements, this might often be observed. As each particle is always in motion, each would be on its wheel of fortune.

Matter could be symbolized by the wheel and the wheel, divided into four parts, as the dividing lines would run to each of the directions: east, south, west and north. The Pythagorean placement of the basic elements, as given by Eugenius, puts fire in the east from where comes the sacred fire, the fire of the Sun. In the west, to balance fire, as a counter, would be water. Sunwise from fire, air would be in the south, and this, balanced by earth in the north. Air would blow toward the north where the Castle of Death is. Each element does not readily mix with the element which it counters, but in every case, will easily mix with those to either side; so the elements might go sunwise or counter sunwise. Sunwise would be with light, toward consciousness. Counter would be into darkness and the unconscious. The wheel represents wholeness, the resolution of the four elements: Jung. Isidorus also has a compass which has fire balanced by water: earth, by air.

The four elements: Earth is the name used to represent solids and the name symbolically represents the heaviest of the elements; though, it is not, in all cases, physically the heaviest; Water represents liquids and symbolically represents the heaviest of all but solids. Air represents gas and symbolically is lighter than all but fire. Fire is the lightest element.

In a cycle, the weights of the elements are a controlling factor as they are a chief influence over a wide variety of other forces, forces which controle a great range of qualities. The heavier the element, the more of its qualities are felt to relate to the female, and the lighter, the more relate to the male. Also, the two heavy elements represent the female and the two light, the male. Heavy elements, as a rule, influence toward imagination, artistic expression, dream, hallucination, fantasy, insight, inspiration, insanity, deception, romance, mystery and emotional natures. Light elements, as a rule, would influence toward mathmatics, logic, exact science, generosity, quickness, discovery, boldness, aggressiveness, clarity, rule of law, health, joy and penetration. The female elements relate to even numbers and the male, odd numbers. The odd numbers are an influence toward existence, life. The even numbers tend toward darkness and death. As Cavendish explains, the even numbers would have points which would pull away from their center leaving an enlarging hole which would give the feeling of falling into a dark abyss.

Particles of matter are ever in motion and as they shift, there would often be a change in influencing elements, in the elements which, in a cycle, would be an influence at a particular time and place. A knowledge of the influence would be an aid to prediction. In some cycles of time where prediction would be of interest, the influencing basic elements might be discovered and so, be of use. Help in discovering the influencing elements might be obtained from a study of the heavens and from the knowledge which past students of the heavens have obtained. The happenings in the heavens which would be most useful for prediction would be the movement of forms and elements which they spiritually represent. Heat, light and gravity are in calculations and meteors have brought predictions; but other than that, activities or objects on the physical stars would likely not be known. Spiritual activity in the heavens has, however, been seen to relate to earthly activity.

Philosophers of old identified, in the heavens, forms and objects which, among other forces, held forces associated with the elements. Along a belt which circles Earth is a series of these forms and twelve of these divide, between them, nearly all of the perimeter of the circle. And these forms alternate in representing, one, the spiritual aspects of a male element; the next, a female element. As the forms circle, shifts in influence would take place. These twelve forms are known to affect activities on Earth; especially, those related to the two large circles which are, each, divided into twelve sections plus a small left over. Each of the twelve sections is named for one of the twelve forms. And the two circles: one, the circle of the year; two, the circle of the ages. Each age covers about 2150 years. The forms, as they each contain a formation of stars, are constellations.

In the great circle of the ages, as scholars such as T.D. Worthen have shown, the activities of each age have related to the significant element of its constellation. As each constellation moves into and through its age, it slowly develops its strength, passes its peak, then fades; its power and influence being replaced by the incoming constellation.

Among the stars, one might see how the sinking of a constellation related to sinking actions which might seem to have pulled it down and, through actions related to the sign, or constellation, pulled in the next age. Over the last ten thousand years, ages have been shown to relate to the spiritual weights of their constellation, then to change as the constellation moved on. Under the constellation Leo the element was fire. The male was important. Strong animal hunter protectors set the example and deities had these animal attributes. Cancer replaced Leo, brought in the influence of a heavy element. Man began growing things. Women and children were needed and men's part in getting children wasn't generally recognized. Then as Cancer sailed on, the Mother Goddess became less featured. To protect crops, warriors and battle leaders were needed and developing city states needed men to govern them. But the states grew and became difficult to govern. The instability became noticed also in the heavens. The North Star had slipped out of place, had left a hole out of which came monsters from the Underworld, one of which, a great snake, defeated gods and became a threat to mankind. The Earth Goddess was called on to protect the lands. However, as battle forces grew in power, the Goddess was thought to have failed. The Sacred Ox of the Goddess was sacrificed, was sent to the Underworld. Slowly, gods of logic and science came into power. And this was begun in the time of the Fire Sign, Aries; and under its influence, advances were made in mathmatics and other sciences. And central governments came to be organized and strong. And gods were praised because they gave order and protection. The Pantheon of Gods was male led, led by a respected father; but, as Polybius and other classic authors write, the Pantheon, as a unit, was much feared. This tended to unite populations. And from Lucretius, there was a balance of deities for birth and of those against life. Pleasure balanced against the punishments and mysterious Terrors of Hades. By this, populations were kept in check. And people in general believed that there were powerful gods keeping order and they were conspicuously gods. And, according to Tertullianus, the Romans were powerful because they were pius and honoured them. As communication became more widespread, more deities became known, were given places of honour and people were free to honour them. There were disputes among the deities; but according to Dionysius, envy had no place. In mid Aries, Zeus rode his winged chariot, there were many happy spectacles and processions. There was general contentment.

  As the constellation of the fiery warrior, Aries, sailed on, characteristics of the element of fire got stronger, snowballed. At the same time, characteristics of the heavy element, water, were building up. As fire qualities increased, they became a burden to Aries. Many virtues became failings. Abilities in communication permitted the exchange of conflicting points of view, caused confusion. Because of many advancements, science gained much favour. The scientific method was brought into religion. Worship of the deities grew to be scientific and exact, but so dependent on clergy who could work the science that masses of the people lost interest. Marcus Aurelius said that prayer needed to be verbally precise. But many were losing confidence in the deities. For religion, people wanted something they could get excited about whether or not it made sense, for deities who had been relied on were losing stature. Deities began to seem too limited to care for the vast areas which had been said to be their charge. In the past, said Tertullianus, Olympus had been treated as if it were the heavens. But it was foolish to think that Jupiter in playing with a few thunderbolts could have much to do with the vast expanse of skies filled with thunderbolts. He said that the failings which were attributed to the deities were many. He claimed that Jupiter was often immoral, as when he had incestuous relations with his sister and when he had conflicts with his father. Tertullianus said also that Jupiter could be unjust, as when he slew the Goat Goddess. And he said Jupiter's power was not as great as was by many thought; as Jupiter, by swearing by the Stygian Swamp, indicated some greater power. Also, it was thought, Jupiter had a fear that Phenon would replace him as chief god. Lactantius was critical of Hercules and said that although Hercules showed physical strength, he didn't conquer shame or lust. One, he brought shame on himself by being Omphala's servant; two, by being guilty of adultery. As activities of the deities were scrutinized, many of these critics felt the deities weren't setting good examples of moral living. As communication improved and information was exchanged, doubts were raised about the outlandish things deities were said to have done. And the power of statues came into question. Minucius observed that no harm came to animals who pissed on statues of deities. To Minucius, as to much of classic Europe, classic deities seemed limited. This was one of the causes of unrest. With the dissatisfaction with the deities came a dissatisfaction with governments and this led to turmoil, to conflicts, to wars. There came a lack of justice. Populations, it seemed, were becoming crude and ill mannered. There came natural disasters and the lands became troubled by monsters. Law giving bodies fell apart and populations became fluid; teaching, difficult.

The downfall of order seems again to have been triggered by disturbances in the heavens, by the instability of once relied on heavenly forms. The constellations of Aries no longer gave their relied on protection.

Aquila, the Star Eagle, no longer rose to announce the rising of the Sun. It is said, as in the heavens, so on Earth. The heavens seemed to have their reflections on Earth: city swallowing disasters.

Thinkers there were a plenty, but these added to the confusion. One, they were often misunderstood. Some, when they spoke of an all powerful force, or everywhere existing spirit, called God, many people related it to an anthropomorphic father figure. It was widely thought that this little understood god was bringing a wonderful religion from far away. The hope and wonder, which came in with the new god, drew and held excited masses.

Contributing to their own fading away, by removing themselves further from the people, were the priests of the pantheon which had been a support of Aries. In the sacred temples, the priests didn't need the people, for their communication with the deities was through more and more complex formulas which the masses of the people weren't expected to understand. The priests could act on their behalf. But the bright light of enlightenment and power, which had shown when Aries was at its glorious height, was now covered with a shade, a shade which had collected such distractions as spider webs and dust. Such as smoke and fantasy obscured, much of the time, the pure flame.

Science and philosophy, with the few, continued to move forward. Marvelous things continued to be invented, but the great masses of people became impatient with the theories and solutions of thinkers, with dry logic of scientists and other thinkers. They wanted not reason, but excitement and passion.

The age of the element of water, Pisces, was in. As the age is that of a heavy element, it is an age which does not favour reason; however, insight and intuition were favoured and becoming stronger. With the coming of the Age of Water came an increase of fantasy, nightmares and other terrors. Deception and illogic were on the increase. Men of that time became haunted by grotesque, demonic monsters and so haunted; many came themselves to act like monsters. To the acts of men, Nature added her cruelties. Death took his toll and often, in cruel ways, from fields filled with love and beauty. The new god from the East would now, to many, seem more of a monster than gods who were gone; as, for the new god, many people were burned.

There was not a sudden shift from characteristics of Aries to those of Pisces. At a point in time, those of Aries were overbalanced by those of Pisces. The attributes which had been Aries' strong points now seem conspired to cause it to fade. Inventions made cities more difficult to defend and added to confusion. Aries characteristics continued, but did not rule. Nor did those of faded Taurus.

As the balance caused Pisces to rise, what had been failings now rose to become virtues. The former virtues would often find themselves at the bottom of a new scale.

Again, the circle of ages rolls toward a new transition: Pisces into Aquarius. Characteristics of Aquarius are rising to the top and those of Pisces are sinking. This would affect prediction. Aquarius would not have the pure force of Fire, but reason would play a significant role. The Goblins of Pisces would not be as likely to startle the unconscious into revealing hidden knowledge. One might expect less from insight.

Beside the heavenly signs, communication might be the most obvious force which would be pulling the age from the ways of Pisces. The failings in communication, which had caused confusion toward the end of Aries, had been one of the causes for the rise of the Age of Pisces. Toward the end of Pisces, the advancement of skills in communication might be seen as one of the reasons for its fade. Information which had been considered history, which had supported Piscean Age fantasy; became, among the masses, shown to be largely untrue. A spread of knowledge about the physical heavens would cause a worry and a fade of interest in a limited One God. Toward the Age of Aquarius, the polytheistic forces, and their histories, became more generally, and better, understood.

Advances in technology would be another force which would bring in the Age of Aquarius. Controle of the skies might have spiritual aspects, but predicting weather would nearly all be done by figures derived by technology. One might use, and appreciate, the predicting in which technology lends its help. As Whewell says, seeing the way elements are regulated and controlled gives one a chance to know something of how the Universe is governed and the effects of its parts combined and balanced. However, from the Age of Aries, predictions by the use of observations of Nature, which were recorded, do give an indication of spirit relationships which in many ages a person might, when predicting, find to be of use. Aratus, a philosopher who made many weather observations, observed an ability which birds have of predicting weather. And these predictions of physical events might be symbolic of other events: perhaps, of spiritual change. Crows, according to Aratus, gather and squawk before rain. A heron, predicting a gale, comes landward with disordered flight and many a scream. Aratus speaks also of oxen. He said that, before rain, they gaze at the sky and sniff the air. Prophetic messages related to these observations might be obtained from representations of birds or the oxen. Nearing the Age of Aquarius, messages would fit into the total picture which would have Aquarian influences, but the person looking at the images might not be enough out of Pisces to be able to receive the messages steeped in Aquarian spirituality: would be better prepared to read those from images out of Piscean nightmare.

Spirituality is a physical property of matter; so, is able to be used in prediction. Spirit might be thought of as mental creations. And these would generate waves and these, in combination, would create a climate of thought. The waves are motions of matter and, as does all matter, they contain the quality of vibration. Vibration permeates all matter in the Universe and binds it together, so that there is no place which is not linked to every other place. So, every motion is in the great network of cause and effect relationships. These relationships require that every action must have a balancing action. And it is the quality of vibration which permits this, and every other law to function. Brainwaves would be bound into this system, would be linked to every other vibration. Man has learned to tie brainwaves to various rhythms of the mysterious forces and to give shape and character to some of them. These forces, given shape and character, are what might be called deities. These deities are clarified by myths. Personalities emerge, give off vibrations. These personalities would affect people where the vibrations of the personalities are strong. Jung has found deities appearing in dreams of people who had had no prior knowledge of the deities. In places where deities and their myths have developed, they appear in dreams to educate even people who knew them not. Although many people in the Age of Aries thought of deities as super human individuals, philosophers, such as Lucius Apuleius, correctly identified them as superessential natures. He goes on to say that they are present at the same time everywhere: that they could appear at the same time in more than one place.

Deities are shaped by cultural consciousness.

From Zimmer: "Collective cultural consciousness collects chaotic forces of an outer world and organizes them into inner world realities."

The personality of a deity would not be static, but would change as times changed. The changes would be governed by the changing needs of societies. It would be usual to find the ethics of a deity progressed to be just beyond the horizon from where man in general was at any given time. And the deity would not think in an animal type way. It would act in order to fill its position in the system. The deity is part of a rhythm which man, in his need, has learned to identify. Objects and locations in the heavens have been found to contain forces relating to one or more of the deities; so, the names of deities have been placed on places and objects, each object and place taking the name, or names, of the deity, or deities, to which it relates. Intuitively, spiritual leaders had the perception needed for determining appropriate names for celestial forms and objects. Intuitively, places were left in the heavens for seven planets even though five are thought, visible. The Moon and the Sun were put in the places of the hidden planets, but it had been realized that these were not the planets.

The spirit forces are not found only in the heavens, or floating in an ether of their own: they are in the aspects of the environment. In flower, rock, river and animal, one might recognize deities and with some deities, one or another of those forms might be considered their most significant. Jacob Grimm has said that the history of the religion of Europe would be much like the history of trees, as many deities have trees as a significant form.

The placement of the spirit forces in the heavens and in the environment, and the need for their doings, as determined from ritual and story, would provide keys which might be used in predicting. It might be a small thing which a deity brings which fills a need. Size is often not the way of locating the needed key. A deity is as large as it needs to be in order to provide its required service. In somewhat the same way size can be altered in the physical world. A star seen as smaller than a pin head can, by use of a scope, be increased to greater than human size. It might be shown to be of a greater size than Earth.

An aid to prediction is math. Math has two aspects: counting and measuring. Many correct predictions have been made by measurements. In predicting, a more complex use of measurement would be in determining influence from an estimated correct size and this may or may not relate to actual size. An example, the Sun might be given as one sees it: the bright ball which flies over flat Earth. There is a reality in the way one sees a situation. Earth presents herself as a wide, generally flat ground. Or, the Sun might be seen the size of a giant human.

In predicting, one often has to consider the mysterious forces involved with counting. Each number has its many meanings. As has been said, odd numbers would relate to the male and even numbers, to the female.

One holds the singleness of Fire, and of the Sun. One is the bright focus: eye being the one eye, arm being the one arm. One eye would represent and symbolize all eyes, would represent the quality of eyeness. Lugus, the Sun Hero, achieved the perfection he needed in order to be the Sun by giving up duplicates of his perfect features: his second eye, his second leg, and his second arm. One is the single candle lighting the way to birth, the torch lighting the way to the Otherworld. See one fox, it is good luck; see more than one, bad luck. One is the prime source, the birth, the fountain of life.

Two, the number of Earth, represents a durable strength – and stability. It promotes balance, getting centered and a resolution of opposites. Two is the number of copulation. It is a sacred number used on many symbols and sacred items: the double headed axe, the two horns of an alter, twin lions and two birds: these, from a list given by W B Crow, would relate to Earth. Two represents the concept of opposites: dark, light; day, night: life, death; first, last.

Three is a magical number associated with sacred trinities and sacred triads. It is the number relating to air. Mercury, a God of Air, is sometimes represented as a three headed snake. Martianus lists three as the number of Mercury. Three is the number which unites three forces, as they come from the Otherworld, to form life; so, three might be called the number of life. It would be the number of change. Change, in one case, is youth, maturity and age. This is sometimes represented as three goddesses; each, representing an age of the Moon. Three relates to knowledge. It relates to the Seeing Eye at the top of the Triangle; to sacred triads and especially to those in the field of mental abilities: the three master poets, the three sacred astronomers, the three witches. Three of items or objects, the number gives them a sacredness; as, the three sacred gifts. According to Jung, three is not a natural expression of wholeness.

Four is the number which relates to the sacred chalice, to the sacred pool. It is the number which defines the circle. It is the number for the four parts of the circle. Their four basic directions, four basic elements. Four is the number representing the door. Jung calls it the ground plan of the unconscious. It relates to stability. It forms the cross which brings the resolution and unity of the basic elements, the resolution of opposites. It represents completeness. It is the number of the crystal, the number of the diamond. It is the number of valences of carbon. Through the four leaf clover one might see the Otherworld.

Five is the number which symbolizes mankind and especially, the female. As a symbol, it is often expressed as a pentacle. Relating to the human, the normal body has five senses and five major organs of intake or excretion. Five is especially sacred to Juno and Ariadne, the Goddess of Death. It is an active number which promotes change. Five is used in centering and it provides a window toward the Halls of Death. It might represent loss, as a lost love. Five might represent a cross with a center; so, expressed as a wheel.

Six relates to the six directions. It can be expressed as a triangle pointed up and a triangle pointed down; so, representing birth and death. Beside the female, as two threes, it also relates to the male. Six promotes copulation and sharing. It aids crafts. Nails would relate to sex. There are hidden dangers in the number six.

Seven is called the magical number, as so much of creation is formed in, and responds to, sevens. The ancient peoples listed seven planets. They also formed seven days to the week. Colour revolves through seven rainbow bands. In a major system of music, after the seventh note of a scale the first note is repeated, but at a different level. Steps of spiritual progress would also number seven. And, according to Leadbeater, this seven step scale would likewise be divided into seven steps. According to the ancients in one school of thinking, steps of advancement through light had its opposing scale of advancement through dark. If one reached the top of one scale, he would find himself at the bottom of the other. There would be no ethic content in the terms light or dark. The different spiritual bands might be recognized by people who are sensitive to changes in the vibrations. Seven would relate to the sword which cuts at limits. Seven promotes spiritual growth. It implies a need for attention to details. It warns of a step into a new way and, perhaps, into another world.

Number eight relates to reaping and to change and this, sometimes sudden change. It has the characteristics of wholeness and harmony. It has strength, joy, glory, balance and darkness. It promotes fellowship. It relates to the eight directions. It is a number for new opportunity. It relates to the abyss and to death.

Nine is a magical number related to the magic of the Moon. Nine relates to conception, birth and death. Nine days is the length of time it takes to get from this world to the Otherworld. Nine is the number of sacred woods burned in Midsummer fires. Nine brings dreams and is an aid in reading dreams. It aids in developing understandings. It inspires cleaning. It brings change. Nine herbs were given by the Sacred Snake. Nine can hold three sacred triads. Nine absolute conceptions are listed by Whewell: goodness, greatness, power, virtue, truth, majesty, wisdom, duration and will. Nine is a number favored by the Moon.

Number ten relates to the wheel and to sexual relations. It holds, at its center, a dark abyss. Ten holds a completeness. It is the sum of the sacred first four numbers.

Twelve, in one aspect, is the sacred temple formed by three circles formed by fours.

Fifteen would hold the strength of three goddesses, each represented by the number five.

Seventeen is a number of change. One aspect, the circle ten; plus seven, and this might be seen as the celestial Lyre, the notes of the seven strings forcing a change.

The meaning held in shape is a way to prediction. Each shape can hold the power of a great spirit. The power of a shape would not need to be pictorially related to what it represented. An R shape might hold the power of motion yet not seem, a picture of an object moving: However, as Flowers had said, it might suggest motion as being a half wheel under a wagon. With a somewhat different look, Agrippa has it representing an evil spirit. To recognize meaning in shape is difficult; however, from most ancient times, men have, through intuition and shared knowledge, learned from shapes. For their magical power, as shown by Frobenius, ancient men have carved geometric shapes on rocks and trees. Kepler studied the meanings of geometric shapes in the heavens. A vertical line, from its top, to the right, a short diagonal and below that, another short diagonal; might give a feeling of song which would bring great ecstasy, would bring inspiration for creative activity. It might give an impression of a great wind bending the tops of the trees, and perhaps a great wind would. The diagonals from the vertical line slant earthward.

And prediction is affected by colour. Colours might not be obvious, but intuitively perceived in auras or spirit substances. Symbols, W E Butler says, might generate spirit seen through astral realm. Some colours have a generally agreed on influence. Red would relate to passion, combat, love, vitality, energy, enthusiasm and rage. Its influence would depend on how it was combined with the other influences. Orange relates to enthusiasm and creativity. Ouseley relates it to mental force. Yellow relates to joy and clarity. Ouseley calls it an aid to the intellect and the nerves. Green is a healing colour and it inspires growth and regeneration. It aids preservation and brings harmony. Green is restful. Blue, Ouseley says, is restful to the mind. It is peaceful and cool and aids in communication. Cobalt aids intuition. Purple relates to leadership and spirituality. Shadings in colour are complex.

Pythagoras used colours in healing the sick. W. E. Butler tells of a healing done with the colour blue.

In influencing actions, movements; colour, shape and number move matter. Pythagoras not only said that matter is moved by the force of numbers, but suggested that the gods might be created of numbers.

The Cross Tarot
The Symbol

A distinguishing feature of human civilizations over the entire world is the use of symbols. Language, its letters and words, is constructed of symbols. Each symbol communicates a complex portion of what it symbolizes. This portion would, in part, depend on how the symbol was constructed and how used. Great networks of meaning might depend on a small difference between one symbol and another. The darkening of a line in the spelling of the word cow might make a big difference in the way one saw the object represented by the symbol; or, thought about the object represented. Large rewards can be gotten because of gaining correct understandings from a symbol.

In Tarot, one has a highly developed, complex use of the symbol. In this, complex networks of symbols are displayed in order that one might gain understandings of the present and the future. The symbols used on the Tarot suggest the magical and often seem to move and shift under one's gaze. Every symbol would have its mystical aspects; however, many of those used in Tarot have a long history of mystical and magical communication so that they often suggest cryptic meanings. The ancient symbols would go back in time to days before they were used on cards. Before there were cards, there were images representing mental and physical realities: water, fire, pain, love, light, darkness, beauty, food, fornication, trees, animals, cold and objects in the heavens. As aids to instruction, symbols such as these were put on temple walls. People, from ancient times, have been taught to understand these symbols and the relationships which exist between each and others and how these relationships change; as, an animal's relationship to the Sun would be different in the summer than it would be in the winter.

With Tarot cards, as with symbols in a temple, one is given symbols to relate to. A question might be put, what are the special problems about each symbol which a person's attention becomes focused on, that attention should be drawn to it? Then, how do those aspects of the symbol relate to other realities found to be in the environment?

Symbols have power to give knowledge and awareness and to inspire action. They are the mysterious sign posts by which many people have gained understandings.

Tarot cards, with their symbols, have been developed through the Age of Pisces, which is a heavy element; so, would have a close relationship with intuition and emotion. Cards, like demons out of nightmare, are for, in part, their shock value; presented in order to shake up normal patterns of thought, so that truth, out of chaos, might be seen.

As Time moves toward the age of a lighter element, a greater weight would be given to logic and clear thinking and this might be reflected in the symbols presented by Tarot cards. The demon which has been thought to be all evil would surely become less on the scene, as would the figure who calls himself as the only All Good; perhaps, the only one who could be correctly defined as a god.

The images would still have a shock value and this, perhaps, even greater; as the goblins of old have masked, somewhat, the depth of the darkness into which one might fall. As the masters have said, one might listen to lectures by teachers or social workers, might agree with them, but it might be that the full force and understanding of the truth comes only when the Tarot card, with its startling symbols, is placed in front of him. That might be when a different sort of thinking begins.

Making Changes

The Age of Pisces would hold great numbers of people who term a single force as God. All forces other are called by other names. The God is honoured, worshipped, or both, as champion over other forces. Tarot has been formed to fit into that system; filled, as it is, with illogical claims for what the god has done; or, can do. The Tarot is filled with goblin like figures designed to, and might well, fall suddenly and startle the reader and the questioner and instigate a fear, or concern, for the huge questions related to time and space, so that he suddenly looks again at his relationship with God. With this, answers to smaller questions would come to the surface and permit an intuitive look at how they would fit into a larger map of a path which would run from past to future. The tendency of the Age of Pisces would be to, many times, gain understanding by intuition rather than by logic.

The coming age, The Age of Aquarius, while not throwing out intuition to the extent which an Age of Fire might, would hold a larger place for logic. Many forces would come to be honoured and might be termed, "God." An Aquarius Tarot might give more weight to the long down played forces.

Age of Aquarius: 2059 — Rudhyar

Elements

As air is lighter than the liquid element, the Age having to do with air would have more of an influence toward predicting from cause and effect relationships than would the earlier age. However, insight and intuition would still be prediction's major tools. With symbols, there would still be vague meanings cloaked in mists; however, meanings might be seen as having greater clarity. Chief guides would be the bare symbols of the elements and their meanings, not clouded by the difficulties of added elaborations which would give few logical directions.

One is Fire, the Sun, the Diamond. It represents math and logic: exactness. The Diamond relates to gold and it is often thought, the more gold, the better. Gold relates to purity and exactness. The Ten, as the Wheel, holds a completeness, and with Diamonds, that would indicate power.

Two is Earth. This has the two meanings of the Spade: the spade to prepare Earth for births and the sword to slay.

The Three is Air and relates to the sacred Triangles which hold the Universe together.

The Four is Water and the number of the Cauldron from which life comes and into which life falls. As points on a Cross, it is the wheel of the Sun and in its center, the fifth point: the Sun.

The Four held life giving liquid, one of which liquids is blood. It was a custom for people to give, for protection, a bit of their blood to travelers.

Insight into the strange twists which some future might hold might come from the picture cards, but understanding the pictures can be difficult. One might be certain that a picture holds great value, but like an admired abstract painting, one might have no way of telling what that value is.

In a reading, perhaps the heavy lifting should be done by the cards which, each one, show aspects of one of the four basic elements. Even with these, one has more than a hat full of shadows.

Elemental Cards

Driving forces which shape a persons path, the four basic elements, are named Earth, Water, Air and Fire; are named for the four basic forms of matter: solid, liquid, air and fire. The four forms are given comparative weight symbols. Solid to fire, the symbols would represent most heavy, heavy, light and lightest. The weights represented by the symbols would have qualities which, in prediction, would serve as guides. The qualities, physical or spiritual, would seldom, more than in a general way, relate to physical weight. In the physical world, a solid might be found which would be lighter than a gas. Some liquid might be found which would rise above a gas; another, which would sink below a solid. The usual is to have solids as a bottom layer called heaviest; water, representing liquid, next; then gas, then fire. The weight types would hold these same positions any place in the Universe. The matter forms, as spirit forces, are in directions of the compass. To give light, Fire rises from the East, faces West, its adversary, Water. From the South, Air carrying the key to the Otherworld, blows toward the North. Around the circle, Sunwise: Fire, the lightest; Air, the next light; Water, the next in weight; then, in the North, Earth.

The symbols used to represent the basic forms of matter are, according to deGivry and others who have studied the work of anthropologists, most ancient. The symbols evolved from depictions of tools used in the dawn of the human race: the head of the arrow or spear, the staff, the sword or spade, the pot or bowl. These basic forms represented spiritual forces and were put on surfaces in sacred places. The shaft, the staff, the cup, the knife, the stone, were tools of deities.

The tools represented the jobs the deities did, the jobs which communities of people needed to have done. These were jobs which people, in earliest times, needed someone to do so that their societies would stay knit. And the people who did these jobs found a need to identify themselves and how better than by the pictures of magical tools of deities who had related functions. People used their symbols on signs and on chips of wood used as debt tabs or calling cards.

One occupation of importance would have been the distributer of goods, or the merchant. He might have pictured himself, and been pictured, as representing the Sun Lord. Ancient Suns were shown with spear headed, or arrow headed, shafts. The stone by itself, without the shaft, was sometimes used for throwing. The symbol evolved to be the diamond, and this came also to represent the King of Jewels and the gold coin. Gold coins flow from the Hall of the Sun. The symbol came to represent wealth and power.

A second occupation was one which formed a connecting link with the deities. This would have been the wandering shaman, as only much later were communities organized to the point where they would have had priests. The signature and emblematic tool of the shaman would have been the staff. It was a tool needed by a wanderer, so related to the wandering god. As a wanderer was considered to have magic, this tool would have been considered part of it. If the staff was forked at the top, this would have had meaning. Two prongs might have given a window to the Otherworld; three, the uniting of three spirits was indicated.

A third occupation was the job of supplying food and drink to a community. The person who had this position would, in times most ancient, have been the community leader. As communities evolved, the job might have become that of a designated hall keeper; later, an inn keeper. A picture which would have identified a person having this job would have been of that object which held the food or the drink: the cauldron or the cup.

The fourth job was that of a defender; perhaps, the chief defender, of the community. Holding that job would have been a warrior hunter and his symbol would have been a knife or sword. As communities developed, farming became needed and the defender's chief occupation became farming. Then he defended the land he farmed. The symbol evolved to a sword like object which could also have been used for digging the land. At this time, peoples had not organized to the point where there would have been full time warriors. The digging tool would have represented the sword of the Sky God who copulated with Earth.

Symbols related to pictures of most ancient of jobs have come to be called diamonds, clubs, hearts and spades. The heart is sometimes seen as the cup and the spade, the sword. Symbols representing the ancient and important jobs became, more than with the jobs, associated with the deities related to the jobs and to the directions to which the deities related. The symbols are complex; each, having a wide and complex net of meanings. On the cards, visual suggestions as to what these meanings might be would, in most cases, be less than helpful, as they would likely detract from the power of the basic symbol, would give misleading information. The visual elaborations to a basic symbol would certainly limit, and detract from, its range and power. The basic symbol is valued for the wide range of information it might give. Each might suggest a deity, a direction, but that direction would not be its gaol, nor that deity, its gaoler. Sometimes a symbol's meaning might seem to come from left field. A diamond might be a stone from the Underworld; a club, a rooted tree and be representing powers of Earth. Or it might be a stick used for making fire, or for finding water.

Being suggestive symbols, not pictures of tools, expands the range of their meanings. Each symbol, beside the force of its more usual associations, would hold a spectrum of less obvious and of hidden meanings. Form itself holds meanings independent of representations. The fact is, if no understandings were to be gained by looking at the symbols, little good it would do to see them on the Path; and through the ages, many have looked and many, learned.

Few guideposts would give a better indication of what is on a questor's path than what his relationship is to the four basic elements. The four basic elements relate to the balanced powers of the deities. The number of elemental cards, fifty two, is sacred to both male and female deities. For each elemental symbol, there are thirteen cards. Thirteen is the number of transcendence through spiritual transformation. Each element holds together a powerful coven. Each coven would face its opposite, would form a balance. Coming equally from the four directions, the elements would form a cross, at the center of which would be a resolution of opposites, and this resolution would form a door through which would come a knowledge of factors forming the balance and an understanding.

Each element has its peculiarities; however, in each element's ability to provide pleasure and pain along the Path, there would be equality.

At the East, representing Fire, the Diamond holds wealth and power. The Diamond would be the tip of the shaft of Fire. It favours gold and promotes learning, order and copulation. Not only does it aid reproduction of others, but it is said, according to Fernie, to have the power to regenerate itself. It supports advancement of logic, math and physics and is an influence toward truth, purity and clarity. It supports the force of laws. It aims for perfection, promotes the one at the top.

The usual driving force of the elemental coven would be the Ace, and this would surely be true of the Diamond Coven. One would recognize, in the Ace of Diamonds, a symbolic Sun, King of Fires. It would hold the sacred oneness of the Sun, and this insures its purity, truth and power. The perfection of its truth is demonstrated by its symmetry. The Diamond, the King of Stones, is, as reported by Kuntz, the stone of fearless invincibility. The Ace would bring enlightenment, would bring an ability to see into matters and to grasp complex meanings, and would bring encouragement for taking charge and it might foster a need to rule. The Ace would encourage physical fitness, good health and a dedication to take advantage of these gifts of nature. The Ace would generate a need for winning, would encourage self promotion and would direct the way toward pleasures and happiness. The Ace dislikes the Lodestone and would be little swayed by magnetic forces.

The Diamond has ties to the Underworld, so can be looked to for Underworld knowledge which might be fathomed by omens; especially, by those related to birds. One way of gaining omens was to face East, create a frame in space, then watch for movement. The Diamond can produce somnambulism and can bring invisibility. Red on a diamond can bring blood and death – to its owner, or mark a dragon slayer.

The Diamond King would be powerful and prosperous. In one aspect, the kings over the elements were the Elemental Kings: Djinn, Paralda, Hicks and Cob. In this, the Diamond King would be Djinn, lean and quick to anger, but his anger would quickly pass – providing it is understood that he, the king, establishes the order, all else fit in. And this is true of all the Elemental Kings, and of the four, King Djinn the most, that the king would set the direction and the pattern of that falling within his province. The King of Diamonds moves with unsympathic force, as those with great wealth are inclined to do. He appreciates music which is well constructed and well performed. And the things fire does come under the jurisdiction of the King of Diamonds, who is the King of Fire.

The Elemental Queens would present quite different aspects from those presented by the Elemental Kings. The Elemental King is the ruler of his domain: the Elemental Queen, a personification of the domain itself. To those within the domain, as a rule, the well being of the queen would be more important to them than would be that of the king. The Diamond Queen is Fire and her flames might be seen touching any other, or every other, card to be seen on the path. Beside the elemental influences, the human aspects of the king and the queen would take their places among the other influences. The Diamond Queen is thought to be generally happy and fond of gaiety. She would be demanding, forceful, and would expect attention, but less so than the great, powerful Diamond King.

The jacks, in human form, would cover a wide range of possibilities. He could be a good man with a sword, or he could be the man who runs the kingdom. The Jack of Diamonds is thought, a fine warrior and a good battle leader. He is honourable, proud and inclined to be selfish. With wealth, he is tricky to deal with. As Spirit of Fire, he might be a solar hero, a Sun form, sailing through the sky slaying monsters; or, he might be Phaeton, creator of disasters.

Numbered diamonds, ten to two, generally represent good fortune as they would be riches and shafts of fire. They might be the gold coins which come from the Hall of the Sun. The seven of diamonds would have special value as the diamond gives value to number placement and the seven holds the seven steps of progress in systems. The Sun, the sacred seat of Fire, we learn from Callistratus, has a lyre of seven strings and the seven steps of music equal the number of muses.

The Eight of Diamonds might represent a seachange. It might reverse the meaning of the other cards on the layout. A person might see in it, new opportunities. The Ten might seem, a powerful wheel of fire shedding Sun qualities throughout the other cards on the layout. Seeing the ten might bring pleasure as diamonds tend to look like money. The pleasure might be increased if, with the ten, one or more of the kings were seen on the layout and, especially so, if the Diamond King was seen; as one of the duties of a king is to give gifts. The Two of Diamonds might signal the coming of an unrewarding pleasure. The Ace might send up a red flag: perhaps a wedding ring in the future. The flag any card would send up would depend on its relationship to the total layout. The Ace might be the deadly Thunderstone.

At the South, the Club is the Magical Staff. It is the One Tree which holds the Universe together; or one might see it shifting so as to provide an opening for the awful snake. It is the Staff of the God of Wind, and in this, might be bringing the Winds of Change. The Staff of the Wind God has three heads and these would be the three forces uniting to form the Spirit of Life. The Club is the Staff and it represented, and was carried by, a variety of persons. It was the staff carried by the poor wanderer whom people suspected of being somewhat magical. It was the power staff of one so forceful he was treated as a demigod. The staff might have great power, be a great mover of forces which could part the veils to the Otherworld. It might be a stick thought to be in some way magical, but how it is to be used is unclear. The symbol, the Club, represents the great wand which many deities use as a key for passing from one world to another. It is a magical force which holds together the three spirits, which combine to form the essence which is life, and the key that opens ways. From the shape of the symbol, one might intuitively feel the driving force which makes it work.

The Club, as a symbol, might suggest one or more of a whole range of characteristics of clubs and wands; beside, a host of subjects quite unrelated. As a wand, the Club might act in unpredicted ways. It might be an especially tricky symbol for those who have little grasp of the use of wands. As recorded by Buckland and others, an important feature of the wand or staff is that, for the shaman, it established a brotherhood with a tree. There would be an agreement by the tree to give the wood, then an exchange of gifts. After this, a custom is to have the Sun, by the first rays of the morning, energize the staff or wand. As Cremonensis has said, the Sun is a friend to Mercury, who is ruler of clubs. In the consecration of the wand, as Simms and others have documented, the element Water has been made use of. This would give the wand a great range of connections and so, uses. Then, the wand can be tricky and magic sometimes backfires. In the long run, an ability in the use of wands might not be to the questor's advantage. As a guide in prediction, the Club is difficult.

The Ace of Clubs represents, first, the Staff of the God of Air. On a layout, as a black ace, it tends to create major changes. However, for power, it should be seen with the branches up. With the branches down, it might be of little more use than a walking stick. But branches up, rising from the Underworld, it might well be bringing knowledge and power, and the strange things which, down under, are usually kept hidden away: dream, illusion, fantasy and mirage. As it deals in magic, it might seem to be casting spells. It might don the Wind's Coat of Darkness, turn up in some unexpected place; or, where it is and what it is doing, seem to be lost. With its interest in deception, it might come masked; or present kaleidoscopic animations, shifting virtues and moods. It might come like ignis fatuus to lead one astray. It might come out of the sky to promote quick wit, alertness, trickery, healing abilities, sham, speed, agility and theft. It might be showing to help breathing ability, to aid in communication, locate passageways, to find water, or, with the willow, point out the correct place for a burial. As a warrior's club, it might bring death. A major focus of a Club Ace might be transportation. It might instigate travel. The Ace might be bringing important news. It might have come to aid in the giving of an important speech.

For knowledge and power, the Club Ace might reflect that of the spirits of trees, and trees connect this World with the Otherworld, and with this influence, aid in prediction, balance, insight, adaptability and might give one an entirely new view of life.

Upside down, the Club Ace might serve as some useful tool, or might work some mischief, but usually small mischief. It might inform one of a way to a store or bring news of a welcome letter.

The King of Clubs would have much power. He is thought to be affectionate, but bad tempered and quick to anger. He is said to be tricky and dangerous. It is a king's responsibility to make judgements and to instigate chastisements, and in this, the Club King's performance is thought to be uneven. Also, giving is an important function of a King, and gifts from the King of Clubs have been considered sacred and his tokens have been carried as charms by travelers. The sacred gift, the communion with the king, might be a power object or being with which the questor, through concentrated visualization or meditation, could become familiar and find of use. Or, the king might give a gift of a token which could be used to identify the questor. Or it could be a gift of healing. Healing is an ability given to kings, and the Club King is known as an able healer. Not only has he a strong healing touch, but the king keeps contact with powerful snake doctors.

The Club Queen is a powerful, capricious witch, though not as powerful as the King of Clubs. Her pleasure is, in part, in her vast herb gardens. She is thought, witty and agreeable; sometimes, most helpful.

The Club Jack is a competent warrior, a skillful ambassador and a useful messenger. He is tricky, cunning and quick tempered and not entirely to be trusted. As do others in his house, he makes use of witchcraft. And he is likely to go off on wild goose chases.

In Clubs, the numbered cards tend to bring surprise. Often, they would bring news from other places. Often, the news would be brought by the eight of clubs. The club numbered cards would often be involved in the exchange of goods. Often they would deal in deception. The club numbered cards would often draw importance from the magic of their numbers. The three is a powerful, magical triad, a Rule of Three. And this is a charm. The power of the charm extends from the Triangle to spoken magics, to sacred trinities, as the Three Oldest Animals, the Three Great Astronomers, the Three Great Concealments, the Three Revelations, the Three Grey Ladies, the Three Fates, the Three Cold Lords, the Three Birds of Epona. The Oldest Animals: the Salmon, the Eagle and the Owl: might, to the clubs, be bringing hidden knowledge. The Three of Clubs would have power. It might make arrangements of threes, or fit the questor into a triad, or it might be involved with a birthing, or a creation of some new thing. The nine, like the three, relates to birth and to death. It takes nine waves to give a birth and nine waves to make a trip to the Underworld. It takes Walpurga nine days to run from this World to the Underworld. In power and influence, the nine would be greater than all numbered clubs except the three, which is the number sacred to Air. The nine would encourage understanding and the development of inner resources. It might relate to a journey.

With clubs, cards seven, six, two and four would have their magical aspects. There are seven segments to the basic spans which are tied to the construction of the Universe. The two is two triangles, balanced against each other, related to death, and to life, promoting copulation. Six is related to the dark abyss; the four, to the erratic Four Winds.

With clubs, the numbered cards are covered with complexities and are likely to send up one or more red flags. Samples of what red flags might show have been recorded by Chambers and many others. One flag: the seven of clubs warned of danger from the opposite sex. The samples are a suggestion of the great number of things a card might say.

When the questor looks at hearts, he might see flowers, romance, dreams, fantasies and love. He might get a feeling of comfort, when a more realistic look at the symbol would give a feeling of insecurity. The fantasies could draw the questor into an ambush, or into a bog.

The Heart is the symbol for the basic element, liquid, which is called water. The shape given to the Heart would resemble more the Cup and the Cauldron, which are tools sacred to Deities of Water; but it isn't a picture of either. It can be all things, or any thing, related to the Cup, the Cauldron, the Heart and all things suggested by these more specific symbols. Its vagueness increases its ability to draw information from its mysterious depths. The Cup and the Cauldron are magical tools involved in creation and in drawing creation into the darkness of death. The Cup has no limit in size. It might be represented by the Sickle Moon. It might hold an ocean and its gifts might be inspiration, food, or life itself. Facing down, it returns these gifts to the Otherworld. And as it is a symbol which represents the heart, the symbol might suggest that it is at the center of things, that it is at the place where the lines from the four directions cross. In one aspect, the Heart sends forth a life giving, or life sustaining, liquid. As the symbol does not picture any cauldron, cup, or heart, one is not drawn to ruling out any of the wide range of associated concepts. The Cup, holding water, would hold the veil between life and death.

The Ace of Hearts is a powerful symbol which serves as a balance to the Diamond. It would be related to major concerns of humans: birth, love, copulation and death. The Heart is a symbol of Love and as such, it is somewhat masked from its darker associations. Related to Love, it is often shown in an environment containing beauty and illustrations of happiness and gentle pleasure. Subjects might include flowers, singing birds and lace. The pleasure of Love mask the relationship of Love to Death. Death might add to the beauty of Love and Beauty mask the pain of Death. Love inspires Copulation and Copulation creates Birth. Love is an eternal force present in all matter. As Simplicius, the philosopher, has said:

> "The World was brought out of Chaos by Love."

Certainly, the deity most thought of as the personification of Love is Venus, and she is associated with the Heart symbol. Not only are humans and other animals of interest to her, but flowers and fruits are under her care. Wine and intoxication are related to Venus.

The Heart is also the Cup with its many aspects. It is the Cup which holds the vast Waters and the personality of the Waters. It holds the limitless sea from which one, who reflected on the image, might get the feeling of flowing away through endless space; or, of floating, lost in a space, a space filled with hidden terrors, shifting moods, mystery, confusion, insecurity and a feeling of lostness, of being out of one's depth in an unknown where fantasies and illusions come out of the darkness. Learning might come also, come from the vast Waters, come from the Ace. The Waters might discover, or they might conceal. They might wipe the slate clean and so, purify; but by so doing, destroy. The Cup holds the personality of Neptune, who is the personification of the vast sea.

The Ace of hearts is the Grail from which sacred spirit liquid flows. It is the Sacred Cauldron, the Crescent Moon and the Magic Well. With the Heart, one thinks of sacred things: spirituality, love, birth, death. The Heart gives and it takes away. The heart is the center from which life springs. It is the Cauldron which accepts the Sun in his going to the Underworld. As heart means center, the Ace of Hearts would tend to indicate the point around which other things revolve. An Abode of the Ace of Hearts would be the Castle of Arianrhod, the revolving Castle of the Dead, which is most difficult to approach, so that its most magical gifts: life out of death, and knowledge beyond what seems possible for humans to have, and a place in the Chair of the Master Poet, and the place of a knight worthy to be a sacrifice to Love: these from the Sacred Cauldron; these, from the sacred elixir of the Ace; even deities had difficulty in obtaining. But the Cauldron at the Castle of Arianrhod serves wonderful drink, but serves none but those who are worthy to drink of it. And the pure, holy Fisher King guards the Grail from those who are not worthy to see it. The Grail, from which the sacred, spirit liquid flows, inspires creation and draws the dedicated warrior to the Otherworld.

The spiritual drink from the Heart would be different for each questor. It might lead one into a path where he is out of his depth; or, lead one into a birth, a birth into a changed life; or, lead to a search, then to discoveries. The questor might be led to discover a way into love, into copulation. Water inspires copulation. In festivals honouring Poseidon, God of Waters, the phallus is often carried in the processions. And Aphrodite, Goddess of Passionate Love, rose up naked from the waves. If the Ace says copulation, one might expect an action which would have noteworthy ramifications.

With the Cup turned up, the Ace of Hearts would be likely to promote passion, healing and feasting. The Sacred Cauldron of Bran the Blessed brought dead men back to life. And it gave an endless supply of what ever food was needed. The Cup or Cauldron would likely hold dream, fantasy, imagination, beauty, liberation, fertility, mutation, revolt, instability, joy, loss, inspiration, nourishment, love: all or any combination of these. The Ace might give warnings: be alert for hidden dangers, for mirages: be careful in a choice of loves.

The Ace of Hearts turned down, it might well be indicating a death. Eros, God of Love, on memorial stones for the dead, is pictured with his cup turned down, a returning of a love to the Underworld: a sacred libation – of love to the Underworld.

The King of Hearts is thought to be good natured, but obstinate and not easily appeased. He is generous, but his gifts do not always bring a durable happiness. He is a healer and especially so, for the heart and circulatory system. The king is calm, composed and not easily moved.

The Queen of Hearts is inclined to take charge and is often thought, more the ruler than the King. She is thought to be faithful and loving, strong in influence, and a dealer in illusions and dreams. She is a gift giver, but capricious and demanding of attention. She might resemble Juno, or Venus, or Doris, or Tethys.

The Jack of Hearts would be a strong warrior, a defender of the king and especially, the queen. He might go on rescue missions or on quests which might seem foolish. Often, he is an idealist, given to sacrifice.

The influence of the hearts would be toward the imaginative, the artistic, the joyful, the passionate, the fertile. They entice people to satisfy sensual pleasures. An influence of hearts is toward instability.

Of hearts, with numbered cards, their force would depend on shifting, magical values. One consideration would be, if the symbol is seen up to hold liquid, or down to empty it. A display of many hearts might suggest feasting. On some path layouts, it might indicate an orgy.

The Four of Hearts holds the magical, sacred number of the Cup. As such, it might be expected to aid in prophecy. The Five of Hearts is tied to the number symbolic of Mankind, and especially, of Woman. Mankind has five major holes in the body and five obvious senses. Nine is magical, and especially, to Woman, as it relates to the Moon and to Woman's relationship to the Moon Cycle, the Lunar Cycle. The Four might tend to keep stability; but, as with hearts, it might put one at sea and in the doldrums. The Four, being heavy, would affect the balance of the Path. The Nine of Hearts would often relate to spiritual learnings. The Five often deals with love and death. And hearts tend to throw up many flags.

At the North, the symbol would be the Sword, or Spade. The Spade is the Sword of The Sky God with which the Sky God copulates with Earth. The Spade would also represent the plowshare and it might be equated with Escalibur, the mighty sword of the Bear King. The Sword would hold a relationship with Fire, but it defends the land; so, Earth. Mars has a tree form; so, becomes the forest defending its land. The Sword, as the Spade, suggests the underground, graves and death. The underground suggests the Underworld, which is dreaded, as is its ruler, Hades; so, a questor might expect from the Spade unwelcome gifts. The questor's feelings about the symbols and their powers might be different from the reality which an astute reader might discover.

The Spade symbol suggests might, honour, valour, cruelty, loyalty, sacrifice, maliciousness, leadership, toil, ruin, polarization, spirituality, victory, asceticism, copulation and love. Pointed up, the symbol suggests a sword; pointed down, a digging tool. A feeling is, Spades relate to death.

The Ace of Spades is a card with much force. As Escalibur, it comes from the stone and is used by a Lord of Earth. It is also the sword of the Lord of the Sky. On many layouts, it announces Death; but, also, it guards against deaths. It is the force of Iron. It is all swords, knives, plowshares and spades. Digging tools are honoured as they copulate with Mother Earth. Plowing is considered a sacred ritual. Plowmen observe the correct times for plowing; so, establish relationships with Earth and deities of grain. And Epiphany Eve, Chadwick reports, his plowshare is carried around a straw fire. The ritual not only honours the deities, but combats malicious beings. The plowman carrying his plowshare, as Dalyell reports, is avoided by malicious beings. Among other things, the Ace represented the deities of grain. When harvest comes, the Sword sends the deities to the Underworld. When the deities are no longer needed in the fields, they put on their Cloaks of Darkness; so, relate to Deities of Air; go to the Underworld. From there, they come again as Deities of Earth. The Sword, then the Spade. The dead are buried so there can be new birth. More need for protection would follow.

Often, if the Ace of Spades should fall into a layout, it is with some dread it is seen. It is a big mover of space and one tends to fear negative aspects. The negative aspects of spades would include toil, battle and death; and these, lead to ruin and grief. But the Ace might be bringing an entirely different look. Pointed up, it might be a great sword bringing victory; or, bringing love and other blessings related to copulation. It might be bringing influential friendships. It might be bringing strength and so, suggesting for the questor to take a stand. Pointed down, by its power, the Ace might be bringing balance, stability and peace. As a sheathed sword, it might be thought to be giving a needed stroke, perhaps, in a far off future. Or, it might come as a spade to dig a direction changing grave; perhaps, that of some person of huge stature. The Ace would certainly be bringing a complex web of aspects; each, with its mix of desired and undesired effects. As Epictetus has said, whether a thing brings pleasure or pain depends on how one sees it. And one would not always see the same messages sent by the Ace as another would, or have the same opinion as to its major function. However, even though it would, at times, be but indicating a job ahead of digging a garden; the Ace of Spades is a big card, and one would be likely to see the waves from it rising and falling down along the Path.

The King of Spades is called stern and powerful, and he has a reputation of being unscrupulous and ambitious, and he is certainly melancholic. The King makes laws which favour military efficiency and sees to it his laws are enforced. Gifts he might give might aid in having orderliness, might help one to be a winner.

The Queen of Spades has a dominating personality and is thought to be malicious. She is, by some, thought to be widowed and it seems likely, she is not the mate of the Spade King. The queen of an element would not necessarily be the mate of the elemental king.

The Queen of Spades brings things to a close, makes changes. She is a reformer and her look at the way things are is critical. She contains a coldness and her touch is often the touch of death, so she has been called the Queen of Death.

The Jack of Spades would be a great warrior, a powerful organizer and an expert administrator: the one who makes policies of the king work. One of these: he gives protection. He is a champion of what he thinks are worthy causes. And he would tend to be cruel.

Often, the numbered spades would represent the stout members of a community. When the land needs defending, these would be ready with swords. In a time of peace, when food would be needed, the swords might be beaten into plowshares and spades so crops could be planted; the dead, buried. There would be new birth. Again, the land would need defending, so the spades and other digging tools would be hammered into weapons. As a rule, the more spades there would be, the better; or this would seem so if one wishes for strength.

The spade numbered cards tend to promote intuition, imagination and spirituality. Birth and death, also, are related to spades. Not only digging, but also slaying is considered a form of copulation. The two of spades might indicate a significant future copulation. In flags on spades, the relationship of the prediction to the number on the card might be hidden. While with spades much might be revealed, much would be buried.

What any card might have been expected to say before being added to all other factors might have little relation to what is said when all was considered. The Jacks, usually loyal, in some layouts, would seem quite the reverse. In a layout; a Jack, quite out of character, might appear as a knight who felt the need to chase a mysterious beast. The meaning of the chase might be cryptic; the knight placed on it, seem foolish; but along the Path, the Jack is going out of his way to say something.

One symbol acting in some odd way, as seeming to go widdershins against some harmony, might activate the pollinating power of other symbols so that one might feel the Life Force, which resides in all things, altered to produce a changed reality. It might be, a usual way of thinking of, perhaps, a concept is turned to a thinking which is new and startling.

The layout is magical. Ones mind flows into it, gets the feel of what is where. The symbols, by drawing down movement from out of the vastness of space and time and placing them in a familiar setting, have the power to alter thought. All information given by individual cards, including those with flags, would not be likely to be the important things which one might want to gain by looking at the Path. What one might experience from looking at the Path is an understanding of the majesty and wonder of the total life experience. One might try to avoid being like a chess player trying to snip off a castle when he should be trying to gain a concept of the movement of the total board.

The Path is a trail which moves this way, then that, in the way it must, due to the interaction of the various forces. From the interactions, one gets the feel of where the Path is going: One has himself, with the cards, with time, with history, with the environment. And the symbols teach in mysterious ways. From the Path, one might get the feeling of a meaning, even when he can't explain what the feeling, or the meaning, is.

The cards on the Path give a fresh look at familiar things, give new ways of seeing. One might have had what lay ahead explained as common sense, but still not grasped its reality, but when he saw the symbols turn up on the layout, that reality might have appeared as would a bolt of lightning. Suddenly, it is there. As Zimmer says, if a person won't permit himself to get knocked off his feet by an exploding symbol which pulls from the depths of the imagination some fresh way of looking, some fresh concept, which breaks away from self satisfied dogmatism; then he is missing an experience of great value, an exposure to wisdom of the ages, a chance to converse with gods, to hear the mysterious songs.

Symbols are unpredictable, yet consistent. In a wink of an eye, when one thought he had a symbol captured, the meaning would have shifted, an obvious change when done, but he might have thought the symbol laughed at him. There was his Jack. His Jack then had a fresh new meaning. Yet, ages old: Old Pan.

Environmental Cards

Each environmental card suggests what might be found physically and spiritually along a questor's path. What a questor finds, he should consider to be tools with which he might shape his life. Each environment presented contains tools and problems. Tools would also be potential problems and problems will, at some point, evolve into tools. What one is usually concerned with is how problems will be solved in the near future.

Along the Path, the questor would find animals, minerals and plants; along with spiritual forces to which they relate. Deities are to be met with in animals, minerals and plants. Especially, the Plant Kingdom gives a way the deities might be communicated with, as many of the deities, at times, take plant forms. As Jacob Grimm has said, the history of European Spirituality would; in many ways, resemble the history of trees.

On a card, environmental influences will often become emblematic. They represent advantages and disadvantages that a certain section of time is giving. In the plant group, there are big, symbolic things which a plant does; then, added to this, the details which make up the plant's personality. These, in their way, are emblematic, as they represent the small details of what a person might find in a season. Details are important. A plant is relatively small. It is often called a wort, which means word, which is a small thing. But a word is a key to knowledge.

Each person brings a personal picture of each season with its host of details. This, a person brings to a card and they are added to the details which the card might make the questor aware of.

Part of a magical power would come from an ability to integrate into the total aspects of the environment. One might instinctively take the step, use the hand, walk under the tree, which would lead to what would be seen as the maximum good fortune. One would be helped by a knowledge of how to handle the various tools which would be found; as one would know the correct time to pick some plant for some purpose which was desired. It might be an herb that would be the way onto the path that would lead into a beautiful environment.

The Path winds in a way which might, to some, resemble the Crane

Dance through the Maze of the Goddess of Death. It is mysterious, foreboding, intimidating, – or, it can be.

Cards XIV through XXIV focus on the mental aspects of the trip along the Path.

Flags

The flag would be the card which would, on the Path, jump to give a message. The message might be difficult to fit into the reading of the total Path. As a rule, the flag is most easy to fit in when the message of the flag relates, in an understandable way, to the flag's graphics. If a flag predicting a sea change was a Seven, the reader should find the situation easy to explain. It would be understandable if, by that flag, the meaning of other cards on the Path had become reversed. If the flag was a Six of Spades, the reader might expect a burial. If he saw a Three of Clubs, he might expect an important message. As Ten, the total of the first four sacred numbers, relates to completion, one might expect a Ten to predict a thing which would be completed. A Five of Hearts might predict a thing related to joy and sex; a Three of Diamonds, a thing related to a person who is bright. An Ace of Spades is known to relate to towers and gaols; a Jack of Clubs, as that Jack at times will wear a Cloak of Darkness, to that which is hidden: perhaps a hidden meaning.

However, often the message given by the flag has no understandable relation to the graphics on the card, nor does it fit easily to the total meaning of the Path. A reader, seeing a Seven of Diamonds, might say that there is gossip about - - -. She gets that because she has become aware that there are times that card will point that way, and she has come on one of them.

In a reading, it is likely that there will be flags.

Vegetation Influence Along the Path

The Path around the Circle of the Year, which each person is on, is a path through vegetation. The vegetation would have an influence on each person on the Path. That the influence is large would, in part, be due to the closeness of the relationships between the Plant and the Animal Kingdoms. The relationships have a closeness that has been recognized by nature religions. Jacob Grimm said that the history of the old religion of Europe could be said to be the history of trees. One link between these two kingdoms is the property in common of having recognizable auras, auras which are sometimes quite visible. These auras are a way, according to W E Butler, animals have of forming friendships and animosities with plants. Attributes can be shared through these auras. As one travels along his path, he or she might find he or she is favoured greatly by some certain plants or some groups of plants. He or she might be favoured by, in general, some environment, including much vegetation, which some section of the Circle of the Year offers. It is understood that all matter is, in fact, united: all matter, physically and spiritually, linked. Small bits of herb might cause a great event to take place. A bit of herb might be hidden in the room of a subject to cause that person to fall in love. Media used herbs to stop the flow of rivers and to check the flight of stars. This, from the writings of Apollonius Rhoduius.

The wheels of cause and effect tie the trees, even to the smallest of herbs, with the great turnings of the starry heavens. Subtle connections between an herb and a distant star can throw the balance of an event toward one direction or another. It is said, "Every herb knows her loving star."

Renterghem Lists

Heart	Female Genital	Lord
Club	Staff of the Priest	Priest
Diamond	Head of a Spear	Soldier
Spade	Farmer's Spade	Farmer

Numbers Related to Trees

According to some calendars, there are thirteen months: twelve, of thirty days each; one, of the days needed to take the old year to the new.

The thirteenth is called the Time of the Unhewn Stone. The old order, at the end of the twelfth, had come to an end and the new, had yet to be formed. Constellation Ophichus, the snake doctor who had thrown the orderly system out of balance; would, at this time, be an influence, as this is the time when he sticks his tail into the Zodiacal Belt. This is the time of the Fool King, to whom Holly and Ivy are related.

The Birch would be the first tree, the tree of Capricorn, the time of the birth of the new Sun. It would relate to Epiphany, would give the Fool his first traces of personality. Birch gives gifts, such as the ability to tell where love flows.

The trees, in their turn, give gifts. The second tree, the Rowan, gives the ability to solve mysteries. The third tree, the Elder, gives health and protection. The fourth tree, the Alder, is a royal tree which leads warriors in battle. It is the hottest tree to fight. It gives the ability to tell what illness a person has and the ability to work cures. The fifth tree, the Hawthorn, gives an ability to relate to Otherworld populations. It is a guardian of the way to the Otherworld. Its fruit, like that of the Apple, holds the Sacred Pentacle. The sixth time relates to the Ash, the tree of the Winds and of the great sky horses. The Ash gives the ability to go between worlds, travel to the Otherworld, and to predict weather. The Oak is also listed as sixth, as it is the tree of Midsummer. It is called the Door to the Otherworld.

King William Rufus was sacrificed against an oak by a man standing under an elder.

The seventh tree, the Willow, gives the ability to discover secrets. The eighth tree, the Oak, is the tree of the Sky Father. The Ash, called the Axle of the World, is also called the sacred tree of the Sky Father and listed as the eighth tree.

The ninth tree, the Hazel, gives wisdom. The tenth tree, the Apple, gives health, youth, love and life. The eleventh tree, the Blackthorn, gives protection and the ability to work charms. The twelfth tree, the Yew, called the tree of purity, gives the guarantee of rebirth. The Holly is called the tree of sacrifice. It gives protection.

The Trees

Tree
Number

1.	Capricorn	First Moon	Birch
2.		Second Moon	Rowan
3.		Third Moon	Elder
4.		Fourth Moon	Alder
5.		Fifth Moon	Hawthorn
6.		Sixth Moon	Oak, Ash, Poplar
7.		Seventh Moon	Willow
8.		Eighth Moon	Ash, Oak
9.		Ninth Moon	Hazel
10.		Tenth Moon	Apple
11.		Eleventh Moon	Blackthorn
12.		Twelfth Moon	Yew
13.		Thirteenth Moon	Holly, Ivy
14.	Chestnut		
15.	Plane		
16.	Walnut		
17.	Fir		
18.	Laurel		
19.	Elm		
20.	Poplar		Oak
21.	Linden		
22.	Beech		
23.	Maple		Vine
24.	Pine		Juniper

Assigning Value

Placing the Fool Card and the Death Card on a value scale would be difficult. As Zero, the Fool has been said to represent all Underworld, or negative values; so, be half the deck; with all the other cards, the other half. In that, the Fool would have a type of value.

Death, as a number, is associated with contemplation of death. Death, as death, is the true zero. Zero times any card is zero. It is the abyss into which all other cards, everything, will fall.

The Trump Cards

0 ~ Fool

The Fool has been called half the Tarot Deck. All the other cards, the other half. M. de Givry said that the influence of the Fool might pervade the whole pack, yet have no determined purpose.

The Fool has been called the modifier, as he modifies cards which present positions, numbers or agendas, but he is less and he is more. As less, the zero has no prescribed value, but it is not an absolute zero. The symbol is a designation, not a measurement. The Fool might suggest a thing of which he had a zero quantity, as a cup of water, when one drinks the water, is empty, but it still refers to water. The Fool, in one aspect, is the person empty of person; or, empty of personality.

On the other hand, the Fool represents the scope of possibilities on the other side of the abyss. So, he might be on the scale to balance sophistication: society with its virtues and failings. He might exist at the point where an accepted truth of one place has been extended to a place where it is not any longer truth and he'd be the one to cause others to question.

Case speaks of the Fool as younger than a new born babe, yet older than night or day. The range of possibility within him some see as limitless.

When the Fool is placed into a layout, the meanings of all the cards previously placed would be likely to shift, excepting the Thirteen. Waite said that in a reading, when one placed the Fool into it, the confusions of all the other cards previously placed would be reversed. In this, the Fool might supply the key to the mysteries.

The Fool would be going in no goal driven, or desire driven direction, but he might inspire a different way of looking at life. The Fool might inspire one to question. As the Joker, he might lead others into foolish ways. Zero, the Fool, is completely guided by nature. He accepts everything that comes to him. Having nothing to do with reason, the Fool would be immune to praise and blame, both of which need reason. Traits associated with the Fool are those of insanity, extravagance and rapture. As he would have no controle over his action, he would be free from guilt, and from prudence.

The Fool has been given a mask and a rattle, and the rattle duplicates the Fool's own head. Like the Fool, the rattle wears a cone shaped hat which has bells on it. The rattle would be phallic, would represent, and be a symbol for, the penis.

The Fool is dressed in a clown suit and bells are on his pointy toe shoes.

The Fool is an unknown quantity. He might represent a readiness to learn. Or, a readiness to blunder. Sometimes, from the Fool comes wisdom, the flip side of foolishness. The Fool is the Wild Card. He might be anything.

At the top right corner of the card is the birch switch. Being switched by birch would bestow on the Fool his first gifts. Some of these would be virtues of the Birch, virtues such as purity. And the Birch gives the gift of awakening. For this, it is the custom to birch mad men. And as an aid to learning, masters birch scholars. The Birch represents authority. Roman lictors carried rods of birch and, as a symbol of authority, an axe wrapped in birch rods is carried.

To be born, a new person might need, as a way out of the Underworld, to pass through hoops of birch. Then the birch switch would take possession of him and keep him from sliding back into the Underworld. The birch would represent a break from the past.

The Spirit of the Birch is a gift giving nymph. Her leaves, when given, are said to turn to gold.

Where is the Fool?

The Fool is where he is because he needs to be in that place. That place might be a place which others of his society saw needed to be occupied; so, as a place holder, he would be seen to have value, as being in a place which others would not have liked to have been in. Frazer tells of a man constructed of straw to serve as a place holder. It was a fool; as, constructed of straw, it had zero personality other than what was given to it, but it could serve as the spirit of a tree when the tree needed to have an object to hold and continue its spirit. Something needed to be in the tree serving. The tree's farmer and the farmer's friends would have found that place inconvenient; but the straw man; called, in one place, The Great Mondard, held that place very well.

The Fool who was, as Kightly said, "without laugh or smile," sent with a letter another mile, was another holder of a space which needed to be filled, but which others would likely not have wished to be in. But The Fool might have been the needed element which would have bound his unit of society together, would have kept each member from flying off and going his own way. Or, The Fool might have been the factor which kept the unit from hardening into a freedomless mechanism.

The Fool would be born into an environment. He would learn from investigation and from being instructed. The Quester might take the place of The Fool; might, with the aid of the cards and a reader, gain knowledge. Zimmer said that picture cards might have served in an initiation into the status of Magus. A picture might be a magical step into an event. A step to having an event occur might be to picture it happening. As a magic, for help in their hunts, cave men drew pictures of themselves slaying the hunted animals.

I ~ Warrior

The Warrior is a force which moves ever onward. It relates to neither evil nor good, but strikes that which is in its way. It relates to the Force of Life, the Plant growing. It gains power by binding forces together, by moving as a team. The Spiritual Force of The Warrior is sometimes a Single Sword rising from a mound of Earth. The Sword, called the most noble of weapons, is the symbol of The Warrior, and of all weapons.

Philosophers, as Eliphus Levi, have related Tarot Cards to the planets. The number one card holds redness. This relates to the Planet Mars.

In the upper left corner of the card would be the head of The Ram. In the upper right corner, The Rooster. Below The Rooster, a yellow hen and below the hen, dawn coloured eggs. At the top of the card, above and to the left of The Rooster, is a limb of an alder. The Alder was called the tree hottest to fight. To the rear, in the distance, one left and one right, would be an unclad woman archer.

In the center of Card Number One, The Warrior stands in his chariot, his sword held up, the tip of it pointed skyward, his round shield held before his chest, and in its center, a ruby.

Through a field of daffodils, two horses pull the chariot on which The Warrior, in his red tinted helm, rides forward. There is a dark reddish colour to his face, and red glints off his shield, his body, and off his chariot.

Along the sides of the card, comfrey and nettles are over violets.

The Warrior is vibrant, lusty and dangerous. He promotes copulation and, in vegetation, seeds.

II ~ Flower

The Time of The Flower rises out of darkness with an abundance of flowers. In the center of the card, above a field of primrose, is a mallow. It would stand not only for all flowers, but for flower meanings, flower qualities and for the concepts of blooming. The Flower represents all growing things.

The Mallow might seem, a rose coloured musk mallow, and would be near to the size of the unclad goddess, who is a step to its right rear. The goddess wears a crown of flowers: cornflowers and smallage. Over a shoulder, the goddess wears a garland of flowers: cornflowers and king cups. Left and to the rear of the goddess and The Mallow would be a blooming hawthorn, bright rags tied to some of its branches. To the right rear of the goddess, on a green hillock, is a Maypole, bright ribbons extending from its crown of flowers. The Maypole is a central feature of Mayday, a festival which is the high point of the Time of the Flower. Mayday, May dew is gathered before sunrise and, thought to be magical, women put it on their faces to increase their beauty, and use it to freshen their linens, and they find other uses for it also. Yarrell said it was thought, two turfs covered with May dew, put together grassy side inward, would produce eels, and the Eel was thought to be a type of snake.

Near the top left corner of the card would be the head of an ox, and around his neck, a garland of flowers. The ox would be a form of Belinus, a god who banishes impurity and infirmity.

In the top right corner would be a maple flute by a sprig of maple, as music from the maple flute would bring in the summer.

From each top corner, flowers would fall.

In darkness, in each lower corner of the card, would be an emerald. The Emerald is related to the Underworld, and it is a sacred stone of Venus. It represents calm and truth. It calms storms and sexual passion and counters magic and the Juggler's deceptions. It enhances, in animals and plants, growth, fertility, abundance and good health. It promotes wealth. The emerald gives quick wit and visions of the future. Looking at an emerald is thought to improve eyesight. Powers of the emerald are enhanced by its colour: Green. Green relates to the Underworld; The

Underworld, to the flower's power in growing.

In the Time of the Flower, Orion, with his club, would be defending the fields. As Maltwood has shown, stars relating to Orion form a sacred pyramid; and this, at this time, gives Orion added power and influence in architecture and hunting. Orion taught how to organize hounds into hunting packs.

In the Time of the Flower, a major force would be the goddess Maia. She is the force of the New Day, the Spring Season and the mating and birthing of plants and animals.

Flora, also, is a forceful goddess at this time, and she has a special day, which falls a short time before May Day. Flora holds The Power of the Flower. She promotes, especially, reproduction and blooming.

Maia and Flora would relate chiefly to light and air; but as the Time of the Flower is a time of balance, their forces of light would be balanced by forces of darkness. Flowers are considered, most powerful, as they draw powers not only from the forces of light, but from the forces of darkness. They draw from the Underworld, powers of growing and of controlling movement. It has been said, a congregation of flowers, acting in concert, can change the mood of a country. A single flower can cause a major event. The power of the flower is used in love charms. As charms, flowers are hidden in the rooms of the intended. It is said, Medea used flowers in blocking paths to The Moon, in changing the courses of rivers and in stopping the movements of stars. In making bonds, chains of flowers have been used. Flowers blooming out of season might cause or predict harm. The Primrose, a joy in May, it thought to cause harm when blooming in August. The way one treats flowers can determine what harm or good those flowers would do. Many flowers, including yarrow and stitchwort, are said to serve best when picked by a naked picker. Flora favours the unclad body. As the Time of the Flower has its dark aspects, the Time of the Flower is a dangerous time. Many of its flowers are near the gates of The Underworld. As flowers relate especially to the spring; young people, especially, should watch their steps.

The observer might see the scene with differences to the way in which she sees it illustrated by another. The Flower is an object of wonder which might tell many things. It might hold a tear for some sorrow, as flowers are caring. As one is told, they even mourn the deaths of other flowers. Flowers, by the suggestions of a scent, might indicate a change in fortunes. Edward Bach, as Heselton points out, used little more than spirits of flowers to work many cures.

On the Flower Card, one might see The Emerald shine through a great darkness, as it can hold the dark webs of the Underworld. From these, one might gain knowledge of the future.

III ~ Juggler

Card III is the Time of the Juggler. He would be a floating figure in the center of the card. Above his hands would be three golden balls. He would be wearing winged shoes and a winged helm. Beside him would be the winged staff, around which would twist two snakes. Over the horizon would be a long golden cloud island, the island of Aeolus, King of the Winds. It is a land of copulation, and joy. It is land of the ever blowing Winds. Cloud relates to winds and the cloud has been called a symbol of sex. The cloud island, said Fiske, is the first place to receive light and the last to lose it. From that island, said Boethius, the Winds are instructed to blow their blessings: Zephyrus, from the West, in plants, revests freshness; Eurus, from the East, brings in Flora with her flowers.

Near the lower right corner of the card would be the vase, Kantharos. And rising from it, a snake. This, a Vessel of Wind and a Vessel of Cures, is the Vessel of the Snake Goddess of Healing, Iaso. And it is a vessel for the dead. The Kantharos has a handle on each side, and each handle begins at the lip, curves up, then down to the foot. Mercury, according to Ogilvie, was also associated with a vessel. And he, like Iaso, would at times take snake form. And snakes are associated with healing. Apollodorus told of a doctor who watched a snake use a plant as a cure, so followed the example of the snake.

On the left side of the card, in the distance, is a tree, and in front of the tree, a leaf and three acorns, which betoken the tree to be an oak, a tree which is looked to for protection. When people have knocked on wood, it was often to gain a gift of protection from the oak. On the other hand, oaks can be dangerous. Also, they might be the homes of elves or fairies, which might be dangerous.

In the lower left corner would be three Jacinths. The Jacinth is at times, by the dead, taken to the Underworld in order to insure a hospitable reception. It is a stone sacred to the Underworld God, Hyacinthos, who relates to the growth and well being of vegetation; and to Mercury. Mercury made the Jacinth the memorial stone for the warrior god, Ajax. The stone banishes bewitchments and phantoms, and protects against disease, injury and lightning, and it augments riches; and, in its owner, encourages prudence, and it protects the traveler. It will change colour to warn of danger. Its normal colour is bright orange, the orange of sunlight, and of healing. The Jacinth stimulates creativity and enthusiasm and generates energy. To gain creative energy, a triangle of three jacinths was at times formed. At times, especially at Midsummer, when the Jacinth is close to the Underworld, the Jacinth brings pride.

The Juggler himself is usually thought of as being Mercury. Mercury is smart, tricky, quick and creative. His creativity is tied to his relationship to the number three, to his manipulation of triangles; as, with his balls, he is seen to be doing. Mercury, in fields of interest, would focus on invention, communication and commerce. With his interest in invention, he would have an interest in witchcraft. He would have, with communication, included poetry and charms, such as Mother Goose rhymes: as Little Bo Peep, which might hold secret meanings. Mercury is a joker. He might trip up a wise man, then pardon a crook. Especially in summer, he is fickle.

The Juggler is over a field of daisies. Parsley, chicory, ribwort and yarrow might be seen along the sides of the card. These are among the many plants who play important roles; especially, in the Time of the juggler; so, when looking at the Path, might be well to understand.

Daisies relate to the death of the young. A faded daisy is not likely to be seen. Daisies are here, and then they are gone.

The Ribwort is called the soldier's friend. A companion of the Cuckoo, it is associated with flying.

Yarrow also has an association with flying. It is used in witchcraft, as it is associated with The Underworld. It serves best, picked naked.

Associated with the Underworld, Parsley is considered, dangerous. It is thought, dangerous to give away a root of parsley.

Chicory, spoken of by Theophrastus, is a girl given a flower form by the Sun. She relates to air, to the invisible. She is a guardian of roads.

The major celebration which relates to the Time of the Juggler would be that held at Midsummer, for at that time, the Sun goes into decline. As the Sun turns toward the Underworld, as it struggles against the Dark Forces, the Forces of Light and Dark are celebrated. Light Forces are represented by the Sun, and Dark Forces, by the Dark Moon.

At this time, the Dark Moon is honoured as The Bear Goddess. Since the earliest times, she has, when in that form, been honoured. For her, rituals were done which related to the Underworld. These would have included form changing rituals and rituals for calling totem beings from an Otherworld.

Bears have been considered sacred. At times, they were honoured with ritual burial, and at times, their graves were enclosed by a protecting circle of ox horns.

For the Sun, at this time when it was felt he could use help, there would have been energy giving rituals, such as the sailing of burning discs, the rolling of burning wheels, the lighting of bonfires and the performance of dances, many of which would have included leaping.

The Sun's rising to peak strength, then shocking drop toward the dark, causes major disturbances of Air, and the disturbances are reflected through out nature. Chambers said it was an ancient custom, at this time, for people to break off tree limbs and put them over their doors to protect against tempest, thunder and other violence. As air often takes snake form, the disturbance is reflected in other snake forms. There is riotous copulation, and this calls for much purification. At this time the dead might be found walking.

The Snake and the Oak are honoured at this time, as they are the link between Dark and Light. The Snake is a slayer and a birth giver. The Oak is considered to be the Door between This World and the Otherworld.

IV ~ Crystal

Card IV is the Crystal, and this relates to the Sacred Spring and to water everywhere. The circle of the Sacred Spring, the Great Circles of Water everywhere, relate to the Moon and so, to Juno. Juno relates to Time measured by the Moon and regulates Circles everywhere. In a larger sense, as a mate to Janus, Time every way.

Card IV has the night sky. Under the sky is the dark water of the Ocean. In front of the Ocean is a garden of white lilies and from this, rises a white pedestal on which is a crystal globe. The lily represents the female genital and is the sacred flower of Juno. Near the left side of the card are hyssop and dark blue iris. At the bottom of the card, in front of the hyssop, is King Crab.

On the right of the card, hanging over the garden, are branches of the Willow. In the sky, left of the Willow, is the Full Moon. In flight below and left of the Moon is the dark shape of a goose, and it would be carrying darkness from the Underworld. In the sky, but not seen, is the Argo, an ancient ship of sad trips which related to the Moon. Also in the sky, also not seen, is the magical dog, called the Little Dog, which is sacred to Diana.

A Moonstone might be in the bottom right corner of the card.

The form of The Circle is sacred. It relates to the Crystal and is especially honoured in the Time of the Crystal. As Buckland has reported, the form of the Circle has been much used for giving protection. Allcroft reports that sacred circles have been obtained from cords tied to hazel rods. Instead of a hazel rod, one end of a cord might be tied to a sacred stone. Cords for making these circles were made from twisted withies.

The Circle relates to the Sacred Spring. Objects, as clouds, seen on the surface of the spring, would not be found on the surface, nor anywhere under the water's surface. They would be in the Otherworld.

V ~ Lion

The Lion is the spirit of the high point in the time of the element, Fire. The Lion has been called the Nemean Lion, who was said to have covered the far eastern hills with fire. The Nemean Lion would have been a form of the lion headed goddess, Lamasthu, and Lampetia, who was called Daughter of the Sun. The Sun is the home of the Element of Fire. The Lion represents the regenerating power of the Sun.

It is remembered, Jupiter is Lord of the Element of Fire. Posidonius Athletes states: In the cosmic sense, Jupiter is thought of as primary. Before a king went to war, he sacrificed to Jupiter. If the sacrifice seemed favoured, the priest took a brand from the fire and carried it in front of the army as the army went into battle.

On a green, dandelion covered mound would be the lion headed goddess, Lamasthu, unclothed and having on her arms, legs and head, a quantity of golden hair. Out of her mouth would come a tongue of fire. From the East, Lamasthu was thought to have often brought pain and misery. In her right hand would be a red rose: the symbol of flowers and of all blooming things. Blooming relates to flame. The Rose, a symbol of all blooming things, is a flower of great power.

On the far left would be a tall ash spear, which would represent the great force of bright royal days of high summer: Jupiter. Jupiter represents the drive to take charge, and to be responsible. In the center of every month, Jupiter is honoured. Worshippers look up to where his statures rise up from behind high alters, rise up, so that thought rises to his tall skies. Worshippers would feel his presence.

Also, The Spear is the Symbol of Lugus, Lord of the Sun, Master of War, Master of All Crafts, King of Lions.

A limb of the Ash Tree is at the top of the card, reaching out from the right. It is a sacred tree, guarded by wood spirits and elves and favoured by gnomes. It is related to The Horse. Horse shoes are buried beneath the roots of ash trees. Ash smoke chases demons and snakes.

On the card's right, on a post, is the King Eagle. In a claw, he holds thunderbolts of Jupiter: these, the sign that Jupiter is alert. Jupiter's lightning let people know that he was looking for injustice. The King Eagle, said Lactantius, represents The Spirit Ascending, The Winged Sun.

Along the sides of the card would be chamomile and columbine, which are favoured by the Sun. Dandelions and Marigolds would be along the bottom of the card. The Marigold, said Lucius Apuleius, is sacred to the Sun. Dandelion restores and enhances fertility. The golden flower is a symbol of the Sun and, said Lactantius, it holds the purest essence of gold. And in the center of the bottom of the card would be the Diamond, King of Stones, which represent the Sun. It protects against insanity, but in general, it is concerned with power and death, and not so much with healing. It is a dangerous stone that can bring death, and especially, if it contains a spot of red.

To the rear on the card, left of center, would be a hill, and on its top, a bonfire. Fire is the energizing Spirit of Life. Said Hartmann, there is essential and hidden fire in all things. Said Benedictus, it matures and purifies in man: in the material and in the astral body. Fire makes the house sacred, said Hocart. Pythagoras, according to Villinganus, could not think of worshipping a deity without lighting a light.

VI ~ Reaper

Seen in the sky during this section of Time is the Reaper, and she is holding a sheaf of grain; and, it is widely thought, this would be Ceres in her mature, giving phase. On Card VI, the Reaper, in a cloak and hood, stands in a field of wheat. In her right hand is a sickle; in her left, a sheaf of wheat in which are a few red poppies, the sacred flower of Ceres. On the lower left is a bee hive, and there are honey bees, which are sacred messengers of the gods. The bees were brought by Ceres from the Underworld. Back, to the right, is the Hazel, and under it, the Sow. At times, Ceres takes the form of a Sow.

Three peridots set in gold are in each bottom corner of the card, as this is a stone favoured by Ceres.

Left center, toward the rear, would be a stack of wheat and around it, fruit and vegetables: apples, walnuts, pears, carrots, figs, squash, plums, grapes. Many of these would be filling, and overflowing from, baskets.

On the lower right of the card would be lavender and meadowsweet; on the lower left, balm.

Ceres relates to the Underworld, which is the land of the dead, so holds a mysterious darkness in which there would be danger. At times, she held a relationship, as mother to daughter, with Proserpine, Queen of the Dead.

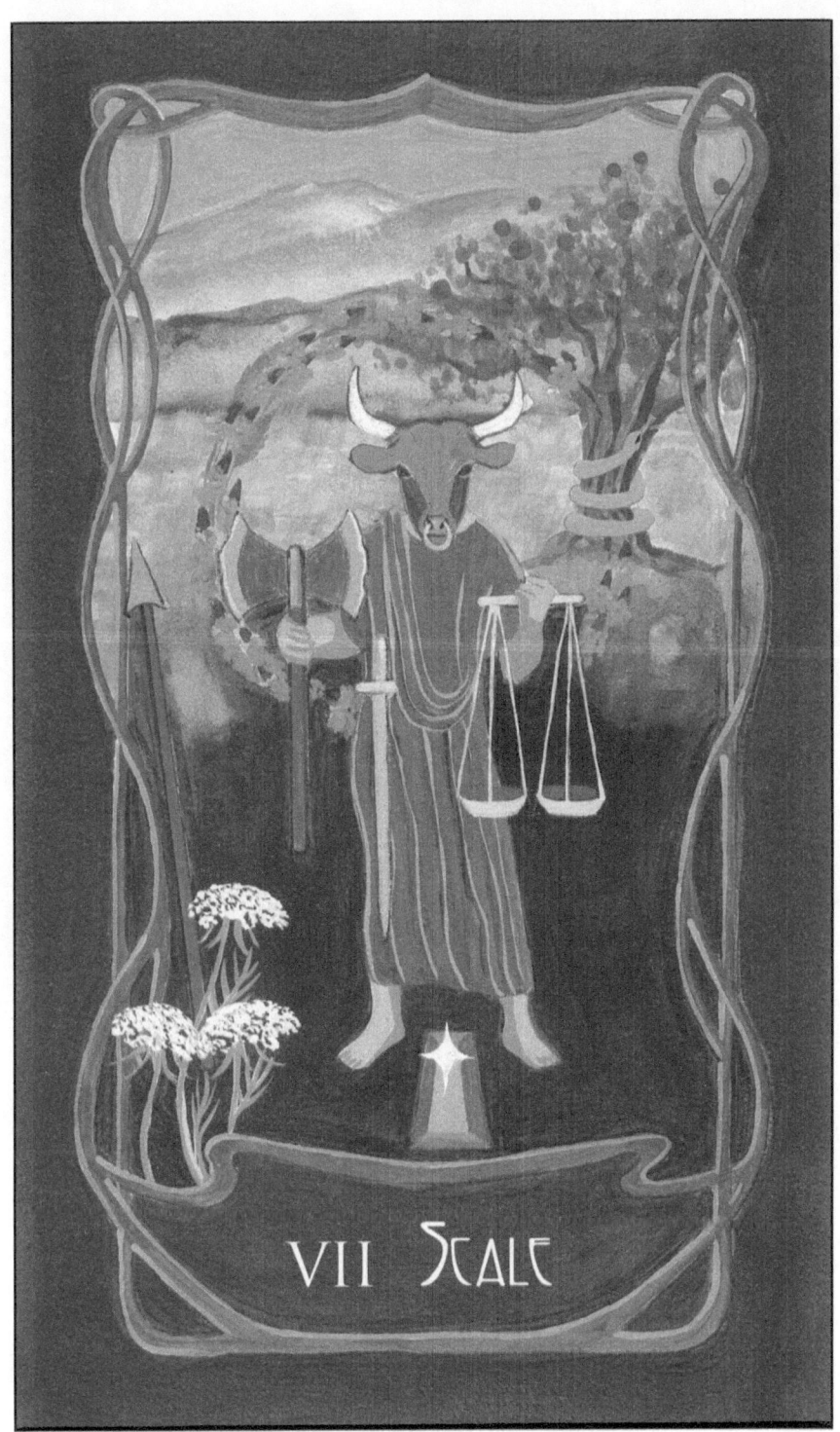

VII ~ Scale

The Scale is an illustration of the necessary force that insists that all creation have balance. For balance, there is judgement. Card VII has a chief judge, Minos, holding the tool used countering one force against another. Pythagoras determined, by mathematical calculation, he would be holding the scale in his left hand.

On Card VII, in a circle outlined by vervain, stands Minos, ox headed and in a purple robe. In his left hand is the Scale. In his right, the Double Blade Axe, the axe which cuts sacred segments.

On the left of the card stands a spear, the symbol of Europa. And this rises from a patch of wild carrot. Europa, the wide seeing goddess who, from over the eastern rim of the world, keeps watch, gives powers to Minos. Power is also given by Nemesis who comes down on that which is out of line.

To the right, in back of Minos is the Apple Tree, around which is a snake. These are symbols of death and rebirth, and these relate to balance.

An amethyst, at the bottom of the card, inspires balance in living. Purple mountains, at the rear, in the distance, hold wisdom and strength and inspire spirituality. They relate to the unknown and to that which is strange.

The resolution of opposites is a function of Time. At some point in time, each force would become one with a counter force. As a rule, the deities would not have been promoting balance, but would have fit into the necessity of the interplay to form balance. The Ram, as Manilius said, might have been against balance, but he would have met a force equally against, but pulling against him. The Scale would function, as Dionysius has said, because of the irreversible coherence of all that exists. The high and the low would have balancing ups and downs. At times, one force might seem, for an extended time, out of balance with its counter force, but this would be an illusion, an illusion at times caused by the greater visibility of one of the forces; as, one force being the richer; or, the taller. The smaller gifts are not as easily seen; or, are those who get them; and, as Callimachus said, the gods give small gifts to small men. But, the Scale measures each movement, tips at the point where balance forces change.

Balance is found to be of use to those who seek for ease or good health. Isidorus said that, for good health, one should strive for a balance, in the body, of the four basic elements: fire, earth, water and air.

The Time of The Scale is focused on changes: the end of day, the end of a season. For those who have begun, the ends would likely be more of interest than the beginnings. There would be an honouring of grandparents, a look at their steps into the Underworld. Attention would be given to contracts, to legal agreements. Ghosts do not escape the Scale. There would be a sadness in the falling leaves, in the sunset's purple glow.

In the center of Card VII would be the ox headed judge from the Underworld. In his left hand, he has The Scale; in his right, his double headed axe. And that, gives sacred segments. As Minos chops, his only concern is that each segment be of the correct length.

VIII ~ Demon

The Time of the Demon would have a relationship with the Underworld. Its number, eight, relates to the abyss, so has a dark hole in its center. Suggesting the dark hole, on the lower left of the card is a cauldron. And by the cauldron, a goblin, which is a form of demon. Demons are usually thought to cause harm; however, some demons; even, sometimes, goblins; might give pleasure.

On the lower right of the card, looking somewhat demonic, is a warped, rotting Jackolantern. By its carved face and by thoughts directed at it, it would have gained a personality. Around the cauldron, the Jackolantern, would be stalks of catnip, nightshade, henbane, monkshood and mint, and clumps of basil.

On the right, back from the Jackolantern, is a twisted blackthorn, and it would be protected by fairies. Blackthorn wands are used in black magic.

On the left, back from the cauldron, is the margin of a body of water and near it, a scorpion. The Scorpion is a symbol for darkness and death.

From the bottom of the card, a path extends to the center of the card, forks; each fork making its own way toward distant hills. The fork, according to Pythagoras, symbolized life and represented an important choice which would put one toward one type of life or toward another. Forks are considered sacred and spooky areas which relate to the Underworld. By the fork is a pile of stones on which an offering has been left for Hecate, Goddess of the Dark Moon and of Witchcraft.

Near where the path forks, on either side of the path, is a dark, howling dog. Theocritus said that at road forks dogs meet and bark. Road forks pick up psychic traces from many people who pass through the spirit energy of the fork: said Heselton.

It was thought, a person, at midnight on Samhain, at a road fork, seated on a three legged stool, could hear secrets.

Forks are considered sacred and spooky, areas which relate to the Underworld. Horns of beasts, wishbones and other forks are used in witchcraft.

In the sky, left of the blackthorn, is a thin, Sickle Moon. Below and left of the Moon is a witch on a broom, in her conical hat; and behind her, on the broomstraw, a black cat. Beyond and above the witch a couple of bats fly.

At the bottom of the card is a blue spinel. It would represent the Sacred Well, so would be a dark way to the Underworld, would hold the water veil, which is between life and death.

The number of the card, eight, relates to The Wheel, and in common with four, six, ten and twelve, has a black pit in its center. Pull the number apart and things are sucked into the pit. And as eight relates to The Wheel, and in The Time of the Demon, The Wheel of the Year, it is a dangerous time of the year; and, especially, as the year is getting old, dangerous, especially, for old persons. At this time, one might feel himself merging with the Spirit World.

And eight is the eight step octave, and the eighth step. It is the jump off into the unknown. Strange shapes vaguely seen might seem to lurk in a shadowy world, might seem dark shadows of dangers. This relates to the Water Veil between life and death. In the Time of the Demon there is an influence toward maliciousness. Assassins might be expected to have their birth at this time. Or so said Petronius. Moon fairies would lurk in the blackthorns. The Time of The Demon would be a time of witchcraft. Dangerous herbs: basil, monkshood, catnip, henbane, black nightshade and mint would be most powerful.

Concentrating on the images on Card VIII, one might manifest, or invest, a spirit.

IX ~ Archer

The Time of the Archer is the Time of the Longhaired Suns, Old Suns who are on their way to the Underworld. Card IX, Time of the Archer, has a Longhaired Sun sinking toward distant, rose coloured hills. In the right center of the sky is the Centaur Archer. In the meadow, left of the Archer, is an old, spreading yew. Near the yew, sheep would be on a path toward distant hills. In the sky, on the far right, near where the Longhaired Sun is sinking, is a harp and a single blade axe. In the left side of the meadow, near at hand, are three crows. Herbs in the fields, close by, might be identified as valerian, centaury and sage. At the bottom of Card IX is a topaz set in gold. It would relate to wisdom.

The Long Haired Suns are gods who had been suns, but are now wise judges. Their influence is toward wisdom and durability. A tree of this time, the Yew, is looked to for wisdom. The herbs promote long life. It was said, said Gomme, the Sage favoured King Arthur. Valerian favours smiths.

X ~ Horned Piper

Card X relates to the First Moon. The Time of Card X is a time of bright joy over darkness and mystery. A time of darkness and bleakness had thrust upon it the madness of the time under the Thirteenth Moon, when Ophiuchus stuck his tail into the Circle of the Year. On the card is the celebration of the New Sun. In the center of the card is the hearth, the alter of Mother Earth, and the way to Mother Earth's alter is never blocked. Left of the hearth is a pine hung with gifts for Saturn and Hades, and with other gifts, which would be blessed by the deities; and hung, also, with decorations in honour of the deities. At its top, to honour the Star Goddess, is a Five Point Star.

In the fireplace would be the Yule Log. This represents the death of the Old Sun. Oh a platter in front of the hearth would be a roast boar. He would be the Old Sun who sacrificed himself to be food for his people and went to the Underworld. The apple in his mouth is the key to passing between the worlds; so, provide for coming back into this world. In his honour, he would be decked and crowned with sacred plants: rosemary, thyme and bay. These have, each, its powerful magics which fit into the magic of the celebration.

To the right of Lord Boar would be gifts of the harvest: bowls of fruit and nuts and a bowl of wassail.

Above the Yule Log, on the mantle, would be holly, fir and juniper. Evergreens act as a charm against malicious forces. Holly and ivy would be across the top of the card and from these would hang bells, which would purify the air.

From the top of the card, in the center, would hang the magical mistletoe, and this would give magical protections.

In front of the fireplace, to the right of the Yule Log, would be the Fool King. He would wear a holly crown, be decorated with holly and would carry a holly club. On the right side of the card, ass eared and wearing a crown of pine, hairy, holding a mug of wassail and his pruning knife, would be Sylvanus. To the left of the Yule Log, holding a sack and a broom, would be Nick. On the far left of the card would be the Horned Piper, Pan. It is said, Pan and the Satyrs were the first to become aware that there was a problem with the King of the Sky. Pan would have his pipes. Not pictured on the card, Amalthea, the Goat Nurse, who gives care and nourishment to people and deities in her area. Also not pictured are the dark, bleak, ice covered cold landscapes and the dark lonesome forests. And, among the disorder of change, the struggle for new birth. After mad disorder and disrespect, after sacrifice, there is purity of new birth and a silence of vast snows and peace. Holly is the Tree of Sacrifice and the spark of new birth.

In the bottom corners of the card would be tourmalines, stones of a shiny blackness which send out glimmers of red and green, which is called malignant fire.

The Tourmaline, it is remembered, is a dangerous stone, in that it tends to become part of its possessor.

Seen on the hearth would likely be a sieve, as Yule Log ashes shaken through it is a way to tell fortunes. Not seen on the card would be the many candles which would be lit; lit, in part, to encourage the brightening Sun. Not seen on the card, the tree holding gifts for the birds, including the Wren. The Wren, was said to predict disasters.

XI ~ Cup Bearer

Card XI relates to the Second Moon, which might inspire wild projects. Card XI, The Cup Bearer, pictures a bleak, cold landscape. Over this, a god, on one knee, is pouring water from a large cup. The god would be Phaenon, Cup Bearer for the Sky God, Uranus. When Jupiter was having trouble extinguishing a fire which Phaeton, a Sun God, had started, Uranus sent Phaenon, and Phaenon put it out. The power Phaenon had shown worried Jupiter and Jupiter would have sent Phaenon out into space, but Uranus ruled against it. Grey Uranus, in his grey robe, is not obviously present on the card, but he is the Grey Sky, which is grey with a suggestion of grey cloud. If the card were showing night, Latona would be there also. In the distance, on the right side of the card, would be a dark bear. In the lower left would be a small rowan. In each bottom corner would be a garnet. Between them, a grey green leaf or two of alehoof.

The grey Uranus gave spiritual need to form. Without form, it would be difficult to find meaning in life. And spiritual meaning, said Whewell, can be realized in the properties of figure. From form, one can gain sensual and supersensual states of mind. And these would relate to Uranus.

The fact that a deity featured in this time period is pictured with a cup, which is a major symbol for water, should not obscure the picture's major theme: the importance of Air. And to its role as the first Air Sign since the birth of the New Sun. Air, at this time, would likely be cold, pure and reliable, but the picture would relate to Air in its many forms. The Lord Air, said Isidorus, is likely to be fickle, although not as much in the winter. And if Fire is above Air, Air should become light and pure. He said that with Water below Air, Air becomes heavy and disturbed.

XII ~ WAVE

Card XII, The Wave, relates to the Third Moon. It tolerates new knowledge. Card XII, The Wave, represents the Sea and Water every place. A tall, curling wave is seen rising above the Sea. Behind the Wave is Neptune with his trident. Somewhat distant, one, far right and one, far left: two unclad goddesses: Doris and Tethys and Tethys' head and arms showing somewhat of a shape change, which is usual for sea deities.

At the bottom of the card, an Onion in the right corner; a sprig of Elder, in the left. The Onion is a money minting god. The Elder is a witch goddess. But these are pictured in their plant forms. At the bottom, between the two, is an aquamarine. Left of the Onion is a clover leaf. Clover, as Chadwick has said, is a Symbol of Spring.

Hidden in the field; in order, as a gift from Tethys, to gain protection; might be a round stone on which a cross has been carved.

XIII ~ Death

Death is pictured as a skeleton in a raggedy black hooded cassock swinging a scythe. On a hemp rope belt he has an hourglass. The ground would likely be bare; the sky, dark and cloudy with lightning; or, a suggestion of lightning.

XIV ~ Craftsman

On Card XIV, the Craftsman pictured is Vulcan, the Lame Smith. With his hammer, he is at his anvil. He can craft tools which are magical.

Vulcan is a God of Fire and, as Fire, he is a purifying agent. He is called, arbiter of the purifying process. As Fire, Vulcan can express anger. As a craftsman, Vulcan is associated with Earth. He relates to animals; especially, to horses and pigs and, it is said, if he saw a horse which needed a shoe, he would put one on.

Card XIV, Vulcan is in front of his smithy, a cave formed of huge boulders; its entrance shaded by a chestnut tree. Behind Vulcan is a fiery forge. Wisps of smoke rise. From a hill behind the smithy would rise a tongue of smoke. On the ground in front of the smithy, here and there, are clumps of valerian. Valerian, as it is an herb favoured by Vulcan, is made part of the Vulcanalia Festival. On the sides of the card is fennel, which is said to hold sacred fire.

In each top corner of the card is a horseshoe, the open side up, so that it will hold fortune. The crafting of horseshoes relates to music. Cassiodorus said that Pythagoras discovered the need for music from hearing smiths hammering on horseshoes.

The chestnut, which shades the front of the smithy, has a relationship to the Underworld. Its flowers were used in making a woman who sent the Sun God to the Underworld. The Chestnut is a favourite tree of the Divine Sow. Ghosts favour chestnuts. Chestnut wands are used for acts of theft. Chestnut sticks are used for gaining knowledge of the future. Chestnuts are used in charms for gaining copulation. Chestnut tea is used for treating coughs and fevers. Chestnut wood is used for carpentry, and often, it has been the wood chosen for the construction of shrines and temples: places which hold spiritual relationships.

XV ~ Tower

The Tower is a focal point of protective force. It is a sacred Temple that holds protective magic. The Tower number, fifteen, is the total of the three number fives, as five is the number which represents each of The Tower's three chief protecting deities: Athene, Rhea and Pallas. The Tower is protected by other deities also.

The tower pictured would appear as a tall, round building; however, its non visible force lines would give it a pyramid shape. The Tower would attract lightning and lightning would be seen striking the tower pictured. The lightning seen might be any one of a multitude of things. The lightning might represent a stroke of spiritual energy. This energy might destroy a concept; so, make way for a spiritual awakening; or, a new mental awareness. The lightning might be destroying an object to make way for a new object; perhaps, an object which is needed. As The Tower, in one of its aspects, represents The Great Penis, the strike of lightning might generate the Great Orgasm, create a birth which would shake an Age. It might create a wave of births; or, it might represent a single birth which would be hardly noticed in its own family. Births represented might not be physical human births, but the creation of an object, or the birth of a concept. The lightning however, might be a physical stroke which, perhaps, did little more than dislodge a few stones. And The Tower, at that time, be giving shelter from the storm.

Lightning creates balance. It sends energy to that which lacks sufficient energy.

The Tower holds a force, which includes spirit powers, and with this force it protects itself and others. Courage is one of the weapons which The Tower holds. Often, The Tower is most helpful to those who trust in the help from The Tower.

The beginning of The Tower is The Dream. At the top of The Tower would be a window, a far seeing, magical eye, and this would give protection.

No tower lasts forever, but a tower within its limits will give needed protection to those who are in a position to call for it. Many things have been found which have had physical or spirit aspects of The Tower. The

Tower gives great and small birthings.

In the bottom left corner of the card would be a plane tree leaf and five plane tree balls. In the bottom right corner, an olive tree wreath. Between them, the head of The Ram. The Plane Tree would represent Rhea; The Olive Wreath, Athene; and The Ram, Pallas.

In the top left corner would be The Owl. In the top right corner, The Bee.

XVI ~ Gaoler

Card XVI is The Gaoler. The Gaoler is the King of the Underworld. He would be pictured in the center of the Underworld, seated on a stone. In his left hand, he holds a two pronged pitch fork. The prongs represent the dual aspects of all things: night, day; hot, cold; light, dark. It also represents the forked way, the choice where one option has to die.

Hades, King of the Underworld, is a ram horned god with, for a face, only dark shadow. His feet rest on a snake. The card is dark and shadowy. Goblin like figures merge into stone walls. A severed hand is in the bottom left corner. Such hands are used for doings which a normal hand could not do. In the bottom right corner is an angry dog, a guardian of the Underworld. In the top left corner is a crow. From the top right corner extends a walnut tree branch, which is forked; so, an echo of the pitchfork of Hades. The fork would be a window for looking into the Underworld.

The Walnut Tree is a link breaker. It gives the freedom to change and the strength for new ventures. And it was said, said Ellis, gods sent out prophecy which was read in walnut twigs. Twigs were cut, peeled and marked. After a petition to the gods, the sticks were cast; then, three twigs selected to be read. For working charms against ailments, spiders were put in walnut shells, said Gerard. Women in order to obtain sterility, roasted walnuts before their weddings; then, after the weddings, planted the roasted walnuts.

The Walnut is a tree related to melancholy and gloom. It is favoured by Diana and relates to The Moon and to witchcraft. Witches have had a custom of meeting under walnut trees.

XVII ~ Star

The Star is the Selected Star from a field of many stars. It is the Star Goddess, Ariadne. She sits in her circle of stars, which is the Castle of Death. From Earth, she seems a protecting, caring point of light. Or, the goddess might be seen as an unclad girl spread on a falling, five point star. In her circle of stars is her glittery castle, which has been called her Silver Wheel. As she is a spider goddess, said Rutherford, her wheel would be a spider web. It is also her Maze in which she holds her Dance of Death. From early times, her maze has been carved into rocks. The center of the Maze, as Cavendish has said, was thought to hold the Secret of Life and Death. Maze dances are done as rituals of rebirth, and it was thought that through these rituals, the Inner Secret of Life and Death could be gained.

The Maze of the Goddess would be a toxic web. It is the web of the Goddess of Silver. The Universe has been considered to be her maze. The Maze is sometimes placed in the center of The Cross. It might be seen in a rock at the bottom of the card.

The Castle of the Dead, seen in the Circle of Stars, would have no place in the physical world. If a bird were to fly toward the Castle of the Dead, it would never get there by flying. There is no physical direction by which one could get there, as that castle rests within another dimension. One might see the Castle of the Dead in the Northeastern Sky because one expects to see it there.

On the card, in an upper corner is the Castle of the Dead, the Corona Borealis. At the bottom of the card are the dark tops of fir trees. The Fir relates to birth. New born babies are blessed with fir, and firs are put on buildings which are being built.

A second star one might see in the night sky might be a second star goddess, Sirona, whom Rhys said was a Symbol of Night. And he said that she balanced Apollo, who served as a symbol of Day. Sirona has been shown with corn and fruit.

A third star would be the Goddess, Astraea, who represents justice. It has been said, she is the last major deity to have been seen on Earth, as she needed to see justice was done.

Stars are loving and healing. Plants, said Father Young, know and watch for their loving star. In healing, it is said, a star will complete the work of a medical herb. Ariadne gives a loving welcome to all those worthy of her love who climb to her.

The Star Goddess, spread out on her Five Point Form, is falling. Every star is a falling star. Every star is a Star of Wonder, a Star of Light, a Star of Royal Beauty. Many appeal to it:

"Star Light, Star Bright, First Star I've seen tonight; I wish I may, I wish I might, have the wish I wish tonight."

XVIII ~ Sun

Card XVIII, the Sun, is the Spirit of the Sun with all of its attributes. These, beside heat and light, would include prophecy, athletics, healing, music, beauty, mathmatics, logic and creativity. People picture Apollo as representing the epitome of clear thinking, as bringing order out of chaos. However, some felt that he added little to excite the imagination. But he did inspire beautiful art and for him, beautiful temples were built. Apollo is Lord of the Land of the Apple, an Otherworld Land. Often, Apollo got poor treatment from women, but he loves the woman who became the bay tree. Apollo favours dolphins and delphiniums, which were once dolphins. And chickens are sacred to Apollo, as the Rooster announces Apollo's rising. The Spirit of Apollo is in gold, so gold coins are minted in the temples of Apollo. Apollo demands honesty. Apollo is not always friendly, but he deals honestly.

On Card XVIII, Apollo is the bright god in the Sun Car. He is pulled by two white horses. In the sky are white, sheep like clouds, and below the Car, a shower of gold coins. In the lower right corner of the card is a dolphin, and in the left corner, delphinium. In the top corners would be yellow hens with golden eggs and between them, a white rooster. At the bottom of the card, in the center, would be a bay tree, and on either side of it, branches of apple trees. On either side of the apples would be marigolds.

The Sun reveals secrets. Also, it might conceal secrets. The Setting Sun protects hidden secrets.

In the Sun Car, The Sun God becomes The Eye of Day. He holds a bow and arrow, and with him in the car is The Golden Harp, which relates to The Sun Car. Number XVIII, The Voyage of the Sun: nine jumps to the Underworld, nine waves to bring The Sun again to This World.

The Sun might be a powerful wheel shedding Sun Qualities throughout the other cards on a layout.

XIX ~ Moon

On Card XIX, in the sky is the Full Moon. On each side of the card elms rise from the ground. On the ground between their dark shapes is a circle of light. In the center of the circle is the naked, drawn down Moon, standing tall, her arms raised to form a vee. On the far left, in the shadows under the tree, is a rabbit, which is a symbol of eternity. On the right, a bow and three arrows are near the bottom of the elm. White flowers are here and there on the ground. Ivy, which has been called wanton, runs a third of the way up the sides of the card, and at the bottom of the card, in the center, ivy encircles a water filled cup.

Lady Moon gives uncertainty, gives beauty, gives love, gives fantasy, gives dream. And in dream, said Lucretius, the glorious divine figures of the deities first appeared to the souls of men.

The Moon gives insight. The Moon, over what seems formless dark, organizes forms, charms and controles releases of knowledge, selects glimpses for learnings. Shapes out of the unknown, half lights and lurking shadows, are directed by the Moon to reveal knowledge. Where there is more darkness than light, the knowledge given by the Moon might be caught out of the corner of the eye, when a hard, straight ahead look and conscious study would, in knowledge from the Moon, give little or nothing.

On the card, the ivy and elms would indicate that the goddess would be Selene, Goddess of the Moon, and of Moonlight. She is gentle, she is beautiful. And her influence floods over that which she touches. Monday's child is fair of face.

Selene might be in the sky, in a car pulled by White Oxen. Selene might be found in a lonely meadow riding an ass. And she might be caught in a cup of water.

XX ~ Teacher

Card XX is the Teacher and the teacher pictured on the card is Minerva. She has been called the Goddess of a Thousand Works. Minerva has a wide range of areas of interest. Minerva integrated fields of philosophy into teachings in the crafts. At her festivals, teachers and craftsmen who work in a variety of fields are honoured. In teaching, Minerva directs education to the seven forms of learning. In crafts, she has a special affection for weaving, spinning and the making of ropes. And Minerva is a warrior and teaches military skills.

In the center of Card XX is Minerva, a stately goddess in a dark robe. In her right hand she holds a spear, and in her left, a round shield. To the rear of Minerva, on the right side of the card, is a spinning wheel. On the card, to the right front, would be a distaff. On the left front, would be a bucket and from the bucket, a rope would run to the top of the card. On each side of the card would be a beech with their top limbs extending over Minerva.

In the top left corner of the card is Minerva's messenger, the Owl.

Along the bottom of the card would be flax in bloom, and below the flax, on the left, a snake. The Owl would carry thunderbolts. Images of owls were often buried with those headed for the Underworld.

XXI ~ Hanged Man

Card XXI has the Hanged Man. He has gone counter to convention and been trapped. He hangs, by the left foot, from a limb of the Linden Tree. He is naked. One can be certain, he is not having fun. It can be seen, the hanging causes surprise and discomfort and, likely, pain. But he is hanging between worlds. There might be joy beyond disgrace. He might be taking himself to a different place.

On the ground under the Linden are three mandrakes. Dark, snaky clouds might be in the sky.

The number of the card, XXI, is three sevens. Seven is the number of segments before a big change to a different group of segments. The Hanged Man is making such a change.

Often a Hanged Man, going widdershins against the sunwise flow, was the one who knit the community together.

XXII ~ Strong

The figure on Card XXII, representing The Strong, is Hercules. The mighty Hercules stands unclad in the center of the card, his oak club in his right hand and on his shoulder, his bow and arrows. To the right rear, on a pink cloud, is the spinning wheel which authorities ordered Hercules to work at. As it sailed over Earth, the spinning wheel with Hercules would have been the Sun. The spinning wheel was like the one owned by the Strong Woman, Omphale.

Hercules wore a poplar crown, and poplars would have been at the bottom of the card. In the top right corner of the card would be a hammer. From near the hammer, lightning would fork in the sky.

On each side of the card would be a pillar.

Hercules as Strength gives much pleasure.

Posidonius said it was a custom to celebrate triumphs in the Temple of Hercules. Statues were draped and beside meat from the sacrifice, other foods, as boiled smoked meats and loaves, were served.

The strength of Hercules was a great marvel. According to Pomponius Mela, when Hercules was leading away the cows of Geryon, he met and slew two great giants, Albion and Bergyon. These, in the World of the Spirit, would have been England and Eire. This relates to the perpetual conflict between the Sky Gods and the Sow Goddesses whom the giants would have represented. The power and durability of the Sow Goddess, as Collingwood has said, has been underestimated. The two giants, being Harvest Gods, would have been reborn.

XXIII ~ Love

Card XXIII is Love, The Goddess of Love is Venus and she stands in the center of the card, unclad, holding a bow and arrows. Unclad is Venus, except she wears golden sandals. In her left hand she holds a mirror.

In each corner of the card is a red heart. At the bottom of the card is a limb of maple, and at the top, a dove. A grapevine, with grapes, winds around the card and, inside the vine is a circle of flowers and fruit: apples, pears, strawberries, violets and red roses. Among the flowers and fruit are green leaves.

Crimson is a colour favoured by Venus. From Theocritus: For love vows to be protected by Venus, bands of crimson wool are entwined.

The Love card and the Strong card relate to the planet Venus.

XXIV ~ Megalith

Card XXIV, The Card of the Megalith, pictures a place of chaos. The card represents the small section of Time unruled by the major forces which rule all other Time in the year. The deities who are usually strong in upholding the law, avoid this Time. This is a time for sacrifice and rebirth. In this Time, Saturn rules, and the Spirit of this time flows past its bounds and into that which follows. This would be called The Time of The 13th Moon.

In the Time of Card XXIV, there is a great feeling of equality and regulating laws do not keep order, and this leads to much loud laughter. In this Time, beings representing crude beginnings gain powers. The Megalith is honoured and recognized as being powerful.

Pictured on the card, the Megalith stands on the left and beyond the area being used for celebration. To the left of the Megalith, and nearer to the celebration, is a pine; and this is decorated with coloured cloths and on it are gifts for Saturn and Hades: dolls for Saturn and masks for Hades.

There is a fireplace built of stones, and in that, a Yule Log. A long, board table sits on rocks and on the table, a boar crowned with bay holds an apple in his mouth. On the table are bowls and platters filled with food and drink. Vases are filled with holly, juniper and bay and these, tied with bright cloths. To the right are screens hung with ivy and bay. To the right of the table stands Saturn, a thin, old man with a white beard, and the Holly King, and he is decked in holly, holds a holly club and wears a holly crown. Saturn wears a ragged white robe. He wears a rope belt from which hangs an hourglass. In his left hand, Saturn holds a sickle. Likely not pictured is the celebrating crowd; or the mad party, a party which would attract odd beings, as goblins and witches, and the horses skull in a hooded garment, and there would be Satyrs, and the Goddess of Earth would be represented. At the party, which is not pictured, there would be Saturnalia gifts, each with its sprig of holly.

On the left, toward the bottom of the card is a juniper bush. In the center, at the bottom of the card, is a pair of dice. Coins, which are popular at Saturn's celebrations, would be left of the dice. As Saturn favours money, money has been kept at Saturn's temples.

From the top of the card hangs mistletoe. Ivy runs up the sides of the card and across the top; and this, mixed with holly. A couple of crows are below and left of the Megalith. In the upper right corner is an owl; a skull, in the lower left.

The Megalith stands tall, strangely shaped, oddly textured. With the stone, there is a suggestion of movement, of shapes taking living form. The Megalith, as it relates to Saturn, and to Uranus, and to remote, Otherworld deities, has a relationship to judgement . This relationship has been recognized by Eliphas Levi, and by W W Wescott. The Megalith also is known to do healing, and to do predicting. It is considered sacred. Lucius Apuleius said that every property owner should have a sacred stone on his property.

XXV ~ Magician

Card 25 is the Magician. He is in white; a white sleeveless slipover, nearly knee length. This is his only garment. He stands barefoot on bare ground. From a chain around his neck hangs a cross. In his left hand is a crystal ball which is held toward Earth; in his right hand, a brown wooden wand held high and pointed toward the sky. Garment, wand, crystal, chain and cross would be tools of the Magician, but would also be extensions of the Magician's body, of his personality. And the Magician would have many other tools. His tools would be all the things he could reach with his senses which he chose to use. These might include distant stars. But he would usually select items closely related to him and these would often be ones he would usually find sharing with him, sacred space.

Each individual tool would have its powers and personality. The Magician would consider if he and the tool, or the combination of tools, that would efficiently fit together to together get to the place where he wanted to be.

Tools considered the most sacred, the most powerful in spiritual work, would usually be made of wood or stone. The first tools mankind used and the first considered magical were certainly of one or the other of these materials.

First, the wand is ancient and magical. It is an extension of the sacred tree. Trees are especially sacred to deities and many of the deities will, at times, take the form of a tree. To determine which tree to select, from which to request the gift of a wand, one studies trees. The personality of a tree can be studied because the auras of trees have shown themselves to be similar, in many ways, to those of humans. An aura would be the spiritual aspect of a physical force field which every object would have. Every object has a force field; so, an aura, or spiritual aspect; but auras of minerals seem not to be ones to which humans can easily relate. Because of the similarities and bonds which things living, in our sense of the word, have in common, the natures of flora would be more easily recognized than those of minerals.

A magician might find a tree which had many characteristics which would be of use to him and which would, as a friend, like to join forces with him. If the tree would be happy with it, an exchange of gifts might be made and the magician, gain a useful wand.

The Magician's wand is an extension of his personality and of the personality of the tree. One personality would compliment, or help to shape, the other. The selection of a tree to work with would, in part, depend on how a magician saw the path ahead, on what problem solving he expected to be doing. The deities with whom a tree tended to work well would be a consideration in the selection of a wand. The Magician would have a wand from the Tree that held a key to the Underworld. And the Tree would reach up to connect Earth with Sky.

And stones have been treated as living things and as spiritual forces. Great stones nave formed centers of spirituality. Powerful gem stones have shaped energy flows and so, caused changes in the histories of nations. Stones are sacred to deities; some stones, to many deities. There would be few sacred places where most sacred stones would not be welcomed.

The crystal, held in the Magician's left hand, would represent the Sacred Spring and so, be an entrance to the Underworld. It would represent the Moon and so, be sacred to the Goddess of the Moon. As the crystal connects this world with the Underworld, it would hold a knowledge of the past and of the future.

From a chain around his neck, the Magician would wear a cross. The cross is the magical shape designating the place where the 4 elements come together and are balanced, each with each. It is the place where differences are resolved. The Cross marks the place of the Magician who is where he needs to be: the exact place at the exact time he needs to be there. For this reason, he would be pointed to as the major cause of an event and so, called the Magician. The cross and chain of the Magician would be of bronze, the metal which Janus would hold as most sacred.

The Magicians clothes would be tools of his. His slipover would be of the neutral. Some magicians would wear a conical hat, its peak in the eye of the pyramid. Some magicians would wear a belt, perhaps one obtained in a traditional ritual, one which would establish him as a magician and which would certainly hold magical power. And the Magician might be working skyclad. With wand and crystal, cross and chain, in his circle, he is seen to be causing significant movement in his environment. He directs circles of energy from Sky into Earth and around, from Earth to Sky and around.

A magical person seen turning a great wheel might be recognized as the Magician. To be magical, and known as magical, the person would likely be working in a system in which he had faith, one which he was confident he could make work. A step in working magic might be visualizing the magic working. As drawings of animals being caught is thought, a step in catching them.

Dedication might be the mark on the person who would be the Magician. It might be seen in the selection and preparation of the magical tools. For a wand, there might be a trip to find the correct tree; the establishing of a rapport with the tree; the agreement with the tree to an exchange of gifts, an exchange which the tree would be happy with; then, the cut of the limb, carefully done with a purified and worthy knife while sympathy is being shown for the tree; perhaps, by the magician cutting a limb of his own so that he is sharing pain. Then, the gift given: perhaps a libation of honey and a chant of thanks. The magician might sit with the tree until the Sun's rising and the time has come to hold the wand over the head in the Sun's first rays. And to request, of the Sun, empowerment for the wand. The wand might then be trimmed, rubbed with linseed oil and purified with the smoke of selected herbs. And the Sun is not looked to once and then forgotten, but looked to each morning; the wand, regularly reinforced by the Sun's rays. Or this, with a magician, might seem irrelevant. He might find, or be given, a stick; wave it, and cause great cycles to turn. He might continue to take steps, wave hands or sticks, so people would see waves made, wheels turn, as if the elements had waited for him, the Master, for his very stick. His magical clothes would be the ones he happened to be wearing. They would be exactly the ones, as they were doing the job, turning the wheel, uniting the elements.

A magical person, to picture himself as a magician, even to his own eyes, might feel a black or white robe would be needed to set the mood, to establish that concept. For his magic, he might feel he needed an alter. Those rooted most deeply in tradition would be of wood or stone. Stone would carry the weight of those most ancient. As a tool, the alter would be needed for organizing other needed tools: those needed on the alter and those prohibited from it.

On many alters, tools representing each of the 4 directions are felt to be needed. East: a stone arrow head or stone knife, according to Pythagoran tradition, could represent the shafts of light from the Sun. South: a ceramic or stone plate, to represent Earth, would be for holding clay or loam. West: a glass or ceramic bowl or chalice would, to represent water, hold water which sometimes needed to be from a brook or spring. North: a bell or an incense holder or both would represent air. On some alters, other tools might be felt to be needed. One might be a crystal globe and its holder, which would be of ceramic, stone or wood. If wood, the wood selected would be important. Willow, elm or blackthorn relate to water and would be usual selections. A ceramic vase and a candle holder are tools which a magician might feel he needs. For the holder, he might feel he needs a bees wax candle. For purity, a saltcellar for salt might be felt to be needed. A glass, decanter like bottle, for the alter, is sometimes felt to be needed. It is sometimes kept off the alter. A wooden or bone wand would certainly be welcome on the alter. As it lacks productivity, salt is kept off the Earth plate. The tools for The tools for the North and the tools for the South were at times reversed.

To be on the alter, it was, and is, felt that an item needed to be purified and ritually prepared, to be accepted by a useful network of deities. It is usual to prohibit iron from being put on an alter and often, any metal. Sacred tools which contain metal, and those which lack purity and ritual acceptance, might be put by the alter. Others would be put by the alter because though needed, are not needed on the alter.

Tools in front of the alter might be a knife, a staff, a cauldron, a bottle and a broom. The staff is a tall wand, so it is size which makes it more fitting for a spot on the ground.

The knife is an important off the alter sacred tool; off the alter as it has a blade of steel. The tail would be of wood or bone as a rule and the wood, a wood harmonious with the blade: perhaps, ash. The knife is not a dilettante, a display item, a replica or a decorative, symbolic representation. It is a friend, glad to be helpful in appropriate ways. It should be used, and a person, to serve the deities, should have a quality knife. The knife at the alter, representing Knife, should be of the best. The knife which one presents to the deities for their blessing should be clean, sturdy, well balanced, sufficiently sharp. The knife which performed well would honour the deities and would be treated as an honoured friend. There are times when a magician might need an honoured knife.

The broom might be, as a person, with an elaborate ceremony, initiated into a magical team. In a ritual, a broom might be dressed in a cloak or robe, purified with incense and bells and treated as a participant in dedication chants. The broom might be bound together with hemp. The broom is used for cleaning, purifying and banishing. Put by a door, it would banish malicious energy.

The cauldron might be used in brewing spells. It might be of iron, brass or bronze.

The bottle would hold useful water.

All the tools would be made with care and cared for with respect, as the materials used in their construction would have their sacred aspects.

A tool which performed well would honour the deities which sponsored its dedication.

The Magician is standing in a circle, which is a symbol of protection. The circle is the basic structure of magic and of all existence. All matter moves in circles of space and time. Each of us is at various points in many circles; all of these, tied together in a complex network of cause and effect relationships. The magical nature of circles has long been recognized. The Magician seems to manipulate circles to cause magical happenings. Manipulation of circles is ages old. Pictures of the magical Circle Dance can be seen on rock walls where they were drawn by artists of the ancient Stone Age. The Circle Dance is written of by anthropologists and writers of early history. Today, witches dance in circles to create cones of power. Other magical circles: circles of stone which represent ships. The dead are put in these ships and the ships set sailing to the Underworld. Other circles of stone are formed which relate to the Castles of the Dead, which are in the Underworld. Stones are placed so that they would have relationships, or significances, to Underworld structures.

To create a stone circle, a rapport with the spirits of the intended location is established. On this location, the related Underworld structure is visualized. Stones which seem happy to be part of the structure are selected. One structure represented as a stone circle is the Star Castle of the Dead of Ariadne, Queen of Death. The circle is constructed of 19 stones; of 7 stones around which are 12 stones: the Maze of Death. When the castle is constructed, there is a magical Maze Dance in and out around the 12 stones. All bodies have Astral bodies which relate to the Underworld and this world has laws of its own. With the Maze Dance, the Magician would turn the wheel in both worlds. The Magician, aware of his astral body; would know just when to give the wheel a push. There is a time when the condition for the magic is right. When the condition changes, the vision of what looks magical is past.

When the stone circle is no longer needed, the stones are thanked for their participation and ritually returned to the places from which they were taken.

The Magician, his hand on the circle, is aware of that which is beyond his scope of physical awareness. Suddenly, he can see great wheels turning, see himself in controle, though he would realize his controle is part of what is controlled.

Circles are used for the manipulation of other circles; the small wheel turning the big wheels; so, the Magician's wheel drives bigger wheels. The Magician puts a circle around himself. The person in the center of the circle is not better than other people. Nor is he worse than other people. But he is different than other people. His movements flow into events seen as magical. It is certain, he would not have asked how to work magic, but he might have asked himself, why to work magic.

The Magician is in danger from his own magic. But he has no choice. He is the Magician. Trapped in his circle, he is programmed to turn the big circles and they, turn him. He is Merlin grinding himself into his Tower of Glass.

"Oh Father Merlin," said King Bagdemagus, "What are you doing here? You are the wisest of men."

"Yes," said Merlin, "and the greatest of fools."

The Magician has a feel for where things are on the wheels, then he steps in, as destiny requires, and, with a flick of a finger, makes a change which might cause a city to fall. The life force which resides in all things is altered to form a changed reality. The Magician might become aware of that part of himself which would exist outside of his protected circle and this might be creating himself as part of all creation, as part of magical force.

The Magician runs the Wheel of Fortune, but is trapped in the wheel. The Magician controls it, but is controlled by it; so, would not take his magic lightly, but would use it when the wheel needed to be kept going, kept turning. As Joseph Campbell has said,

"Where magic is, there is no death."

A person might consider, what form, as a magician, he would have? What tools would be available to him? What symbols might he wear? What clothes, what tools, would he carry onto the stage? From them, what effects might he expect? To have his circle, he would cast around himself a part of himself which exists beyond that which is considered the physical and the normal. From in that circle he might create an other world, an other self, and might gain a vantage point.

A person might draw a circle around him or herself, protect and concentrate powers; perhaps, then, he or she would do a thing seen as magical, or many things seen as magical.

Path Finding Cards

Laying out cards moves energy in the Spirit World. One might get the feel of that flow of energy and, as if by magic, receive insights. But also, useful knowledge might be overlooked if careful attention is not given to details. Small things make big changes, as saxifrage seeds have cracked big boulders. In looking at the layout of cards, one might remember, there are details which are not on the cards. These would, however, as all matter is connected, relate to the cards. It is the cards, however, with their objects and shifting symbols, to which attention is largely directed. The shifting would change balances, would cause balance shifting in cycles great and small. The reader might consider the situation. Discovering the balances might be the key to prediction.

On the cards are included items and energies of environments which would influence events to come. There is no dividing line between what is spiritual and what is mundane. A haw might represent chemicals, nutrients needed for health, or it might represent the powers of a god in tree form. At one level, it is both of these things and others beside. Trees, rocks, animals, deities: each is a center for special types of forces. Other centers are stars and star formations.

One might consider what might be, at a particular time, an appropriate way to look at the environment. The environment as it presents itself, Earth is flat. The ball of the Sun rises in the East, sets in the West. It is usual not to be concerned with the physics and math of an environment's literal qualities. Although the Sun and the planet Mars might seem impressively larger than our eyes see them to be, and one knows somewhat of their actual size, one does not experience their hugeness much more than in the limited physical qualities of learned facts. What is physically happening on Arcturus would be of little concern to one's environment as long as it did not affect the way one saw it in relation to other stars.

Earth one experiences is, except for rises and falls for such as mountains, is flat. It represents the bottom element, even though water might weigh more than a light soil. Actual weight would seldom be more than a small footnote. Earth, as it appears, is a spiritual force. The star, which one sees rising and setting, is a spiritual force. These relate to other forces to form the path which one follows. Each force would fit into the pattern which would guide each person along his destined path.

In an attempt to form some likeness of his path; one might, along a structure representing the path, lay out cards representing forces which would be giving meaning and form to the representation of the path. Symbols would relate to a time of day, a season of a year, an age. The time in which the symbols are observed would make a difference in how they are read. Read in Aquarius, they would have a different meaning than they would have if read in Pisces.

Looking at a layout, seeing a card; emotion might cause one to act, might stop an activity which a card seemed to suggest would be bringing harm. But by heeding that card goblin, one might get led into a swamp by a card which seemed good. Meanings are complex and often hidden. According to Joseph Campbell, if one can see his path laid out in front of him, he should be certain, it isn't his path.

In the Cross Deck, there are seventyeight cards, and these fall into five classifications: the Fool, Death, the Magician, the Elemental Cards, and the Environmental Cards. The Elemental Cards are bare and numbers two through ten are devoid of added detail, as each symbol holds many meanings and each of these, with many ramifications. Added detail might detract from the meanings and power of a symbol.

On a layout, it would be important, how the cards sat, in relation, one to another. The place of the layout would be an environment to be considered. The reader, and what the reader wore, would be factors to be considered. The reader might be dressed in white, might be in a special ritual garb, might be in a conical hat.

Of the various card spreads, each has its individual personality, but which spread one is destined to select; it is certain, there will be a beautiful path to follow. The Path will be him for whom the cards have fallen. It is said:

"Thou canst not travel on the path before thou hast become the path itself."

"Each will travel his path toward his goal though his goal," as Eiseley has said, "might be light years distant."

A look at the path, being struck by its wonder and its beauty, might bring a person into a relationship with spiritual forces.

While the cards are making statements about what is going on.

In a flash one sees himself, himself extended through everything; himself as the Path, the intricate system of balances.

Paths of Awareness

The movement of the universal system, of all matter within it, guarantees that each segment of the great body of matter will hold a focus of awareness time and time again. This focus will generally struggle for an expanding awareness: an ever increasing awareness of time, of space and of relationships with the other forces which present themselves. The Focal Point's Awareness struggles outward, through time and space, toward the infinite. And it generally attempts to prolong its aware condition. The need which mater has, to become aware, and to prolong and expand its awareness, is a reason why one looks at the Path; at the prospective forces, at the prospective personalities, which one might meet on the Path, which is set in the determined pattern, as are all paths. Each path, with its network of forces, is set, as it ever has been, in its external cycle. Each would be an Odyssey, the acting out of which would provide the needed way for the attempt to expand the understanding of the meaning of existence. And the paths lead outward, through the depths of space and beyond.

Some persons, as focal points of awareness; have, among the network of other forces spaced along the zigzag paths of their Odyssian trips, one or more card readings: each, certainly, involving a reader and one or more cards. One might ask, is a reading a cause of effects which, projected into the future, would, to the subject of the reading, seem large? One can be certain it would be.

A reader might look at the way a layout sits in its environment, make an artistic assessment of its meaning, then influence the subject of the layout toward one direction or another. Or the reader might be a tired pro at a festival who had decided to do one more reading before going home; then, on a whim, given the cards one more cut so that a Two of Hearts was turned up. The reader might have had little to say about the Two, but it might have suggested to the subject that he would like to go to a bar and have a drink. At the bar, he might have met a person who would have gotten the subject into a different lifestyle. Without the two of hearts, the subject might have headed for home, run a stop sign, slowed up a line of cars and so, made changes in many lives.

In a layout, each card contributes its influence—and each would have both malicious and pleasurable contributions to make if extended far enough into the future. So, the cards might be considered neither good nor evil—even though they might lead directly into pleasure or into pain. One thing the path of cards does is change directions which matter is to take. And, as all unaware matter is waiting to be reborn, all movement would be important to some matter; so, laying down a path might, in some way, be like planting a garden. When one plants a garden, she is selecting matter which is soon to have rebirth. Laying out a path with cards is similar to planting a garden.

One might find himself on that flower filled Path among the stars. One might look down, see marvels stretched out toward the distance, toward Dreamland, toward the Otherworld. One does not know if it is the Good Path, but it is his Path. And he must follow it. The Path goes on without end: dark balances light, then the light is balanced by dark.

The Reading

Each living thing has its path. Matter needs to know itself: that is the reason for the Path. In one relationship, the Path is a layout through the Stars, and these are governed by inflexible necessity. Then there will be regulation by deities: the forces of the material and spiritual elements. A look at the Path would be an important event. For that look, mental preparation would be in order.

The reader has been selected: that important person who is to be the guide along the way. To proceed, there should be purification: a ritual bath; purification, then, by herb smoke. In dressing, the clothes selected should be ones in which one would wish to be presented to the deities. Dressed, one gathers his tools and goes to the place selected for the reading. If this place is recognized as a sacred area, one might, as Apuleius recommends, demonstrate some respect for it: touch one's fingers to one's lips; and, if a sacred object is present, recognize it; perhaps, by bowing or dipping the knee.

The questor then should, as likely would the reader, get the feel of the location: relate to the trees, the plants, to Earth, to the total environment. The questor might find an advantage in, before the reading, meditating and clearing his aura. He would want a bright aura and spiritual strength for looking on the path ahead.

There would often be trees against which the questor could lean while he meditated. W E Butler notes his experiences with some of them. Some trees would have more spiritual energy than they would need and would be glad to share their excess. Among these, Butler often finds firs and pines. He has found apple, oak and beech often helpful. Butler found that at times a tree short of energy would take some from a person who chanced to be near it. Or a tree might, annoyed at being petitioned when it was itself short, send out negative vibrations or drop a limb on the petitioner. Butler suggests elms might do this. Elms, on the other hand, can be the very best of friends, can wonderfully clear an aura and give much encouragement as the questor looks down his path. The questor should give a libation, and perhaps, other gifts also, to the tree from which he hopes to obtain help.

When the questor has meditated and has become comfortable with the area, he should make certain that the surface, which is to hold signposts for his path, is in keeping, as best he can make it, with the direction in which he intends to send energy. If he wishes to communicate especially with Gaia, he might find bare Earth the most appropriate surface. To communicate with Mercury or Mars, clover might be the better surface.

Before the reading, the area had best be blessed and purified. Some readers would have it swept with a prepared broom, sprinkled with sacred water and the air, purified by the ringing of a bell. Likely, in honour of the deities, a candle would be lit; the questor and reader, direct their thoughts to the spirit world.

The reader would lay out signposts along the Path. The questor would establish a rapport with the flow of energy, the flow linked with that of the spirit world. The magic of the layout would have the power to drive the search forward, to part the veils, one after the other, so that one can behold distant horizons.

In a layout, driven by the power of the symbols and guided by the ways of the stars, the questor is guided into beholding; through the web of cause and effect relationships, along the symbols, with their layers of shifting meanings intuitively perceived; but which, words can't do more than suggest; the wonderful Path. The Path is suggested, not exactly known, as no two individuals would see the same card in exactly the same way. But often, one gifted reader would see many of the same things as would another. But with different readers, it would never be quite the same path.

Seeing the cards on the Path permits vision beyond that which verbal explanation would give, as there is understanding beyond intellect. Waite said that a man unmoved by logical argument might understand quite well when he saw the symbols drop from the reader's hand. The subtle balances between symbols might indicate trends grasped by the subconscious before they would be realized by the conscious. Some meanings might be felt rather than understood through reason.

The Path the questor beheld might have meanings some aspects of which would not be revealed until some future date, some later time. Some aspect which would seem to the questor to be negative might trigger some event which the questor would find quite favourable. So, balances are formed: dark brings on light and light, dark. One thing dies to make space for another creation's birth. Building a house destroys the arrangement of the land where the house is being built. And the land might have had a realized, or unrealized, value so different from that of the house that the two values couldn't be measured, one against the other. The house was built because forces needed it there. Forces place matter where it is needed. If a singer is forced into the light, it would be because some other singer has gone dark, has become silent. Darkness would create the need for light; light, for dark. Dark and light would each have its virtues. However, both those in light and in dark would think of glamour as being the place where they are not: the banker seeing glamour in driving trucks and the trucker, in working in a bank. So a value in looking at the Path might be to see the symbols that indicate coming changes, changes leading into glamour.

The Path laid out before the questor would certainly reveal wonderful creations, exciting adventures. As on a physical trip, one might see magical things along the way; mostly, tending to be serendipitous, as one traveler found, hidden in an overgrown garden, the Blowing Stone which had once stood near the White Horse of Uffington. Truly magical things can be around the next corner, be indicated by a layout. These might be tomorrow's sunset or the next Moon lit field. These magical scenes might be indicated by the questor's path. The path might take the questor out on the road to Walsingham, Watling Way, which continues out among the stars, which is the Milky Way. The questor might find himself on a flower filled path among the stars. Along the Path, the questor might see marvels stretched out toward the distance, toward Dreamland, toward the Otherworld.

The questor does not know if this is the Good Path, but it is his path. And he must follow it. He, like Pellinore, must follow his beast until he and it together fade into the dark. But the Path goes on without end: dark balances light, then light is balanced by dark. As to what is best, no one knows what is best in the long run.

For any layout, for any look at a path, it would certainly be wise for a questor to select a reader with a wave length which corresponded, in a gentle way, with his own; as the trip might be long, long as a trip to the sacred castle of Ariadne, long he will watch the 7 lights of her castle get brighter as the beautiful goddess sits silent on her high throne and he will realize that she is Goddess of Death. Then he might view life as a spiral going ever upward and downward. It might be an unnerving trip. The symbols are magical, as they act in their own right and tend not to obey the intent of the questor or reader. But they present a path which, as his imagination grasps it, will become part of the questor's future. And the reader, looking on the path, might see a thing here, a thing there; might say,

"This will happen here."

The word "will" suggests mental force, so that the statement might have meant,

"I will that to happen here."

The reader is an important part of the total picture. As a strong mind seeing the picture, he might guide its elements as they fall into place. His personality would bend the reading.

A person might want a reader with a wave length which would fit, in a comfortable way, with her own, as the trip along the Path might be long, as it leads to the Castle of Ariadne, the Goddess of Death. The questor would watch the castle lights get brighter as, high above, silent on her high chair, would be seated the beautiful goddess.

The cards present a path which will be part of the questor's future. The symbols will act in their own right; as, a Nine of Spades might say, "For you, I represent time spent at spiritual functions." To another, it might have said, "Hard work ahead."

The reader might understand, the card said the word which was needed for the balance of the Path. Then the reader, seeing, would say, "This will happen here."

An impression might be that the will of the reader forced the elements to fall into place. So, in the Big Picture, did not Dame Fortune select the reader?

Little things to watch for: how the card is placed would affect the value given to its symbol. An example: the Six of Hearts with most of the hearts placed so they could hold liquid, they would likely be bringing a beneficial substance. Most of them points up. Most might be giving a libation to the ancestors. With the Six of Spades, points up, the card might represent winning swords. Most of them points down, the card might suggest digging graves. Even slight unusualness in the laying down of the card could indicate a thing to the reader.

Looking at the Path

In looking at a path, one can not see all the details; but it might be, a concern with seeing many of the details might leave one with less knowledge of a true nature of a path than would another approach to looking. At times, one sees a truth out of the corner of one's eye, a truth which one has missed when giving the scene a steady, concentrated look.

The Path is more than the analysis of its details. One might look at a seascape and get a feeling of music which one would not have gotten if she, when looking, had concentrated on the geometric forms or the chemical composition of the water. Bright sunlight might not give as complete a knowledge of the scene as one might wish. One might wish to see it again by moonlight where thoughts could wander among moon shadows. She might investigate possibilities in that way presented, might discover feelings revealed by half lights and lurking shadows. As if by magic, shapes from nearly forgotten dreams might flood into the scene. With the night, one might get a feeling that life has more in common with the vast unknown than it has with all that is known. Under the Cloak of Darkness, one might see pale fingers of moonlight touch shapes half masked by the darkness, half concealed, but suggestive; so that shadow is turned to dream, dream to truth which is felt, if not exactly known. One truth which is known might be, one is beholding a beautiful Path.

The Winding Path of Progress

This path is toward the Gate into the Unknown. One can look down the path to get an impression; to see, beyond the layout of cards, other cards, perhaps cards not in the deck, evolve into a landscape going into mists of a distant future.

In looking at a path, the questor looks at shapes which hover between life and death, between awake and dream. In looking at the path, the questor could not see all the details. In trying to see them all, he might miss a relation which is not open to a study of details. He might be left with less knowledge of a true nature of the path than he would have obtained from a glance to gain a general feel of it. At times, he could see a truth out of the corner of his eye, a truth he had missed when giving the scene a steady, concentrated look. And the path is more than what is discovered by an analysis of its details. One might look at a seascape and get a feeling of music which he would not get if he concentrated on its geometric forms, or on the chemical composition of the water. Bright sunlight might not give as complete a knowledge as one would wish. One might wish to see the seascape again by moonlight where one's thoughts could wander among the Moon shadows. He might investigate possibilities in that way presented, might discover things revealed by half lights and lurking shadows. As if by magic, shapes from nearly forgotten dreams might flood into the scene. With the night, one might get a feeling that life has more in common with the vast unknown than it has with all that is known. Under the cloak of darkness, one might see pale fingers of moonlight touch shapes half masked by darkness; half concealed, but suggestive; so that shadow is turned to dream, dream to a truth which is felt, if not exactly known.

The Winding Path is a mysterious, if not spooky path, which, like the seascape, might be best observed by moonlight.

The Solar Wheel Spread

```
                5     13
    12          4
 9       8      1     7     6
                3           10
         11     2
```

Toward Light

```
         11     9
                8           10
 5       4      1     3     2
 12             7
                6     13
```

Toward Dark

The Solar Wheel Spread
Can be Very Bright or
Very Dark

Three Octave Spread

This has been called the Cosmic Ray of Creation. It is the rearrangements of material as a succession of events, forming the steps of an individual life into an octave; or, into a series of octaves, the octave, with that to the front and that to the rear, forming a triad.

```
1 2 3 4 5 6 7 8
        1 2 3 4 5 6 7 8
                1 2 3 4 5 6 7 8
```

This spread relates to colour.
As we learn from Ouseley,
each colour has 7 aspects.

Questions

What are the controlling forces for my body?

How am I to be effected by my ego?

How is my intellect to affect my life?

How am I to be effected by my memory?

To what extent is my will to controle my future?

What are the projections for my total self?

What is the future for my hopes?

What is the future for my desires?

What is the role of the spiritual aspect of my mind?

What is the character of my astral body and what effect will it have on my future?

How is the spiritual aspect of my living to project into the future?

How is my ideal self to affect my future and how much actually, is actuality, going to resemble the ideal?

What is to be the future for the spiritual aspect of my life and for my spiritual self?

On a 13 card layout, a question might be assigned to each card.

The Big Picture

Light needs darkness. Darkness needs light. Balances turn the wheels of the Universe. Change brings creation and creation needs destruction. The builder destroys in order to get building materials. Some events which look unfavourable trigger the creation of things thought to have value. Building one thing destroys another. Improving an object might cause its demise, as an object's strength might put it on the shortest path to darkness. But things go where they are needed. The reason one is in the dark is because she is not yet needed in the light. If she comes to the light to sing, it is likely because some other singer has gone to silence. Darkness creates the need for light, so is a seed which brings light.

Often people look up the Path into the future. Often, because the light seems to be where they are not, as that is where the grass is always greener. Often, the banker would see life as a truck driver to be romantic, while the truck driver would see the romance in the banker's life. So, each might look into the future in order to see change. But by stepping out on the Path, the questor might gain understanding, or a feeling of having understanding, as the Path lay spread out, filled with incredible creations. Wonderful deities will appear so as to lead her forward. And to be there, the deities need Man to walk the Path and see them. They are in the magical sunsets, the Moon lit fields. The Path is a trip toward Dreamland and toward an Otherworld.

Cards can be a step through The Veil. They appear on the Path, so that one is out along that way. Perhaps it is the road to Walsingham, which has been equated with the Milky Way. Then one might be on a flower filled path among the stars. But one does not know if it is the Good Path. But it is her path and she must follow it. She, like King Pellinore, must follow her beast until she and the beast together fade into the dark. But the Road goes on without end. Dark balances light, then the light is balanced by dark. As to what is best, no one knows what is best in the long run.

Trump Cards and Associated Plants

I ~Warrior

Lupine	Leguminosae
Coriander	Umbelliferae
Nettle	Urticacea
Sow Thistle	Compositae
Chard	Chenopodiacea
Barrenwort	Berberidacea
Black Mustard	Cruciferae
Bucklers Mustard	Cruciferae
Charlock	Cruciferae
Red Nettle	Labiatae
Comfrey	Boraginacea
Daffodil	Amaryllidacea
Violet	Violacea
Cowslip	Primulacea
Bugle	Labiatae
Buttercup	Ranunculacea
Alyssum	Cruciferae
Charity (Sweatroot)	Polemoniacea
Burnet Saxifrage	Umbelliferae
Garlic	Liliacea
Hops	Urticacea
Blackberry	Rosacea
Marjoram	Labiatae
Arsesmart	Polygonacea
Hairy Woodrush	Juncacae
Peony	Ranunculacea
Mandrake	Solanacea

Many times, flowers, such as yarrow and stitchwort, serve best picked when the picker is naked.

II ~ Flower

Bluebottle Cornflower	Compositae
Primrose	Primulacea
Sweet Woodruff	Rubiacea
Johnny Jumpup	Violacea
Herb Robert	Geraniacea
Toad Flax	Scrophulariacea
Red Campion	Caryophyllacea
Great Stitchwort	Caryophyllacea
Tufted Milkwort	Polygalacea
Butterwort	Lentibulariacea
Savory	Labiatae
Smallage	Umbelliferae
Lovage	Umbelliferae
Wood Betony	Labiatae
Cuckoos Orchis (Mascula)	Orchidacea
Greenman Orchis	Orchidacea
Moschatel	Caprifoliacea
Groundsel	Compositae
Wood Sorrel	Oxalidaceae
Strawberry	Rosacea
Fritillary	Liliacea
Sheepsbit Scabious	Compositae
Bluebell	Liliacea
Ragged Robin	Caryophyllacea
Purple Foxglove	Scrophulariacea
Tansy	Compositae
Teasel	Dipsacea
Narrow Leaf Bellflower	Campanulacea
King Cups (Caltha)	Ranunculacea
Vetch	Leguminosae
Wake Robin	Aracea
Scilla (Peruviana)	Liliacea
Blue Mallow	Malvacea
Musk Mallow	Malvacea
Twinflower	Caprifoliacea
Lucerne	Papilionaceae

III ~ Juggler

Hypericum	Hypericacea
Parsley	Umbelliferae
Dill	Umbelliferae
Greater Celandine	Papaveracea
Eyebright	Scrophulariacea
Dyers Rocket	Resedacea
Cinquefoil	Rosacea
Hyacinth	Liliacea
Black Bean	Leguminosae
Elecampane	Compositae
Speedwell	Scrophulariacea
Germander	Labiatae
Anise	Umbelliferae
Orpine	Crassulacea
Fenugreek	Leguminosae
Ribwort	Plantaginacea
Weybroed	Plantaginacea
Tarragon	Compositae
Pimpernel	Primulacea
Chicory	Compositae
Bistort	Polygonacea
Wood Anemonae	Ranunculacea
Dogs Mercury	Euphorbiacea
Vincetoxicum	Asclepiadacea
Daisy	Compositae
Red Rattle	Labiatae
Yarrow	Compositae
Saffron Crocus	Iridacea
Stranglewort	Asclepiadacea
Roundleaf Rampion	Campanulacea
Horehound	Labiatae
Sainfoin	Leguminosae
Wood Sanicle	Umbelliferae
Stoncrop	Crassulacea
Fennel	Umbelliferae
Lily Of The Vally	Lilacea
Great Mullein	Scrophulariacea

Moth Mullein	Scrophulariacea
Brake	Filices
Maidenhair	Filices
Spleenwort	Filices
Birdsfoot Trefoil	Leguminosae
Yellow Loosestrife	Primulacea

IV ~ Crystal

White Lily	Liliacea
Flax	Lilacea
Purslane	Caryophyllea
Hyssop	Labiatae
Saxifrage	Saxifragacea
Ladys Mantle	Rosacea
Blooming Sally	Onagrariacea
Herb Paris	Liliacea
Colewort	Cruciferae
Burdock	Compositae
Iris	Iridacea
Sweet Cicily	Umbelliferae
Chervil	Umbelliferae
Wintergreen	Pyrolaceae
Morning Glory	Convolvulacia
Venus Looking Glass	Campanulacea
Feverfew	Compositae
Honesty (Lunaria)	Cruciferae
Wall Flower	Cruciferae
Quick In Hand	Geraniacea
Honeysuckle	Caprifoliacea
Mugwort	Compositae
Southernwood	Compositae
Wormwood	Compoistae
Amaranth	Amaranthacea
Walewort	Caprifoliacea
Enchanters Nightshade	Onagrariacea
Purple Loosestrife	Lythracea
Acanthus (Bearsbreach)	Acanthacea
Asarabacca (Birthwort)	Aristolochiacea

Uva Ursi	Ericaea
Day Lily	Liliacea
Martagon Lily	Liliacea
Summer Snowflake	Amaryllidaceae
Moonwort	Filices

V ~ Lion

Rose	Rosacea
Rue	Rutacea
Borage	Boraginacea
Burnet	Rosacea
Agrimony	Rosacea
Chamomile	Compositae
Dittany Fraxinella	Rutacea
Marigold Calendula	Compositae
Rockrose	Cistacea
Columbine	Ranunculacea
Heliotrope Turnsole	Boraginacea
Dandelion	Compositae
Mezereon	Thymeleacea
Churnstaff	Euphorbiacea

Jupiter Favours Plants With Smooth Leaves: So It Was Thought, Said Fox.

VI ~ Reaper

Red Poppy	Papaveracea
Periwindle	Apocynacea
Lavender	Labiatae
Balm	Labiatae
Oats	Graminacea
Wheat	Graminacea
Barley	Graminacea
Rye	Graminacea
Meadowsweet	Rosacea
Black Bryony	Dioscoreacea
White Bryony	Cucurbitacea
Black Hellebore	Ranunculacea
White Hellebore	Liliacea

Plumbago (Leadwort)	Plumbaginacea
Pennyroyal	Labiatae
Crosswort	Rubiacea
Millet	Graminacea

VII ~ Scale

Queen Annes Lace	Umbelliferae
Vervain	Verbenacea
Lobelia	Lobeliacea
Evening Lychnis	Caryophyllacea
Asparagus	Liliacea
Goldenrod	Compositae
Corydalis	Fumariacea
Caraway	Umbelliferae
White Campion	Caryophyllacea
Spikenard	Compositae
Forgetmenot	Buraginacea

VIII ~ Demon

Monkshood	Ranunculacea
Henbane	Solanacea
Black Nightshade	Solanacea
Basil	Labiatae
Catnip	Labiatae
Spearmint	Labiatae
Gourd	Cucurbitacea

IX ~ Archer

Dock	Polygonacea
Red Centaury	Gentianacea
Sage	Labiatae
Valerian	Valerianacea

Bouncing Bet	Caryophyllacea
Corn Cockle	Caryophyllacea
Woad	Cruciferae
Dusty Miller (Cineraria)	Compositae
Coltsfoot	Compositae
Arnica	Compositae
Cocklebur	Ambroisecae
Shepherds Purse	Cruciferae
Felwort	Gentianacea
Masterwort	Umbelliferae
Wood Pink	Caryophyllacea
Yellow Gentian	Gentianacea
Deptford Pink	Caryophyllacea

X ~ Horned Piper

Rosemary	Labiatae
Thyme	Labiatae

XI ~ Cup Bearer

Alehoof	Labiatae

XII ~ Wave

Onion	Liliacea
Clover	Leguminosae
Bitter Cress	Cruciferae
Delphinium	Ranunculacea

The Cross Tarot

Volume II

THE FINER POINTS OF THE
26 TAROT TRUMP CARDS

I ~Warrior

The Warrior, the Force of Life, moves forward, Life against Death. Neither Life nor Death relate to good or bad.

The Warrior might be represented by Mars, but many other deities also represent combat. These might include deities whose major thrust is in areas other than war: Aphrodite, Goddess of Love; Aurora, Goddess of Dawn. As warriors, Aphrodite and Aurora extend the spirit of combat into the realm of chaos; so that, against whatever force, winning is the issue. Spiritual force is extended to extreme limits of the nature of the deity. They are the power of Love, the power of the Dawn.

The force of the Warrior moves to the forefront of need for spiritual response, March 17, Agonium Martiale. It inspires stomping and leaping. At feasts, warriors with spears and shields leap to encourage growth of vegetation. To honour Mars, there is a parade which features leaping and stomping. The parade not only encourages vegetation, it is also considered a war dance. The feasts, at which there is much boisterous drinking, honour, especially Mars and the vegetation god, Liber. The parades are often elaborate, containing many types of musical and visual performers. They blast in the new life and banish the forces of Winter, Darkness and Death. At times, the parade carries a figure, representing Winter and Death, to a body of water and throws her in, so she is washed away until she returns at vegetations death. The day, sometimes called Marzana, signals the coming of the fires of new birth.

To honour the festival, women crowned with ivy sell cakes which, when sold, are sacrificed on hot grills to deities being honoured at the festival. The festival gives strength and encouragement to growing vegetation and, for coming battles, to warriors.

March 18, Lucarium, also, Sacred Groves Fest is a feast day honouring Athene and Mars. Athene, beside being regulator of the home, is protector of lands. The day is celebrated with music contests and torch races. On this day, King Edward the Saxon was sacrificed.

March 19, Quinquatrus, honours Minerva, Mars and the warrior god, Quirinus. It is the custom for men in tunics and cloaks, made in an old style, and in bronze beast plates; to carry bronze shields, which they beat with clubs, in a dance through the streets, while they sing ancient chants invoking and praising Mars. At the end of the dance through the streets, there is a feast where there are loud cheers for the military and many young men take this time to join military outfits.

At the feasts, Minerva and Quirinus are also praised and given honours. During the day, there are rituals for Minerva who was not only a goddess of battle, but a Goddess of Teaching and of Crafts. On this day, scholars, in honour of Minerva, celebrate and teachers are honoured. There is a parade where Minerva's white garment is carried. In the parade, it is usual for dignitaries to wear olive crowns, carry olive branches; these, followed by warriors with spears and shields; these, followed by women carrying water in pots, then men wearing millet crowns, then women carrying ritual tools in baskets. Minerva is celebrated with song and poetry, with rituals to aid teaching and, especially, rituals centered on spinning and weaving, which represent all crafts.

March 23, Tubilustrium, Mars is honoured and the focus is on war trumpets. The trumpets are cleaned, purified; then honoured with a parade featuring the blowing of horns down decorated ways, past shrines and public places decked with bay. Horns are highly respected as having power. They drive away malicious spirits and purify the land; so, prepare for growth and battle. Some horns have caused major events which have, sometimes, been great destructions. It is said that, at this time, the Ram makes certain that the cars of Night and Day run even.

This day also honours the battle goddess, Nerine. She also relates to copulation. She is called Nerine the Strong.

March 24, Bellona is honoured. She is the Spirit of Aggression. War and peace deals are conducted under her authority.

March 25 is Lady Day. A major influence is Rhea. Her crown represents the fortress. Her magical tool is the double bladed axe. She is the protector of her domain, Earth. Her milk, which was seen trailed across the sky, supports creation. Lady Day is a time of joy.

March 28 is Hiketaria. On this day, Theseus and Arianrhod are honoured and prayer is directed to Apollo. Theseus, as the Sun, destroys the Minotaur, who is Darkness. Ariadne, Goddess of Death, leads Theseus out of her Web of Death. Then Theseus, as the Warrior Sun, needs to move away from the Death Goddess. Some past thinkers, giving Theseus human feelings, could understand that warrior moving away from the love relationship. He had never established a romantic bond nor made a binding declaration. And life is too full of action to permit the warrior to be bound into the limited sphere of a lover. The Sun was moving away from Darkness and Death. Theseus, as the Sun, slays all combatants who stand in his way; not because he dislikes them, but because they stand before him in opposition. He held games in honour of Sinis, a warrior whom he had slain.

April 1, April Fool; also, Aphrodite Day; points to the element of foolishness in people in general. This suggests that the most sedate and serious actions might have the element of foolishness in them; might seem, in some lights, quixotic. In the fabric of life, there is a place for foolish things, for foolish people. Life, to hold together, needs balance and foolishness is one of the elements which give it balance.

Jest is a form of foolishness which can be an important tool in holding things together. Some things can be said or done in jest which, to hold things together, needed to be said or done, but couldn't have been said or done but in jest. Things said or done other than in jest might lead to tragic results when, if done in jest, wouldn't have upset things.

A foolish person is sometimes the charm which makes of a group activity a thing of value. On a frozen pond, all but one might be of like dress and all these in like dress, skating sunwise. One, in a strikingly different dress, might be skating counter to the Sun, winding in and out among the other skaters and so, weaving a memorable web which all there would remember. The picture would hold together and would, as a memory, move into the future and maybe one or more of the skaters would need that memory.

As serious contending forces are seldom interested in fools, being a fool would give protection. As the men of Gotham were thought to be foolish, army recruiters passed them by. Demons and Underworld forces avoid foolish people. Fools are often seen as objectionable; sometimes, dangerous. In this, they are thought to, at times, give protection. It is thought, foolish antics and insane laughter confuse malicious beings, beings from the Underworld. Straw Fools are, in April, put in apple trees; then, at the end of harvest, a man is designated to eat the last apple, the Straw Fool is burned and the apple eater becomes the protecting fool and is the protector until the Spring Fool is put in place.

There is a relationship between the April Fool and the straw man who sits holding the Spirit of the Tree. Both relate to being born and to prebirth protection which is given to the Fool. A touch of the fool's protection is a thread binding a community into a more durable fabric.

April Fool is a day for a person to be a fool on and on which to make a fool of others. It searches out the foolish aspects of generally ordinary people, or searches out ways to cause ordinary people to look foolish. The person who is a complete fool would certainly not be classed as an ordinary person. As Ure said, he would be indifferent to directions dictated by his desires. His continued existence would certainly need to be provided for through the interest of others. The ordinary person becomes ritually a fool in order to fill a needed spot in a picture to give the balance which would be needed for moving life forward in an orderly way. April Fool is a day for bringing balance. It is a day for lies and wild goose chases. Practical jokes are in order. Making a person trip is a thing which would make him and others look foolish, and so, produce a ritual fool. April first, people are asked to answer foolish questions, or to get foolish objects, such as left handed hammers. On April fool, boys make cardboard saws, powder them, then slap people on the back with them. Effigies of old ladies are filled with nuts, then broken so that people will make fools of themselves scrambling for the nuts.

There is a relationship between the Straw Man in the apple tree and the April Fool. These are ritual fools. The April Fool might also be put into a learning situation, so become part of a ritual birthing. A lad, the fool letter carrier, who, without a laugh or smile, is sent another mile by the person who reads in the letter, "Give this lad back the letter and send him another mile."

This would be a birthing ritual, said Kightly. So the lad would be given the protections given a fool, plus those given to the newly born.

Fools, although serving a community, might be bringing harm to themselves, as the Three Wise Men of Gotham might have done – when they went to sea in a bowl. But the deities give protection to fools and to societies which have fools integrated into their fabrics. Pennick said that a fool would keep a society from becoming too rigid. The fool would give a flexibility, which would relate to durability.

Fools are considered to be in need of learning, but, also, they are often needed for teaching. They might be teaching many others. A fool might provide a new way of thinking about a situation. An environment might look entirely different with the actions of the fool added into it. A person's thought might evolve into new concepts. A fool might act in a way not permitted to any but the fool, then that action might show a needed way of problem solving.

The Cuckoo is associated with April Fool, associated with foolishness and, especially, foolishness in connection with romance, as the Cuckoo lays eggs in other bird's nests. It is said, the Cuckoo selects foolish ways to bring in the spring: warm weather comes when a hag lets a cuckoo out of a basket. The Cuckoo, to end its season, it buys a horse and rides away.

It is said, the men of Gotham tried to hold onto warm weather by trapping a cuckoo within a hedge of thorn trees. A nutty or silly person is called cuckoo.

April first is also called Aphrodite's Day. Aphrodite, Goddess of Love; is focused, as Aristophanes has said, especially on the physical aspects of romance. She relates to April Fool in that love makes a fool of people. Love caused Mars to get caught in Vulcan's net. This is a day for making sacrifices to Aphrodite. Bloody sacrifices are not permitted on her alters. On this day, a boy may ask a girl to be his Midsummer Lady.

April second is called Battle of the Flowers. As a sham, or mock, Battle of the Trees, the spirits of this world against those of the Underworld; it is a hilarious extension of April Fool. The day, full of the throwing of flowers and confetti, is to show honour to Spring's victory over Winter. Hidden in foolishness, people sneak in charms against Winter. Spring flowers, as charms against Winter, war against things which favour Winter.

April sixth, Delphinia, honours Apollo, the Spirit of the Sun. The day is focused on purity. When Apollo slew Python, he demonstrated the importance of purity by, after the battle, cleansing himself. Girls dress as suppliants for Delphinia and, carrying branches of laurel, go to a temple of Apollo and ask for well being for their community and for themselves. Then, by priests, they get purified. For purification, branches of laurel are used for sprinkling purifying waters.

Alters and shrines, for the holiday, are decorated with delphiniums and other flowers. Especially, the alters and shrines of Apollo would be decorated.

April eighth, Mouninchia, Artemis and Iphegenia are honoured. Moon Goddess Iphegenia has been shown riding on the horned Moon. In human form, she is said to have located a sacred statue of Artemis. She and Artemis have been involved in human sacrifice. Artemis has, beside human and moon forms, bear forms.

On April thirteenth, Libertas, troops of boys go down the streets blowing horns.

The goddess Easter, on the Solar Calendar, is celebrated April seventeenth. In the fifth century, a custom was established of celebrating her on the Lunar Calendar. Easter, Goddess of Dawn and Spring, is a warrior goddess who comes to take lands by force. Hens, eggs, rabbits, lilies and daffodils are sacred to her.

Easter is celebrated by hunting coloured eggs which the rabbit has laid among the flowers. Easter would have touched the eggs with colours of the dawn. Often those eggs found are put into decorated baskets along with egg shaped candies, imitation baby chicks, trinkets and flowers. On this day, people often dress in bright clean Easter clothes. Easter eggs, at times, are rolled down hills. Rabbits are sacrificed to the goddess, then made into pies. The pies are often cut up, pieces handed out and it is considered good fortune to get a piece.

Some Easter Eggs are marked with magical symbols and put on graves to assist rebirth. From springs, jugs of water are drawn. The water drawn is called Water of Life and some of it is poured on flowers near the spring, and flowers, especially daffodils, cowslips, lilies and violets, are put on shrines of Easter and other goddesses. Men who have drowned on Easter can ride back on white horses to attend Easter celebrations. At these celebrations, it is a custom to copulate on the newly plowed fields.

April nineteenth, called Cerealia, honours Ceres, who sponsors all that grows from the soil. It is celebrated by processions and other rituals. A traditional highlight of the festival: torches are tied to the tails of foxes; the foxes, released and chased through the streets. The fires purify and so, prepare for new growth. Mars plants the seed.

At this time, Warrior Woman Rheada is honoured.

The center of the Warrior Card would hold the one who would most represent the Class of Warrior: Mars, God of War. His dark red face would be shadowed by a red tinged helm. He would hold up a red tinged sword, would hold a red tinged shield which, in its center, would hold a ruby. On a chariot, pulled by two horses, he rides forward.

Mars is considered second only to Jupiter in influence and power. He is the defender of the law, of order, of vegetation and of the land. His leadership provides victory in battle. He is an organizer who knits forces together into a team. Mars, said W E Butler, has a special power over connected energies. Said Nagy, he joins objects and energies and sees to it that they work. The Spirit of Mars would be in the form, in the Heavens, called Aries. The same energies, according to Lyndoe, would be observed in the Planet Mars. The force of the god covers a wide area. As Collingwood has said, Mars is a god of widespread honour. Agrippa has Mars dressed in red and associated with the Horse.

Mars has a power which is often called for. Ordericus has recorded; at times, libations of human blood are given to Mars. However, Mars does not win every battle. As he is the personification of the Alder, his strength would, as would that of the tree, wax and wane. In season, he is firm and brave, with a strength seeming on a par with that of, perhaps, even Jupiter. Out of season, he could lose battles to Apollo, and to Athene, and could get caught in Vulcan's net. He is selective in what challenges he meets. He did not, with Jupiter, stand to meet the great dragon, Typhon.

Mars has the ability to link energies and to cause auras of energy to vibrate in chain so that the power of each aura can be augmented, can draw power from the vibrating chain. This chain would link all other things. Each thing has energies which link, directly or indirectly, to all other things, and there is a flow of energy from one thing to another, but some forces have more controle of energy flow than others and energy flow depends, also, on relationships, one energy to another, or to others. Mars, with his power over connected energies, is looked upon to harmonize activities; especially, military forces. His name has come to be associated with harmony. He is the good soldier who joins things together and sees to it that things work well together. He is the patron of joiners, of builders and of teams of horses and of oxen. Mars copulates and promotes copulation. Mars can be tempestuous, merciless and an instigator of violence.

Mars, as are other gods of war, is associated with Wind, as Rhys has said. For winds, men of the sea might call on Mars. And Gods of Wind, as Castor and Pollux, were associated with war. And Mars, as were other gods of war, is associated with metals. The Sword is a form taken by Mars. He has been represented as a Sword standing in a mound of Earth.

Mars has a tree form. Trees, to some extent, like Mars; have abilities in aural energy controle and relate well to mankind. One may be fed energy by a tree or might feed a tree, as do some people, like some of those said to have a green thumb.

Mar's tree form is the Alder, which dons a robe of royal purple to show that it is a king indeed. Purple is also the colour of invisibility, which relates it to the Spirit World, to the Underworld. Related to the Underworld, Alder is a tree of enlightenment. It can give knowledge of the future, and it has the ability to detect, and inform about, diseases.

As the Alder has a Spirit of Fire, it contains a fiery energy. It inspires determination and tenacity and gives the ability to march forward, to struggle on when one is committed. In conflicts, it gives protection. There is a tradition for boats for the dead to be made of alder. Venus holds the Alder, sacred.

Alder is used for treating dyspepsia, diarrhea, haemorrages, inflammations, swellings, sore feet, sore eyes and fevers. For cures, alder leaves are gathered while the dew is still on them.

The great Warrior Spirit will be, at times, as Agrippa points out, seen in a woman. As with men, many of the women warriors are thought of, first, as authorities with some other jurisdiction. The Morning Star, Aphrodite, is first, a goddess of Love. She is associated with Spring, and with Dawn. She is a man killer, a grave digger and a huntress. In the morning, she adds help to the rising Sun. She takes part in battles. At times, she is called on to be a battle ally. Aphrodite's alter is honoured with prayers, and pure fire, and many flowers, and the flowers she favours are the Violet, the Anemonae, the Lily and the Mandrake. She promotes love, courage, youth, health and copulation, and in this she takes pleasure. For Aphrodite, the month of April was named.

Aurora, Goddess of Dawn, is a lusty warrior goddess. At dawn she opens her gates, opens the way for the Sun. When filled with desire, she rushes through her gates, grabs a warrior of her choice, keeps him at her service until she tires of him; then, grabs another. She captured the great bully, Orion, and forced him to serve her pleasure. And as she is a healer, when Orion was blinded, she restored his sight. Delphinium and Chamomile are flowers she favours.

Mighty warrior women include Pallas, Keeper of the Sheep of the Dawn, Nerine the Strong and the Spirit of Aggression, Bellona. Hippolyte and Marpessa are mighty women warriors. Otrere holds the Spirit of Battle.

The chief animal for the Time of the Warrior would be the Horse, a great companion to the Warrior. The Horse pulls the Sun, the Chief of Fires. The Horse intuitively goes in the right direction, does the right thing. Horses come from Water. They are a gift from the King of Water to the King of Fire. They are brave and strong, have the fiery spirit and work well in teams. The Ram, favoured by Aurora, Aphrodite and Mars, is an influence in the Time of the Warrior. The Warrior, like the Ram, will overcome obstacles and continue to move forward. It is said, people of the Time of the Warrior, like the Ram, tend to be butters in.

The Woodpecker relates to the Time of the Warrior. The Woodpecker is Picus, a warrior king who was put into woodpecker form. He is an herb healer and a great friend of Easter's and of Mars: He is an advisor to horse trainers and was an advisor to Aneas. He protects sacred trees and he is the Guardian of the Oracle of Mars. He has a gift of prophecy and will forecast storms. Flowers he favours are the Peony, the Anemonae, the Daffodil and the Wake Robin.

Roosters and hens relate to the Time of the Warrior. Hens lay eggs and eggs are magical as they relate to the Otherworld. They are a sacred emblem of Easter. Egg shells have been used for crossing waters, as waters are the veil between the worlds. It is said they have been used to cross the River Styx.

The Nettle relates to the Warrior. It represents the sting of death. Warriors use the stings to warm and treat body parts which have suffered from cold weather. The stings also stimulate the sex organs of men and beasts. Nettles timidly touched will give a good sting, but grasped with vigor, feel good. The juice from the nettle is an antidote to its own sting. Nettles hold a powerful magic. An old nettle passed three times, one hand to the other, will then be ready for use as a weapon. Young nettles are used in love potions. One, holding in a hand nettle and yarrow, would be free from fear, fantasy and hallucination. A person anointed with nettle; if, holding nettle and leek, he gets into water where fish are, the fish will gather around him. To be rid of fevers; one, on three consecutive days, pulls up a nettle root. Fevers might also be lowered by a person pulling up the nettle while naming the sick person and the sick person's parents. Nettles make good cloth, cloth sometimes made into garments for Otherworld beings. Nettles covered with rain water, left standing two weeks, make good pest killers and fertilizers. In spring, as a potherb, nettles improve appetite and aid memory. For nursing mothers, nettle tea improves milk flow. Also, nettle tea strengthens the circulatory system, lowers blood pressure, kills worms and is used to treat sore throats, dropsy, piles, anaemia, dysentery, urinary trouble and neuralgia. Nettle lotion is used for treating rheumatism and wounds. It is used, said Dodonaeus, to stop bleeding.

Nettles are magical warriors which protect against demons and lightning. The stings, said Leyel, are said to protect against sorcery.

Nettles counter poisons and nettle cloth is worn to protect against Otherworld forces. Nettles protect milk from being affected by demons. They grow where elves and demons have their dwelling places and grow where innocent blood has been spilled. Nettle smoke disperses storms. Nettle leaves are put in shoes to prevent tiredness. Gathered before dawn, nettles cure cows. Chickens favour nettles and they are fed nettles so that they will grow big and strong. Nettles clear the mind and quicken the senses. They clean and purify.

Dodonaeus said that there are two types of stinging nettles. One of these is large and strong, and this one would contain male energy. The smaller, less strong nettle would have female energy.

Dodonaeus said that there are nettles which do not sting, and these, called dead nettles, are, in virtues, much the same as the stinging nettles. One of the dead nettles is the Red Nettle. If eaten in March, it aids memory, promotes sleep and keeps decline away. If pulled before dawn, it protects against lightning. As a tea, it is used to treat dysentery, kidney trouble and to bring vigour. In gardens, said Marion Davies, it chases potato bugs and improves the flavour of vegetables. And it is favoured by bees.

Marjoram, created, it is said, by Venus, is an herb of the Warrior. It brings affection, so is put on graves to bring loving feelings to the spirits. Marjoram brings joy. Planted on graves, in healthy growth it was thought, said Grieve, to bring peace and happiness to the dead.

Marjoram enhances sexual bliss. Added to food, it acts as a love charm. In ritual, it is used to petition Venus for love. As it protects newly weds; marjoram, in wreaths or crowns, is often given to them.

Aphrodite touched Marjoram, which gave it power and a sweet aroma. It protects against witchcraft and thunder, so it is put by milk so that neither of these will spoil the milk. It wards off malicious spirits and brings prosperity.

Favoured by Mercury, marjoram is used for prophecy and is thought, especially useful in predicting coming poverty, coming riches, or the coming of a lover.

Marjoram is used for treating consumption, convulsions, dyspepsy, dropsy, rheumatism, colic, coughs, jaundice and wounds. It is used to counter toxins and to bring good health.

The Daffodil is an important herb in the Time of the Warrior, as it holds a special place with the lusty Warrior Goddess, Easter. It relates to dream, to death and to the Underworld and their beauty caused Proserpine to stray so close to the Underworld gate that she got herself captured.

Daffodils are worn by Hades and by the Furies, and they wreath the hair of the Eumenides. Daffodil wreaths are sometimes worn by the dead, and they are placed in coffins. The fragrance of daffodils is said to produce dullness, madness and death.

The Daffodil is an Underworld aspect of the Sun. In keeping with this, daffodils combat snakes. They cure snake bites. Put at gateways, they keep out harmful influences and sorcery. Planted near graves, they provide nourishment for spirits while the spirits are in this world. Wrapped in linen, they are worn in order to drive out malicious spirits and to protect from injury. They are used for treating ague and swellings, but to eat one could cause death. Also, they are used in cleaning and purifying. Daffodils are bells, but only babies can hear them. The first daffodil to bloom brings silver and gold. Beside Easter, Mars and Aphrodite relate to the Daffodil. Seen as a symbol, it might suggest unrequited love or lack of confidence. The best time for collecting daffodils would usually be at the Waxing or the Full Moon. They are sacred to Saturn.

The Buttercup is favoured by Mars. It relates to the Cuckoo. Buttercups instigate memories of childhood. They aid in gaining wealth. To cure madness, one might; during the Wane of the Moon, or when it is in Taurus, or in Scorpio; put buttercups on the neck. If rubbed on the correct spot, they will rid a person of the plague. Buttercup lotion is used to treat rheumatism, gout and sciatica. Pigs enjoy buttercup roots. It is said, a way to die laughing is to eat buttercups.

The Cowslip is a sacred flower of the goddess, Easter. April 17, her alters and shrines are decorated with cowslips. The Cowslip is the key which unlocks Mother Earth and awakens forces of nature. Cowslips are used in the Druid brew of inspiration and fairies make their homes in them. Cowslip balls thrown up and caught with the right hand can predict how much longer the thrower will live. Cowslip tea makes the senses stronger. Cowslip wine is a narcotic and sedative used for treating rheumatism, false apparitions, frenzies, cramps, falling sickness, palsy, convulsions and back pains. Cowslips are used for treating headaches and wounds and for calming nerves. They are hung over doorways to keep harmful energies out of houses. Also, they inspire the increase of charm and attractiveness. They are a flower of the Underworld.

The Violet is an herb of the Warrior said to have been created by Jupiter to be a food for Moon Goddess, Io. He had violets spring forth to feed Io, the Wandering Moon Cow. The Violet is a sacred flower of Aphrodite and Venus and it is the flower which some areas have chosen to be represented by. It represents love. Violets influence toward gentle love, faithfulness, truthfulness, cooling peace and modesty. The Violet is also associated with death; especially, death of the very young. Coffins, in some places, are covered with violets, as violets guard against the fumes of death. In a person's garden, the death of a loved one will cause the violets to wither.

The Violet is a flower of enchantment. In dreamtime, violets lead people to otherworlds. Fairies love violets. Violets inspire dream, take people to the World of the Fairy.

Violets, as a food, promote balance in the gastrointestinal system. They promote calm, love and general good health. Worn about the head, violets dispel fumes of wine and prevent headaches. As Culpeper has said, violets cool the body inside and out, or, the inward and outward heat of the body. They bring relief to inflamed eyes, and they are used to treat headache, nerve disorders, falling sickness, jaundice, ulcers, rheumatism, gout, quinsy, pleurisy, sore throat and ague. B P Apuleius found violets would cure new wounds and old. Athenians used violets to moderate anger and to strengthen the heart. Violets are used for treating cancer and for purifying the blood, and they are used as an antiseptic. Violets oppose wicked spirits and counter malicious magic. They inspire serenity.

Influenced by Venus, violets rekindle past loves. As they are associated with the Moon, violets weave spells. Mixed into a goatmilk bath, violets give beauty. In some funerals, the penis of the dead is crowned with ivy and violets; the violets, as Venus' gift to the dead.

The Violet is associated with Easter, and with her holiday. And it is considered a flower of Mars. Diana hid the beautiful Violet in a flower.

A magic to bring sleep is to soak the feet in water from violets and go then to bed with violets bound to the temples. Going into sleep, they provide the Violet Dreamworld.

Sweatroot, or Jacobs Ladder, is favoured by Vulcan, Aphrodite and Mars. It encourages war. It is a favourite herb of cats and is protected by fairies. Sweatroot is used for treating inflammations, headaches, pleurisy, nerve complaints, colds, fevers and falling sickness and for curing snake bites.

Chard, an herb of the Warrior, is favoured by Mars and by Apollo, to whom it was served on a silver platter. It is used to treat problems of the liver and spleen. It cleans the blood, combats anaemia and regulates menstrual flow. It is a cleansing herb which opens obstructions. Put on the temples, it cures inflammations of the eyes. Put in the ear it aids hearing. On the skin, it heals rash, itches, sores and wounds, and it is used to treat venomous bites and stings.

Comfrey is favoured by Mars and, like Mars, it is a unifying force: it brings things together. It is called knitbone, as it brings bones together and heals them. Albertus has said, a steak cut in half and put in a cook pot, then comfrey added to the water, the two halves of the steak would knit back together.

Comfrey is used for unlocking secrets and for getting in and out of hidden places. When travelling, it is put in shoes for protection and for protection, water off comfrey is sprinkled on clothes, and it is sprinkled on clothes for gaining success in dealings. And people carry comfrey in order to give a favourable impression.

Comfrey protects the heart. It takes away pain from, and heals, wounds, sprains, swellings, bruises, piles and ailing genitals; and it is used for treating ruptures, coughs, gout, dysentery, ulcers, scrofula, asthma, leucorrhea and problems of the lungs. As comfrey gives courage and chases away depression, warriors put it in their drinks.

An herb of the Warrior, Alyssum is a warming herb and it is used to combat snake venom.

Coriander is a powerful herb of the Time of the Warrior. If picked in the Moon's last quarter, it is a powerful aphrodisiac and would promote long life. Clothes, so that they bring good health, are washed in coriander water. In a garden, coriander protects the garden and the home and its residents, and it is much favoured by bees. Coriander is an influence toward peace and love, but can bring anger.

Coriander is associated with the Underworld. It is an herb called for by many different potions. For an easy childbirth, thirteen coriander seeds are strung on a linen thread; the thread, tied around the left leg and near the genitals. After childbirth, it is quickly removed. The thread used is often red.

Coriander cures headaches, aids digestion, strengthens the heart and brings down fevers. To treat skin problems, it is mixed with olive oil. To freshen air and gain other blessings, people hang coriander in their houses.

Lupine relates to Mars. It sometimes represents small amounts of money, or dejection; however, as food, cattle and horses find much value in it. Lupine, to even a beggar, might seem of little value; but to a horse, or to a man with a horse, it might seem a fortunate thing to come upon. Earth herself favours Lupine and blooms with vigour where Lupine lives.

Lupine is an emmenogogue, is an opening and cleansing herb. As a lotion, it is used to heal sores, and its oil is useful in making soap.

Peony, as a cure, is put over sleeping lunatics. The herb is sacred to Apollo and Mars.

The Bugle, an herb of the Warrior, is favoured by Aphrodite and by deities related to thunder. To pick a bugle would, it is thought, cause a thunderstorm. Bugle inspires love. Blooming out of season, it predicts misfortune. As a tonic, bugle cures coughs and ulcers. As a lotion, it heals sores.

The Mustards, herbs of Mars, are a number of herbs which promote good health. In health, the use of the mustards was taught by Aesculapius. The herbs produce heat and are made into warm ointments used for treating rheumatism, sore muscles, colds and other throat and chest ailments. The mustards, used in a foot bath, aid sore feet. Mustards stimulate appetite and aid digestion and the leaves are a health giving food.

Usual mustards are black mustard, white mustard and charlock. Charlock is often an herb of choice for pulmonary ailments and Dodonaeus speaks of its value for giving a burning oil.

Arsesmart is an herb of the Warrior which is favoured by the Horse. It is friendly to horses and on them, it keeps them free from hunger, thirst and fatigue; and, also, it cures their sores. With humans, it is used to treat piles, jaundice, ulcers, dropsy, rheumatism, lethargy, palsy, apoplexy, stone and falling sickness. Also, Grieve lists it as a treatment for gravel, gout, dysentery and coughs. Under riders, it keeps the horsemen from getting tired.

The Blackberry relates to the Warrior and is sacred to the Goddess of the Dawn, Aurora, and is sacred to Aphrodite. In grave yards, it makes straying out of graves difficult for ghosts. Bending hoops of the bramble are magical and one can gain strength by crawling under them.

Crawling through bramble hoops is a way to banish boils, and a child with a hernia is passed backward and forward under a bramble hoop when the Waning Moon is in Aries.

Blackberry fronds are used in destroying malicious, or negative, energies – and to fight opposing magics and charms. Ailing cows, as ones which shrews have walked over, are cured by being dragged through hoops of bramble.

Blackberry leaves are used in treating sores, ulcers, dysentery, constipation, piles, gout and the stone. As a lotion, they combat venoms and improve the complexion. And blackberries make food and drink for the deities, and for humans until the Braderie, and then, Nick pisses on them.

The Mandrake is a powerful herb with a heavy influence in the Time of the Warrior. It sits in the middle of Aphrodite's garden. As it is associated with Medusa, for workings with Hades, Hekate, Saturn, Venus, Diana, Circe, Mercury and Aphrodite; the Mandrake is an appropriate herb to use. One use is to burn incense made from mandrake fruit or root during the workings, or when searching hidden knowledge.

The Hairy Woodrush and the Barrenwort are stout herbs of the Warrior.

The Time of the Warrior is a time for using healing energies. At this time, Yarrow and Betony are useful as healing herbs. From Homer, it is recorded that Cheiron taught Achilles how to heal wounds with Yarrow. And Betony is eaten by animals to be cured of wounds.

The Time of the Warrior would inspire a quickness in identifying and moving to solve problems. The wisdom of Mars would be an influence and Aurora is a healer. Healing wounds would be given priority. The deities directed healers to magics which worked. Hyginus said that Telephus was healed by the treating of the weapon which caused his wound. Clodd said that swords were rubbed with a correctly made powder to cure those whom they had wounded. Rulandus said that the person who had caused the wound healed it with rust. It has been observed that although iron and brass cause wounds, they have healing powers. To bring cures, they have been passed over the bodies of sick person.

The Time of the Warrior is a time when there have been many dreams which have predicted events and it was thought that these dreams were often sent by Jupiter.

On the card, Mars moves forward pulled by two horses. In the foreground are daffodils. The daffodils are on the border between life and death. As do many of the flowers which relate to fires, the daffodils have bright flowers, blooms which invite copulation with bees. In the bottom corners of the card are stalks of nettle.

The Time of the Warrior is given the number One: the number of the Sun, Lord of the Seat of Fire. Fire has the colour Red: the colour which radiates courage, anger, desire, force, strength, vibrancy, passion, lust, love and quickness. With the Warrior is an excess of violence, for nothing succeeds like excess.

Number One relates to focus, to unity. The Time of the Warrior would promote focus and unity, and would promote harmony, strength, vigour, determination, courage, health, lust, love, poetry and music. Number One relates to pain and death. In each bottom corner, below the nettles, would be a skull. Warriors have worn skulls.

The Number One Card holds a redness. In the upper left corner is the head of a ram. In the upper right corner, a rooster and below the rooster, a yellow hen and below the hen, dawn coloured eggs. At the top, from the right, a limb of the Alder. The Alder was called the tree hottest to fight. To the rear on the card, in the distance; one, to the far left; one, to the far right; are women archers. Up the sides of the card, comfrey and nettles are over violets.

In the center of Card Number One, the Warrior stands in his chariot, his sword held up, the tip of it pointed skyward; his round shield held and in its center, a ruby.

The Ruby would be the stone favoured by Mars. One would grace the center of his shield. Rubies are worn so that the wearer might have success in controversies. Crow lists it as representing health and strength in the physical World, action and passion in the Astral World. Kunz said it was believed that the Ruby, worn on the left side, would protect a person's home and lands, and that in its center, it contained an inextinguishable fire. The Ruby was thought to give protection from storms and to give success in battle.

In the card's center, through a field of daffodils, two horses pull a chariot on which is the Warrior Mars in his red tinted helm; his face, dark red; red glinting off his shield. He rides forward.

"Why do you go on, battle after battle?"
"Legion, my friend."
"And will you go on and on to the end of the Earth?"
"Aye, to the very end."

II ~ Flower

The Flower is symbolic of the time when growing things are in their glory of bloom. This segment of time might commence April twentieth, which the ancients, as one might learn from Fox, decreed should be given to the honour of Flora, Goddess of Flowers, and it was given the name, Florilia. Flora represents reproduction, growth and blooming. She appreciates beauty, including beauty of the human body, so many of her Moon lit rituals are done in the nude. In the day, there are parades of dancers and flower decked musicians; these, followed by flower covered wagons from which medallion charms and beans are thrown to the outstretched hands of people in the celebrating crowds and of the medallions, many are obscene. Goats and rabbits, animals favoured by Flora, are let loose into the crowds and there is a scramble to catch them, as the animals bring fortune in procreation. Then night, there is bawdy dancing around fires. Dance relates to copulation.

The next day, Parilia, honours the Goddess Pales and the Birth of Rome is celebrated. Pales is protector of the Sun's sheep, of sheep and cattle in general, of lands, of vegetation, and is a goddess of Dawn. In observing her rites, sheepfolds are decorated with wreaths and green branches, and they are swept and purified with spring water and sheep are purified with smoke from rosemary, fir and the shells of beans. Households, also, are purified with smoke and decorated with bay. Floors are swept with bay and sprinkled with spring water. At dawn, people face East, say four prayers against harm, wash their hands in dew off bay; then, for purification, each person jumps three times over a fire made with bay and bean stalks and sometimes, fragrant woods, as juniper and pine. Offerings, such as the dried blood of sacrificed horses and the ashes of sacrificed unborn calves, are given to the fires. Cows and sheep are driven through the smoke. From the cracklings of the fires, omens are deduced. Then, people sing of the Parilia and offerings of milk and millet cakes are given to Pales. There is music of pipes and drums and people ask Pales to forgive any slight against Nature committed during the previous year and not overlooking the smallest slight, so that animals would bear healthy offspring. Warm milk is offered to Pales and people drink milk mixed with must and eat millet cakes. This, from Pater.

Later in the day, there is a picnic where libations of milk are poured to Pales. After eating, there are games. Flaming Cupid arrows are shot at trees. An evening custom is to have a girl, dressed only in flowers, go from place to place singing charms which call for caressing rain. She makes herself into a cloud and, as she floats through the sky, petitions the deities. All along her route, people pour water on her. Her route is made to include local springs and brooks.

April twentysecond, Plenteria, Minerva, with spinners and weavers, is honoured. Clothes are washed and women hang their clothes from fruit trees.

April twentythird, Green George Day, honours Jupiter, Venus, George the Dragon Slayer and Green Man, and Shakespeare. The master poet was born and died on this day. As on other special days, omens are looked for. This date, the year a long haired star was seen, many were slain in the Battle of Hastings. Green George Day, to honour Jupiter and Venus, flowers are planted in a public place. And celebrations include flower decked parades with floats and bands and one man on a horse, designated as Green George, and he might be expected to make a speech; then, might have other duties: slaying a dragon, driving nails into a willow, getting himself thrown into water.

Green George represents the Sun. Being pushed into water; then, helped out, shows the Sun is trusted and helped to be reborn. The Sun, the Spirit of Fire, is swallowed by the Dragon, the Spirit of Water; then, slays the Dragon and is reborn.

Often, sheep and cows are decked with wreaths of flowers, and girls make offerings of herbs to Venus.

April twentyfifth, Robigalia, honours Robigus, God of Corn, God of Agriculture. Robigalia is a day on which there are many fairs and entertainments. There are parades to carry sacrifices of red dogs, dismembered, to Robigus' candle lit alters. Grain, also, is sacrificed. Then, there are solemn prayers so that Robigus will give protection from blight and mildew and not let the Dog Star destroy the crops. The Dog Star, thought powerful and feared, has ties to the Underworld. Oaths are sworn by the Dog.

On this day, also, the Cuckoo is honoured and the day is sometimes called Cuckoo Day. The Cuckoo is looked for, it is said, to bring in the summer. It is also a bringer of omens. A man having missed a meal, hearing a cuckoo, might expect the coming year to be lean. The first cuckoo call of the season, if heard at night, would be bringing death. The first cuckoo, heard before breakfast, would be bringing ill fortune. The flight of a magpie toward a house would indicate a sudden arrival of strangers. It is said, the cuckoos eat wood sorrel to improve their singing.

April thirtieth is Beltane and this has been considered the start of summer. Beltane goes into May first, which is Mayday, named after Maia, Goddess of the Fires of Dawn. She celebrates the blooming of all life, its madness and intoxication. She is a mad warrior goddess who brings, among much else, death. She promotes copulation, reproduction and joy. She is a mother goddess. She is called the Mother of the Winds; so, of Mercury. She is a Star Goddess. Her form can be seen in Maeve and her influence, in the madness of the Maenads who for rituals dressed in wild animal skins and acted the part of carnivores. Intoxication, fucking, eating, slaying were all part of the Maenads' mad rituals. As representing blooming youth, Maia copulates and sees that others follow her example.

The Flower represents the female genital.

Maia is the Queen of Fairyland, so, has a relationship with the Land of the Dead. As Queen of Fairyland, Maia does some things which seem harmful to people of this world. Some of these things, such as tangling the hair of animals or people, seem little more than mean jokes or pranks. Some of her actions are more harmful, even deadly, to those of this world. People who, in quests for honour, come up against Fairyland, often fall into great sorrows.

As Queen of Fairyland, Maia moves in the theatre of witchcraft. Under her sponsorship, some women have become skilled in those arts. Fairy magic is dangerous. Fairies are a threat to carry children away.

Fairies hold festive dance rituals on Beltane and these are sometimes seen; sometimes, this is by the aid of herb ointments. Sometimes a bright radiance over a field lets one know that fairies are there even when they are not seen. If one sees the fairies' dance, one might see intricate colour patterns which, through their dance, they form. The patterns might be seen as a structure, a form of temple. Wonderful music is sometimes heard playing for the dances. It is sometimes heard when the fairies are not themselves seen. If fairies are seen, the fairies would usually be in the Otherworld into which one might be granted a rare look. The walls between the worlds are thin at Beltane and at Samhain. Any from the Otherworld who have come into this world, the visit is usually short.

Touching iron or passing over a body of water would certainly be enough to whisk any one of them back to the Otherworld.

Beltane is a festival of celebration and protection. As veils to the Otherworld are, at this time, thin; this is a dangerous time. At Beltane, a major god looked to for protection is Beli, God of Light, God of the Moon. Also known as Belus and Belenus, he was sometimes called a son of Neptune; sometimes, thought related to Apollo and was considered a guardian of the Underworld – and a protector of the Delphic Oracle. An Ox God, Beli rode in a chariot pulled by dragons. As Belenus is a god of magic, this is a time for doing magical things. Belenus is a God of the Plow, so clumps of plowed turf are put under the nests of hens in order to have protection from hawks and thunder. Belenus will grant protection.

The Tree of Belenus is the Willow and it is related to magic and to the Moon. The Ox is the Guardian of the Moon.

At Beltane, a central focus would be on animal husbandry. There are animal and land protection rituals to be observed in order to correlate with the deities in providing for the satisfactory turning of the cycle of nature. Often, an early ritual at Beltane is beating the bounds. This is done in the name of the deities in order to secure rulership. Men carrying birch whips and willow whistles ride around areas under their jurisdiction and at points, especially border markers, junctions and water banks, they beat the ground and blow their whistles. After this protection, people make ready, then have a parade to the top of a hill, which would be the site of the Beltane fire. The parade would be a form of dance intended to inspire growth. The parade would usually be athletic, full of vigourous jumping movements; and noisy, noise from bells, whistles, cans, drums, horns and things.

At the fire site, it is usual to have a magic circle drawn, deities summoned. There would be a ritual lighting of the Beltane fire. It is a custom to give a selection of sacred flowers to the fire. A usual selection would include tansy, teasel, wood betony and savory. Often there will be a Bel Carl selected. One method of selection; cakes are passed, one to each of the men and boys as far as the cakes go. One of the cakes would be made of burnt barley and he who gets it is Bel Carl. Another method of selection, a hat is passed containing pebbles, one of them black and he who pulls the black pebble from the hat is Bel Carl. The Bel Carl is required to jump 3 times over the Beltane fire; then, over all of his skin, he is made black with charcoal. He is then pelted with egg shells and then, must not speak until May Day has passed. Others speak of him as if he were dead. He is a sacrifice. In some places, in times past, the Bel Carl took on himself the transgressions of the area, then was whipped through the streets and from this, he often died.

The fire is chiefly for purification and for feeding energy to the Sun. Cattle are passed over part of the fire to be purified and to be rid of any demons which might be on or following them, which might cause them harm. Also, for blessings from Belenus, cows' udders are switched with rowan switches.

As the Willow is sacred to Belenus, it is a custom to make a figure of willow wicker, have it take on personality and energy of the god; then give it to fire. It would give energy and fertilizing power to the Sun. Sometimes other beings are put in the Wicker Man when he is given to the fire. It gives added energy.

It is a custom, an oaten cake is baked with 9 square knobs, each knob dedicated to the protector of flocks. Also, in a cauldron, a caudle of oatmeal, butter an eggs is made, then bits handed out. All those with caudle would stand with their backs to the fire, ask blessings of Belenus for the coming year, then throw the caudle over the left shoulder, into the fire. Then there is music and dancing around the fire combined with bawdy activities.

Toward the dawn, May Day, May dew is gathered on silver spoons and put in silver vessels. Girls, for their complexions and to bring love, wash their faces in it. It is said, "The fair maid who, the first of May, goes to fields at break of day and washes in dew from the Hawthorn Tree will ever after handsome be."

May dew is recorded to bring forth births. Two dew covered turfs, put together, was said to create eels.

The Hawthorn is the favourite place from which to gather dew. It is also thought good to gather dew from ivy. Some people, feeling a need for extra potent dew, might gather it from new graves. There is a practice of collecting it from specific flowers for targeted ailments. May dew is sometimes used for cleaning and whitening linen. For this, the linen is left out all night to catch the dew. Dew ponds, partly formed from the water of dew, are thought to give knowledge of the future. May dawn dew pools would be looked at.

At dawn, ribbon decked May baskets are filled with flowers while maple flutes are played for the Goddess of the Dawn. Maple relates to love and to death and encourages the coming in of summer.

In many places, after breakfast, a parade is formed: people in bright clothes and many, in costume. There might be, beside the music makers, whip crackers, a hobby horse with a hobby horse teaser, and representations of Robin Hood, nymphs, satyrs, elves and brownies, and others also. The parade would make its way to a place where there would be a Maypole, a tall pole set up, usually, with a crown of flowers at its top from which ribbons of various colours would depend.

One custom, at the Maypole, a May King and May Queen would be crowned with flowers. The May King would represent the Green Man, the Spirit of Vegetation. Robin Goodfellow and Robin Hood are forms of the Green Man. From Skene: The people were, at the Maypole, honouring Robin Hoode with tabor and horn.

The King, after he is crowned, would be expected to start doing his kingly duties. In some places, a duty assigned to the King is to shoot an arrow into an oak. He might, from the direction which the Beltane Fire smoke blows, predict when summer weather will be in. Smoke blowing toward the North would mean summer weather would be coming late. Often, to inspire growth, the King would call for a high stepping, stomping Morris Dance. Shooting the Oak would demonstrate the King's authority. He would be Master of Games. The games are light hearted, seemingly frivolous; but many, suggestive of death. The celebrator's laughter at the suggestions; might seem a bit like whistling in a graveyard. The closeness to the Otherworld in May tells people, there is a great danger from death when one is at the peak of bloom. The closeness to the Otherworld at Samhain tells the old to get ready for death is near. Beltane brings warnings to the young.

The games, Ring Around the Roses, London Bridge, Drop the Handkerchief, all have death messages to communicate. The first has, "Ashes, all fall down;" the second, "here comes the chopper to chop off your head." "Drop the Handkerchief," leaves always a person out of the circle of the living.

Another game, "Nuts in May," is about collecting the nuts whom Death should have carried away at Samhain, the appropriate time for gathering nuts. One by one, nuts are assigned to be carried to the Otherworld.

There would be dance games presided over by the Queen of May decked in flowers. Often, a tugowar would be waged, Winter against Summer. The setting up of the Maypole is a ritual sometimes done at this time. The two hoops of flowers at the top of the pole would represent the crown of Maia. To music, there would be various dances with the Maypole ribbons, ending with the dance to bind the ribbons to the pole.

The Hawthorn is a big part of the Beltane May Day celebration. It is considered a great lord, a guardian of the way to the Otherworld. It is a custom to decorate the elder hawthorn and have dancing around it. As it is at the Gate to the Otherworld, fairies often hold their rituals near it. Related to the Birth Goddess, the Hawthorn encourages copulation. Old hawthorns are often avoided, as they are thought, filled with strange and harmful magics and to have attracted dangerous beings. To harm a hawthorn is thought, likely to bring disaster. The crown of King Richard III, after his loss at the Battle of Bosworth, was found hanging from the limb of a hawthorn. The Hawthorn is an ogre like god who guards the graves of mighty warriors, and guards wells, sacred springs and temples. At Beltane, requests are made of hawthorns. For justice, three priests go to a chief hawthorn, stand in a circle around it; then, holding it, they face away from it, state their problem and say, "King Hawthorn, we ask that justice be done."

The Hawthorn is a tree of purity, a tree of cleansing. Its branches are hung over doors for protection; however, to collect the hawthorn, one should have permission from the Hawthorn. Moss off a hawthorn brings sleep, but the moss should be removed before deep sleep, otherwise the sleeper might not wake up. Hawthorn flowers in houses are thought to bring ill luck. They might invite the goddess, Cardea, and that goddess might eat any children whom she finds. Cardea uses a wand of hawthorn. Satyrs relate to Hawthorn.

Hawthorn is used to treat heart trouble, kidney ailments, dropsy, sore throats and other infections. An horizontal slice of a haw reveals the Sign of the Goddess, which is the Symbol of Mankind. At Beltane, often chief hawthorns are honoured with rituals and decorations of bright cloths which are tied to the hawthorn's branches.

The Broom is in the Beltane May Day environment. It is often decorated and carried in the May Day parade. Brooms are also used in May Eve rituals, especially those which honour Walpurga, who runs through the lands with a sheaf of grain and her triangle mirror. Goddess Walpurga relates to the Moon and, also, to witchcraft and the Broom is a tool of witchcraft. To sweep the house with a flowering broom is to invite death. It is said, to sweep the house the First of May is to sweep the head of the house away. Broom flowers are favoured by fairies, so protect from witchcraft.

May Day is, in a big way, a celebration of flowers. Flowers are often showy or odoriferous so that they attract the affections of butterflies, bees and bugs, attract flirtations which relate to copulations. To demonstrate this aspect of flowers, girls make balls of flowers, throw them into the air; then, if they catch the balls, expect good luck. Boys make rings of flowers, put them on poles, then girls take the wreaths from the poles. Many flowers are used in decoration, in decorating homes and the wagons, platforms, costumes and other things used in the May Day celebration. Nymphs and Satyrs would be decked in flowers. Some nymphs take the form of one flower or another. Nymphs have been considered affectionate but shy. Personalities other than nymphs would sometimes have flower forms.

On May Day, the identifying image would be the Maypole, usually a tall pole which would conduct a god's shaft of fire down to fertilize Earth. Any one of a number of trees might be the one selected to provide the Maypole. Birch and Rowan are trees often selected. A third is the Maple. The Maple, a tree sacred to Venus, holds the Fire of Love. Love encouraging maple flutes are blown on May Day, and these are magical. It was a maple flute which revealed the murderer of a princess. Venus, beside her interest in the whispers of lovers, is interested in justice. It is under a sycamore maple that King Arthur, each May Eve, sits to judge the battle, the King of the Unknown against the Guardian of the Underworld for the hand of Cordelia, Goddess of the Sea. The Maple also relates to Vulcan and Vulcan honours Maia on May Day, as do the priests at his shrines.

The Maple is an emblem of quietness and reserve. New babies are passed through the branches of maples so that the babies will have long lives. From the roots of the Maple come cures for liver complaints and sore eyes. From its sap, a health giving food is made. For whips, the wood chosen is often maple.

The bird honoured at May Day is the Robin. It is the sacred bird of Belenus.

Beltane saw the birth of Taliesin, of Mordred and of the Duke of Wellington.

Toward the middle of May, the Spirit World and the dead tend to occupy more and more of peoples' thoughts. May 11, much attention is given to ghosts and ill omens are looked for. A solar eclipse on May

11 announced the death of King Erkenbert and also, in that year, a great plague.

May 13, Lemuria, makes a statement on May's relationship with Death. On this day the dead visit old haunts. In the middle of the night, the man of the house goes to the front door, faces the darkness and, with a thumb through folded fingers, makes a sign which is for all his house. He then turns and throws nine beans over his left shoulder and welcomes the ghosts, saying,

"These I cast to redeem me and mine."

The number of the Flower is two: the unity of a thing with its opposite; night and day, heads and tails, dark and light, life and death. There would be two scales of value for an object or an action. What is best in the light might be the worst in the dark. As one climbs a ladder toward the top of the good; he might, at the same time, be climbing a ladder down on a different scale. A deity of Earth needs but to turn her coat inside out to become a deity of Air. She puts her coat of invisibility on. Number two brings strength. It binds two things together. It is a number of revelation, as it relates one thing to another.

The focal image for the Time of the Flower is the Flower. The Primrose is a flower favoured by Maia, Flora and Venus and is a favourite of fairies. A good while before Beltane the blooms of primrose can be seen filling waste places with variations of what is known as primrose yellow. It is a magical herb which leads people into carefree dreamlands and into otherworlds; these, often worlds in the Faery Kingdom. It might cause one to float down a metaphorical path: a feeling of well being, of joy. The Primrose might lead one to see the world through rose tinted glasses, to see a world of the imagination. Associated with the Primrose is a wistful sadness. Primrose is said to be the son of Flora and Priapus, who ever mourns for his lost love. Primrose is a gentle herb which heals wounds and sores. It is put in baths to bring attractiveness and affection. As a tea, it is calming and dispels gout, headache, rheumatism, insomnia, nervous disorders and phrensie. Primrose combats intestinal worms. A bunch of primroses taken into a house, the number of blooms will relate to the number, in the barnyard, of chicken eggs hatched. Taken into the house, or given as a gift, a bunch of primroses must contain at least thirteen blooms, or, if not, the number made up by violet blooms. The bunch, otherwise, would be dangerous. The five petals of primrose form a sacred symbol of the Goddess. With fruit, primrose flowers are put on alters of

Flora, Maia, Venus, Aphrodite and Cupid. Chiefly, primroses lead a way out of the world of toil and care and inspire song.

The Cornflower, or Bluebottle, is important at this time. When Cheiron was wounded, by an arrow, in the foot; a man treated the wound, so Flora turned the man into the Cornflower. It is used, through Flora's influence, to attract women. The Cornflower combats poison and venom. Snakes flee from cornflower smoke. Bad air is banished by cornflowers. Cornflowers in baths relieve gout. Cornflowers, as a tonic, are used for conjunctivitis, liver ailments, plague and ulcers; as a lotion, for cuts, wounds and sore eyes. On the eyes, cornflowers might give an ability in clairvoyance and in seeing Fairyland.

The Blue Mallow is valued much and especially at the Time of the Flower. It is much used in May Day decoration. The large, showy flowers attract bees, promote copulation, bring love. They are used to increase fertility. The use of Mallow in healing dates back to the dawn of Mankind. It is known to have been used for over sixtythousand years. It heals wounds, sores and ulcers and cures problems in the pulmonary and digestive systems. Vaginal problems, kidney troubles and problems with tissues are treated with mallow. Mallow cures gout and treats problems with the eyes. It removes the pain from stings. For sore throat it is found effective when mixed with honey. The Greeks for its healing abilities have called it Althea, from, "to heal." It is picked at Full Moon.

To gain love or ability in reproduction, mallow is taken as a tonic, worn as an amulet, carried inside the pants or, as an ointment, used on the genitals. Mallow is eaten by women for an increased breast milk flow. As a food, it is considered to be nutritious. Also, it is thought to give protection from witchcraft.

Mallow is favoured by Venus, Juno and the Moon. Jeanne Rose gives its meaning as delicate beauty. It is given a place at funerals, put on coffins and planted on graves. The Mallow, among other flowers, forms the paths for the dead, and the Mallow helps the dead into the Underworld. Mallows are close to the Gates of the Underworld and are often seen at the water's edge, as water is the veil between the worlds. Mallows are honoured in both worlds – and it is said, Rhadamanthus, the great Underworld Judge, said that one should pray to the Mallow, as it could lead one out of Hades.

In the Time of the Flower, Wood Betony is an herb felt to be needed. It is important to Beltane, as its flower is part of the magic of the Beltane fire. Betony is a controlling herb which directs thought. It brings courage. It is planted around houses to keep away malicious beings, nightmares and, as Leyel has said, dream fantasies. And it is planted in graveyards to keep order among spirit forces. And it is often worn as a charm. Apollonius Tyana lists it as an herb of magic. As Betony has a relationship with dragons, a circle of Betony put around a pair of snakes will make them fight.

Betony is a major healing herb. Caesar Augustus said that it was shown to cure fortyseven diseases. Others have said that is could cure even more. Its use was taught by Aesculapius and his aid, it is said, should be requested when using it. It is said to cure body and spirit. It is said to cure ailments from toxins, witchcraft, malicious spirits and elf darts. Gerard lists it as a cure for sciatica pain, colds, ruptures, convulsions, cramps, mad dog bites, snake bites and epilepsy. Culpeper adds jaundice, dropsy, palsy and gout to the list. Antonius Musa recorded it as a cure for headaches. And it improves the appetite and heals wounds. Grieve said that wounded stags are said to search out betony, to eat it and get cured.

Betony is used to combat troubling dreams, fearful visions and despair. It has intoxicating leaves which relieve stress.

It is thought, the best time for gathering betony is in August, and before sunrise. In collecting wood betony, no tool containing iron should be used. A girl would feel lucky if her lad was the first to find the Beltane Betony, and pick it. Betony is a flower loved by fairies.

Another flower favoured by fairies and important to the Time of the Flower is Herb Robert. It is under the special protection of Robin Goodfellow, so Robin and the fairies would likely punish anyone who was caught harming the plant. Herb Robert is a healing herb. Its leaves heal sores and wounds. As a tonic, it is used for ulcers, sore mouths and throats and intestinal disorders. As an ointment, it is useful for piles.

An important herb for the Time of the Flower is Tansy. It has importance especially on May Day, as it has a part in May Day rituals, one of which is the eating of tansy cakes. And tansy is one of the herbs thought needed for the Beltane fire. Tansy is the powerful herb given to Granymede so that he would become immortal. Because of this power, it is put on graves and is carried to attract love. Its life force causes it to grow even in a pocket when it is carried. This is said to cause, or indicate, a growing love. Tansy is favoured by Venus, Maia, Jupiter, Juno and Flora – among other deities. To inspire rebirth, it is put with the dead. To guard against ague, people put it in their shoes. Tansy is used to treat jaundice, dyspepsia, gout, fevers, bruises, burns and liver and kidney ailments. It is used to combat intestinal worms. Tansy makes a health giving tea and, in the garden, it drives away ants and flies.

Teasel also is important to the Time of the Flower. It is thought needed for the Beltane Fire.

The Teasel relates to procreation. The juice of the Teasel, mixed with that of Mandrake, is given to women to cause conception. If a tooth of the baby conceived because of that potion were put into a drink, everyone who drank any of it would get quarrelsome. Teasel Flowers, cup shaped, are called Venus cups, and the liquid which collects in them is said to have had the Spirit of Venus descend into it, so it is valued as a medication and, especially, for the eyes. From Teasel root, a salve is made which is used on abscesses, fistulas and skin blemishes. Teasel infusions are used for treating jaundice and liver obstructions and for cleaning and strengthening the digestive system. Also, teasel is used as a protection against witches. Worms from the teasel heads are hung from the neck to combat melancholy, depression and the ague.

As it represents the Goddess, Teasel has become the symbol of cloth makers and is used in cloth making.

The Butterwort, favoured by Belinus, protects cattle and children from elves.

Of the Time of the Flower is the Foxglove, a favourite flower of fairies. It has power in the World of the Fairies. In its flowers, the fairies are said to have a special delight. When foxgloves bend over; it is thought, it is for some reason in the Otherworld. A foxglove bent over might be offering itself as a resting place for some fairy. The red spots found on foxglove flowers are said to be places where fairies have put their fingers. It is said, fairies make gloves for foxes and for themselves out of foxglove flowers; that they are put on foxes so that the foxes might tread quietly. Foxgloves are often seen around rabbit holes where they would be convenient for foxes. The leaves of foxgloves can restore a child who has been bewitched by fairies. Fairies favour the rose and purple flowered foxgloves over the yellow flowered ones which usually come later in the year. Foxgloves favour honey bees and the bees take pleasure in foxgloves. The bees alight gently on the doorstep of flower after flower and these and many other beasts and bugs avoid harming the plant. As the Foxglove relates to the Underworld, it is used by those who wish to establish a tie to the Underworld, but it is tricky, dangerous to use and through the Foxglove, the Underworld might get a person in its grasp, drag him under. Foxglove leaves are used in healing wounds and sores; the flowers; ulcers, dropsy and as a strong medicine for the heart. They are also used to counter poisons. Fairies might have many uses for foxgloves, as it is thought, foxgloves are gifted in music. The flowers are called fairy thimbles, a name which suggests they might help with work. It is dangerous to take them into a house. It is suggested, they might be most useful left standing in the gardens. Where they can use people as they wish to.

The cousin to the Foxglove, Toadflax, is also favoured by fairies. And toads like toadflax. They like to rest under the leaves and when ailing, eat toadflax to be cured. Witches, who like toads, grow toadflax in herb gardens. Toads are often totem animals. Also, they give toad stones which, worn as charms, protect against illness and malicious beings. They can also keep ships from sinking and houses from burning. They bring prosperity and encourage victory.

Toadflax is used to treat jaundice and other liver ailments, scrofula, dropsy, ulcers and, as on ointment, skin problems and piles.

The Toadflax welcomes visits from the Honey Bee, but it is the Bumble Bee it invites to dinner.

A flower favoured by Flora is the Bellflower, and the first Bellflower on the scene is the Narrow Leaf Bellflower, which, blooming early, honours the Queen of May with its bloom. It symbolizes constancy and inspires love. It is a cure for stomachache and tuberculosis and, for skin problems, it is put in lotions and in baths. If the lotion darkens the skin, it predicts a cure. As it is a favourite of fairies, it is unwise to pick it. Wandering in woods where bellflowers are, people are likely to get lost and, perhaps, lost forever, even if the woods is a familiar one. Blue Bellflowers bring death.

The Wood Sorrel is a flower favoured by Venus. Associated with the Cuckoo, it is sometimes called the Cuckoo Flower. It is said, cuckoos eat it in order to have improved voices. The Wood Sorrel sponsors maternal care. It cools the liver and strengthens the heart. It cools inflammations, the heat of agues and brings down fevers. It is used to combat venoms. It is a health giving food.

The Cuckoo Orchis blooms in time to welcome the Cuckoo with bloom. Orchis is the son of a nymph and a satyr. Slain for his rudeness, his father got him turned into a flower. The Orchis relates to death. It promotes lust, so is effective used as a sex stimulant. Lovers might share an orchis root so the root would provoke an explosive orgasm. A withered root would hinder the orgasm. Orchis treats intestinal problems.

The Green Man Orchid represents a gallows from which those who have sinned against the Greenwood are hanged. Satyrs eat the roots of orchids to gain energy to attack women and copulate. Some orchids are called Dead Men's Fingers.

Wake Robin is also associated with the Cuckoo and is sometimes called Cuckoo Pint. It restores bears and birds after a hard winter. The juice of Wake Robin can be used as a cleaner, but might be harmful to the skin and deadly if eaten.

Savory is an herb of the Time of the Flower which is favoured by satyrs. It inspires mirth and pleasure. It is felt needed for Beltane fires and is one of the nine herbs included in wreaths given to Midsummer fires. Bees are fond of Savory, so to please them, it is planted near bee hives. It improves eyesight, is good for colic and, as a food, brings general good health and feelings of light hearted well being.

Groundsel is important to the Time of the Flower. Venus favours it and with her support, it cures wounds, and especially those caused by an iron weapon. Birds favour groundsel and it supports birds. In horses, it combats bot worms. It is used to treat sciatica, jaundice, falling sickness, stomachache, gout, colic and king's evil. It combats fevers. In collecting it, no tool which contains iron should be used. It is favoured by fairies.

An herb of the Time of the Flower, Smallage is called an Herb of the Spirit and it is useful to magicians. It brings sleep.

Lovage, a Flower of May, is an aphrodisiac. It is put in baths that it might bring love and beauty. It is put in wedding wreaths and, as it brings happiness, it is worn in the hair. Lovage cleans the air and adds freshness. When used in confections, it aids digestion. As a tonic, it is used for pleurisy, jaundice, intestinal ailments, urinary trouble, gravel and ague and as a lotion, for sore eyes, venomous bites and stings. Lovage brings feelings of radiance.

Woodruff is a valued herb of the Time of the Flower. It is the distinctive ingredient in the magical May Wine, which is used in May Day rituals. Dried, woodruff is hung in rooms to freshen the air, and is put with linens to keep linens fresh. Woodruff tonic removes obstructions in the liver and strengthens the heart. Woodruff ointment heals wounds and sores. For aid in battle, warriors wore woodruff, said J. E. Meyer.

Butterwort and Milkwort are favoured flowers of Flora and Venus and the Strawberry, which gives health and pleasure, is favoured by Venus.

Beside the personalities of the host of individual flowers, the power of flowers includes bodies of flowers acting in concert and the great power of flowers in general which, in a big way, is represented by the symbol of the Flower.

Philosophers have spoken of the judgements of flowers, the approval of flowers and the fear of flowers, as if the disapproval of flowers carried significant weight. A body of flowers can say,

"Do the right thing,"

or, "What you are doing is wrong."

They can say, "We are still here."

And so, give an example of strength; so, give encouragement.

They have said, "Yes, you are a wise man. See, you do know."

And, "Yes, you may call yourself a philosopher."

And, "You have our permission to call yourself a naturalist." This, from Father Young.

The Time of the Flower rises out of darkness with an abundance of flowers. In the center, above a field of primrose, is the Mallow. This is a rose musk mallow, much like the blue mallow, but a larger flower, and here, quite large. It would stand not only for all flowers, but for flower qualities, flower meanings, for the concepts of blooming. The Flower represents all growing things. It sends forth a radiance. With this come feelings of gaiety, sensual pleasure, love and a knowledge of childhood death.

To the right rear of the Flower, unclad, stands Flora. On her head is a crown of flowers: cornflowers and smallage. Smallage flowers are soothing. As was a custom, guests have been crowned with smallage and smallage put on tombs of relations of the guests. From a shoulder of Flora, a garland of flowers would fall across her body in a bend sinister. The flowers of the garland would be cornflowers and kingcups. Kingcups, if put before one's door on Mayday would bring one luck, said Marion Davies. But, said she, these are dangerous flowers and put in front of doors before Mayday, they would be likely to cause harm.

To the left of the Mallow, up and to the rear, is a blooming hawthorn, bright rags tied to some of its branches. These rags would likely be what people had torn form their underclothes and given to the tree.

To the right of the Mallow, on a green hillock, is a maypole, bright ribbons extending from a ring of flowers. The maypole symbolizes the copulation, Sky with Earth. The ribbons suggest the sunwise dance around the pole. The dance would generate energy for growing, blooming and reproducing and would supply energy to aid the Sun.

Left of the Mallow, near the top of the card, would be the head of the Ox and around his neck, a garland of flowers: cornflowers, vetch, primrose and woodruff. The Woodruff was called Master of the Woods and, by battle leaders, was worn into battle in order that they also be the masters. The Ox would be Ox God Belenus, God of Light, Ruler of the Plough. He is, in part, an Underworld God and relates to the Moon. And at this time, the Moon would be an influence. It brings integrity, purity, devotion, beauty, fantasy, contemplation and dream.

In each top corner of the card would be a maple flute: music from the maple to encourage the coming in of summer.

On the card, each side is covered with flowers: kingscups' bright gold, cornflowers' blue, purple orchis and Robin Goodfellow's flower, red campion, which women wore in their underpants to attract love.

The card would suggest Mayday, a time when the King and the Queen of the May would copulate, do sex magic, so that life would be conceived and would bloom. And it was thought best if festival goers should see them doing it, take part in spirit and get confidence that the coming season would be productive; as in this, the magic would have increased power. And Pan, Belenus, Flora, Maia and Pales would share in the joy in it. Pales enjoys rustic pleasures. She favours the modest farmer, the thatch covered shed.

The Flower is close to the Gate of the Underworld. Guinivere, a Moon Goddess, one Mayday, when out picking flowers, was stolen away to the Underworld.

If the card illustrated the May Night instead of the day, Orion might be seen in the sky with his club. He would be defending the fields. If the focus of the Sun is on this section of his road through time, the mathmatics and architecture of all nearby shapes on the ground and in the sky would be thought to be having an effect on events.

Even in day, there is a darkness around the edges in the Time of the Flower.

In the darkness, in each bottom corner of the card is an emerald. The Emerald represents calm and truth. It calms storms and sexual passions and counters magic and the Juggler's deceptions. The Emerald is related to the Underworld, so is looked to for visions of the future. The Emerald gives quick wit, and looking at an emerald is thought to improve eyesight.

With being green, it promotes growth, good health, abundance, fertility and wealth. Green relates to the Underworld, and is a sacred stone of Venus. And Venus has a special relationship with flowers. Flowers, as love charms, are sometimes hidden in the room of the intended.

Flowers are considered, most powerful. The Witch Medea used flowers to change the courses of rivers, to stop stars and to block paths of the Moon. A congregation of flowers acting in concert can shape the mood of a country.

III ~ Juggler

The major influence of card III is the element of Air. Air is the breath of life and a force which carries us on our life cycle. One recognizes that Force as the God Mercury. As Air, Mercury could be Great Wind; or, King of Winds and as King of Winds, he is Ruler of Roads. As Air, which includes the Breath of Life, he is the Great Doctor. His jurisdiction extends through light and darkness. As God of Darkness, he has authority in magical happenings. Because he relates to darkness, it is a custom to give him, at meals and rituals, the last libation of the evening. Ulysses observed this custom. As Breath of Life, Mercury relates to the Spirit World and, as key to that world, carries the staff which holds the three energies which combine to form life. Early representations show him holding a branch. When one needed to communicate with the Underworld, Mercury was often called upon. His help was needed in recovering the Vegetation Goddess, Proserpine, whom Pluto had taken to the Underworld. Mercury went to the Underworld to get the Sun Ring. He helped Hercules steal Cerberus from the Underworld. As Mercury was not only a communicator, but a diplomat, he was sometimes able to get persons back from the Underworld, persons such as Theseus and Protesilaus. As Mercury is King of Roads and all roads lead eventually to the Underworld, people take care not to let any of their hair or nail clippings get into a road to, perhaps, be picked up by Mercury, taken to the Underworld and so, attract the attention of Underworld beings who might get the owner of the hair or nail clippings picked up. As King of Roads, Mercury would supervise traffic, including that coming and going to and from the Underworld. He lends the use of his name to merchants. He is called Hera's messenger; however, as he went to make changes and solve problems, he might be called, as Seymour suggests, an ambassador. Mercury flies between Heaven and Earth, said Rulandus, bringing the spirit of generation, birth and inspiration from the other dimension, the Otherworld. Mercury has been called on for aid and protection on journeys. As monuments to Mercury, piles of stones were made at road forks and crossroads and before journeys, people went to these to ask for blessings. Some of the monuments held heads on their tops. And roads, as under the authority of Mercury, were themselves held sacred. The Great Trip is the path that goes on forever: the Road to Walsingham which becomes equated, as Sitwell says, with the Milky Way.

By incense and prayers, merchants, said Fairbanks, sought assistance from Mercury.

In preparation for a trip, the aid expected, or hoped for, from Mercury is supplemented by other help. For this, people carry stones, magic signs and herbs, some of which relate especially to Mercury. If the trip is all, or in part, by flying, special mental and physical preparation would be made. One preparation to be rubbed on one's body would have aconite, cinquefoil, soot, water parsnip and belladonna. Then, celery seeds, or smallage seeds, are eaten so that the flyer can keep from falling. This, from J. Rose. For an Otherworld trip, Rose lists poplar, soot, hemlock, monkshood, mistletoe, and opium. Robbins lists monkshood, deadly nightshade, soot, water parsnip, cinquefoil and baby fat, and said that the broomstick to be ridden was also rubbed with the herbal mix. This way leads into the unknown which, as Waite said, would hold mysteries which the intellect could not know.

Mercury, as King of Roads, would be Lord of Communication. As all matter is always in motion and each part linked to all other matter; or, as Marcus Aurelius said, gods, nature and the Universe bound together and all moving, conforming to order, and each part affecting all else; this would give Mercury wide authority. Communication can be seen as a ruling force. Communicating is accomplished visually, audibly and by intuition and dream.

With visual communication, learnings are given through realistic and through symbolic representations. With symbols, there would be the clearly stated meanings given so that the symbol would have a desired utility. Then there would be the shades of meaning a symbol would attract to itself. And forms themselves have meanings. Some of these meanings would seem magical. Sometimes, as Flowers said, meanings have been discovered intuitively; sometimes, by trial and error. Discovered meanings might become part of tradition. Some of the magical shapes given by Flowers are a four point star, which is said to provide good things and a stable harmony; an acorn, thought to bring masculine sexuality; a raindrop, which holds the meaning of nourishment and dynamic water and might be used to cause rain.

Symbols can be magical signs of great power. Basic representations of much used objects would be likely to be considered symbolic. The symbolic images, Aldus Huxley said, would have a brightness by which they might be recognized as symbols. From the collective unconscious their characteristics of given reality might be recognized. H. M. Chadwick saw ancient representations of a mirror, a comb, a stag, a wolf, a goose, a fish, a bear, an eagle which were recognized as symbols used for their magical power. Said Steiner, the pentagram is a symbol representing the mobile life force in Man, which flows through the body and away from it in five directions, and this symbol is much used by magicians. Elbee Wright explained how it is used for invoking and for banishing. It is, with the middle and index fingers held out straight, inscribed in air sunwise for invoking. For banishing, it is inscribed widdershins. The magic of symbols gives an indication that divine beings exist and shape the progress of events. And Zimmer said that before symbols, one should maintain proper humility. Some astrological symbols, called sigils, are said to have power of stars conjured into them. A sigil inscribed within a pentagon, said Villinganus, was used to drive away spirits.

One thing people hoped to gain through visual communication was knowledge of the future, and as Mercury has authority in both light and darkness, and areas of his authority extend into the Underworld, he was often called on to give this knowledge. And much of this knowledge was communicated by signs and by dice.

Mercury had a special interest in dice, so that Aristophanes called him the God of Dice. But people, realizing that much of Mercury's teaching could be tricky, would often not trust it unless it came supported by other authority. Hocart said dice have been used in ritual from earliest times. Dice were not always as they are today. The dots on the sides, said de Givry, could have numbered from one to twelve and might, in some uses, referred to symbols. Opsopaus said that this gives them a relationship to the Tarot. Through the ages many have found dice to be scary. This seems suggested by Blackstone's comment:

"Look at a pair of dice. There is absolutely nothing frightening ---"

Dice were used at an oracle of Hercules.

Mercury communicated much prophecy by signs. Observation and evaluation of observation was a method of divining favoured by Pythagoras. All signs need not only their observation, but as many as can be gathered of the circumstances surrounding the observation. Vocations to do with the ability to read signs were developed; but many signs, seen as omens, were available to the general public. If a person's foot itched, said Trevelyan, it was thought, he would soon be treading unfamiliar ground. Oxen were considered beasts of power, so it would have been considered important to note their movements. Before rain, it was said, oxen gazed heavenward and sniff the air. A frisky ox would predict a wind storm. Trevelyan said that a strange looking cow in a herd was thought to bring ill luck. Talbot said that a guest spilling wine was a traditional omen expected to bring misfortune. Theocritus said, it would be noticed if town dogs howled where three roads met. At night, if dogs howled in the town square, that would have been noticed and an ill event expected, said Pausanias. As dogs were generally considered guardians of the Underworld, as Maltwood has said, they would have been considered to have sensed problems. Cats, also, as they are associated with deities, would have been expected to give prophecy. Ceram believed that the warning of coming misfortune a black cat gives by crossing a person's path has been given in times more ancient than the Kingdom of Babylon. Horses, rabbits and pigs were also looked to for signs. White horses, said Tacitus, were considered oracles and were kept separate and their snortings and neighings were observed. Poseidon, it has been said was more likely to give prophecy through horses than through waters.

In Rome, the highest rank of official diviners were the augurs. These, interpreted messages from deities which had been sent by birds, as birds are related to Air and so, to the Spirit World. Many times, said Halliday, it was birds which carried the messages from the gods. Ovidius said the augur Thestorides foretold the victor and length of the Trojan War by seeing a snake swallow seven birds. Tacitus said, many felt that before getting married, the wedding needed to be approved by a bird. In a grove of Diana, said Livius, when birds forsook their nests, that was reason for great concern. As is seen in Shakespeare, the cuckoo is related to adultery. The owls, said Albertus, gave knowledge of the future. They were known as Athens's messengers. If a person had heard an owl hoot, he would have been likely to throw salt into the fire as an appeal to Vesta for protection. To augurs, some birds were more of an interest than others. Lapwings, said Rhys, bring messages from the Underworld. Jackdaws, magpies, cuckoos, wrens and crows were all of special interest and carefully watched. Among other things, weather was predicted by birds. Aratus said that if the heron, from the sea comes landward with disordered flight and many a scream, it predicts a gale. Jackdaws and crows gather in flocks and squawk before rain. Crows were said to bring rains of summer. From birds, people other than augurs got predictions. Armstrong reported, a girl would throw a stone, a bone and a clump of soil at a crow. From the direction in which the crow flew, the girl would discover what type the person would be whom she would marry. And Lovarcus said, woe to the sick one who hears the cuckoo sing.

From Ingersoll: It was said, drinking dragon blood gave one the ability to understand birds.

A major method of communication is communication by the use of sound. In this, the Juggler is a major force. He regulates the fluency of speech and, with inspiration from the stars, marries sound to reason. He inspires quickness of wit.

There seems, a magic in sound. Words hold so much power that those gifted in their use are sometimes called magicians and many people have become afraid of them. Highet said that Ovidius and Vergilius were called magicians. Ovidius was also considered to be a prophet and cosmologist and was said to be able to read with his feet. Prestige and physical rewards were given to poets in part, because it was thought, their words could bring blisters and cause other harm. Poets had power over reputations, so that warriors would be slain in battle rather than be treated ill by poets.

Said Layamon, Merlin lifted stones with a chant.

Incantation can be magical. At times, form and movement is needed with the vocal to make it function. An example given by Spence: a poet would sing a charm through his fist over a person from whom he wants information. Some beckoning charms, Skelton said, are extensions of non verbal, telepathic message sending. A chant might be sung a magical number of times, then suddenly stopped. In the silence, a happening would then be visualized. Chants can be so powerful that they seem separate from, and might physically affect, the poet.

Music also is magical. Mercury was gifted in music and taught the craft, in one case, to Orpheus and it is said; Orpheus, with music, according to Callistratus; charmed rocks, which moved to the music and so, changed the courses of brooks; and charmed trees and these, ordered themselves to the sound of his music. Flutes, said Hocart, bring messages from the gods. Maple flutes bring love; also, flutes bring in the summer. Harps are considered magical. They can cause tears, laughter and sleep. Stolen harps can change the fate of nations. Jack stole the harp of the awful Giant of the Sky. And so, destroyed the Giant. A master harper, Rutherford reports, restored a dumb man's speech. Mercury made Amphion's harp.

Other sound which Air carries can have momentous meaning. Disembodied voices or other ominous unassociated sounds, said Putnam, would have been thought to portend some trouble or other noteworthy event. Wheatley Stokes reported that when, with no chariot present, chariot wheels were heard, it was thought that the birth of a king was being announced.

As Lord of Darkness, Mercury has a relationship with sleep and dream. His help might be sought in understanding the knowledge which dreams give; especially, prophetic teachings. Dreams might touch into some Otherworld which would have its own meanings and laws. Said Jung, it is a superhuman world that surpasses understanding. Through the Dreamworld, its influence might be felt. It might tempt, make demands, form bonds. Leland says, one can learn through mysterious intuitions; some, quite weird; or, mad. The Otherworld is near Dreamland and Mercury is familiar with its gates. Dreams, it was thought, were divine messages which it would be a sacrilege to ignore. Dreaming of rabbits put one on the spiritual path. In a dream, Eiseley saw Death as a huge, white python. A beast of Air, it would relate to birth, copulation, wisdom and death. In dream, Mercury might teach what is concealed from the awake body.

Mercury also used oracles for giving knowledge. An Oracle of Mercury was at Pharae. From contact with the Underworld, Mercury would have vision into the future. At the oracle, for gaining knowledge, one burned incense on the oracle's hearth; then filled the lamps, one on each side of the hearth, with oil. These, then were lit. Then a brass coin was put to the right of a statue of Mercury, which would have been behind the hearth. The questioner then covered his ears, went out into the market place, uncovered his ears. The first words he heard would have been considered prophetic. At the oracle, sacrifices would have been made, and not only to Mercury, but to Athene, to Glaucus, to Mars and to a female Centaur, Tritea. For Athene, a cock was the usual sacrifice.

Mercury makes himself known at other oracles. Said Nutt, messages might have been written on leaves which the Wind might have blown away. Messages which told Aeneas how to find his father were written on leaves.

A usual way for the deities to send messages was by smoke; especially, the smoke of sacrifices. Mercury would have delivered the messages or himself provided the information. Winds and breezes would indicate the mood of Mercury. Information is provided by observation of the Wind's direction.

Many people gave messages from the deities serious consideration. Said Tacitus, many books on signs from the deities were written and studied. People realized that correctly reading signs was difficult and that false divination could occur, said Iamblichos, when the spiritual would become involved with the body; so, interrupt divine harmony. However, many people did not treat the messages with a great deal of respect. Aristophanes said some people kept messages from the gods as playthings. Some, like Epictetus, did not worry over the messages. Said Epictetus, when a raven croaked with foreboding, it was with his will that he would make any predicted event work in his favour.

Mercury is the Spirit of Air, of Communication, of Trickery and Delusion. As a Juggler, he juggles many energies that are on his roads. He balances the light of the conscious against the dark of the unconscious.

Mercury is the Spirit of Quicksilver and as this spirit, said Junius, he is the Spirit Principle in Plants. This is the spirit, or vital power, of life. It is feminine, supple, volatile, etheric and plastic, according to Junius. It forms a spirit unity with salt and sulphur, according to alchemical systems. This is reflected in the staff of Mercury: two snakes around the center pole as three united as one, and these represented the three forces united to form life. This is reflected in the lightning which Jupiter held, which was three forked, as was reported by Ovidius. From Rulandus: Quicksilver purifies gold. It relates to weather, as, in an enclosed instrument it measures temperature. An amulet against pestilence calls for quicksilver enclosed in a walnut.

Mercury is found in many forms. To Agrippa, his body would be fair, cold, and moist, with affable speech and in human shape. He would be clear and bright and in motion, like silver coloured clouds. This, he said, would be Mercury's usual form. Other forms, some frightening, in which Mercury is thought to be seen are of a bear, a staff, a magpie, a dog, a cloak of many colours and a three headed snake, and in this form, Jung saw him rising from a chalice. At times, Mercury was pictured as a crow. Clodd said that for cures, people went to boundary stones which were sacred to Mercury. These stones, when they were prayed to, were considered to be Mercury himself. A winged sandal, or the representation of the staff of Mercury, the Caduceus, was thought to hold the Spirit of Mercury. As

Air, Mercury was invisible, so related to the invisible spirits of the dead. As Zimmer said of Merlin, Mercury was the force that inhabited and moved nature. He was the atmosphere which was there when needed. He gathered together other forces, other deities, when they needed to act in concert.

Mercury was the erratic genius of magic and trickery. He was noted for mental agility, physical agility, teasing and hoodwinking. Some of his jokes have caused disasters, but doctors and inventors have learned from him. He was apt to favour those with curious minds. He is thought to have assisted diplomats, vagabonds, heralds, travelers and thieves, and he was sometimes forgiving when other deities were not expected to be. He had been a thief himself; had stolen sheep from Apollo, a girdle from Aphrodite, a spear from Mars and arrows from Artemis. His wit got him out from under the bad humours of those other deities. Rogues cleansed themselves of wrongdoings by going to a shrine of Mercury and getting themselves sprinkled with water off bay leaves.

Pausanias said that Mercury has been called the Chief Shepherd. He protects and cares for celestial flocks and shepherds sought his aid in the care of their flocks. It was considered an honour for a man should he be selected to carry the Ram of Mercury to a Mercuriala rite.

Mercury had a sword and with it he slew the many eyed monster, Argus. A master sword came from Findas, a Kingdom of Air, said Blamires. Beside power to slay, as Beyerl has said, knives and swords would hold counter magic. They ward off harmful energies and disturbing energies and break spells. The Juggler can be dangerous. He bound Ixion to an ever turning wheel. Mercury and Athene made Bellerophon able to slay the three headed dragon, Chimera. He put the Cloud Children on the Golden Ram from which one of the two, the girl Helle, fell and went to the Underworld.

Mercury is represented as a lame king. A live king, it was thought, should be perfect; however, kings were lamed in order to keep them in the Land of the Living. He is lame, but wears winged shoes, so is known to be quick. Being lame would have indicated that he would have been intended for sacred duties, not for working or for fighting. And as King of Air, he would have an invisible self, as would spirits of the dead.

As were other gods of Air, Mercury was often seen in snake form, and as a snake grows a new skin, would be involved in rebirth, rebirth of others from the Land of the Dead and in his own rebirth, and this is a way of getting out of the Underworld. Mercury brought Zeus back from the dead after Zeus had gotten torn to pieces by the dragon, Typhon. As rebirth is related to healing, snake gods are master healers. As King of Snakes, Mercury is God of healing.

Mercury has been represented holding a branch and this, to indicate that he has a tree form; so, would relate to spring rebirths; so, the relationship with Maia, Goddess of Daybreak and Spring Awakenings. Maia, Goddess of Rebirths, would be called the mother of the reborn Mercury, who with his staff, his key representing his tree form, would pass from one world to another; the three part staff, the three forces which make up life. The staff could cure and it could slay.

Mercury, the Chief Juggler, is quick, quick of wit, shrewd, inventive, eloquent, tricky and capricious. He is a trickster and his pranks and jokes can bring joy to many with alert and curious minds. Keightley said that a stone thrown into a sacred lake might cause a tempest to rise. This would be an example of his tricky nature. He is an entertainer who brings forth multitudes of intriguing schemes and surprising displays. However, even his little actions can have huge ramifications. The Juggler is a Lord of Change, which some might call, "The Wind of Change". Often, this is quick change; often, tricky; but often helpful; sometimes, when situations are critical. His changes might be a sudden reversal, as from black to white. He gave Pandora the box that took the World out of the Golden Age.

The Juggler is sometimes the Great Doctor; sometimes, the Mountebank; sometimes, seeming like a carnival magician. But Man likes to believe snake oil is a magical cure. Blackstone has said, being fooled can be entertaining. And it can be educational, as lack of attention to detail can be the cause of error. And dealing with a juggler, having a serious warning mixed with foolishness can cause a problem. But he is there when one needs to take a chance; perhaps, needs a spokesman. But the Juggler is ambivalent and changeable. But Spes is never far off.

Mercury, the Chief Juggler, controls the circles and might be seen juggling three of them. The three circles symbolize the three forces forming life. The Juggler, a creator of illusions, is a shifter of vast energies. He manipulates circles to get the magical triangles which change the happenings of the world. Ammianus said that Mercury has been called the Intelligence of the Universe and was thought to arouse activity in people's minds.

Mercury became a god of choice to call for help, in part, because of

Maia. He has been called the son of Maia. It was a custom to summon Mercury, as the conveyer of magics and incantations, to ceremonies of magicians. This, one learns from Lucius Apuleius.

Julian the Blessed would awaken himself in the middle of the night to pray to mercury for learning. From Mercury, he is said to have learned balance in justice. From Mercury, Julian learned, also, how to awaken when he wished.

Gaufridus reported that it was Mercury whom Hengist considered Chief God and Mercury who guided Hengist across the seas.

Mercury relates to the little finger. It is associated with mental agility and an ability to picture tools solving problems. It is used in magic.

The Planet Mercury joined to another good planet increases goodness. It relates to intelligence, knowledge, adaptability, balance, responsiveness, skills and magic. The Spirit of Mercury would be in the planet.

As a healer, and as he has a tree form, Mercury would have a special relationship with plants, and many come under his special attention. For protection from witchcraft, Mercury took Ulysses an herb. Herbs have many powers beside that of healing. Through communication with plants man might gain knowledge and this, at times, would be of the future. Theophrastus gives some of the messages which trees send: sweet fruit trees going sour is a message that bad times are coming; sour trees giving sweet fruit, worse times might be thought coming; grape vines changing colour of grapes, bad times might be looked for; a fruit tree bearing fruit not in its nature, a disaster might be looked for.

Sometimes plants give extraordinary powers. Plant combinations have been made into ointments intended to give invisibility, to give a super ability to see, or to give an ability to fly, or to do some other desired work. To see beings in the Otherworld, instructions for making an ointment to be used is given by Rose. Thyme is to be picked from the spot where a being from the Otherworld had been; this, mixed with rose and marigold, picked while facing East, and with hazel, olive oil and rose water made with water from a spring. Nicholas Remigius tells of an ointment which permits a witch to rise aloft and disappear from sight. Some herbs are carried for protection. Onions, favoured by Mercury and related to the Snake, are killed and buried with dead warriors. This, from Magnusson. Other herbs, also, give protections in the Underworld. Said Vergilius, when Aeneas went to Hades, he needed his wand of mistletoe. Some plants give off energy which can be of help to humans. Sometimes humans give excess energy to plants. Some plants and some people are especially looked to to give energy. People recognized for this are sometimes called a green witch, or a person with a green thumb.

In the time under the sponsorship of Mercury there are important aids to the valuable communication with members of the Plant Kingdom. One, there is the high which life in general gets from sharing in the joy of the Sun as it rises to its height. Another is the aid from the birds, as it is a time when many of them would be most likely to be of help. And birds not only aid in communication with the Plant Kingdom, but give much other knowledge and other blessings. Many seekers of knowledge from the Otherworld specialized in gaining knowledge from birds, as birds relate to Air, so to the Spirit World. And relating to the Plant Kingdom, birds which eat corn would take on spirits of corn. And Frazer said, it was thought, some forms, as they become spirits, take on the forms of dark birds. Some birds, for giving aid in health, were looked to.

Swallows are gifted and used in healing and teach the magical use of herbs. E. V. Lucas said that powdered swallows' nests were used for cures. He said that the nests of robins and wrens have also been used.

The Juggler underlines the magical aspects of plants, of their link to knowledge and communication. One communications method is through vibration, and this, as Edward Bach has said, might be instigated through aroma, so the plants can channel thought toward particular virtues, and chase harmful spiritual vibration. Plants, through aroma and vibration, bring forth and chase emotional problems and bring changes in mental outlooks. Directing the mind is an important aspect of health. Maple has pointed out, many illnesses might be traced to unconscious conflicts of the mind. Wearing certain herbs might be done to attract favourable influences or to protect against negative influences. Combinations of herbs might be worn or otherwise made into charms. Clodd said that dolls made to represent an ill person were filled with the particular combination of herbs designed for that particular person.

In communication, to the careful observer, herbs give keys to their personalities. The key, called its signature, would, as Leland has said, represent the ideal spirit of the herb. The key, like a seed in spring, might expand virtues in the mind of the observer. Some observers, as Linnaeus, might determine an herb's sex, and this might give a better understanding of a plant's virtues.

Through plants, people communicate with deities. On alters of the deities, sacrifices of herbs are made. Said Pater, the herbs burning with a clear, tall flame would indicate the pleasure of the deities.

In many ways plants lead people to wisdom. As Monaghan has said, one might go into the garden to understand.

Mercury is, as a rule, good humoured and glad to give instruction on how plants are to be used. There are instructions not only how plants are to be used, but, how they are to be gathered. Some herbs, said Theophrastus, are best gathered from windward, some plants, best gathered by day; some, by night. Some people, when gathering hellebore, would first have anointed themselves with sacred oil. Sometimes, very complex instructions are given. And Mercury is a help to healers by relating markings and colours to uses to what each plant is to be put. Leland said each plant is marked with an indication of its ideal spirit from which its help would come. The Spirit of a plant might treat not only the ailment; but, as Paracelsus said, the cause of the ailment. The long life of a plant might be considered a signature. Skull like seeds, said Bartram, indicate its use for headache. Blue flowers suggest a use for nerves; yellow flowers, a use for liver ailments; orange flowers, for problems with the spleen. Also, purple flowers under Saturn are thought good for treating the spleen. Spotted leaves would indicate a use for skin problems. Reading comfrey and columbine would discover their use in healing sores. Plants, said Plinius, lose their virtues if, after being picked, they are permitted to hit the ground.

A major influence in the Time of the Juggler would be the Oak; the mighty, magical door between the worlds. By the tree; especially, by the Oak, Sky copulates with Earth and restores it and so, connects this world with the Otherworld. Midsummer is the spiritual Time of the spiritual Door. The Oak, in one aspect is a form of the Sun, and in another, the Club of the Sun. For the Oak, a magical time would be when the Sun reached its highest point and headed toward the Dragon of Darkness. Oaks are hugely influential. They are symbolic of strength, law, masculinity, justice, wisdom and fertility and these they promote. And they promote copulation and they, by lightning, copulate with Earth. They attract lightning and some powerful oaks are thought to bring rain, storms and sunshine at their pleasure. As a door between the worlds, the Oak is looked to for knowledge and especially, for knowledge of the future. Oak leaves are thought to whisper secrets. Augustus Caesar was said to have been announced by the revival of a dying oak. Oaths were sworn by the

Oak. Plants, as fern and mistletoe, by growing on oaks are given extra virtue. It was thought by some, oaks could produce honey, and, some thought, even bees. Oaks, considered magical, are favoured by elves and spirits and stands of old oaks are thought to be haunted. When passing old oaks, one is advised to turn his cloak, "for fairies dwell in old oaks." By turning a cloak, one would be more in sympathy with the Otherworld. As the Oak is thought to be on the brink of the Otherworld, it would be looked to as the sponsor of transitions of many kinds and to be the protector of laws. Porteous said that it is on falling oak leaves that elves fly away to the Otherworld.

The Oak is a giver of gifts. Its wood is used for sacred fires. Fires and especially, oak fires, are thought to feed energy to the Sun. Oak is used for the sacred fires of Vesta. Oaks are often associated with sacred wells. Distinguished oaks are gone to for wands and for blessings. On some oaks, candles and decorations have been put. If an oak would be host to a sacred mistletoe, it is not likely it would be disturbed for any reason not relating to the mistletoe. Some old and respected oaks have been given large gifts. White oxen have been raised especially to be sacrificed to oaks, and in many places it is against the law to harm an oak. A felled oak is said to scream and to attract lightning.

For the power of its influences in many areas, some of which are justice, courage, power, health, leadership and hospitality; oak leaves are worn, acorns are carried, or clubs or wands of oak are used. Men who have distinguished themselves have been given oak leaf crowns. As oaks represent wisdom, loyalty, courage, strength and justice, it is under oaks that judgements are made, that contracts are signed. In order to gain its attributes, people have climbed oaks.

The Oak brings balance and stability, and it protects laws. It supports Terminus and just boundaries, and at some boundaries, it was a custom to read rhymed laws under an oak. The Oak gives security to possessions and heritage. It favours dignity. It inspires resolution.

All parts of the Oak hold their magics and their virtues. For its virtues and its special magics, of great value is the acorn. One, it has been a very important food. And the acorn has been used as a charm for gaining for a person some request. At times, it is carried for protection. For telling fortunes, the acorn cup might be used. The acorn, powdered, is used to neutralize toxins and to counter the effects of alcohol. Oak galls cure horses.

From oak bark a tonic is made and this, used to treat goiter, ague, bladder problems, kidney stones, piles, vaginal trouble, liver trouble, sore gums, intestinal problems and to drive away worms. As a lotion, oak bark is used for infection, rashes and swellings.

One might learn from the Oak about the weather. For information, one would notice in the spring, if the Oak or the Ash leafed out first. The saying is, as Grieve reports, "If the Oak before the Ash, you will get but a little splash. If the Ash before the Oak, expect a soak."

The Oak, as The Door, is a guardian of the way between worlds.

As the Spirit of Mercury, in one aspect, would be the Staff: the Tree bound by the pair of snakes: the one, with the Light; the other, the Dark: he might be said to be the Plant Kingdom tied to a vocation of the snakes: healing. Nine herbs, especially, were given by the Snake, and these would have their special magical gifts. In honour of this gift, nine herbs, picked before sunrise, were put into the Midsummer fire. Herbs given by the Snake are Mugwort, Cress, Fennel, Chamomile, Weybrod, Nettle, and Chervil. Those listed as selected for the Midsummer fire are Vervain, Sambucus, Artemisia, Yarrow, Ivy, Orpine, Weybrod, Hypericum and Chrysanthemum Segetum: this is one list. Other lists have included Mugwort, Betony and Tansy.

For the use of plants, one does not depend only on the instruction of others, but plants themselves communicate, and by this, instruct. Wort, which many plants are called, means word. Words are tools of communication.

The herb representing the high point of the Time of the Juggler would be the Hypericum. As it represents the Sun, it would be considered over all. Midsummer Eve, when it is often gathered, it is often seen to have a golden glow. On other nights also, it is seen to light up. On Midsummer Eve, women went on flower collecting missions. Kightly reported that in order to get pregnant, women took off their clothes and collected hypericum while naked. For attracting money, it was thought, it should be dug up with a gold coin. It would increase business.

Hypericum inspires truth, purifies areas and destroys hexes. To counter witchcraft, it is hung over doorways and juice from its bark is put in babies' eyes so that the babies will be able to recognize witches. It is said, hung on the wall of a bedroom, it will cause a maid to dream of a future husband. Put under a pillow, it is said to chase away ghosts. Women put it in their crotch so that they would be free from demon lovers. Hypericum gives protection from lightning and malicious spirits. It is worn under the left armpit in order to bring peace and plenty. It is given to children to keep sickness away. It is used for treating cramps, itch, stitch and other ailments caused by fairies, and for treating jaundice, wounds, ulcers, pulmonary trouble, dysentery, gastrointestinal problems and to purify the blood. It is put in invisibility potions and in love potions and in shoes as protection from fatigue. Put in fires, it is thought, the smoke would chase away goblins. It is said that eaten, it might cause sunburn. Gathered on a Friday under Jupiter, then hung from the neck, it chases melancholy. As Hypericum relates to the Spirit of Fire, it inspires love and aids copulation. For its ability to heal wounds, warriors carry it into battles. Hypericum, as a chief herb of the Sun, is said to be over spirits. With an owl's head which has been put on a hazel staff, hypericum is used for raising up ghosts. Midsummer Eve, a stepped on hypericum would turn into a horse which would suddenly rise from the ground and carry the transgressor until sunrise. At sunrise, often a great distance from where it rose up, it would suddenly sink into the ground. For medical use, it is thought, hypericum is best collected, Midsummer, after sunrise. For all other use, it is collected Midsummer before sunrise. If a person's hypericum quickly withered, it would likely be sending a message, death is near.

For Mercury, the first named herb might be Parsley. Beside Mercury, Hercules, Proserpine and Venus favour Parsley; and, as it is favoured by Proserpine, it is often used in rituals relating to the Underworld – and in potions intended to be used for summoning demons. Parsley is used in baths, as it opens communion with the Goddess of Earth and the Goddess of Love. Pregnant women, and women wishing to become pregnant, take parsley baths. As parsley is thought of in relations to purity, it is valued for cleaning the human body.

Hercules honoured Parsley and wore it as a wreath; so, to honour Hercules, said Pausanias, wreaths of parsley were given to winners of the Nemean Games. To honour Hercules, parsley wreaths were also given to, among other games, winners of the Isthmian Games. Parsley was considered the symbol of strength and agility.

At banquets, garlands of parsley were worn as a way to avoid getting drunk. Also, it was worn at banquets because of its influence toward honour, strength and sobriety.

Parsley was said to have sprung from the blood of Archemorus the

Forerunner of Death, and it was fed to his horses when they were on their way to the Underworld. It became a custom to feed it to chariot horses so that the horses would pull the warriors to the Land of the Dead. Also, it is fed to horses to increase their speed and sure footedness.

Parsley is used at funerals and wreaths of parsley are put on tombs. And parsley is planted on graves. It is considered dangerous to transplant it, as it is thought that would bring misfortune. Those who sow parsley, said Rago, might expect a death in their family within the year. And those who sow parsley, there is a custom for them to curse as they sow. Some, to avoid sowing, put the seeds where the wind would scatter them. It is said to bring ill luck to accept a parsley root, but the leaves may be accepted and they bring luck. Parsley is an influence toward material gain, so to give away a parsley root is to throw away luck. To pull up a parsley root while uttering a person's name is a way to send that person to the Underworld. Parsley is said to grow best where the woman rules. If one's parsley withers, death is forecast; however, if it flourishes, peace and plenty are forecast.

Parsley is listed as one of the five opening herbs. It clears the mind and gives clear vision, so is put in dream pillows. Prophetic dreams inspired by parsley are thought especially useful where love is concerned. For banishing demons, parsley is found to be useful. Parsley removes obstructions in the liver and spleen and expels kidney stones and gall stones. And Buchman finds it of value in provoking urine.

Parsley is used to stimulate mental activity. It stimulates copulation. Another use, said Pitman, is to improve digestion and assimilation of foods. Apuleius Platonicas found it useful in treating snake bites and sore muscles. It dispels fatigue, said Bartram, and combats dropsy and ailments of the womb. Jaundice and bites and stings are treated with parsley. And put in a pond, it will cure sick fish. Parsley is used as an anti spasmodic. Sheep with ailing feet are treated with parsley. Marion Davies said it promotes the health of tomatoes and roses and increases the power of other herbs. She said that parsley must go to the Underworld and back seven times, as folk knowledge has it, before it will grow. Parsley guards food from spells, and bees favour it. According to Beyerl, it is best gathered on a Friday and under a Waxing Moon. Women, in rites for separating from mates, have used picking parsley.

A large influence in the Time of the Juggler would be Yarrow, and for its virtues, Yarrow has been valued from ancient times. It is recorded to have been used around sixty thousand years ago and has been listed as one of nine herbs considered most important in classical times. It is an herb which Cheiron taught Achilles of its virtues and with it, Achilles healed the wounded Telephos. In the Trojan War, it was used to heal the wounded, and was especially effective in healing wounds caused by iron. Put on wounds, it stopped bleeding and performed healing. For cures, it was rubbed on the blade of the sword which did the wounding.

Yarrow has been called the Flower of Death. It is a mystical herb which has many mysterious powers. It relates to the Underworld, so is valued as a way to see into the future. For this use, it is thought best if picked off a grave and often, care would be taken in the selection of the grave. The yarrow would be best picked at midnight going into Midsummer, and best, in the Dark of the Moon. Permission might be asked of the yarrow for its use. After being picked, it would be carried silently to a sacred place, or to the place where it would be used. For telepathy, it might be put on the eyelids. Or yarrow stalks might be used for looking into the future. For this, the stalks are usually dropped onto a prepared surface. A freshly picked yarrow stalk might tell secrets without being dropped. With words woven into a charm, the yarrow might be questioned and, as the yarrow is favoured by Venus, often the questions would be concerned with love. Put in shoes, the yarrow might give one the ability to see his or her future mate. In shoes, the yarrow is thought to attract love. Or the yarrow might be put in a dream pillow in order to inspire prophetic dreams, and as yarrow is favoured by Venus, the dreams would often relate to romance. It is thought best, if in or under a pillow, not to speak between the time of picking the yarrow and sleep. Or, before putting it in the pillow, the magic charm of "Jack and Jill" might be chanted to it if romantic dreams were wanted, and the dreams, to be prophetic. Another charm, documented by Grieve, which was intended to give a vision of a future husband or wife, called for sewing yarrow in a cloth, then saying to it:

"Thou pretty herb of Venus' tree,
Thy true name is Yarrow;
Now who my bosom friend must be,
Pray tell thou me tomorrow."

This, she obtained from Halliwell's "Popular Rhymes".

For an affirmation of love, one might have put yarrow up the nose. It this caused the nose to bleed, this would have affirmed a true love.

For another use of "Jack and Jill" in finding a mate, the rhyme would be said to the Yarrow, the Yarrow slept on, then put in the left shoe.

Ledwidge gives a method of dreaming of a true love: one strips the leaves off a stalk of yarrow, puts them under the pillow.

Yarrow is a dangerous herb and people have avoided keeping it in the house; however, in the garden, it chases demons and protects other plants. When gathering yarrow, a charm might be said and the charm might mention the virtues one hoped to gain from the yarrow. Often, as Yarrow is favoured by Venus, it has been used in love charms. Combined with Parsley, it makes a love charm which is said to hold its power for seven years. For protection, Yarrow and Basil would be tied together with a white string. For an ability to fly, Yarrow would be combined with Rue. Rago said that a malicious person going near a yarrow plant would cause the plant to vibrate.

Yarrow is used in cleanings and purifications. As a tea, it takes away fear, banishes depression and drives away melancholy. It is carried for giving its blessings and as protections against snakes. And it is used to cure snake bites and other wounds, to treat piles, urinary trouble, ulcers, mouth sores and gastrointestinal problems. It is used for colds, flu and rheumatism and it stops bleeding. Kloss recommends it for measles and chicken pox. Extra healing strength would be gained by, while on the right knee, pulling up the yarrow with the middle finger and thumb. Yarrow will drive away harmful insects.

A useful plant given by the Snake is Weybroed, a plant favoured by Mercury, Venus and the Moon. The Weybroed has a lady form and is called the Mother of Herbs, as it is used not only by itself, but as an important part of many other healing potions. It is the symbol of loyalty, so is carried by warriors. It is used, by them, on scrapes, rashes and wounds. It gives magical protections and is used in some flying ointments. Rubbed on the forehead, it cures headaches. Weybroed is taken to relieve fevers, to treat toothache and to cure ague, dropsy, ulcers and other gastrointestinal problems and kidney and bladder problems. It is especially effective in treating piles. Albertus lists it as a cure for men's ailing genitals. Weybroed leaves are put around the ears to ease earache. Put in the ears in oil, Dioscorides said that they would aid hearing. Feet suffering from wear, Apuleius Platonicas suggests, could be given relief by weybroed soaked in vinegar. For headache, it was suggested, three times scratch five weybroed leaves with the thumb and little finger and bind them to the head. For healing wounds, weybroed is said to have a magical way of bringing flesh together. Plinius said, to demonstrate this, two cuts of meat with weybroed might be put in a pot and be seen to join together. For snake bites, Dioscorides recommends taking weybroed mixed with wine. It is said, dogs, also, can be cured of snakebite by eating weybroed. People and animals can, by eating weybroed, rid themselves of the toxins they get from the bites of spiders and the stings of insects. As an ointment, weybroed is used to heal burns and the itch. Gerard said that as a cure for ailments, three roots of weybroed were hung from the neck. These served also as preventions from ailments and especially, from air born toxin, which an enemy might send, and venereal disease. Weybroed is also used to combat worms in the intestines. One method, which Apuleius Platonicas suggested, was to put weybroed juice on the navel.

An herb related to the weybroed is the ribwort, and it, for healing, has many of the virtues which the weybroed has. For wounds and skin problems, it is not as effective, but it is thought, more effective for curing pulmonary trouble. Ribwort is an herb used in flying ointments, as it is a companion to the Cuckoo; a bird, more than other birds, related to ghosts. And all birds would have some relationship to ghosts. Each ribwort, once every seven years, if dug up at the exact correct minute, would turn into a bird. One ribwort, if dug up at exactly midnight, Midsummer Eve, would have a stone at its roots which, as long as the finder keeps it, would keep him or her in good health.

Ribwort, as a charm, is carried to repel malicious spirits of Air and to ward off death. Without protection, a spirit might enter the body, as through a sneeze. Ribwort, like Weybroed, gives prophetic dreams. It is a mysterious plant which relates to Mercury, Mars and Venus. As it holds prophetic knowledge and relates to warriors, this knowledge is sometimes obtained by making conflicts between two ribwort soldiers. In one way, two ribwort flower stalks would be wrapped in a dock leaf and, Midsummer Eve, put under a stone: one, representing yes; the other, no. At a future time considered to be correct, the stalks would be examined to determine whether the yes or the no stalk would be the victor. The Moon; especially, the Dark Moon, favours the Ribwort. Under the pillow, it leads one to achievements.

Also, Fennel is a plant given by the Snake and it would be in bloom for Midsummer, which is the high season for the Snake. Said Opsopaus, Fennel is a plant in which the Serpent rises up through the stalk. Snakes eat fennel and rub against it to sharpen their eyesight. And, said Gerard, it is used as a tonic to improve the eyes. It clears eyesight.

Fennel has fire hidden in its stalk and it is this fire, it is said, that Vulcan got from the heavens, set in his forge and spread over Earth. Vulcan brought it with him hidden in the Fennel stalk. This fire gives fennel plants powers. Spicer calls Fennel an herb of protection. Put in keyholes, the power of its fire would keep ghosts from entering. Floors are sprinkled with water off fennel stalks in order that they be free from unwanted demons and adverse witchcraft. Also, for this protection, fennel stalks are hung over doors and windows. Fennel is used for establishing and for sweeping out sacred circles. "Pick it, it brings luck:" Howel the Good.

Fennel favour maturity and is an herb of the Archer. It is favoured by the Long Haired Suns and, especially, by Cheiron. It is a sacred herb of Vulcan and is honoured by Mercury and Jupiter. It secures long life and gives virility, vitality and strength. It gives courage and ability to face adversity and danger. As it has a hollow stem, it would be known to relate to the pulmonary system and the gastrointestinal system and it is used to work miracle cures of both. It cleans the digestive track and cleans the blood. It counteracts toxins and cures jaundice, gout and the agues. Bartram called it an ancient remedy given by the gods. Fennel is used to summon demons as well as banish them, and it is thought to inspire insincerity. It is used to symbolize flattery and deceit. This symbolism was used by Shakespeare. Fennel banishes problems. It opens obstructions in the liver, spleen and gall and breaks the stone. It provokes urine. It is best gathered Midsummer Eve – as a usual thing.

Chervil is an herb given by the Snake which is valued at Midsummer. It is favoured by Jupiter and Juno and it relates to the Sacred Well, to the Cauldron. It is a key ingredient in charms. It is used as an incense to transport people through the veil to the Underworld and growing chervil would permit a person's mind to slip through the veil. Called an herb of immortality; Chervil is, in part, in the Underworld. The fragrance of Chervil gives communion with the Spirit World. Chervil gives insight and imagination and brings love. It is grown in graveyards so it will give its virtues to the dead. Chervil sends down women's courses and expels the afterbirth. In spring water, the powdered root of chervil breaks spells. Catullus said that the smell of chervil gave him great happiness. Marion Davies enjoyed it as food and said that it aided digestion and purified the blood. Rago said it restores youth, and Gerard, it provokes lust. Bees favour it. It is sown with the Dark Moon.

Cinquefoil is an herb of the Juggler and it is extra powerful where Mercury has jurisdiction, or a special interest. Cinquefoil is an herb for enchantments. As it relates to Air, it is found useful in flying potions. Cinquefoil is carried in order that the bearer might have eloquence in dealings with authorities. It inspires courage and negates spells. And cinquefoil is useful for mental journeys and meditations which give knowledge of the future; especially, in the realm of love. And it might help one find a mate. It is used in many potions and many of these would be love potions. In some love potions it is combined with smallage, monkshood, black nightshade, water parsnip, baby fat and soot. An ointment with cinquefoil, which was intended to protect from enchantments, had in it monkshood, smallage, wheat flour and fat off a baby from a newly dug grave.

Cinquefoil aids communications, heightens awareness, gives connections with the Spirit World and with nature and brings joy. As a tea, it chases away griefs and brings happy and, sometimes, prophetic dreams. Cinquefoil tonic is used to treat jaundice, gastrointestinal problems, influenza, sore throat, palsy, pox, kidney stone and the ague. As a lotion, it is used to treat rashes and wounds. As Cinquefoil is magical, many of its workings are achieved by magical manipulation, as the correct number of stalks included in a potion; the number, adjusted to the exact requirements of the work. Use would be made of the plant's repeated number fives.

For protection, cinquefoil is best collected when Planet Jupiter is angular and strong and the Moon, in good relation with it. Mercury joined with Jupiter would increase its goodness. For most uses, Midsummer Eve is a good time for collecting cinquefoil and it is best, if the Moon is Full. Frogs enjoy sitting on cinquefoil plants.

Chicory is a girl who was given a flower form by the Sun. It relates to Air and can give invisibility. To gain invisibility from it, a person would pick it a midnight going into Midsummer, then put it into his, or her, shoe. It is said, it is the root which gives invisibility. Chicory is a guardian of roads; and, as it relates to the Spirit World, especially of roads leading to the Underworld. It is put in love potions and travelers carry it for protection. Made into a tea, chicory flowers are said to give understandings and wisdom. The tea would be made from flowers picked when they are fully open; then the tea, left where the bright Sun would bring virtues from the flowers. It leads one to productive ways. It opens locks.

Chicory is called a cleansing herb. It gives gastrointestinal health and is used to treat gout, gravel, jaundice, the ague and ailments of the spleen, liver, and kidneys. As a lotion, it is used to improve vision and aid the skin. From the root is made a health giving beverage. The best time for sowing chicory is said to be under a Full Moon. Chicory is favoured by Apollo and Jupiter.

Dill is an herb related to Wind and to Death. It is favoured by Belenus, Io, Mercury and the Moon. As it is favoured by Mercury, it sharpens the mind, gives clarity to thinking and to the mind, brings calm. It induces sleep and brings prophetic dreams. Dill is an herb of protection which blesses the home and hearth. To give protections, it is grown beside doorways and put in wedding wreaths. It repels negative energies. Warriors carry dill as, beside protections, it gives endurance and success in battle. War heroes are given crowns of dill. Dill is used in charms for countering the spells of witchcraft and for attracting riches. Dill is used in ritual cleanings and purifications. It chases demons – and protects from the evil eye. To chase demons of epilepsy, Pythagoras said one should hold a stem of dill in the left hand: this, from Leyel. From Wright: Dill steeped in hot wine is drunk to excite passions. Dill is included in love potions. It is tranquillizing and settles the stomach. It increases a woman's milk and it is used as a cure for rheumatism, sciatica, dyspepsia and colic. As an ointment, it is used for swellings and pains. Dill ashes, mixed with honey, cures the itch. Dill promotes menstruation. It sponsors longevity. Bees favour dill and Vergilius called it a pleasant and fragrant plant. Dill breaks spells, obsessions.

Elecampane is an herb of the Juggler which is a favourite of elves. It relates to elven magic, some of it harmful, as elven magic corresponds to the capricious nature of elves. Dealing with elven magic can be tricky. An elf spell might be broken by stabbing the root of an elecampane with an iron knife. It is a custom to leave gifts for elves by selected elecampane plants.

The Elecampane has long been known to be magical. Helen of Troy was holding a bunch of elecampane when she was carried off by Paris. And as she was carried away, where ever her tears fell, elecampane sprung up.

There are methods of gathering it which are thought compatible with elven magic. One method, from herbalist Rago, is to select the plant, then draw, with a ritually prepared knife, appropriate symbols around the plant. Next day, before dawn, and without speaking; the collector, using no tool which contained iron, would gather the plant and take it to a ritually prepared place. No word would be spoken until the plant was secured in a ritually prepared place. It is a custom to speak respectfully when in the vicinity of elecampane.

Elecampane relates to the Time of the Demon. This relates it to the octave, to the scorpion, to the wheel and to the abyss. It relates to reaping, to death and to darkness, to power and to strength. Helen of Troy had it counter the venom of snakes. It will kill worms.

Elecampane cleans and purifies, so is found useful in consecrations. It is used as a cleansing tonic. It sponsors clarity, sustains the spirits, brings mirth and aids eyesight. It encourages humour and happiness; especially, if charms had been sung over it. Worn in the hat, the Elecampane drives away crooked people and attracts good fortune. Elecampane smoke is used in purifications. Elecampane lotion, for sciatica and ailments of the skin, and as a tonic, for dropsy, pulmonary problems, coughs, consumption, convulsions, cramps, kidney stones and digestive complaints. It promotes menstruation and aids the flow of urine. It strengthens mucous membranes and brings health to teeth and gums. For good health, elecampane root is eaten. It is said, Lady Julia Augusta regularly ate it. Elecampane is used to cure ailments in horses and in sheep.

Celandine, Chelidonium Majus, is related to Midsummer, the high season of the Sun. Favoured by Jupiter and Mercury, it relates to the Lion, the Eagle, the Hawk and the Swallow. It is favoured by birds. It comes into bloom, so we are informed by Plinius, when swallows arrive and fades when they leave. And it is said, it springs up when eagles make their nests. It is a sacred herb of swallows. Swallows use it to improve their eyes and the swallows instructed men in this use. The dew off celandine, gathered Mayday before sunrise, is thought, especially effective in improving eyesight and the wellness of eyes. For aiding the eyes, juice of celandine has been mixed with milk. Celandine root is given to hawks in order that the health of the hawks might be improved. This, from Gerard. If one has celandine with the heart of a mole, said Albertus, he can overcome his enemies in all arguments. Celandine gives the power to win debates. It sharpens articulation.

Celandine increases mental alertness. Mixed with honey and wine, it can produce dreams which have prophetic meanings. In brandy, it is used to treat neuralgia. Mixed with lard, it is used for headaches. It is used to remove obstructions in the liver and gall, to purify the blood and to treat kidney stones. Celandine is used for jaundice and asthma, to heal wounds and to improve urine flow. It is put on corns and on ringworm. Fernie said it is used to stop toothache and that, for this, Queen Elizabeth used it. Celandine flowers have been used for treating scurvy.

Celandine is an herb often selected to be a gift to the Midsummer fire.

Related to Air, Horehound is a guardian of roads. An herb of the Juggler, it is used to counter witchcraft, to break magic. Horehound is an aid to positive thinking, to moving forward with clarity and balance, to ingenuity in problem solving. It clears the mind, stimulates inspiration and increases intuitive powers. It frees the mind from prejudice. It promotes creativity and balances energies.

Horehound is used for cleanings and purifications, including a freeing from undesired psychic energies. It kills worms, including those which attack trees, and kills harmful bugs. It gives protections from dog bites. And it cleans the system of toxins and is used to treat coughs and pulmonary problems. It purifies the blood and protects against small pox. It cures the ailing stomach, liver and spleen. As a lotion, it heals sores and rashes, clears the eyesight. As a tonic, it is used to treat asthma and jaundice and to tone the muscles. Horehound is made into health giving candies and put into ales, which put drinkers onto pleasurable paths. Horehound is used to attract bees. It is best gathered when in bloom. Horehound is, certainly, a bringer of good fortune and its blooms are treasured by many.

Pimpernel is an herb of protection and for this, is taken on journeys. It is an herb of the Juggler and is favoured by Jupiter and by Gods of the Sun. Called Scarlet Pimpernel, it protects from illness, accidents and enchantments. It banishes witchcraft and melancholy. It is worn as protection from sad thoughts and depression and put under the pillow to bring soothing dreams. And pimpernel brings joy. It is thought, holding pimpernel, one might gain second hearing, second sight and an understanding of the voices of birds and beasts. Pimpernel gives one the ability to move against the stream: or, counter clockwise.

Pimpernel is used in cleaning, purifications and consecrations. In consecrations of tools, this might be done under a Full Moon (pimpernel mixed with the blood of a rabbit which had been sacrificed to the Moon; then, the tools would be anointed at midnight). Pimpernel is worn as a symbol of honour and victory.

For healing, pimpernel is highly thought of. It is used to treat venomous bites and stings and to heal wounds, even bites of mad dogs. It removes thorns and splinters and, with honey, heals sore eyes. It cures inflammations and swellings and cures sore throat and ulcers. And it is used to treat epilepsy and problems of the liver. Said Bartram, Pimpernel brings euphoria and free laughter. Pimpernel opens for the Sun. If one found it closed, he should expect rain.

The Daisy, in full glory at Midsummer, is favoured by Artemis, Venus, Helios, Mercury, Diana and Juno. Daisy is a Dryad, Belidis, who turned into a flower to be free from the god, Vertumnus, who had become enamoured with her. Fairies have a special love for daisies and for them, the joy of summer comes with a field full of daisies. The daisy is sacred to Venus, so is worn as a token of love and a sign of fidelity. To honour loves, warriors wear daisies into battle. Symbols of innocence, they send messages of innocence. – Daisies are friends to warriors and are quick to heal the warriors' wounds and bruises. It is said, daisies rule fields of battle. Daisies have a relationship with Death and are often seen on graves of babies.

The Daisy aids in the ability to learn and to absorb information. And it brings knowledge from the Otherworld. From the Daisy, one looks, especially, for a knowledge of love. For a yes or no answer to a question about love, petals are picked from a daisy: each, in turn, representing a yes or a no. To dream of his love, a lad might sleep with a daisy root under his pillow. The roots of daisies boiled milk, given to puppies, it is said, would stunt the puppies' growth.

The Daisy gives protection from lightning and it works cures with viral ailments which might seem magical. So Bartram speaks of these cures. One poet has said, more than any other flower, the Daisy reminded him of death.

Daisies are used to treat arthritis, gout, fevers, jaundice, nerve problems, sore eyes, digestive and pulmonary disorders. Daisies bring joy, love and happiness and for this, people make daisy chains. Daisies like the sun bright day and will close their petals before rain; so, predict the weather. Daisies are called the Eyes of Day and none have seen a faded daisy, said Father Young. They are ever young.

An herb of The Juggler, Eyebright relates to Air, and to the Sun. It is valued by bees and linnets are said to use it to improve their eyes. Linnets, it is said, taught humans of this use. In aiding eyesight, eyebright is thought to give psychic vision and a clearer thinking, and to aid memory and to bring wonder, joy and mirth. Eyebright promotes logical thinking. It is used to overcome the tricks of fairies and to treat colds, hay fever and pulmonary problems. As a tonic, it brings general good health. It would relate to the top of the Pyramid. It would clear the Gate of Perception.

Favoured by Mercury, Germander sharpens the mind. It is called Hind Heal, as hinds use it to cure sickness and to heal wounds. Charles V of France had the gout, so took germander and was cured. King Teucer of Troy praised it. It is used to treat fevers, headache, uterine obstructions, rheumatism, digestive troubles, dullness of spirits, ulcers, coughs, wounds, inflammations, sores and palsy. It cleans the blood and kills worms. It is a stimulant. It chases melancholy.

The Rampion, an herb of the Juggler, is often found in witches' gardens and is valued for its magical powers. It is set to guard valuable items and sacred places, and this would include at least one passage to the Underworld. In one of Grimm's accounts, Rampion, called Rapunzel, guarded a secret stairway to the Underworld. One learns, from Grimm, of a woman who had a desperate need for a rampion. It is said, Apollo called for rampions and they were carried to his temple on golden plates.

Rampion is said to incite quarrels. As a medication, it is valued for treating inflammations and ailments of the mouth and throat. As a lotion, it is said to enhance a woman's beauty. In human form, Rampion had been a beautiful princess whose tears had contained magical, healing powers. Rampion flowers are used at funerals and on graves.

Orpine, from its durability, has been called, Life Everlasting. Healing powers it has were said to have been revealed by Telephus, who was called the Son of Hercules. For procuring sleep, one put it under the pillow of the person to whom one wished to give the gift of sleep; but to gain sleep, the recipient must not know that the orpine is under the pillow.

With orpine divination is done Midsummer Eve. Death or attraction between people are events which are often predicted. Orpine purified in Midsummer smoke would hold its magic. On Midsummer, orpine garlands are made and it is thought, they will keep ailments away as long as they keep unwilted. Malicious persons near orpine, it is thought, would make it wilt. For curing ailments, it is said to have been used by lake fairy women. One use was to cure sterility in women.

Stonecrop, an herb of the Juggler, is used to give protection. On rooves it would give protection from lightning and from witchcraft.

Stonecrop is used for gaining knowledge, for learning of the future, and it is especially helpful in matters concerning love. People look to see which way stonecrop stems fall in order to know whether or not loves are true. If stems entwined, they would predict a coming together of a man and a woman. Stonecrop is said to do the most predicting at Midsummer. As a medication, stonecrop is sometimes used to treat scurvy, dropsy, piles and ulcers.

With a stone, Mercury, by accident, killed a boy. Mercury dipped the boy in dew and the boy became the Crocus. Praised for their colour and aroma, crocuses have served as a bed for Jupiter and Juno. Medea, from crocuses, made a life giving potion. Crocuses have also been used in flying potions and have served as aphrodisiacs. And they are used for treating gout and digestive disorders.

Mullein has been called a Rod of Power and it is said to be related to the Dragon. It was called, by Lucius Apuleius, an herb favoured by Mercury. Mercury gave a mullein to Ulysses when Ulysses needed protection from Circe. Mullein is used to counter magics and spirit forces and, by witches, for working magic. For some spells, witches put it in their lamps. Or mullein stalks might be ridden. Mullein torches, for protection, are used at funerals and to light the way to, and from, the Underworld. Pausanias said that Ilithyia, Goddess of Birth, is represented carrying a torch. Hecate, Guardian of Roads to the Underworld, was said to carry a mullein torch. The torch leads the way into the world and out of it. Many witches carry mullein torches when they march in procession.

Mullein is a calming herb. As a medication, it has many virtues. It is used for treating piles, ulcers, constipation, colic, croup, dysentery, dropsy, swollen glands, swollen joints and pulmonary troubles. Gerard said that, as a beverage, it is given to cows to improve their breathing. For preservation, figs and other fruit are wrapped in mullein leaves. Full of large flowers, mullein predicts a severe winter. Snakes and fairies enjoy mullein and give it protection. Mullein is favoured by Saturn, Ceres, Hecate and Mercury. It is best gathered in August. It gives protection.

An herb which has, also, a relationship with the snake is the Speedwell. It is considered dangerous and to pick it, it is said, would cause fires to start. It is an herb favoured by fairies; so, to pick it might cause the pickers, or a member of his family's, eye to get pecked out. Speedwell promotes fidelity. Also, it sponsors quickness and other qualities of air. As it relates to the Dragon, it would be expected to give protection, so has been worn to give protection from malicious forces. Also, it is thought to bring prosperity and other good fortune. From the herb is made a health giving tonic. The tonic purifies the blood and combats asthma, coughs, kidney trouble, gout, colds, small pox and measles. As a lotion, it is used for skin ailments, and to give protection from accidents, and to aid inspiration.

Tarragon, also, is related to the Snake and is called the Little Dragon. It is worn to increase stamina and is used, as are other herbs which relate to the Snake, to treat the bites and stings of venomous beats and insects. Tarragon stimulates digestion, increases endurance and brings general good health. Artemis and Helios favour it.

An herb of the Juggler, Fenugreek brings logic and intellect of the Sun. Favoured by Mercury, it is useful in healing neurasthenia, scrofula, gout, gastrointestinal troubles, fevers anemia and ulcers, and it is used to heal broken bones, inflammations, sores and wounds. Women drink fenugreek to increase the flow of their milk. It brings good health.

The Hyacinth, a flower of the Juggler, symbolizes sadness. It suggests, also, misfortune. It is said, when Ajax was slain by Zephyr, Apollo turned him into a flower and on it, stamped AI. This has come to mean remembrance and it is a symbol which is put on tombs. Spoken, the word gives the impression of a sigh. The symbol is also said to suggest justice. The Hyacinth has associations with the Underworld. It is sacred to the Underworld God, Hyacinthos, and the Underworld Goddess, Chthonia. For these deities, there is a parade when priests wear garlands of hyacinths and a hyacinth decked statue of the goddess is carried. Pausanias said that hyacinths are also used in other rituals for Chthonia. Venus bathed in dew off hyacinths and for this, her spirit in the dew is said to cause the dew to increase a person's beauty. Jupiter and Juno are said to have made a bed of hyacinths. Maple said that pink hyacinths bring good temper. Hyacinths are used to treat leucorrhea and hyacinth leaves, to treat snakebite.

Anemonae, said Theocritus, has a meaning of sadness. Anemonae was, it is said, a nymph for whom Zephyr had affection. Because of this affection Anemonae received, Flora dismissed her from the company which she, Flora, had gathered. Anemonae became sad and lonesome, so Zephyr turned her into a flower. To bloom, she would wait for Zephyr to blow; or, another Wind might serve as well. Anemonaes were said to have sprung from the tears Venus shed for the slain Adonis. Anemonaes have been used as garlands made for cows and often they have decorated the alters of Artemis. Called Wind Flowers, they are worn around the neck as charms against illness. They are used in charms relating to air. Anemonaes are sometimes found to be useful as nervines, but they are dangerous and can cause pain and injury. They are called flowers of ill omen.

Wind Flowers are Wind pollinated and Wind pollinated flowers are usually small and inconspicuous and not much favoured by Ceres or her bees. Anemonae will not open until the Wind blows.

Asarabacca, Birthwort, favoured by Juno and Mercury, is a help in child birth and of use to jugglers in controlling snakes. Drunk, Gerard said that it protects against snakes and venomous beasts. It has a power of stupefying serpents. Asarabacca is used for treating headaches and weak eyes and is sometimes used as a purge. And it is said to be an aid to teeth. Mixed with ribwort, asarabacca is used to clear nasal passages. For this it is used in snuffs.

Amaranth is an herb of the Time of the Juggler which is sacred to Artemis. As it represents immortality, wreaths of it are put on tombs and on representations of the deities and it is given a place at funerals. It is used for treating sores, ulcers, dysentery and vaginal problems and its cures have seemed magical. It is a health giving food. It is lasting love.

Dogs Mercury, an herb relating to the Time of the Juggler, has been said to, by Mercury, have been given hidden abilities. Hippocrates said that it had value for use in healing women's ailments. The use in treatments was external. In treating ague, dogs mercury and a cock were made into a soup. This soup would be made in a magical way. It is said to have been used, in a magical way, for treating ailing ears, penis, ailing eyes and jaundice. The herb, eaten, might prove deadly. It has proved a dangerous purge. It has been called the wicked goblin.

Acanthus, called Bears Breach, is a sacred herb of Artemis, Mercury, Apollo and Jupiter. As it relates to eternity, its leaves have been left on graves and images of its leaves, carved in marble, have graced the temples of many of the deities.

Trefoil is listed by Spicer as a protective herb. Birdsfoot trefoil is said to be related to goblins. It is an herb of the Juggler.

Lily of the Valley Culpeper lists as under the Dominion of Mercury, so strengthens the brain and aids memory, and he said that the spirit of the flowers, distilled in wine, would restore speech. Gerard said that the flowers, put in a stopped bottle and buried for a month in an ant hill; would, used as a lotion, be good treatment for gout. Lily of the Valley has also been used for treating the liver, the kidneys and the heart. As a flower of the Moon, it is held sacred by Juno.

Grieve said of Lily of the Valley, that it was related to Maia; so, favoured by Mercury and that it has sprung up where blood has been spilled. And that, according to Apuleius Platonicus, Apollo gave a Lily of the Valley to Aesculapius and that Aesculapius, in healing, found it of value. It has a value as a heart tonic, as it cures without having the toxic effects of some other heart tonics. And it has been used to remove obstructions from the urinary canal. Dodonaeus used Lily of the Valley in a potion to aid the memory and strengthen the heart. As an ointment, Lily of the Valley has been used to heal burns and ulcers. The spirit of the flowers in wine was said to restore lost speech and to aid those suffering from apoplexy, dropsy and palsy.

Herb Paris relates to the Moon and is sacred to Juno and to Venus. Its leaves form a cross, and the cross is, said Gerard, a true love knot which attracts love. The form of the herb repeats the number four and this relates it to the Sacred Well and to the Cauldron, so the magic of the number can be used; the parts of the herb, used in pairs so they would act in harmony. This magic is used for binding love, for countering witchcraft and elf spells, for countering toxins and for gaining magical cures. Used in odd numbers, the energies would be reversed, would be directed toward misfortunes, the helpful medications become deadly toxins. As medications, Herb Paris is often used for epilepsy, plague, colic, coughs, the itch and the stitch, and it is used as a purgative, and from it, one can gain Otherworld trips.

The mysterious Fern has an affiliation with the Juggler. And, as they sit partly in the Otherworld, they hold Otherworld energy. Frazer said, it is thought, fern seeds would hold magical powers if gathered exactly at midnight, the midnight going into Midsummer. Collected at this time, they might be expected to grant invisibility, to foretell the future, or to give strength. Grieve said that with the seeds, one might expect to gain a strength equal to thirty or forty men. It is said, if one casts the seed on water, prophetic images will appear. Fern smoke is used to drive away unwelcome visitors; including spirits and demons. And burning ferns can bring rain. For solutions to problems, people put the roots of ferns under their pillows.

There are many different ferns and, although they are much alike, each has its individual virtues. The Spleenwort is one of the ferns which is especially good at treating the spleen. Another fern, the Brake, in dream, brings solutions to problems. The Shield fern might be used for driving away worms; the Maidenhair, used in an ointment for repairing damaged bones and joints. All ferns would protect against storms.

Honesty is a sacred herb of the Moon and relates to the Crystal. It is dangerous to step on and should a horse step on it, the herb would unshoe the offender. Honesty opens ways and finds secret passages. It is used to open locks. In a garden, it attracts riches if the garden owner is an honest garden tender. It holds the pure, chaste Spirit of the Moon. It is used for healing broken bones, bruises, dislocated joints, ruptures and wounds.

Colewort is an herb of the Moon which is favoured by Juno and it is held to be so sacred, oaths are sworn on it. It is best planted under the Crab, when the Moon is waning and by women wearing nightgowns. Fairies ride on colewort stalks. One was instructed by Apuleius Platonicas to mix colewort with lard, to put the mix on linen; then, for cures, to put these medications on sores and swellings. For some cures, colewort juice is mixed with honey. Colewort is said to have been for Crysippus, his God. It is said to have sprung from the tears of Lycurgus – and is in harmony with the Spirit of the Great Sea. Its spirit clashes with that of the Vine. It causes vines to do poorly. It deters intoxication. It encourages good health, improves the eyes. Colewort improves the muscles, cures headache, combats rheumatism and gout and banishes bad dreams. Colewort leaves are healing on sore breasts. It is said, none of the colewort family of herbs is toxic. It is said, doctors of ancient times considered colewort to be their everyday herb of healing.

Mugwort is one of the nine plants given by the Snake and it has its high time at Midsummer. Its virtues were said to have been discovered by Artemis – and it is one of her most sacred herbs. Juno, Hera and Mercury also have a great respect for it. It relates to the Moon and the Crystal and is a connection to the World of Dream. Often it is put in dream pillows and from it, one might expect prophetic dreams. Also, it is put in pillows to be put under the heads of the dead. It gives psychic power, heightened awareness, inspiration, insight and a way of looking into the Spirit World. Mugwort is used for cleaning, purifying and consecrating crystal globes, mirrors, prisms and other crystals. It is used to clean, purify and energize tools. For keeping malicious beings and spirits away, mugwort is put in coffins. A bunch of mugwort flowers, tied with a string, is used for blessing rooms and gatherings. The flowers are tied in a ritual which binds the power of the flowers with the Spirit of the Bear. To be free from tiredness, travelers carry mugwort and, from Father Young, it is put in shoes to keep the feet from tiring. However, Midsummer Eve, according to Rago, if one had mugwort in a shoe, the Spirit of the Mugwort might turn into a horse, give that person a ride until sunrise. Mugwort is carried so the traveler will have protection from wild beasts, malicious spirits and beings, toxins, injury and sunstroke, and would gain stamina.

Midsummer Eve, mugwort is often thought to be required by the sacred bonfire. And often, it is felt, a blessing or charm, often rhymed, needed to be said when it is given to the fire.

Midsummer, said Leyel, is the best time for gathering mugwort. It is thought best gathered, by a fasting person, before sunrise. Often, it would then be purified in the smoke of the Midsummer bonfire. Then it might be used in flying ointments, or put in potions for mental journeying, or put in baths. The baths would give strength, health, clear thinking, creativity, insight, joint and muscle ease and aid to the genitals and would solve problems of female health. Mugwort might serve as a valued aid in brewing. It might, with silver, crystal or moonstones, be used to work powerful charms. It might be used for discovering secrets and, at Midsummer, especially secrets concerning love. Or, it might be used as a medication. It is valued for treating palsy, epilepsy, nerve disorders, fevers, ague, wounds, female problems and back trouble. It serves as an aid in birthing and is used in treating ailments in cattle. Mugwort smoke purifies and protects against lightning and malicious forces. Mugwort protects against the evileye, and it makes protective incense.

Mugwort has qualities which make it of value in crystal gazing. It drives off choleric, anger filled and irritated mentality and brings calm, far seeing awareness. Mugwort energies turn toward the North, and this aids the gazer to focus thoughts. To gain, for gazing, a useful lightness, at times one would drink an eggshell full of mugwort juice. This, from Petrus Bayrus.

Midsummer, at noon, one might dig up a coal from under a mugwort root. The coal is thought, said Leyel, to turn to gold and to drive off malicious forces.

Mugwort is often teamed with other herbs so that the combination forms a powerful, new force. Mugwort with thyme and comfrey form a way of seeing into the future.

Mugwort is little favoured by bees.

Southernwood, similar to Mugwort, has many of the same properties. But to instigate and expedite copulation, it is southernwood which is put under the mattress. As it drives away bugs, it is put with clothes. It kills worms and its smoke drives away snakes and other venomous creatures. And it chases away fevers. The southernwood seeds, which should be gathered under a Waning Moon, are made into a tonic and used to treat cramps, convulsions and other muscle problems, and rheumatism.

Wormwood, which is much like Mugwort, is valued for giving prophecy and many other virtues. Its medical use was taught by Cheiron. It aids the liver and is put in sleeping potions. As a lotion, it is used for sore muscles. It is favoured by Artemis and Diana. Wormwood, like mugwort, is often used in drawing down the Moon. And wormwood, like mugwort, is used in dream pillows. From them, one might gain understanding and psychic power, plus dreams which might be fantastic. They might unroll knowledge of a great expanse of one's future. They might cause the White Horse of Dreamland to carry the dreamer through the night, or even farther. The dreamer might come back changed, might make no sense of the World. The dreamer might not come back.

For enlightenment, wormwood is sometimes used as beverage or rubbed on the forehead. It is often used in baths. In baths, it has an invigorating quality and increases fertility. It is an aid, in baths, to menstruation and cures bruises, sores and gout.

Wormwood relates to silver and compliments silver's power, and as silver comes from the deaths of stars, wormwood would relate to astral travel, to creativity in music and art.

The Purple Loosestrife and the Yellow Loosestrife are favoured by Juno and relate to the Crystal. Unrelated though they are, they have many of the same qualities. They both end strife. The Purple, put between two fighting beasts will stop them from fighting. Purple Loosestrife is fastened to animals to keep the animals calm. It cures injured eyes and other wounds and sores and aids vision. Yellow Loosestrife, said Plinius, to keep the oxen calm, is put in the collars of oxen set to plough. For this, the herb was used by King Lysimachus, so ancient histories report. Like the Purple, it checks bleeding and heals wounds. Grieve said that the smoke from the herb would drive away snakes and harmful insects.

Anise, an herb of the Juggler, is used to treat coughs, colds, dropsy and pulmonary disorders. Anise seeds are carried as a charm. As an incense, Anise dispels headache and brings restful sleep. And it gives protection when one is in Dreamland. And it is used to preserve youth. It is used to protect against the evileye and to drive away bothersome bugs. Bags of anise are carried for protection from demons. Part of the communication with Anise, and so, part of its power, would come from its aroma.

Burdock is an herb of the Crystal and relating to the Bear, it is favoured by Artemis. And fairies favour the Burdock. In childbirth, it works its magic. By moving burdock around, the womb may be pulled to where it is wanted. Put on the navel, it would stay the child in the womb. As a medication, the Burdock inspires healing. It cleans the blood and corrects gastrointestinal trouble. And it cures gout, scurvy, dropsy and kidney infection. As an ointment, it is used to treat sprains, skin disorders, glandular swellings, bruises and sores. As a tonic, it is used for ulcers and liver problems. It combats snake and mad dog bites. And it is a health giving food.

Purslane, an herb of the Crystal, is a lover of Water, so relates to the forces of Water. It protects against the forces of darkness, their malicious aspects. It guards against malicious spirits disturbing dreams. It guards against negative energies from celestial bodies and gives protection from demons and from lightning. It attracts positive energies and cancels harmful spells. To gain protection, one method is to rub it on the forehead. Eaten, it brings insight and intuition. As a tonic, it is used to treat frenzy, headache, coughs, pulmonary problems, fevers, ague and liver trouble and to bring happy dreams. Purslane, as a lotion, is used to treat sore eyes, gout, sores and inflammations. Purslane is used to clean and cure the gastrointestinal system. And purslane is a health giving food.

The Convolvulus is a flower of the Crystal which relates to the Moon and the Bear. It does not favour Helios and will turn contrary to the Sun. It is used in magics which relate to binding and is used in cleaning the gastrointestinal system. It is used to treat jaundice, rheumatism and dropsy.

Hyssop is called the royal herb. An herb favoured by the Moon, it relates to the Crystal. An herb of purity, a sacred herb, it is used for cleaning and purifying people, places and things. Priests have washed themselves in hyssop expecting to be made spiritually whiter than snow. Hyssop is used for cleaning auras and, among other things, for cleaning, purifying and consecrating tools. People, in rituals for purification and consecration, are sprinkled with water off stalks of hyssop. Stalks of hyssop are hung up to prevent the entering of negative energies and malicious intruders.

In gardens, walking on hyssop induces sleep. And waking from that induced sleep, one might be given to understand the language of animals and birds. Hyssop strengthens auras and clears the mind. To banish negative energies, water from hyssop stalks is sprinkled on areas intended to be used for sacred work. Hyssop is carried as protection from physical and spiritual aggression. As a charm, hyssop works well with tin. As a medication, hyssop is used for treating rheumatism and for cleaning the gastrointestinal system. It is used also in treating jaundice, dropsy, falling sickness, colds, inflammations, pulmonary disorders, asthma, bruises, sore muscles, quinsy, snake bites, worms and problems of the bladder and of the spleen. Hyssop is favoured by bees.

It is considered best to gather hyssop under the Crab, before sunrise and in the Dark of the Moon. A recommended way of gathering it is to be barefoot and bare headed and dressed in nothing but a white robe. Hyssop then should be gathered with the right hand, cut with a stone knife, then covered with linen and, with the left hand, carried to an appropriate place. Before hyssop is gathered, many would make a gift or libation to it. Wine, honey and bread are thought to be appropriate gifts.

Hyssop was an herb used by Ceridwen when she brewed her potion of inspiration.

Saxifrage is a magical herb of the Moon which is sacred to Juno. For purifying swords, warriors washed them in saxifrage juice and mole's blood. Saxifrage juice was rubbed on the blades of swords so that the swords would cut better. And, by warriors, saxifrage was worn near the heart so that it would aid in gaining victory in battle. Saxifrage is used for providing openings, for removing obstacles and for locating hidden passages. It will split rocks. It can purge the stomach, clean the bladder and break the stone. Also, it is used to heal wounds, to increase the flow of breast milk and to provoke women's courses. Women eat saxifrage as it causes beauty to increase. And saxifrage protects against the plague.

Ladys Mantle, an herb favoured by Venus, relates to the Crystal. For some magical workings, ladys mantle is put in water taken from a spring, the water and the herb, collected before sunrise. This would be called, according to Gladstar, holy water, and it would be used for purification and magical use. One use, listed by Rose, is for magical potions made for curing elf shot cattle. In some of the potions made with this water, copper and silver coins are used. Another use for the potion is to gain an increase in the ability to fornicate and to procreate. Dew off ladys mantle, the dew collected before sunrise, holds a magical power. It is thought, added to potions, it would seal in the potion's power. Ladys mantle is used to lock in other magics also. And for magics of its own, it is used to change one form of a thing into another form, and is used in formulas where change is required. Another use for ladys mantle is for astral travel. And under the pillow, it brings sleep. It is used also to regulate menstruation and to treat vaginal ailments. As an aid to childbirth, it seems to work magic and cures it works also seem magical. It is said to cure many elf dart caused ailments. And it cures gastrointestinal troubles and troubles with the liver and spleen. Ladys mantle, sometimes mixed with honey, is used to cure wounds, sores and inflammations.

Relating to the Spring, Ladys Mantle would relate to the Ace of Hearts, to Juno, to Artemis and to Proserpine.

Wintergreen, which relates to the Crystal, is of value for cleanings and purifications. An antiseptic, it is used for treating bruises, wounds and muscle pains. Wintergreen combats gout, arthritis and rheumatism. An aromatic, it is particularly useful in treating neuralgia. With women, it treats problems of the womb and the overflowing of terms. Epilepsy is also treated with wintergreen. It is an herb favoured by Juno and Saturn.

Venus Looking Glass relates to the Sacred Spring, the Veil to the Underworld. It is a flower of the fairies and is sacred to Venus. It relates to the Mirror, a magical tool which can be used for sending someone to the Underworld. A shepherd once found Venus' magical tool and, looking in it, he beheld a most handsome man: himself become more handsome. This was the nature of the mirror. Cupid struck the mirror out of the shepherd's hand. The mirror fell and turned into a flower. The herb is used as a lotion, as a tonic and is put into baths. The tonic is used for the stomach; the lotion, for skin problems. When used, if the lotion darkened on the skin, a cure was predicted.

Feverfew, an herb of the Crystal, is favoured by Juno, Carnea and Venus. It is used to treat menstrual problems, problems with the menstrual cycle, and birthing problems. It is said, in troubled birth, if a woman sits over feverfew, which is in bath water, she shall have the birth, even if a still birth, and the afterbirth. Feverfew cures fevers and, in a garden, keeps fevers away. Gerard lists it as a cure for vertigo and says that it chases melancholy. Feverfew stops hysteria and delirium tremens. And it is used to treat coughs. A coal is sometimes found under its roots, and the coal is said to have great healing powers.

The Gillyflower is a flower of the Moon. It is planted under the Waning Moon. It represents a love bond with the meaning, always true, and is worn to indicate the lover is true, or the wearer is true to women. In gardens, it is said to wilt where either the master or mistress of the land has died.

The Wood Sanicle is an herb of the Time of the Juggler. Its name indicates that it is a healer. Its virtues include the ability to cure ailments of the throat and lungs, to cure dysentery, to heal sores and wounds and to clean the blood. For fertilization, it looks for help from the Winds and not so much from bees. It is thought best gathered in the morning after the dew has dried.

Enchanters Nightshade is favoured by Juno. It is an herb of the Moon. Found in dark places, it gives protection from elf darts and charms and scabies.

From ancient times, Chamomile has been known as an herb of the Sun, and from the Gods of the Sun and other gods has received many virtues. This has made it able to aid many who have gone to it for help. Apollo, Mars, Aurora and Venus are some of the deities which have been said to have looked with favour on Chamomile. Then, the strength of Chamomile might be noticed when one enters an area where the herb is; especially, if given the blessings of its aroma. Chamomile would be immediately calming, would be driving away restlessness and irritability. It would subdue anger, if anger should be present. And it would, by being there, treat aches and pains in muscles and joints, if these should be present. It relaxes and sooths muscles. It eases anxiety and solves emotional problems and calms the nervous system. It clears the lungs and cleans and purifies the blood and cures neuralgic pains. It refreshes those who are tired. Chamomile chases infections and for this, some people hang it over babies' cribs. People walk in gardens of chamomile to be cured of migraines, menstrual spasms, gastrointestinal pains, skin problems and sore eyes.

The Chamomile is on a classical list of nine magical herbs. It is a caring and helpful herb which serves as a friend and aid to other living beings. As it is favoured by Venus, it is often used in love potions. And people wash their faces with chamomile so that their faces will attract love. As Chamomile is favoured by Apollo, it is used in potions for obtaining wealth. It is used in many charms by itself or with other herbs. The inclusion of chamomile is said to insure the success of a magical working, or of a venture on which it is sent. Chamomile is used for ritual cleanings and purifications. Chamomile drives off nightmares and brings pleasure to dream. And it might well bring the prophetic dream. As a healer, chamomile works wonders. It cures ailments of the liver, kidneys and spleen, heals dangerous wounds, breaks the stone and brings relief from bronchitis, typhoid, delirium tremens, dropsy and the ague. As the Sun dislikes them, it expels intestinal worms.

Chamomile serves as a calming tea. It inspires patience in the face of adversity, drives away melancholy, and brings feelings of peace and joy. In the garden, it acts as the garden's guardian spirit. And it is called the plant doctor, as it brings good health to other plants. It chases away harmful insects, but it is much favoured by bees. Chamomile also banishes harmful spirit forces. Sir Francis Drake played on his garden of chamomile before sailing off on his missions in order to gain helpful spirit energy. Chamomile has been called the symbol of energy.

An herb of the Crystal, Birthwort relates to Juno and Carnea. As it is concerned with the roads between the worlds, it also relate to the Juggler. The herb has shaped itself to suggest its value to birthing. It resists toxins, aids in delivery and cures the womb after birth. It also chases away demons which would often be attracted by a conception. However, misused, birthwort might cause the baby to be aborted, or cause other harm. Besides birthing, birthwort treats other ailments and this, often by its aroma. Ailments it treats include rheumatism and gout.

An herb of the Time of the Lion, Rue is seen as a symbol of sorrow, repentance and grace. It is an herb under Jupiter, but it also has a connection with Hades, and this connection indicates that it would have a use in witchcraft, so one might find it in flying potions, in consecration waters and in dream pillows. In dream pillows, rue promotes sleep and brings visions, visions that might be prophetic. With consecration waters, circles are consecrated with waters sprinkled by sprigs of rue. And the water is used for purifying and consecrating tools and for exorcising demons and especially, demons causing sicknesses such as hysteria and epilepsy. Rue favours purity, so one's face should be clean before rue water is put on it. Some rue, it is said, is so strong that it will blister the face of the person who looks on it. Sprigs of rue, for protection, are hung over doorways and from around the neck. Around the neck, they are worn especially to chase away plague and other diseases. Also, rue is carried to chase beasts. So Gerard reports. Also, rue is worn to prevent walking or talking in sleep and to give protection from spells. One wedding custom, wreaths containing rue with rosemary and lovage are exchanged. If a girl should die unmarried, there is a custom to put rue in her coffin. There was a custom for unmarried girls to raise rue in front of their houses; then, give, intended husbands each, a bunch of rue. Arrows rubbed with rue fly true.

Dioscorides said that rue is used as a counter to dangerous medicines. It is used to combat venoms and as an antidote to toxins. Plinius said, as an anti toxin, rue seemed magical. For headache, rue is rubbed on the forehead. Rue is used to treat coughs, colic, ague, and, as a lotion, pains in the joints and sciatica. And it is said to quicken the eyesight and to cure earache. And rue is said to keep animals in good health. Ailing cattle and chickens are fed rue. For some cures, rue is combined with honey, fennel and the gall of a cock. It is usually considered best to gather rue under the Lion. Sowers of rue, as they sowed, it was a custom to face East and curse. Otherwise, it was thought, their efforts would not be well rewarded.

Dittany is a powerful and magical herb of the Sun. It has Otherworld associations, so is used in seeking knowledge, as in establishing relationships with ghosts. Also, it has been used to contact Proserpine and other deities associated with the Otherworld. From Proserpine, one might gain understandings related to travel between this world and the Underworld. From the other associations, one might gain understandings of the two worlds. Dittany, as an aid in relating to the two worlds, has led to associating this herb with the Sphinx. Dittany aids in understanding the mystic and mysterious questions.

Dittany, as an herb of the Sun and under Jupiter, is related to fire and in the high season of the Sun, it shoots flames. It has the power to shine and burn on hills where it grows.

Dittany works magical cures. It overcomes toxins and Gerard said it is reported to cure snakebites and other venomed wounds and to draw out shafts and splinters. For women with a still born, dittany is called on to expel the baby and to cure the woman who had been pregnant. Wounded goats and wounded deer are said to eat dittany to remove weapons and heal wounds. Venus, to heal wounds of Aneas, used dittany.

Dittany relates to life cycles and this relates it to ten. Its relation to fire, to the Sun, would relate it also to one, to the Ace.

Dittany is used for charms and magical potions.

Agrimony is a bright herb of the Lion which holds magic, as it is favoured by Jupiter. It is used in many magical potions. Put under a person's pillow, it is said, it will keep that person in a deep sleep until the herb is taken away. Called the Elven Rod, agrimony cures goblin caused ailments and chases goblins away. Dioscorides recommends agrimony as a treatment for dysentery, liver ailments and snake bites. It is much valued as a cleanser and tonic for the digestive track. And it is used to treat colds, bruises, wounds, gout and ulcers. As a bath, it cures sores and skin problems. And agrimony purifies the blood and strengthens the eyes. It is used to bring sleep and bring down fevers and banish the ague. Agrimony is an herb of the High Summer and being in its presence might be expected to chase away problems of the mind.

Borage is a much valued herb of the Sun which is highly honoured by Jupiter and Mars. Borage brings courage; so to enhance courage, it is carried by warriors and the warriors add it to their beverages. Borage gets its Latin name from its ability to bring courage. An herb of many virtues, Borage chases away melancholy and, as Rose said, expels pensiveness. It combats insanity, drives away dullness and, as Dioscorides said, brings joy and merriment. It calms the frantic and the lunatic, said Gerard. It settles the mind. As a medication, Borage cleans the blood, combats ulcers, inflammations, swellings, rheumatism, ringworm, fevers, sore throat, colds and the venoms of snakes. It cools the body and stimulates the kidneys when made into a drink. Borage leaves are eaten to strengthen the eyes. As a beverage, it was called, by Homer, the drink of Nepenthe; or, forgetfulness; which took away anxiety. As Borage represents purity, it is used in cleanings and purifications.

Borage gives protection. In a garden, it gives protection to other plants and especially, the strawberry. And bees take pleasure in Borage. Borage flowers are often included in wedding wreaths and in bridal bouquets. The time to sow borage is under the New Moon. As it follows the Sun, it is sometimes called Heliotrope.

Burnet, an herb of the Sun, cheers the heart and drives away melancholy. It guards against pestilence, protects the blood, heals wounds and preserves good health. People have seen the hand of Apollo in the good health given by Burnet. And added to beverages it gives pleasure. It is thought, to be most effective, it should be gathered under the Lion. Burnet honours July with its flowers. Blooming out of season, it predicts misfortunes.

A flower valued in healing is the Rockrose, which is also called the

Sunflower. It cures ulcers, sore throat, scrofula, dysentery and genital ailments. The flowers of the rockrose, by their presence, drive away panic. Rockrose is under the Lion.

Bistort, a flower of the Time of the Juggler, relates to the Snake and is sometimes called Dragonwort. Its root holds the darkness of the Night Sky and reflects the Snake in its twists. It is an herb of love which is said to make a woman more beautiful and lovely and promote in men the will to do that which is honest and becoming. In gardens, it is said to bring virtue and to cause love to come. It is an herb valued by Juno and Carnea. It causes a woman to contain and conceive birth. And it cleanses after the birthing, and it chases elves and malicious beings. Sprigs of bistort are hung over doorways to keep malicious beings out. Bistort expels venoms and worms with which people are troubled. And it is used in treating jaundice, dysentery, poisoning, plague, measles, piles, pox, snakebite and ulcers. Bistort, as do other herbs which favour Wind, does not have flowers which provide the show which invites intercourse with the Bee, but depends on communication with the Winds to supply fertilization for its flowers. Bistort is pictured with the Unicorn, a symbol of virtue. As Bistort represents virtue, it is a custom to eat bistort root at Easter.

The Elder is so much valued as a medication and for potions that it has been included in short lists of most valued herbs. Theophrastus said that men wash their hands and head in elder juice when being initiated into religious mysteries. The Elder is strange and mysterious. It is said, if men drink out of elder bowls, their hands would likely grow out of their graves.

Many herbs relate to Midsummer. Dyers Rocket brings the Sun's gold. Some, including Dyers Rocket and Vincetoxicum, could be dangerous or harmful. Constructive use of these herbs in healing would take skill.

The flora is a most visible player in the movement of events. As this is generally recognized, many members of the Plant Kingdom are recognized as god forms. In the opinion of Grimm, the history of the European polytheistic religion might be called the History of Trees. Trees, and other plants, as they move through the cycles of time, they come more or less to the front in the causes and effects of events, but the roles plants play might seem the greatest under the Juggler. In many tools, the spirits of plants are a force. In the use of these tools, one might manipulate the spirit of the plant, or both the spirit and the physical being of the plant; as, wearing Hypericum would be holding the physical while the spirit might be bringing money. Or the spirit might be manipulated, as in a charm, without handling the physical. However, the physical would, in the charm, have its part to play. If a word charm were, "As fresh and green you grow, sweet Dill, may my love bend to my will", it might be best, as Skelton suggests, that the speaker of the charm have some skill at keeping the dill green and fresh.

Words, a major means of communication, are important tools of the Plant Kingdom. A name for plants in general is worts, which means words. In words, plants tell people what those people would want to know. In knowing how best to move down the Path, the information needed might be given by plants. One might request desired information. If it is given, philosophers have said, one should avoid saying thankyou to the plants, as the added word might throw the statement out of balance, might cause a wrong turn. At the Midsummer season, many of the words of plants would be loud.

Much used tools given by the Plant Kingdom are the cords and ropes, and many of the functions of civilization would be handicapped without them. As they relate to the Snake, and so, to the Wind, they not only do mundane tasks, but play parts in the mystical movements of environments. Cords and ropes relate in a major way not only to Mercury and to the Winds, but to Ariadne, and to Minerva. Minerva, especially, was honoured by rope sellers, and, according to Livius, rope sellers had a custom of making offerings of silver to her.

Ropes can capture, or be endowed with, some of the qualities of the Winds; some of their powers, so that the Spirit of Air can add to the physical qualities of the vegetation. Cords have been used in magical bindings. Powers of the Moon have been captured in ropes. In one working, which Corrigan writes of, the charm is worked in two stages: the binding and the release. In the binding, nine knots are bound and each knot, keyed to a word spoken as the knot is bound. This would be done as part of a ritual to, and under, the Full Moon. When the charms become needed, each word would be spoken again as each charm is sprung. Ropes might form traps and so, be dangerous. Some dangerous ropes were made from linden bark. Ropes are mysterious and mystical and might take a person to the Underworld. But rope traps would have a balance, but the balance, ever hidden. The meanings of ropes, even if not known, might be treated with respect and awe. The rope circle, perhaps a trap, relates to sacrifice, and to rebirth: both honoured transitions.

Some magicians are gifted in the ability to capture winds in cords and, by charm, they are often tied behind three knots. Kepler said these cords are sometimes carried by sailors who untie the knots to release the winds: one knot, mild; two knots, strong; three knots, a gale.

Gomme said that witches and wizards have buried strings of winds in green fields; then, thrown water over the left shoulder, well water, in the directions in which they have wanted the winds to blow.

Other tools relate to the Plant Kingdom and often a personality of the plant, or plants, of which it is made causes noticeable effects. Brooms are magical tools which often have much attention given to the materials of which they are to be made. For a wooden bowl, often a particular wood is felt to be needed. For some uses, ivywood is called for. Skinner said that Bacchus drank wine from a bowl of beech. Containers, as baskets, made of willow often had a personality influenced by the spirit of that tree. From tradition, a witch with a broom went sailing into the sky in a basket. And cloth bags could be powerful containers. Winds, it is said, were captured by witches and, by the witches, put into these bags. Flutes, magical tools favoured by Mercury, could bring winds. For making flutes, box wood or maple were often the woods selected. Maple flutes bring in the Spring and inspire love and copulation.

Certainly, the most ancient tool given by the Plant Kingdom would be the stick, wand or staff; the tool having a name appropriate to its virtues or uses. This is a tool Mercury is pictured as having. A small wooden shaft might be a stick, and if of the Elder, it might be carried to give protection from rheumatism. Or an illness might be transferred to an elder stick and the stick, buried. Rowan sticks, like elder sticks, protected against demons and spirits of the Underworld. They were used to give protection at childbirth and were put on ships to give protection at sea. People took sticks from midsummer fires, according to Spicer, and put them in houses as protections from lightning. A stick used for the purpose of locating minerals, water or other things is called a divining rod. Often it is shaped like a Y and the searcher would hold, one in each hand, the ends of the fork. As the searcher moved over the land, the unheld end would point to the searched for substance. In the search for water, rods of willow or hazel were often selected. Linnaeus used a hazel wand for finding money. Valentinus used seven types of wood for divining rods: one type for each of the seven planets.

The first tree which gives the key to the Otherworld would be the Apple. The Apple would represent the Plant Kingdom. The Plant Kingdom, as a kingdom, would have a relationship with the Otherworld. And from that kingdom, Hercules, a Warrior Sun, needed the sacred Apple for travel to the Otherworld. Apollo who, as a Sun, made trips to the Otherworld, is God of Apples. An Apple Branch, somewhat bowed and holding three apples, is said to be the Key to the Otherworld and, said Spence, it was a custom of a great body of priest magicians to have a wand of the shape which reflected the shape of the Apple Wand of the gods; except, this wand would have been of the sacred Yew, as the Sun would take the form of a Yew.

The Staff of Mercury, which is a Key to the Otherworld, was said to have been of Hazel. It is the staff which represents all staffs and all the abilities of staffs, and a most significant ability would be the ability to travel to the Otherworld.

What staffs and wands do would depend on what the tool is, and who is using it, and what it is called on to do. A staff or wand in its sacred or consecrated form would be prepared to do more than one which was not, and the tool would do more the more, as a rule, it is treated as a useful companion. The magician's tools, wands and staffs, would be consecrated and bound to him or her by ritual and, said Gennep, would be an extension of the magician. This is an advantage which the tool gives. It might strike a surface beyond its user's hand. It might follow a beam, touch a distant star. It might reach out, pick up fire from the Sun, carry it to where there is a need. That need might be to circle some sacred object, or to form a sacred circle. What the tool would do would depend, in part, as Leland has said, on the user's ability to controle will.

In one use, wands and staffs have been used for transformations. With a wand, an Earth Goddess changed the Sun God, Balor, into a White Horse; then, into a wolf, as Jeremiah Curtin tells it. The Underworld God, Math, who has been related to Arcas; struck two deities, Gwydion and Gilvaethwy, with his wand and changed them into deer. Another time, he changed them into pigs and another time, into wolves. This, from the Mabinogion. Spence said that the magician Reachtaire struck his son with a wand and changed him into a pig which had no ears or tail. A wand changed the Children of Lir into swans.

A magician's tools would be consecrated and bound to him or her by ritual. Buckland and others give ways by which magicians obtain and consecrate staffs and wands. The obtaining of the tool is an important ritual. Heselton said he thought it best that the tools be obtained from an area local to where they were to be used. Local is a term that would mean many different things. Heselton felt that there are only a couple of short periods of time during the year when a person should gather his staff or wand. Buckland said he felt that any time of the year would be appropriate, but that it should be gathered under a Waxing Moon. Before gathering the tool, Aborrow said one should become familiar with, and make friends with, the area; then locate a tree which would be best for supplying the tool and make certain the tree would be glad to give the gift. Proper gratitude, it is generally thought, should be shown, and many magicians would say respect and care should be at all times shown during the gathering. For cutting the wood, a sharp, purified and consecrated knife should be used. Care should be made to repair the cut on the tree. Some magicians have said the gatherer should make a gift of his blood, a cut for a cut. And a libation, it is thought, should be made. Sometimes this would be honey; sometimes, wine; sometimes, both. Aborrow suggests, one might do things which the tree might appreciate; as, clean up the area. With the newly cut wand or staff, there would be rituals for bringing it into a family relationship. A ritual Nigel Jackson gives: breathe on the tool three times, make a statement confirming the new relationship, spit on a finger and with it, make three exes on the tool, pass the tool three times through purifying smoke. Buckland also calls for the tool to be passed through purifying smoke. For Buckland, the tool should be cut before sunrise and, before sunrise, it should be taken to the highest rise in the area where it could be held up to the rising Sun. In the Sun's ray it is energized. Then, by breath and thought and visual concentration, it becomes part of the magician.

When a person acquired a staff or wand, he or she might have altered it. Many would have done nothing to have altered the way in which Nature had presented it. Some, as Aborrow has said, would have removed the bark, polished the tool, then rubbed it with linseed oil. That would have been, if that had felt right to the Spirit of the Tree.

A tool might be augmented by symbol, design or colour. A leather hand grip might have been added. Some gods might have favoured the addition of an acorn, a pine cone, or a shell. Any augmentation would have influenced the direction toward which the tool would have gravitated and would have affected the work of the magician with the tool. The more added, the less one would have the pure Spirit of the Tree. But an addition might add one or more spirit forces to the tool. A pine cone might gain the interest of Pan, as he had an affection for the Pine in her female form. With a symbol representing Blaze, or Blaise, a swineherd, Villinganus said, protected his swine: the symbol fixed onto the swineherd's staff. The swineherd left the staff with the swine and went off on other business.

As wands and staffs are from trees which are, or represent, deities of great power, there has been a long tradition of holding them in much reverence; but the trees most honoured, or believed to be most supportive, from one segment of population to another, has differed. Spence said that the population of one large area favoured wands of oak, while another area favoured those of yew and among those who favoured yew, wands of rowan and of hawthorn were also used. Giraldus listed three trees from which wands were often selected: hazel, poplar and chestnut. Jackson listed ash, hazel, rowan and blackthorn. For staffs or wands, Aborrow listed yew, hazel, willow and blackthorn. For staffs, Buckland listed ash, yew, oak and walnut. Those with the Goddess as the center of their ritual practice might have selected willow or elm. In one tradition, said Cavendish, it was thought, a magician's wand needed to be hazel. From one magician's instructions, the hazel wand needed to be nineteen and one half inches long, and needed to be gathered with a knife which had taken blood. With his hazel wand, one magician struck a corpse nine times and demanded that the corpse answer questions.

Wands and staffs are selected from a number of varieties of trees, for one reason, because trees have different powers and different interests. In order to bring rain, poplar wands were used for whipping stones. Flowers said that in fertility rites, birch is used. Also, the birch staff is used for giving learning to fools. Flowers said that for divining, willow wands were often used and, he said, witches and magicians used blackthorn as a blasting rod, and a blackthorn staff was carried for protection and for use in working malevolent magic.

With the staff or wand which holds the power of the Tree, which represents the Plant Kingdom and is the Key, the unified forces pass from one world to another. Each member of the Plant Kingdom would be partly in the Otherworld and, at a point, could be the Sacred Apple: could be the Key. Some herbs would be quick to take one to the Otherworld. An herb, or a combination of herbs, put on the eyes might permit one to see into the Otherworld, permit one to drop beyond this World's space. And, perhaps, herbs would permit those of the Otherworld to reach out into this World. In the web, events might seem, triggered by plants; many happenings, by plants.

In the Time of the Juggler, as the Sun increases his influence because of his rise in energy, the energy in other beings rises also. Much of the Plant Kingdom is, at this time, energized. And the essence which flows through all things, so that the Plant Kingdom and Man are united, would cause Man to be affected by the increased energy, and so, activity, of plants. And the rising flow of energy in Man, as it flowed in motion with all else, would be shaped by the rising forces of the plants. Man, through the ages, has been aware of the great influence which plants have on the way life is lived. From the walls of ancient tombs, it can be seen that from most ancient times, as Pitman has said, how plants have, "Their central role in all aspects of life."

A major aspect associated with the Plant Kingdom is that of health. And Mercury, the Master Juggler, is the major deity who brings the abilities of herbs to the use of others. This not only is knowledge of the abilities of herbs, but he would tell where to find them and when to use them. It might be, as Theophrastus has said, to guide one to a plant which had its young about it, so that the searcher would gain the stronger plant, the one at its best. Or, to cure a wound, Mercury might, as Clodd has said, direct one to rub the blade which caused the wound with an herb.

Mercury, beside being an instructor in healing; is, himself, a master healer. This would be associated with Mercury in his form of a snake. The Spirit of the Snake relates to birth and creation, to a death; then, death to rebirth. By dying and being reborn, the Snake goes in and out of the Underworld. Mercury, as a three headed snake, passes from one world to another. He passes into death, gives a skin to the Otherworld and is reborn. The Snake is Birth and Death. It slays itself and is reborn. As a circle, as slaying and creating itself, the Snake is shown eating its own tail. A phallic tail and a vaginal mouth, slaying and creating, is symbolic of eternity. It represents the basic circle of existence. And this would represent the forces of nature completing their circles; which would, as Ure has said, represent the determinism for all life. A Pair of Snakes, as a duality, as Opsopaus said, forms a circle which feeds on itself. It represents life, as Matthews has said, which passes simultaneously downward and upward. A self destructive nature in snakes has been observed. It was noticed, said Rulandus, that baby snakes often kill their mother. And snakes kill each other. At times, a female viper will bite the head of her mate.

To kill is to produce life, said Hartmann. Said Holzer, objects need creation, and creation needs destruction. To build a house, one would need to destroy to get building materials. Some would not have wanted the new building, but new births must come, come out of the darkness of the unborn. The old singer leaves a place in the light, a place which calls for a birth. There might be a singer who holds a bright lantern and seems ready to step center stage, but until she is there, she is in the dark of the unborn. There is doubt. Then, when the singer is heard, it is because another has gone silent, as Holzer has explained. Darkness creates the need for light; so, brings light. Light needs darkness.

Hiding and revealing are forms of death and rebirth. Ussher said, motifs of hiding, drowning, and swallowing imply a return to chaos. Chaos is a darkness which holds unborn. And with chaos, there is a primal hunger: Chaos must eat and all things are food for chaos. Falling into Chaos might be thought of as being eaten by the Snake, and the Snake might be called the Snake of Time. Mysteries of theology are based on the basic hunger of the Snake. The Apples of life keep one from falling into Chaos, but these are guarded by the Snake. The Snake can guard those in Chaos, then bring rebirth. Worthen pointed out that deities concealed in festival celebrations are deaths waiting for rebirths. In children's games, deaths might be hiding and waiting rebirths. The games might be rituals concealed in play.

The Snake has been called the Dark Side of Nature. That is the darkness of the abyss. The Snake holds the darkness of the Underworld. One gate to the Underworld is called the Mouth of the Snake. In a dream, Eiseley saw Death as a huge white snake. The Serpent of Darkness, said Rhys, lay on the ring of the Sun. The Snake eats Light. Light slays the Snake, and is reborn. The Snake is reborn.

The Snake guards the Apples of Life. The Snake's eyes are always open. A snake's nature is to guard and protect. Pater said that it is said, snakes with sleepless eyes guard the River Styx. Dragons are often pictured guarding mounds of treasure. Athene threw Draco, the King Dragon, to The Pole to guard the sacred Apple Tree. By Atlas, Hercules gets the rejuvenating apples, as Opsopaus explains, from the one who would controle rebirth: the Snake.

As its eyes never close, the Snake is known to hold great knowledge, and this is one reason it is especially favoured by Athene.

The Snake guards, or secures, things. The Spirit of the Snake would be in tubes, in ropes and in strings. These are often used to bind things and so, secure them. Loops and knots might secure not only the physical, but that of the spirit. Theocritus said crimson strings of wool had the power to bind a love vow. In security, there would be two aspects: one, the aspect of protection; two, that of restriction. A guard might be a gaol, be seen as a gaol; perhaps, a trap. With the Snake, there is an unease of not knowing. A thing might be guarded in one way of thinking. The Snake inspires dread. As Hawthorne has said, there is snake like doubt. The coils of the Snake might form a snare. The great snake, Draco, was thrown into the sky, it was said, to guard the Sacred Apple, and was said to be not always reliable. However, the Snake might have had a hidden purpose. The Apple had covered the hole at the top of the World, but the apple, as Worthen explained, had shifted; so, the Snake was there to guard the hole, the Dark Abyss. Typhon, who had come out of the hole to destroy much of life, had caused the Snake to guard the hole. At the Apple, the Spirit of the Snake would have the form of Draco. Against the hole, the Dark Abyss, the only counter would have been rebirth; so, the Snake. It would be dark against dark. The darkness of the Snake counters darkness.

The Snake conducts birth, death and the events along the way, which to birth and death relate. In regulating the trip toward death, the Snake would hold the regulating of healing. Belts and rings could hold the Spirit of the Snake and so, have snake powers. Paracelsus said the belt could be the Snake eating its tail. The Spirit of the Snake might be called up by ritual for aid. Snakes have taught the art of healing and especially, healing by the use of herbs. Apollodorus said it was known that snakes used herbs to bring the dead back to life. Hyginus said that by the use of certain leaves the snake brings a dead mate back to life. Snakes taught the use of powerful herbs, which Jacob Grimm called snake leaves, which repel infections and invasions. In times past, said Leyel, snakes were kept in the houses of physicians. In some areas, said Trevelyan, each house was thought to have its guardian snakes, and these would appear before the master or the mistress of the house died.

Snake flesh is used in cures, and toads, considered to be forms of snakes, are used for bringing cures. For a snakebite, or for the bite or sting of another venomous creature; the toad, as a beast of darkness, would neutralize the darkness of the other beast. Dried tadpoles are put on snake bites so that the darkness of tadpoles would draw out, would draw to it, as Valentinus has said, the dark venom of the snake. Dried toads have been used to check a woman's flow of blood and to check, also, other fluxes of blood. This, from Rulandus.

Toads are quite magical. Women, at midnight, put toads into running water and so, came to understand animals and gained in sex appeal. These women have gone by the name of Toad Women. Frog crossing one's way: good luck: Aeschylus.

Snake eggs would be highly magical, and would have been much valued for their powers. Edward Davies tells of a ritual where the snake's egg was tossed up in the air. Magicians would have, at times, worn snakes' eggs as pendants from around their necks.

Stones from snakes are valued for healing powers. One stone found in the head of a snake is called draconite, and this gives protection from snakes and other venomous creatures. It is said, it must be taken from the head which has been cut off an unsuspecting snake. Other snake stones, called adder stones, have been gotten from the heads of snakes. These, according to Dalyell, were put into pots of water in order to gain healing infusions. These stones have been worn as charms for gaining prosperity and for protection from illness and malicious demons.

A stone is produced by the copulation of snakes and this, also, has been called an adder stone. Giraldus said snakes entwined to create a ball which they threw up into the air. Fernie said it would be made by snakes joining, before the Autumnal Moon, to copulate. The stone was said to be, at times, like a glass ring. All these adder stones would hold a powerful magic.

Snake stones were also found in the heads of lizards. Taken from lizards, according to Sylvaticus, the stones would protect against venom.

Another snake stone, the toad stone, was gotten from the head of a toad, which was considered a type of snake. The protective spirit of the toad would have been in the stone. It protected not only against illness, but against houses burning and boats sinking. It was thought especially effective against whooping cough. It was said, toad stones grown in a king toad would change colour in the presence of poison. Warriors wore toad stones because the stones encouraged victory.

Toad stones, it is said, were obtained from fairies. It was a custom to leave a coin for the fairies in exchange for the stone.

Snake skins were magical healers.

The Onion, as it changes its skin and has a hollow stem, has a Snake Spirit.   R M Lucas said that sliced onions were hung in rooms to keep influenza out.

Ophite, a stone which has snake markings, is said to cure headache, lethargy and snakebite.

The Spirit of the Snake, in one aspect, became the Art of Medicine. Ausonius said he thought that it was the only art which had produced a god. The God, called Ophiuchus, and also, Aesculapius, is healer and preserver of life. He is thought of as the Snake God, but is often pictured in human form. As the Spirit of Healing, Ophiuchus took pleasure in healing all he contacted. So many became healed that Hades came himself out of the Underworld and went to see Jupiter. He told Jupiter that none were entering his realm; so, if any were born, the system would be out of balance. Jupiter, in anger, struck Ophiuchus with a bolt of lightning and threw him into space. But it is the nature of the Snake to be reborn. Little by little, Ophiuchus crept toward the Zodiac Belt until, as Astronomer Ottewell said, Ophiuchus' tail was stuck between Scorpio and Sagittarius. He runs along the outside of Sagittarius and he is becoming more and more an influence, and this might cause Hades, representing Death, to feel uncomfortable. The sign of Ophiuchus is a staff and a snake and Pausanias has seen Ophiuchus pictured with a staff in one of his hands. In the other hand, Pausanias said, he held a branch of pine. As Ottewell said, Ophiuchus was becoming more of an influence. But he would not overstep his bounds.

It was said, a hunter found Ophiuchus; later, usually called Aesculapius. Rome, while having an epidemic, heard that Aesculapius was in Greece, so prayed that he would come to their aid. Aesculapius, Ovidius said, turned from a human form into a crested snake and went to Rome and there, stopped the wave of illness. At Rome he established a temple. Physicians became considered priests of Aesculapius, Manas said, and for their god, demanded the sacrifice of a cock, which is a bird of the Sun. Iamblichos said, after purification, dieting and other rituals, suppliants would have been put into a sleep, or trance. Aesculapius, the sender of dreams, would have identified his problem. A priest would have instructed in the cure. A marvelous number of cures were worked and Iamblichos said the instructions from Aesculapius received while awake seemed to work even more frequently than those received in dream. Cheiron was said to have told Aesculapius much about herbs, and these, especially aloes for wounds, were much used in the temples. Aesculapius, known as a healer of the gods, commanded much respect. Galienus said he was told by Aesculapius not to go north with the army, so obeyed his god. Said

Figulus, Aesculapius could, with a stone, return the dead to life.

Iaso is a Healer Goddess pictured in snake and in human form. She is associated with a tall, footed vase, called the Kantharos, which has, on each side, a handle which curves from lip to foot. The handles represent the two natures of the vessel, dark and light. The natures form a balance. Balance is a nature of Iaso, and of Mercury also. In snake form, Iaso is pictured drinking from the vase. Vases and cups would be Caves of Winds. Mercury has been pictured with a cup, or vase. The dark and light sides of the vessel would, as Jung has said, represent the conscious and the unconscious. Rebirth rituals would tend to do away with separation between conscious and unconscious so that the balance brought would renew inherited instinct. The vase is the symbol of balance, and of the healing power of Iaso.

Healing would be the balancing of elements. Lacinius said this would be the elements brought together by the Moon, the Sun, and Mercury, God of Air. This could be called the Master Medication.

In regulating events along way from birth to death, as all created things have births and deaths, the Snake would be involved in all creation. The coils of the Snake hold the Spirit of Creation. The coils would be ever in motion generating changes. The Winds of Change are certainly snakes. The Snake contains all elements. As Fire, as van Gennep said, is the impetus of change; and this, especially true of sacred fire; the coils of the Snake would relate to the element of Fire. Armies, to have changes go their way, would carry before them burning brands from the fires of accepted sacrifices. Mercury, as the Juggler, works with all elements. When his mood swings toward quick and tricky action, fire would be a useful element to work with. The Spirit Fire relating to the coils of the Snake has been called Dragon Fire. Corrigan told how, through ritual, people have made use of this fire. For the ritual, an important tool would be the wand, as the wand would hold the Spirit of the Snake. Corrigan said it might be helpful if a dragon were carved into the wand, and helpful if the dragon were coloured red.

As related to birth, the Snake would relate to copulation. And Winds, who would have the snake form as their usual form, would have copulation as a major interest.

King of Winds, Aeolus is a lusty king who lives on a cloud island and to this, carries women with whom by force he copulates. Epictetus said Aeolus chooses what winds blow.

Boreas is the North Wind. In some places, however, he is the Wind; or, the Wind in the North. And he is known to be lusty. He snatched up a dancing girl, wrapped her in dark clouds and fucked her. He would have chosen a dancing girl because dancing is related to copulation. Boreas developed an attraction for a beautiful maiden, Pitys; but she, instead, chose Pan; so Boreas, in a rage, slew her. Pitys was then given a pine tree form. In many areas, Boreas was a highly honoured god. Allcroft said that in some places, to honour Boreas, houses were built to face North. So Boreas would send rain, beheaded blacksnakes, as a sacrifice, were hung up by the tail. All the Winds would, at times, be given sacrifices. Pausanias said, for the Winds, a cock was torn in half; each half, carried around a vineyard until they met and there the cock was buried.

Boreas is blustery and dangerous, but the South Wind, Auster, is thought to be more deadly. Zephyr is boisterous, but usually friendly, but any Wind might blow a person toward the Underworld. Kittredge said that Winds related to Waters are dangerous. Athene, said Herodotus, was thought to have rule over Winds and storm.

During the time when the Juggler is the major influence, the celebrations go from dark and shadowy, to loud and filled with energy.

May thirteenth, behind the bright flowers of May are the shadows, the ghosts from the past. At Lemuria, with rituals, the dead are returned to the Underworld. In this holiday, dark and light walk together. There is the rise in bright energy with the coming drop toward the dark. The holiday holds the combination of fertility rites with funeral rites. One, Bacchic and hilarious; the other, Chthonian and sinister. This is the day Mercury led Proserpine out of the Realm of Hades. And ghosts and spirits slipped out of the Underworld. Their powers became strong; so, to prevent harm, doors were painted with pitch. At meals, food fallen from the table was swept out the door for the ghosts. At midnight, the head of the house would wash his hands, then walk barefoot through the house while spitting nine black beans. Looking away from the beans, he would say, "Thus I ransom myself and mine." Then, at the front door, he would, while facing the inside, throw nine black beans over his left shoulder, say a charm to dismiss the visitors from the Underworld, clang two brass urns together; then, again wash his hands.

Beans played a big part in charms for protection against the Underworld. Mysterious plants of Wind, they serve as offerings to spirits of the Underworld. Bean flowers are considered to be sinister and dangerous, and especially so, where love is concerned. They bring melancholy and gloom and attract the ghosts which might be dangerous or critical. And they cloud the vision, and they advance lust. And beans might bring nightmares or madness, but beans protect honesty and work magical cures. To dream of beans would be to be warned of coming trouble. In transactions, beans have been used as counters so that the transactions would be protected by the beans, plus by ancestors and ghosts. Beans are put in rattles for chasing away malicious spirits. Put on warts, with the aid of a spoken charm, beans would make the warts go away. It is said, fairies and witches ride on bean stalks. Pregnant women walking in bean fields would cause the beans to wither. People, to secure aid from Hecate, would plant beans at road forks. For Underworld trips, bean roots might have been eaten. As beans relate to the Underworld, the time for sowing them would be under the Waning Moon.

Pythagoras had a great respect for beans, and it was in a bean field where he was slain. Ceres is said to have called beans unholy.

May fifteenth, Mercuriala, Mercury is honoured and, especially, his relationship to the Underworld. At this time, Hecate, ancestors and lost spirits are also honoured. At forks of roads, bells are rung to purify the air and pillars of stone are built and to these, all inhabitants of the community are encouraged to contribute stones. A ram, followed by people with wands of willow and wearing crowns of flowers and mourning clothes, is carried around the town as an appeal to Mercury, Chief Shepherd, to protect the town's sheep. From Robert Meyer: during the day, there would be solemn parades, often with flags and drums. People would carry branches of bay, and wicker puppets were carried to the water and thrown in. The puppets would be stand ins for old people. Moving through the Water Veil is a property of the dead. At the water, people would dip their bay branches and sprinkle each other with water off the sacred leaves. During the day, rams, goats, cocks, honey and animal tongues were sacrificed to Mercury and merchants sprinkled themselves with water off bay leaves. In the evening, in an account given by Cooper, there would have been a candle parade which would have included two huge candles, and each candle, behind it, would have had a following. As a climax, there would have been a race between the two followings, each trying to be first to get its candle to the alter of Mercury. As the day focused on purity, it was sometimes called White Day. At night, on this day, to honour the ancestors, on the piles of stone at the road forks, candles would be lit and the piles would be decorated with flowers.

May twentyfirst, Agonium Vediovis, and May twentysecond, Hyakinthia, were celebrations dedicated to the Underworld. Agonium Vediovis was a day for honouring Underworld gods. There were feasts for the dead, and black animals were sacrificed to the gods.

Hyakinthia is a day for vegetation god, Hyakinthos. On this day all classes of people feasted together. Garlands of iris and ivy are worn, said Firmicus Maternus. Even though the celebration was joyful, Hyakinthos was brutal and demanding. For him, on his mound, animals were sent to his Underground Realm, and the god demanded that at his alters, worthy women be given to him. It was said that the daughter of Hyakinthos, Lusia, had been sacrificed and buried in his mound. As human sacrifice was not permitted in the city, his alters were not there, but they were out in the wilds. Ritual was led by a man dressed as the Green Man, and there was singing and music by flute and lyre. Graves were decorated with flowers. Warriors, especially Ajax, were honoured.

The stone of Hyakinthos is the Jacinth, an orange stone which protects travelers, brings riches and counters spells. And it protects against poisoned arrows. It raises the spirits and fortifies the heart. And Fernie adds, it is hung from the neck to ward against plague. And it chases toxins and is a specific against cramp. Boetius adds, worn in a ring, it procures sleep and brings honour and wisdom. This stone would represent Hyakinthos and, as Fernie has said, would tell the past history associated with it.

May twentyninth, Ambarvalia, is a most sacred day for dedications to the deities. On this day, according to Lord Ruadh, the deity at the center of attention would have been Ceres. People created a sacredness around themselves and their properties in the name of the deities, and the distinctive feature of the celebration was the walk, three times around the field. And this would have created sacred space, three being a magical number for charms and one sacred to Mercury. Also, Pater gives an account of the holiday celebration. The household shrines were decorated. Shrines of Bacchus, Liber and Ceres were presented with baskets of flowers and, according to Ogilvie, respects to the Lare were not forgotten. Shrines of Venus were decorated with bright shells and with cloths fixed to flutter in the breeze. Oxen which were to be sacrificed to Ceres, so had been exempt from toil, had their managers filled and were decorated with wreaths of flowers. Plows and other tools were decorated.

Then, each farm had its sunwise march around its lands. The marchers, wearing crowns of oak leaves and carrying torches; sang hymns to Ceres and shouted to Ceres and Mars requests for blessings. Three times around the lands they marched and did, according to Lord Ruadh, artless dancing. Other deities, also, were included in prayers and requests for blessings. Ops, Consus, Rhea, Robigo and Hercules would not have been forgotten in prayers, and in respects paid at shrines. Trees, especially, the Oak and the Apple, were shown special honours, so that, in some areas, this was called Oak Apple day. And respects were paid to Sylvanus. It was, as Snell said, one of his special days, as he had special care for apples and oaks. Sylvanus was not so much part of formal rituals, but he was outside the law, so inspired fears. He was little involved with the care and protection of farms. He was not part of the program of rites and respects which other deities, it was thought, expected and cooperated with. It was more difficult to harmonize with Sylvanus and with him, each person was more or less on his own. Sylvanus was considered humourous, but dangerous: somewhat demonic. Animals sacrificed to Sylvanus, it was thought, needed to be eaten at the site of the sacrifice.

After family celebrations, families would join the procession to the central shrine of Ceres. The procession was led by priests in antique, white vestments and, fixed on the tops of their heads, were ears of barley. After the priests, dressed in white, were litter bearers, and on the litters were garland draped statues of deities. Following these were boys dressed in white; some, carrying incense pots; some, pots of holy water. These were followed by boys leading representatives of farm animals; usually, a cow, a sow and an ewe; each, decorated with chains of flowers. Torch bearers came next in their oak leaf crowns; then, bearers of decorated tools; the host of worshipers, following. People wore not only chains of flowers, but, to honour Ceres, as one learns from Plinius, garlands made of grain.

When the host was assembled at the Shrine of Ceres; priests spoke words which, in later times, no one would understand; and no one but the priest would speak, as any sound would change the direction of the ritual. Gestures and actions were done; each, precisely at the correct word. Gifts were given to Ceres. Vergilius said that honeycomb washed with milk and soft wine was a correct gift. Then, herbs were burnt on the alter fires. Burning with a tall, clear flame would indicate the pleasure of the deities.

The procession went from the Shrine of Ceres, to the shrines of Liber and of Bacchus. Chants were given: each word, spoken carefully so as not to cause the displeasure of any deity. It was a custom to then sacrifice sheep. The livers of the sheep would have been inspected to make certain that the deities were calm. Aristophanes said that it was a custom to put the tail into the fire last to determine if the sacrifice was agreeable to the deities. The indicated pleasure of the deities would have made joyous celebrating an obligation, a duty. Feasting and getting drunk, said Tibullus, was thought to honour Ceres. For Ceres, freshly cleaned clothes were worn and, for the day, people had purified their hands in running water. Then, celebrating with music, dance and wine would have promoted stability in the circles of nature.

Later in the day, in some areas, feasts were held in honour of the Oak and often the Oak was asked to speak for the people in dealings with other deities. In honour of the Oak, oak leaves were worn and in some places, those not wearing one were likely to get pelted with oak balls.

A custom was for a procession to form behind a King of Vegetation, or a King and a Queen of Vegetation. The King, or the King and Queen, would have been dressed all in flowers and been wearing a flower crown, and would have led the procession up the highest available hill where, said Kightly, the Queen, or if there was no Queen, the King, would have put on a crown. The marchers would have been wearing garlands of flowers and it was a tradition to include Milkwort, called Fairy Soap, and Ambarvalis, in the garlands. Fairies were said to use Milkwort and Dioscorides said it made milk more abundant in nursing mothers. In the processions, marchers rang bells to chase malicious spirits and to purify the air. Distinctive features of Ambarvalia were the magical walks, the protective processional dances. As King Charles II, on this day, was protected by the Oak, that was a reason why it was thought the Oak favoured the British Crown.

May thirtieth honoured the Dead. It was the Day of Moira, called Moira the Strong One. Also, it was Memorial Day. Moira cut the Thread of Life. Hades and Proserpine were celebrated and many people of fame, on this day, have gone to the Underworld. These include Arcas, who is known as King Arthur, and Mordred, and Joan of Arc. Ajax and Hector are remembered on this day. Flowers and flags decorate graves and a farewell call has been heard sounding from the horn.

In late May, Apollo needed to be purified because of slaying Python, the Great Snake.

June first honoured Juno, Hebe, Tempestas and Carna, who was also known as Cardea. She is Goddess of Doors, Hinges, Locks, Goings and Comings, Birthings, Physical Survival and Domestic Life. Graves lists her also as a Goddess of Grain, and of Inspiration, who has the Key to the Underworld, and relates her to Porcys, Sow Goddess of the Dead. She is a White Sow Barley Goddess who sacrifices her kings. The Hawthorn and the Bean are sacred to her. In her honour, there are feasts of pork and beans and pork and beans are given to her. At the feasts, there are games and entertainments. Hinges and locks were repaired so Carna would bless them, and people made requests for trouble free birthings. And Juno, in her aspect as Moneta, was honoured and the use of money, encouraged. Money, as it was minted in temples of the deities, was treated with respect. As Lindholm has said, one needed to spend it wisely. Also, on this day, Tempestas, Goddess of Storms, was honoured and she was requested to send a bright, sunny June. Fortuna, as Ogilvie has said, was also considered a storm goddess and in some areas, was respected as chief goddess. Ussher said that Castor and Pollux were also considered, Gods of Storm. They were looked to when sailors were in need of aid.

June ninth was Vestalia, a feast honouring Vesta. Vesta is the Goddess of the Hearth and in one aspect, Fire. The Hearth, as Jacob Grimm has said, is a Door to the Underworld. For Vesta, on Vestalia, feasts were held and gifts of food were sent to the Temple of Vesta. As fire was started by the rotation of a staff, mill wheels and mill donkeys were decked in flowers. Millers and bakers observed the holiday and Ovidius considered Vesta most sacred. It was a custom, never to portray her with facial features. Vesta's Fire was cared for by sacred Vestial Virgins and no one else entered her temple. Vesta is a goddess who might be recognized by her spiritual presence. And the hearth is magical, it was said, a cat sitting with his back to a hearth can stir up a battle of high winds. Said Musaeus, battle of four winds causes storm.

June Thirteenth was the Feast of Epona. Epona was called the Divine Mare. She is a river who has mare and human forms. On the holiday, Minerva is also honoured. Flute players, on the day, hold a procession. They play in long gowns and masks, so that even their sex is masked, and this, to show that it is the music that is important. The masking encouraged the flute players to be boisterous and bawdy. Boxwood was the wood favoured for these flutes. The players would usually be followed by dancers, some carrying olive branches wrapped in linen.

In spirit, Epona would have been leading the march. She, in some places, was represented as the naked woman rider leading a procession to the forest. Epona was Guardian of Roads; especially, those to the Underworld. Also, she is a supervisor of procreation and especially, the procreation of horses and kings, and kings rule subject to her approval. She is a protector and supervisor of animals: especially, horses and asses. Lucius Apuleius has her statue on the center support of a stable and pictured her covered with roses. Mac Cana said she was usually represented seated sideways on a horse. She was often associated with birds and music, and these, related to death. And she was considered, a Warrior Goddess.

The energy of nature, which climbed to its peak the Twentyfirst of June, had expression in Midsummer celebrations. Midsummer Day would usually refer to June twentyfourth, into which, celebrations usually spilled over. But the seasons energies, inspired earlier celebration. The peak of energies, in some places, was called Sonnen Wende. And the following day, the day of light, Caevron. The day might also be called Goursav Heol; or, ecstasy of the Sun. The celebrating has as its focus, the Sun reaching its peak of strength, its brightness, and heading toward the dark. The Focus at Midsummer is on the Wheel of the Sun, and on the Sun's turning. As the Sun not only is, itself, a wheel, but represents the concept of a Wheel: Moon Cycles, Nature Cycles, Fortuna's Wheel and other wheels of all types. The Wheel of the Sun and the Wheel of the Year, especially, are celebrated.

The chief duty at Midsummer would have been to honour the Sacred Fire, the Sun. To give the Sun energy as it began its decline, fires were built on the tops of high hills. And, many times, discs of fire and burning wheels were thrown, or rolled, down the hills. The total of Midsummer celebrations would help the declining Sun in continuing his important tasks. Around the bases of the hills there would have been fairs and entertainments leading up to the lighting of the fires.

First, to prepare for Midsummer rituals, there would have been cleanings and purifications. People would likely have cleaned and decorated homes; then, washed and dressed in clean clothes. Then people often would have congregated at fairs where there would have been games, sales booths and entertainers such as hobby horses. At times, pageantry would have presented solar attributes in hope to encourage them. Contests and athletic events were often included in the celebrations, such things as tugowars, which would have encouraged light to defeat the dark. Dance, including circle games, have often been part of Midsummer celebrations. Children's circle games, often included, often held magical charms, and they often related to death. One nursery rhyme ends, "Ashes, ashes, all fall down." Ferguson gives one which has a Jingo Ring, a merry me tansy, a choice of maidens; then, "Twice about and then we fall."

At times, dances were done around oaks. Elves, said Porteous, lived in oaks and loved circle dances and would have had a place in the dancing. As birch trees related to the birth of the new born Sun, they were decorated and danced around. Often, poles representing trees were danced around, and some, according to Linnaeus, were birch poles covered with leaves, flowers and white chips of horn.

Many of the elves and other elementals have loved dance and especially at Midsummer, which was their time of high energy and bright joy. With people, however, elven activity would have been felt but seldom seen. But it was said, there were ways by which one could have seen, even taken part, in elven activity. At the exact time in the Midsummer season, if one had sat under an elder tree, one would have been able to see elves, but if that person had fallen asleep there, he or she would likely have been transported to the Otherworld. And it was thought, one could have gotten trapped in an elven ring, then would have needed a charm in order to get out. Porteous said one might have escaped from an elven ring by turning his or her coat inside out, then putting it on. Spicer said that disturbing an elven ring was said to bring blindness, but that telling of seeing one was said to bring good fortune. Truth, said Giraldus, was important to elves. Trevelyan said that elves stirred up storms.

Other elementals who were thought, especially active at Midsummer were the Selphs. These could have been frightening and sometimes caused panic. As they reveled in the midst of storm, they would, according to Hodson, be seen as black figures with, around them, auras like lightning flashes. Hodson said that in the Winds of bright day, they could create, in people, feelings of buoyancy, of lightness, of joy.

Many deities were celebrated at Midsummer. Furrina, as Hislop has said, was praised and asked to supply blessings. Fortuna was considered a major force at Midsummer celebrations and in her honour, there were games of chance and fortunes were predicted, and the predictions gave pleasure even when their correctness wasn't relied on. One Porphyrius, considered wise, in his, "Book of Oracles," said that the future, because prediction is full of obscurities, is uncertain even to the gods. But

Midsummer was considered, a good time for love divination. Leyel said that for this, at Midsummer, mugwort and hypericum have been found useful.

Hercules was a deity honoured at Midsummer. Hercules protected Earth from monsters and those were especially active at this season, such as the Earth Giant, Busiris, whom Hercules slew. Of this slaying, as an example of justice, Boethius said Hercules gave the same treatment to Busiris which Busiris had given to many others.

Hercules had a devotion to duty. If a duty, in justice, was presented to him, he was certain to do what the duty required. Libanius said that to be a Hercules was to be given an unpleasant task, then to feel duty bound to do it. Hercules was said to have died at Midsummer.

Hercules had an oak form and the Oak was called the Door Between the Worlds. Hercules was called the Doorkeeper for the Gods. The Door, in one aspect, was the mighty, magical door between life and death. This related the Oak to prediction. Lovarcus said, "Dense are the tops of oaks, know by knowledge given to poets." In the twigs of the oaks he read secrets. It was said, ravens rested in the limbs of oaks and gave prophecy. Made of oak, the prow of the Argo gave advice to Jason.

As a door to the Otherworld, the Oak is a sponsor of transitions of all kinds. Meetings where laws were changed might have been made under an oak. By turning the coat inside out, one would have been taking a step toward the Underworld. It would show sympathy for the Underworld. For sexual potency, a red cloth was tied over the center of an equal arm oak cross. The cross would give, also, protection and balance. It was thought, if a person caught a falling oak leaf, that person would be free from colds during that coming winter. Holes in oaks have been called fairy doors and they have been called on to work cures.

The Spirit of the Old Oak, as the Spirit of the Old Sun, was said to have gone to the Underworld at Midsummer, and to have been replaced by a Sun, young and in good health. This was to benefit the land. As the king went, so went the land, said Spence. Often, the drama of this change was presented in Midsummer celebrations. Some areas had a tree which was considered the King Oak. To give it a young spirit, a man would take on the Spirit of the Oak, meet a play acted death; then, have a young replacement who would give his spirit to the King Oak. The clothes from the Spirit of the Old Oak King might have been torn off, put on the new tree and around the land so that the clothes holding the Old Spirit would give protection.

Related to the celebration of the Oak was the celebration of the Mistletoe. It was felt that the only two times when it was safe to have mistletoe in homes was during the days of the Midsummer Season and during those of the Yule Season. At Midsummer, Mistletoe is honoured when in full bloom. Plinius said it was collected from the Oak by men in white robes. In many cases, it was cut with a knife of stone and caught in a cloth of linen. It has been called the male genitals of the Oak and is said to cause death and birth. Mistletoe was given to Aneas so that Aneas could return from the Realm of Hades. Put under the pillow, it was thought to bring prophetic dreams. It was called Heal All, as cures it brought seemed magical. Among the more usual uses, Fiske said the ancients used it for epilepsy. It was used for menopause disturbances and for nervous disorders, and Hippocrates used it as a remedy for the spleen. Mistletoe would bring creativity, productivity and, in women, aid fertility, and it was said to give protection. The twigs, for added power, were tied together with red ribbon or string which was red. At Midsummer, Ickis said that mistletoe was handed out, each piece, with blessings and requests that it might grant divine favours. Women put mistletoe berries in their pockets.

Another tree which was often honoured at Midsummer was the Poplar, a sacred tree of Hercules, and it was also favoured by Helios. It cured Hercules when Hercules got bitten by a snake. When Hercules defeated Cacus, he was given a poplar crown and Hercules wore it to the Underworld and there, fires darkened the tops of the leaves. The Poplar was a tricky tree, gifted at slight of hand and, it was thought, not always honest. It gave messages and was, in other ways also, an aid to communication. It was said, a poplar leaf put under the tongue would cure the inability to speak. At Midsummer, poplars were sometimes decorated with bright shells, bright cloths and painted egg shells.

At the celebrations, the wheel would have been featured, in many ways, as it would have honoured the Sun. To bring good fortune, magical symbols were put on wheels. On some wheels, herbs were placed on the points of the compass so that the Sun would give benefits and especially, in health. One such wheel was given by R M Lucas, and this, put around the circle, mistletoe, elecampane, hyericum, rosemary, vervain and bay.

There were often a number of ritual pageants. One, the Sun Hero defeating the dragon. Another, the Divine Twins riding in a boat to protect the Sun. A great Sky Boat was said to hold Castor and Pollux, two mighty horsemen warriors. Castor was a master of armed conflict and Pollux, of boxing. They were Storm Gods thought to rescue sailors. Ancient graphs show a young Sun being transported in a boat.

There would have been booths serving food and, certainly, drinks. Mercury traditionally got the last libation.

In the evening, a procession would form which would often include musicians, clowns, town leaders and a hobby horse. The march, which was a processional dance, would have been to the highest available hill and there, the sacred Midsummer Fire would have been built. In building it, there were usually customs which it would have been felt necessary to observe. One custom: a sacred space would have been established for the fire. The four elements would likely have been consecrated and, for protections, taken around the circle. In their turn, deities would likely have been called and asked to give protection, and the classic system of Pythagoras, which was given and explained by Eugenius, had Lords of Fire at the East, Lords of Air at the South, Lords of Water at the West and Lords of Earth at the North.

It would have been usual to have a ritual for starting the fire. One custom, from Howard: bone was put on the wood before the fire was lit. To light the fire, a traditional method was by using an oak wheel and staff with birch tinder. Woods used for the fire would have included oak, as burning oak fed energy to the Sun. And the men, usually nine, selected to start the fire would have been considered worthy of the honour. There were usually gifts given to the fire and a usual gift would have been nine favoured herbs neatly tied with ribbons. A worthy maiden would have been selected to present the gift. As the fire burned, there would have been sunwise dancing, and this would have fed energy to the Sun. To honour Apollo, Tacitus said that men would dance sunwise, skyclad, around the fire; then, while music continued, others would join the dance. For blessings, people put stones on the tops of their heads, praised Fortuna, jumped over sacred fire, then threw the rocks into the fire. For ailing cattle, one custom, two four edged sticks would have been burnt with the fire. The ashes from the sticks would later have been mixed with spring water. With the rocks, the sticks and the gifts to the fire, omens would have been looked for in the way the fire burned.

As the dance continued; on trees, fire wheels might have been put to spinning; discs of fire, thrown from the hill; and certainly, burning wheels would have been sent rolling down the hill. Likely, drink would have been blessed and given out.

As the night got older, the darker forces would have been becoming more an influence. It was one of the few times Underworld beings could have been seen in this World. Snakes would have held conventions, would have copulated and rioted, and the toxins caused by that overflow of energy would have contaminated waters and caused other problems, but the smoke from the Midsummer fire would have purified the area and chased away malignant forces. And the smoke would have increased the strength of herbs. Women, to be cured of sterility, would have run naked through clumps of flowers. Hypericum could have been seen, its blossoms, bright like golden fires, as it would have been in communion with Spirits of Fire. Collected before Midsummer sunrise, the dew off hypericum would have been magical.

In late hours, some observed a custom of trance dancing around the fire. For this, people often invoked Artemis or the dark deities to aid in taking on the spirit of another life form. For this, dancers would put on paint, feathers, furs, tokens or other aids to transformation. Herbs were often used. Then, with action, sound, magical signs and visualization; dancers would manipulate the physical self. Through visualization, a landscape appropriate to a new self might have been created. A new form would have then been there: new ways of thinking, of feeling, of seeing. There would have been new desires, new motivations. There would have been different physical abilities, new ways to communicate. Random thoughts would have floated in, brought new experiences and with them, insight and wisdom. The dancer would gain a new spirituality, a way to unite with the Spirit of Nature. Then, the dancer, in form finding, might have discovered his or her totem, and so, new responsibilities. As Eisner has said, the discovered totem can present new taboos; as, for one, one could not eat or kill the totem. And the new learnings and feelings would have brought appreciations, responsibilities and joys. New ways of looking would see new beauty.

At dawn, there would have been a watch for the coming of the Sun: Hyperion, Helios, Apollo. That day would have been the Sun's glorious day of light. When he showed, there would have been the Sun's glorious day of light. When he showed, there would have been cheers and, likely, anthems would have been sung. Torches would likely have been lit in the sacred fire and, for blessings and protection, taken to grain fields and animal pens. The fire would have had a purifying effect and driven away illness and misfortune. And, said van Gennep, Midsummer fire was a protection against storms. Then, there would have been purification rites at the waters to counter the toxins from the rioting and copulating snakes.

The one who was Spirit of the new King Oak would certainly have been requested to bless the fields. He would likely have scattered ashes from the Midsummer fire and, likely, the torn up clothes from the old King Oak. And he would have made a sacrifice: perhaps, a frog. And that would have been buried in the field.

At this crucial time, all needed to go right. Omens were looked for. If a cuckoo sang, ill fortune or death would have been looked for.

So. In the center of Card III would be a floating Juggler and, above his hands, three golden balls. He would be wearing winged shoes and a winged helm. Beside him, his winged staff with two twisted snakes. Low to the rear would be a long, golden cloud. The sides of the card would hold thin, silvergrey columns. These, called Quicksilver, hold the Spirit of Mercury and this is thought to bring magical cures. As a substance, Quicksilver overlaps the bounds of a single element and relates to both the Sun and the Moon. It is used for measuring temperature and for repairing teeth. Cloud relates to Winds and the gold tinged, long island would be the land of the King of the Winds, Aeolus who, according to Vergilius, controls the struggling Winds and the roaring Storms. The island would be a land of joy and copulation, a land for the ever blowing Winds. It is the Hyperboreans' country, which is, as Fiske has informed us, the first to receive and the last to lose the light. From there, The Winds are instructed to blow their blessings. Said Boethius, Zephyrus, from the West, in plants revests freshness. And Eurus, from the East, would have brought in Flora with her Flowers. The cloud has been called a symbol for sex and would be related to fertilization. Aeolus chased cloud beings to controle weather. This, from Frazer.

Near the lower right corner of Card III would be the vase, Kantharos, and rising from it, a snake. This, a vessel of Wind and a vessel of Cures, is the Vessel of the Snake Goddess of Healing, Iaso. And it is a vessel for the dead. Three leaves would be in front of the vessel. Apollodorus told of a doctor who saw a snake use a plant to restore life; so, the doctor used the leaves of the plant to work magic.

Mercury, said Ogilvie, was associated with a vessel.

Above and to the left of the vessel would be a distant tree. Below the tree, in the foreground, would be a twig containing three oak leaves and in front of that, three acorns. The tree was thought to give protection and to gain this protection, one would knock on wood.

In the lower left corner would be the Jacinth. The Jacinth was often taken by the dead to the Underworld in order to insure an hospitable reception. It is a stone of the Underworld God, Hyacinthos, who relates to the growth and well being of vegetation. Mercury made the Jacinth the memorial stone for the warrior, Ajax. It banishes bewitchments and phantoms, protects against disease, injury and lightning, and it augments riches and, in its owner, encourages prudence. It protects the traveler. To warn of danger, it changes colour. The Jacinth holds the bright orange of sunlight. Orange, the colour of healing, stimulates creativity and enthusiasm and generates energy. At times it brings ambition and pride. At Midsummer, it is close to the Underworld.

The Juggler is over a field of daisies. Along the sides of the card would be ribwort, parsley, and chicory. The three golden balls above his hands show his relationship to the number three. Three is the number which locks in a charm or a system into a sacred triad: the three great bards, the three oldest animals, the three astronomers.

Three announces transition into life, into death: three hoots of an owl, three knocks, three howls of a dog. Three rings of a bell purifies the air.

Three is the force formed from three forces, set in a triad, which passes into life; then, into death. Three forms the triangle through the top of which knowledge is gained. There are three Fates. Three can form a trap; three wishes; the third, undue the benefits of the first two and put the wisher on the path to misfortune.

The number of the card, three, is the number of change. It relates to mental activity, to wisdom. It forms the Triangle, which Whewell called the Building Block of the Universe.

The Force of Life might move from Air, to Cloud, to Three Headed Snake, to Mercury with his Three Force Staff, as he is seen as the Juggler, the Cowherd who steals cows from Helios, who drives cows to milking, the tricky Shepherd who steals Helios' sheep. Mercury would be the Chief God of Air and of its aspects, including those of Wind. As he is the God of Communication, and the god who goes to the Underworld and from there, returns, he has been much used as a messenger. As a god tied into motion and change, he would be a cause in the shifts of great things and small. Mercury might be seen as the Juggler, his quick hands shifting things, setting traps. He might send messages, give choices in what to move. Messages might especially be looked for in Mercury's fields of special interest: transportation, communication, or health. If one, intending to go on a journey, stumbled on his doorstep; that might have been a message from Mercury. A wise man might have decided against the journey, or any other less than usual activities on that day. And often, he sends messages to do with health. He is seen as part of the healing pattern of the Heavens. The Spirit of Mercury, in the Planet of Mercury, joins with healing planets to increase healing power. The reverse would be true, according to Junius, with Mars or Saturn aspects. As one might witness in the Heavens, the Planet of Mercury makes quick changes. Mercury might, with the tip of his wand, make a change that would, like an orgasm, explode into a new thing. The Juggler, in keeping with his Snake form, relates to copulation and he gives gifts even to wrong doers. Inspired by the stars, he marries reason to speech, to the fluency of speech. But he can be tricky. And some of his tricks are dirty tricks. The Juggler is a playful, humourous conjurer, and with the humour, said E V Lucas, there is most often an element of cruelty.

A Transporter to the Underworld is the Juggler. He is tricky. He deals in illusion. His fires might be Ignis Fatuus. Many of the Juggler's activities relate to play.

> "Och! That a bachelor's sigh avails not
> For me to invoke the art of Melwas!
> The thief that by magic and illusion
> Took the fair one to the world's end:
> To the green wood that Juggler went,
> To the leafy rampart of a bough:
> And to climb aloft like him,
> That is what I could wish to do."
> D ab Edmwnt Trans. Sir John Rhys

IV ~ Crystal

The Crystal represents the concept of water: the Spirit of Water. It is the Sacred Well, the Sacred Spring, the Sacred Pool. The Crystal relates to the Underworld and gives a look at the Underworld of changed values, dream, fantasy, imagination, romance, intuition.

Of the deities relating to the Crystal, first of the important forces would be Juno. Juno is the Great Circles of Time. The circle of the Moon is included in her jurisdiction. She is the Spirit of the Female. She is Time measured by the Moon. Juno, through the Moon, regulates the cycles of life; especially, the menstrual and other life cycles of women. She presides over birth, betrothal, marriage and the woman's entering a new house. She presides over homemaking, acts as a guardian, but punishes women who neglect their duties. The doorposts of a new house are anointed in Juno's name.

Juno regulates death and rebirth. She celebrates the first sliver of the Moon. Beginnings to Juno are sacred. Then, as the Moon grows toward fullness, as the feminine principal grows toward full power, Juno becomes strong and warlike. And she is sometimes aggressive. In a time of trouble, when a king was slow in opening the Gates of Janus, which was the signal for starting a war, Juno descended from the sky and flung open the gates. That inflamed the people and the warriors rushed out to war.

Women can relate to Juno's cycle, flow with it; with it, gain power. The Dark Moon is the phase in which Juno sponsors new creation, new beginnings, gives them a greatly nurtured start. But regardless of the phase of the Moon, Juno sponsors beginnings. She oversees childbirth. As marriage is a beginning, many women, to honour Juno, marry in June. As fertility pleases Juno; grain, which inspires fertility, is thrown at brides. To flow with the Spirit of Juno, brides are given wedding rings, circles sacred to Juno. Juno supervises the bride's first undressing by her husband.

Juno supervises the circulation of money. Money relates to the circle and the cycles of the Moon. And Juno supervises the manufacture of money. Money was made in the Temple of Juno and that money, since silver is the sacred mental of the Moon, was made of silver. Juno supervises the use of money and is likely to chastise those who commit dishonest dealings with it. Offerings of silver coins are made to Juno and these, sometimes put in fountains. To bring good fortune, it is a custom to put a silver coin in the right shoe. As Juno relates to the water veil to the Underworld, she is looked to for knowledge of the future. She warns of coming dangers.

Sheep, geese and crabs are sacred to Juno. It is a custom to sacrifice white lambs to her. Sea nymphs are her shepherdesses.

As geese have a relationship with the underworld, they are looked for to give knowledge of the future. Geese flying over the Full Moon forecasts travel. Geese escort people to the World of the Dead.

A second force of the Time of the Crystal is Hera, the ox eyed goddess with the roaring voice. Hera has been called magnificent in form and feature. She, in her living, was thought to evolve from phase to phase; this cycle, divided into three. After Midsummer, she was renewed; her statues, taken to water and washed. Hera, in quarrels with other deities, could be difficult. She sent snakes of darkness to strangle Hercules. She is a force of great power.

Hera favours the Pomegranate, the Crab and the Cuckoo. King Crab was dangerous. Boethius spoke of his fiery eyes burning vegetation. Hera sent King Crab to attack Hercules. The Cuckoo is a bird of births and disastrous jokes. In order to seduce Hera, Jupiter took the form of a cuckoo. Kightly said that Hunting the Cuckoo was a wide spread April Fool ritual: the Fool was sent on a fool's mission. This related to being born, learning, then taking on a personality.

A goddess of the Time of the Crystal was the River Goddess Epona. As is true of the goddesses of a number of rivers, she is a goddess of wide authority. She had, beside a River form, a Mare form and a Woman form. Mac Cana said that she was served by three sets of horses, three to a set. She held an apple branch, which was her key to the Underworld. She is a protector of animals and a guardian of roads. She is a supervisor of kings and of horses; especially, the sexual well being of mares. In some places, a ritual expected of a king was that he copulate with Epona, carnated in Mare form. On a horse, said Mac Cana, it was usual to see her represented seated sideways, as horses were thought to eat off her lap. Epona was thought to favour warriors.

In the night, June twentythird, Artemis was honoured, celebrated in her Bear Aspect. The dark forces were summoned, and the celebration was called Buphonia. Around fires, women dressed as bears and acted out bear parts; so, merged with the Spirit World. Faces were darkened with charcoal. Euripides had Artemis and Iphegenia involved in human sacrifice. A man, to honour Artemis, was chased down and given to the Bear because of the dishonour a man had shown to Latona. Artemis, according to Aristophanes, required women to dress in bear skins, but as punishment for slaying the bears, they were required to go to rituals. Artemis had not only a Bear form, but, according to Lethbridge, also, a Mermaid form, and a Tree form. As a Mermaid, she was attended by nymphs and provided protection for ships. Pausanias said she gave protection to travelers and was petitioned for wealth and a happy old age. Callisto, a nymph, also had a Bear form. When in Bear form, she was chased by her hunter son, Arcas, who hadn't recognized her; so; Jupiter, turned Arcas also into a bear and gave them a place in the sky, so, avoided an unnatural fight; this, according to Hyginus. In Bear form, in rituals in the shadow of the falling Sun, Artemis and Callisto inspired copulation and slaying. It was said, the carnation of Hercules had his scrotum cut off. The rituals, said Snell, expressed a mystic creed and fervour.

The coming day was the time, especially for women, for honouring Hera. The celebration, called Heraeum, including cleaning and decorating Hera's alters and shrines and taking Hera's statues to the waters and washing them. In some years, the women held athletic contests. There were three age groups and winners in each. Each winner received an olive wreath crown and a statue representing herself placed on Hera's alter. Men observers were not permitted. At this time, for Hera, waters were, by ritual, purified. In this, herbs often used were lavender, spearmint and hyssop.

This was a time for decorating sacred wells. At times, on this day, water from a sacred well was taken by a woman, and she would have washed her underclothes in the water so that she could get a vision of her future lover. Pausanias said that once a year Hera went to a sacred well and drank its water.

June twentyseventh, Arretophoria, and also called Initium Aestatis, is a day which honours Aestas, who is called, by Pennick, the tutelary Goddess of Summertime. Also, with song and dance, sea nymphs were honoured.

July, said Manilius, was under the guardianship of Jupiter and Juno. Days on which special honours are given to Juno reflect her relationship to beginnings: March first, June first, July first and July seventh. July first was listed as a day for concerns with property and estates. Suetonius said it was a good day for renting houses and for moving into houses. It was then, offerings would have been made to Juno and a correct offering, said Livius, would have been, for Juno, silver.

July seventh was the feast of Caprotinae, and this was a royal festival for Jupiter and Juno. Ancestors and family would have been honoured and homes, appreciated. Juno would have overseen home and family relations and would have watched over any moves. Women, on this day, held bawdy feasts under fig trees, and these were called Wild Fig Day feasts. For the feasts, maidservants were dressed finely; then, afterward, had bawdy games and fights. Attention would have been given to honouring Juno. For her, said Ogilvie, a white lamb was an appropriate sacrifice. And her statues were decorated. It was thought, deities took concern with representations of themselves, said Villinganus. Furius Camillus said that a wooden statue of Juno was reported to have spoken with a human voice. When asked if it wished to be taken to Rome, said that it would. Care of statues was thought to aid deities.

July eleventh was called Panathenaea and was a day for honouring Athene, a defender of lands and homes. And she was associated with horses.

July twentythird was called Neptunalia. The day honoured Neptune and other deities of Water. Neptune was a King of Water in general. Whereas Poseidon seemed most concerned with salty seas and at times, squabbled with deities of fresh water, Neptune was, in spirit, a good part in fresh water. Both Neptune and Poseidon had the Spirit of the Horse, but Poseidon would have taken horse form more often than would Neptune. In copulation, the Horse was a form often used by Poseidon. Halliday said that Poseidon gave more knowledge of the future through horses than he did through his waters. At Neptunalia, Amphitrite and Salacia were among the deities honoured. Amphitrite cared for the animals of the sea. And Doris and Tethys were honoured. With Tethys, Waters were magical. Catullus said, a man was considered dirty if not even white headed Tethys could get him clean. At times Tethys was in Crow form. She was the ancient, shape shifting quality of Water, and the life giving quality of Water who had knowledge both forward and backward through Time. Water is magical. Dalyell said that to keep malicious forces off a person or object, as forces which might have been attracted when the object was praised, it was a custom to spit on the object in order to give it the protection which the Spirit of Water gives.

In the celebration of Neptunalia, Lord Ruadh said that arbours of boughs were erected.

The tree representing the Time of the Crystal would be the Willow. It is a Tree of the Moon and, especially, the Dark Moon, and Juno held it in great esteem. The Willow suggested melancholy, death and love. It is a tree of transformation and rebirth, and it has a relationship with Water. It floats in an atmosphere of fantasy, magic and dream. It relates to witchcraft, wickedness and wisdom; then, might protect against destructive forces. For separations and for ending relationships, willow is used, and it protects new beginnings. It could force confessions from transgressors. The Willow is used in mourning and in attracting new love. For the dead, for holding onto love, wreaths of willow would have been made. When love was away at sea, willow was used to keep it fresh and strong. Willow gives intuition and the power of deception. Willow wands were used in transformations, protections and healings. To protect boundaries, willow switches were used for beating the bounds, but striking a child with the switch, the child would have been in danger of withering away. It was said that unless they were needed for bringing down fevers, willow branches were not to be taken in the house. Willow baskets gave protection. And they were used, because of their sacred nature, to house sacrifices. People and animals have been given to the deities in willow cages. Willow whistles have been used to brew up storms. Willow baskets have been used for gaining the power of flight. Willow was used for cleanings and purifications. Switching with willow was thought to purify. Willow rods guarded against enchantments. For protection, they were wrapped around churns. Willow was worn to ward off storms. Willow wands were used for workings with the Moon. Willow is a bringer of dreams. It promotes music and, especially, that related to melancholy. Willow, at times, was used to gain knowledge of the future, and it was especially useful in gaining knowledge of love and death. With willow, one could be fooled; meaning, be different from what one thought a thing to be; as, some shift in the perceived shape of things. Willow can be dangerous. To burn it is insulting to the willow and so, dangerous. The Willow is strong and can be frightening in the night time. At night, it was said, willows could walk, and they could communicate with spirits from the Underworld. Willow was involved with shape shifting and used in shape shifting magic. Willow relates to travel. Willow baskets were used for transporting people on the sea and through the air: witness, the old lady who sailed in her basket nineteen times as high as the Moon. Magics which were done by shadow and mirror were sometimes aided by willow. Willow was used at funerals. It related to lost love and sad memory. Willow mourned the fall of Phaeton. Willow was used for charging crystals and for giving them healing powers. In rituals, willow was used in healing, in relieving sorrow, in love and in death. Under willows, witches worked their spells. Circe hanged suitors from the limbs of willows. Willows were planted in graveyards in sympathy with the dead and because of their relationship to rebirth. Willow was useful in healing bruises, sprains, strains, rheumatism, colic, gout, dyspepsia and most other pains. It was used in treating pulmonary problems, rheumatic fever and heart conditions. It encouraged the flow of urine. Willow baths were used for relieving tension and pains, and for purification. For relief from ague, people went silently, without crossing water, to a hollow willow, breathed three times into it, stopped up the hole; then, without looking back, went silently home. A willow wand protected Orpheus in the Realm of Hades. Willow ashes drove away snakes. The Willow had a relationship with the Bee. Ceram reported representations of willow and beech leaves on the crowns of ancient queens. Ovidius called the Willow a sacred tree and Rago said it was a sacred tree to poets; with, for poets, a protectress in each tree. Concepts of bent, supple, wisp, witch, tricky, wiley and wither relate to the Willow. Beside Juno; Diana, Selene, Belinus and Hecate have affection for the Willow.

Growing things; especially, members of the Vegetable Kingdom, have their development overseen by Juno. And, in the Time of the Crystal, a number of plants are recognized as having special values. First, the Lily. It is the flower which most symbolizes particularly the female. It symbolizes the female genital; so, relates to physical love. Juno, in her love, once copulated with a flower. The White Lily is the emblematic flower of Juno. The White Lily was said to have grown from Juno's milk, said Gerard. And he said, Juno's milk caused the white colour of the road across the sky.

The White Lily is honoured by many deities; Aphrodite, Easter and Mars among them. Lilies inspire nobility and purity; especially, the White Lily, which is a symbol for purity. And the White Lily suggests Death, and this might have led to the thought that it could bring Death. From Jacob

Grimm: "In a white lily bloom, brave boy, is they tomb."

As lilies relate to sorrow and sympathy, they have been often planted in cemeteries to comfort the dead.

There were other lilies, other than the White Lily, and each had its virtues, and those who honoured the White Lily would have extended honour to all lilies. And fairies might have had a special love for the Marigon Lily. Among virtues, lilies were calming and cooling, and they brought down swellings. They aided those who were bitten by snakes. They have countered poison and plague, and they have served as food. Leyel said that to fall while carrying lilies was to become liable to fits.

Like Juno, Diana was represented by the White Lily.

Another flower, Iris was considered, a great force. It represented coming into life: the force which through the root, through the stem, drove the flower. The three petals were the major forces which made up life. Representations of those petals formed the magical wand which was considered the Royal Scepter of Juno. Representations of this scepter have been carried by many of Earth's kings and queens. The Scepter held power and majesty and its three petals symbolized triads of the important virtues, such as wisdom, valour and faith. The Iris inspired those virtues.

The Iris is the Flower form of the Messenger Goddess: the Rainbow Goddess. And she, like the flower, is known as Iris. She is one of the few deities who could at will pass in and out of the Underworld, and she was a special friend to Juno, and to Hera. As the Rainbow, Iris was dangerous and powerful. In Rainbow form, she could be deadly. Deadly rainbows protected sacred areas.

Iris escorted people to the Underworld, so Iris' flowers were given to the dead to remind them of the kindness of Iris and of the protection from malicious spirits and spells which she gave. The goddess, bright and beautiful, moved quickly from place to place and even to the World of the Dead, to which she took water. Iris, also, said Ovidius, drew up water and fed it to the clouds, and she took water to where it was needed.

Iris was a goddess of power and majesty. Her many coloured coat, said Graves, was made of poison rainbow. She would whish people off to the Underworld. Iris was sometimes represented by a flame.

Iris, as an herb, was used for purifications. It was used for curing snake bites. Iris lotion was used for bringing affection, or love, and for dispelling anger. To improve vision, the lotion was put in the eyes. As a tonic, iris was used for cleaning the blood and to treat coughs, scrofula, fits, dropsy and gastrointestinal problems. For treating bruises and sores, the petals were used. R M Lucas said that the blue iris was used as a stimulant to the glandular system. Beads of iris root were carried as a charm, as they gave physical and spiritual protection. One custom, which Grieve reported, was to have barefoot women weed and care for gardens of iris.

Flax was honoured by Juno and held sacred, in part, because of its purity, which was enhanced by its growing among sacred trees: the sacred pear and the sacred apple. Flax protected against witchcraft. Cloths made from flax protected herbs which had been gathered, and ships were protected by sails of flax. Flax cords, to close out negativity, were used for binding sacred robes. As flax would banish impurities, it was made into cloth used for vestments and in shrines. Children of seven years were sent to dance in fields of flax so they would, by the flax, be made beautiful. Flax flowers were used for banishing negative energies and magics, and for bringing health and joy. For this, the flowers would have been gathered immediately after the dew had left them. Flax worked many cures, many of them which seemed magical. From the seeds, an oil was obtained which was used for ulcers and other gastrointestinal problems, for kidney troubles and for asthma. For external use, it was valued in treating rheumatism, swollen glands, burns, bruises, sprains and sores. The oil was also used for preserving wood and in consecrations. Also, flax was used for treating ailments in sheep, horses and cattle. In gardens, it protected other plants. It was planted in potato fields to protect potatoes. Flax was favoured by bees.

It was said, a child put naked on a field, then flax seeds sown on the child and on the field, the health of the child would be related to the growing plants in the field. Then Earth would see that the flax from the field was well used.

Juno had other herbs in her garden which she valued. In the garden, one could communicate with chervil, gain a feeling of the Otherworld. Chervil relates to the Cauldron.

Honeysuckle, an herb of the Moon, related to immortality and so, to the Underworld. It gave psychic awareness, brought sleep and inspired lustful dreams. It was a calming antispasmodic and it relieved nervous headache. A favourite of fairies, it dealt in illusion. It appreciated the past, so gave a feeling of security. It was used in treating colds, fevers and arthritis.

Quickinhand was found in wet places and it gave a healing lotion for the skin.

Herb teas were effective in the Time of the Crystal and under the Full Moon was considered to be the time best for making them; for capturing, as Gladstar has said, the mystical, enchanted energy of the night. Fresh herbs with flowers were placed in a crystal bowl and covered with pure water. The bowl was put where it would catch the moonlight. At dawn, thanks were given to the Moon, to the deities of the Water, to the deities of the Night and to the herbs.

The Red Rose was thought to symbolize growing things and Juno honoured it. Should a person have put a red rose on a new born baby girl; it is said, Juno would have made the girl beautiful.

Beside plant and animal, stone also came under Juno's rule. A stone favoured by Juno was the Moonstone, a stone with a colour and strength which waxed and waned with the Moon. For gaining fortune, love, predictions and other knowledge, a moonstone was put in the mouth when the Moon was full. Wrapped in yellow cloth, it aroused passion; and for strength, it was often kept wrapped in yellow cloth. Fernie said it had a reputation of being ominous. It related to dreams, visions, and invisibility.

The stone representing the concept of Water and its spiritual aspect is the Crystal Ball. It is symbolic of the nature of Water. It was the Sacred Globe of Juno, who was the Spirit of the Moon and the Night Sky. Jung said crystal might be called the Perfect Water. It would have represented the Sacred Spring. It was, as the Sacred Spring, a window to the Otherworld. The crystal ball related to the Otherworld and gave a vision of an Otherworld of changed values; fantasy, dream, intuition; and these, influenced, by direction from sources related to Juno, toward emotional response and this often included romance. Deities took pleasure in the crystal balls and granted wishes because of them. Through the crystal, they became divine guides. The crystals inspired confidence, poise and peace. From the crystals, people learned what was relevant and what was true. Crystals collected and focused scattered energies. They solved problems. They influenced temperament, so the user became a more efficient personality. Crystals, at times, brought thought into physical reality. They were used, Ridgeway said, for bringing rain or fire from the heavens, and for other weather spells, and for starting sacred fires.

People sent thoughts into crystal balls, and the crystal would drop them into the pool of what was already held within it. Desires sent into crystals could have gotten energized; thought, brought into physical reality. Used correctly, it was thought, crystals had served as powerful aids. They have served as guides and have been used by gazers to bend others to the gazer's will. Crystals were used, mostly, for gaining knowledge and understanding. People gazed at crystals, then were beyond, into a distance; the crystal, out of their minds. In that distance would have been visions; perhaps, of a moonlit Otherworld. Crystals were known to be dangerous. Shadows of doubt, crystals would magnify and distort, and crystals created mirage and illusion. Visions were often vague, but deities, delighted with the brightness of crystals, would often have been helpful and would have granted wishes.

In the use of the crystal ball, the usual method was not to look at the Moon, or at the other source of light. The crystals were at their best when they were used in moonlight. It was not to see the Moon, but to know the source of light was there. And not to have the crystal the object of direct inspection, but one would have usually looked beyond it, so that objects would have slid into one's knowing below the focus of consciousness.

The Crystal would also, as a symbol, have had an influence. Symbols, as the suggestive shadows in the globe, would have slid their teachings into the sub strata of what was known. Looking directly at the symbol, one might have thought on the form and its meanings, but all the while, out of the observer's eye, he might have glimpsed meanings which would not have been gained by the hard look focused straight ahead. The straight look would have given the more limited information. The space looked at would form and reform like clouds in the sky. Meaning is caught from the thing in motion. Nothing is still. Nothing is in a vacuum. Relationships are in continuous change.

Shapes suggested by the crystal would have, as would those from the symbol, an Otherworld relationship, as they would not be located in this World. Seen as someplace beyond, like reflections of clouds on a pool, but less in a place, would be the images from the crystal, would be the host of thoughts and related shapes, and they might be little related to a central image or its associations. Crystals, like symbols, would have been unpredictable. They might have given an unexpected secret: a serendipity.

Cut crystals were also considered, powerful and were honoured by the deities. These, also, had a relationship with Water. At times, they were put in water to make healing infusions. And they were used much in healng and in bringing sleep and dream. Cut crystal held qualities of water, including those that were magical, and in some places it was called water stone. Crystal related to births, deaths, ends and beginnings. Crystals were valued for magical work, and have been generally treated with respect.

It was thought, crystals were best when they had not been bought or sold. To clear away negative energies, they were washed in a brook. To energize crystals, they were left overnight in a garden under the Waxing Moon; then, before dawn, covered with a black cloth. To purify crystals, they were left three weeks buried in a grave, or were buried in sea salt.

Also, the Spirit of the Sacred Spring would have been in mirrors. Mirrors and crystals would have been actors in what Dionysius called the Pythagorean Cyclic Order of the Universe. To take part in a cyclic action, one would have used part of him or herself which would have existed beyond the physical. Mirrors would have been windows to the Underworld, and they would have held the Spirit of the Moon, and this would have tied them to the Circles of the Moon and so, to all circles. They would have had a part in the rapture and magic which other circles contained; except that mirrors were the widdershins to other circles' sunwise motion. They were the left to other circle's right and, as Jung has said, would relate to the unconscious.

Mirrors, as they related to the unknown, to dark places in the unconscious and to obscure places in worlds beyond this world; have been looked on with dread and so, have gained dark powers. Through the window of the mirror, one looked into the unconscious, which was, in the realm of Hades, below the water of the Spring. Frazer said that to dream of seeing one's face reflected in water was an omen of death. Lethbridge said that seeing the Moon's face reversed in a mirror would have gotten the viewer strangled. To break a mirror was said to have brought seven years of bad luck.

Bozwa said that mirrors, as they related to springs, were used as if they were crystals. E. M. Butler said that mirrors and crystals were used for binding spirit forces. One binding she listed: the mirror was buried over a dead man's face; then, buried at a crossroad; then, on a Sunday, put on an alter and left there for three weeks. A dog or cat, after the mirror had been charged, needed to have looked in it before it would have again been safe.

Mirrors were used with sacred waters in order to learn of the future. Pausanias told of one oracle where the mirror touched the well water. The questioner, after praying, looked in the mirror for knowledge. Bringsvaerd said, when a mermaid held her mirror, she was said to have spoken with an oracular voice.

The Mirror, said Firmicus, was a tool of Juno which she used in the slaying of Bacchus. With it, she tied his Circle of Life to a Circle of Death. As Beyerl has said, Life and Death are both circles. Mystic associations which mirrors had were made use of by other deities also. Venus had a mirror. Medusa was slain by a mirrored image. The Mirror, the mirrored image, the Spring, equated with the aspect of Water which caused quick change, or which brought quick change; as, the drop through the Water Veil. Objects have seemed unstable in water. Water deities have frequently changed form. As a balance, water also gives protection to forms. People would put a water barrier between themselves and malicious physical and spiritual forces. Spirits would have been stopped by a body of water. If an item had been praised, it was a custom to spit on it as protection from malicious forces, which might have been attracted by the praise. People have made use of water barriers. These they have put between themselves and harm from the Spirit World. A ghost might have followed someone as far as to the brook which he or she could not cross. And Fiske said that brooks not only were boundaries which ghosts could not go beyond, they could wash ghosts off of people. As water protected and gave blessings, often people have been anointed with water.

The Essence of Juno as the Mirror, or as the Crystal, which served as the Sacred Spring, made of her, the Way to the Otherworld. She was the Cup, the Cauldron of Life and Death. Her Cauldron was sometimes called the Cauldron of the Ruler of the Deep. As Rhys has said, deities of the Moon often owned Cauldrons. Cauldrons, Spence said, received the dead and prepared them for rebirth. The Cauldron was the Sacred Cup which hovered over a round table; which R S Loomis called the magic talisman of plenty which held the property of discrimination. And the gold mounted skulls held Juno's spirit, the skulls which, according to Titus Livius, were used for drinking cups. Juno was the Spirit of the Cup which held All Waters.

The Circle of the Cup related to the Circle of the Moon, to Moon Cycles. Moon Circles correlated with menstrual cycles which were used in connection with magic relating to emotion and perspective. These circles related to circles in general. To be tied into any circle was thought to involve risks. Clodd said that there was a custom, never to completely clear a table, so as not to complete a circle of having food. The circle, with its ends and beginnings, would have a unity with the Underworld. The Underworld, the Mirror, the Spirit of Juno, would hold resolution to circles. Through the window of the Mirror, the Crystal, one looked into the Underworld, which held the Land of the Unconscious, which was in the Realm of Hades, below the water of the Spring, which was a vast sea, one held in the ship of Juno.

For the Time of the Crystal, vision might be influenced by Juno, might touch on one or more of her areas of presence. Juno relates to Time measured by the Moon. Through the Moon, Juno regulates the circles of life; especially, the menstrual and other life cycles of women. Juno is in the Spirit of the Female. Juno has to do with money and the sacredness given to monetary dealings. This would relate especially to silver. In silver's relations to impurities, it could cause troubled visions. But one might see the coming of riches. Juno has to do with birth. One might see her gift of help in birthing. Juno is interested in family and heritage and these relate to rhythms of the Moon. Juno relates to cleanliness and purity. Impure people washing at springs have caused springs to withhold utility. Juno's waters must be kept pure. In her relation to birth, that meaning might be Juno's Spirit with a housewife in labour; or, it might be in a thing quite vast which would have an effect on a great body of people. Juno might inspire a great poet, such as she did with Vergilius, to take the lead in a spiritual awakening, bring unity to conscious and hidden.

The Time of the Crystal is subject to big swings in mood. This is a characteristic of the Moon, of the Sea. It might be from mad frenzy to a dreamy moonlit pool. Visions from the crystal might be troubled. Under a Strong Sun Moon there could be unsettling swings up and down. And the Sea gives and it takes away. Petronius said that born under the Crab, one had a good chance of acquiring wealth on land and sea.

On the Card of the Crystal, a garden of lilies; the flowers, pure white. On the far left, in the garden, dark blue iris. The lilies represent purity. The Lily is the Female Genital. It represents the resolution of forces. It is the Emblem of Juno.

From the lilies would rise a white pedestal on which would rest a crystal globe. The crystal represents Water, the Sacred Veil between the Worlds, where there is a coming together of the four elements, which forms the Sacred Cross. The crystal represents the Sacred Spring, and springs and pools everywhere, all of which have their sacred aspects, so should be treated with respect. Digging a hole, pouring water into it, stirring it around with a finger, might cause a storm, as the pool might have taken a sacred aspect.

In each bottom corner would be hyssop.

Beyond the crystal globe would be a dark sky over water. In the sky, behind a willow branch, would be the Full Moon. In the distance, below and left of the Moon, would be a goose in flight. At the bottom of the card, left of center, would be a crab to represent the King Crab whom Hera had to bite Hercules. On the right of the card, the willow and the Moon.

In the sky, but not seen on the card, would be the Argo, and, also, the Small Dog. The Argo was built so that Jason could steal the Golden Fleece, which was sacred to Apollo. The Argo was built from one of the Oaks of the Dodona Oracle, which was the Oracle of Dione, Daughter of the Ocean and Goddess of the Night Sky and the Moon. Many heroes rode with Jason and these included Castor and Pollux and Theseus. And Hercules rode long enough to get the voyage underway, but then left to attend to other things. For the warriors, it was a sad voyage, but for Jason, Medea did steal the fleece from her father, but paid a price; she caused the death of her brother; then, later, slew her own children. Medea was a powerful witch, but the Argo brought her misery. The Argo is an unhappy ship.

The Small Dog, a favourite of Diana, is magical and tricky. He is a bit of a wild card.

The power of the Time of the Crystal is from the Circle. In foretelling, on the first Monday of the quarter before sunrise, eyes closed, barefoot and fasting, the questor circled sunwise his house. When he reached again his door, he made a circle of his finger and thumb. He opened his eye looking through it, looked for omens. Crossed straws, a good omen. A woman standing, not good: from Spence.

The number of the Crystal is four, the number of creation and stability.

The major force of the Time of the Crystal would be Juno. She is a guardian, a protectress. But Juno has her rules. One should not rock an empty cradle.

V ~ Lion

The Lion represents the high point of the element, Fire. Fire can be represented by the lion headed, fire breathing goddess, Lamasthu. Barnes said the Guardian of the Sign of Leo was the Fire Lion God, Lamas. This would have been the Nemean Lion who flooded the East with hot fire, who burned the hills along the eastern horizon, who rose in the East above a wide expanse of fire. Lamasthu would have been Lampetia, Daughter of the Sun, a goddess who brought pain and misery; especially, to those who did not honour her. And to most plants, she was said not to be a friend. As the Lion was dangerous, amulets relating to the Lion were worn for protection. Rulandus said that lynx toenails were worn as a charm against epilepsy. According to Sextus Placitus, to be rid of apparitions, people ate lion flesh.

A great influence in the Sun's high season is the Sun God, who, especially at this season, is often thought of as Lugus. Lugus rose to the position of first in authority and one reason was that he could do so many things which a society needed. Lugus, in spite of having great strength, does not win every battle; but, at times, must return to the battlefield for his victory. His births are filled with risk and his preparations for his duties as the Sun, filled with difficulties. From his far between defeats, he returns in glorious triumph. In some areas, for the production of life, he is honoured over all other deities. Ladies of the Land depend upon his copulation. Said Aeschylus, the forces of the Bright Sky love to penetrate Earth and Earth aspires to that union. Lugus' Spear was called, said Fairbanks, an agricultural tool of fertilization. Superhot, it must be kept standing in a cauldron.

As is usual with Sun Gods, Lugus is a harper and, as with Sun Gods, his music is magical. Lugus' music, said Rutherford, could bring tears, laughter, and sleep.

Lugus is Light: The return of Lugus, the return of Light, Lugus, as the Sun, holds the Sacred Seat of Fire, is the shaft of Fire.

Lugus was sometimes known as Lucryn.

The major force in the high Time of Fire would be Jupiter, who was also known as Zeus, and as Zeus Pater. Zeus means Sky and Day. Jupiter went from a god who was in charge of the weather to a ruler over all forces. Tertullianus said that Jupiter became All Things and the virtual Fate. Jupiter was the chief Giver of Gifts and the Overseer of Justice. To make that point clear, he carried a fist full of thunderbolts. Libanius said that no one was so rash as to oppose Zeus. The rule of Zeus, said Pausanias, seemed limitless, extending even over the Underworld. Fairbanks said that Zeus was considered, chief ruler over the Ocean and was called, God of Sailors. Seymour said that Zeus, displeased that Poseidon claimed to be Lord of the Ocean over Zeus, gave him a year's worth of tasks to do. Herodotus said, people looked to Zeus as to a great father. Aratus said that always, people had a need of Zeus, of his kindness and inspiration. He woke men, reminding them of livelihood. He gave favourable signs for men's activities. He set signs in the Heavens and will continue to teach man how to read signs of things to come.

Pausanias said that Zeus had a high regard for honesty. Athletes who had cheated, to penalize themselves because of a displeased Zeus, would pay for statues to be made to honour Zeus. Zeus considered it a virtue to be charitable, said Lucius Apuleius. When people received a stranger, said Hocart, they were often so certain Zeus was present, they would pour a libation to him. And Zeus, said Pausanias, was thought to have pity on the down trodden. Reckford said that to harmonize with Zeus, victors in contests were charitable to those who lost.

When Zeus was Lord of All, Fiske said that it was largely forgotten that he had been the Sky God who sent rain, but people still recalled his special interest in the weather and people would often say, "Rain, rain dear Zeus."

And Horatious said that his thunder confirmed the belief that he is Lord of Heaven.

As an enforcer of justice and protector of balance, lightning and thunder could be convincing. Tacitus said that Jupiter, by lightning, struck down a general who had just won a series of battles so that he seemed almost godlike. MacManus told of a king struck by lightning shortly after he had broken an oath he had sworn on the Sun, Moon and Stars.

When a representation of Zeus was struck by lightning, Pausanias said it was obvious Zeus didn't like it; so, a larger, grander representation was made.

Jupiter was thought, also, to have sent stones crashing down out of the Sky and these, called Thunderstones, were thought, magical and to hold the power of lightning. One such shower, said Livius, was reported to have fallen at Eretum. Windle said that a thunderstone was kept in Jupiter's temple and used on sacrifices, and people prayed that should they become unworthy, that they be struck with a thunderstone. To solemnize important treaties, the sacrifice was slain with a thunderstone, said Windle. As a usual sacrifice, a pig was slain by the thunderstone to put the treaty under the sponsorship of Jupiter. Then, for prophetic dreams, people would stand on the skin of the animal sacrificed to Jupiter. In this way, said Talbot, they would get purified before sleep. To get revelations from these dreams, Halliday said that Epimenides slept for forty days.

As powerful as Jupiter was, he was not considered, all powerful, but depended on the correct functioning of the system and the support of the other deities. There had been disputes with other deities. Belinus and Saturn had rebelled and Europa had to be subdued. He had lost a battle with Typhon, then needed Mercury to put him back together so that he, Jupiter, could fight Typhon again. When a number of the deities threatened to revolt, he needed the support of the Sea Goddess, Tethys, in order to stabilize the situation, to get the deities back in line. And the memory remained, said Gomme, that he had once been weak, had been fed the life giving sap of the Ash. But Jupiter is the Great High Sky. Still, said Vergilius, Jupiter admitted he couldn't change prophecy, but only show displeasure with it by shaking his thunder. Ovidius also said Jupiter admitted needing to follow destiny. But still, people said, "By Jove."

Pausanias said Zeus was often pictured with a lion and an eagle. The eagle seen with Zeus would have been the Eagle King, Aquila, who was most wise and, in ancient times, flew into the sky to announce the Sun. Aquila was Zeus' armour and arms bearer. Armed conflicts were said to have been announced by eagles and pairs of eagles would be seen where armies were to camp. A shriek from an eagle was considered, a message from Zeus. Eagles were said to favour smiths.

Armstrong said, the Wren was associated with Zeus and was often seen represented in Zeus' temples.

The Ash is a tree which represented the Time of the Lion. It gave the sap which was said to have been Zeus' first food. Ash sap has been considered a powerful food, considered to give strength, to give protection from malicious creatures and other forces, and to cure major and minor ailments, and these included cancer, rheumatism and gout. And it expelled harmful and unwanted energies. Ash was considered, a mighty chieftain and, with charms, was requested for blessings and cures.

By charms, strength was tied to the leafing of the Ash. Love was tied to an even leafed ash stem. For a hernia cure, an ash was split, the ill person passed through the split; then, the split was bound together and as the ash grew together, the ill person healed. There were charms for the Ash to get rid of warts, to chase away the evil eye and to break spells. To be rid of warts, pins were stuck in an ash, removed and stuck in the wart, removed and stuck back in the ash while a charm was being said. For love, an even leafed ash twig was taken; then, while a charm was being said, the woman passed the twig from a bare hand to a gloved hand; then, put the twig in next to her bare breasts. For some blessings, a hole was made in an ash, the request made, the gift of a shrew put in the hole and the hole plugged up. It was said, snakes avoided even the shadow of an ash. To get protection from snakes, the area to be protected was inscribed with an ash staff. For protection from the Spirit of the Ash, ash staffs and ash milk pails were used. Fiske said that ash rods were used for curing cattle and sheep. For protection from malicious beings and spirits, ash keys were carried. Ash stimulated the blood.

The Ash related to communication. It gave meanings to shapes and the mysterious shapes could be found on the trunk of the Ash.

The extension of the Ash served as a Pole of the Universe. However, the tree standing in the way between the worlds would have been the Apple, which was named Thuban. The shifting of Thuban, as Worthen has said, left the hole which needed to be guarded by the Snake.

A number of flowers relate to the forces at the top of the summer. The list would include the Dandelion, the Agrimony, the Marigold, the Rue, the Borage, the Burnet, the Rockrose, the Columbine, the Churnstaff and the Rose.

A flower favoured by Jupiter, and by many other deities also, would have been the Rose. The Rose, as a symbol, would have stood for the Flower as a concept, would have stood for all blooming things. The Rose, representing the Flower, presents the essential element of love and states that copulation is an integral and inseparable ingredient of it. Love, represented by Cupid, is held responsible for the birth of the Rose. It was said; Cupid, when carrying a cup of nectar, slipped and spilled the nectar which, on Earth, turned into the Rose. Venus put thorns on the Rose. Cupid shot it with an arrow, which turned it red. The Red Rose brought the fire of love. The Rose inspired lust and required truth, chastity of the spirit and purity. The Rose is the symbol of the secret nature of love, and of secrecy in general. It is the symbol of the secret. Roses have been given out at banquets and at conferences to remind those attending that the things said and done there were to be kept secret. Meetings have been held in rose gardens so that the roses would suggest and inspire secrecy. Queens and kings have worn roses to indicate to, or to remind, those whom they were with, not to repeat that which they heard.

Deities, especially Venus, were said to protect the secrecy of the Rose. The Rose has been carved on tombstones and over doorways to inspire secrecy and silence. Venus covered the body of the fallen Hector with perfume of the Rose. Zephyr favoured the Rose. Ship sails have been so perfumed with rose that the Winds have grown love sick. Said Albertus, Rose was used in returning life to a sick pearl.

Suetonius said that not only were roses used in banquet halls, but that guests slept on beds covered with roses.

Roses were used in love potions and in magical medications. People ate roses to break bewitchments. It was said, if a rose picked Midsummer, wrapped in pure white paper, if it kept its true colour until Christmas, the pickers love would have been true. But it would have been necessary for the picker, after picking the rose, to have carried it walking backward to the place where it was to be stored. Roses have proved to be dangerous. Charms whispered to roses have brought deaths. The aroma of roses was a powerful medication. It aided memory, eased stress, aided skin, stimulated romance, solved problems with reproduction and conception and chased apathy.

The Dandelion, the Tooth of the Lion, suggests the rays of the Sun. It has been called the fairy clock because of the regularity of its opening and closing. Dandelions have been found useful for making daily living predictions. In clear weather, if dandelion seeds would suddenly puff away, a storm would have been forecast. To answer the question as to if one was wanted in the house, one might blow three times on a dandelion in seed. If, after three blows, any seeds were left, one was. If dandelions were blooming in April, a hot, wet summer was predicted. Dandelions gathered at Beltane protect against witchcraft.

Dandelions, like the Sun, cleaned, purified and opened ways. They cleaned the blood, liver, gall and spleen. They removed obstructions, including urinary blockage and stones. A number of ailments have been cured by the Dandelion: scrofula, scurvy, dyspepsia, dropsy, rheumatism, jaundice, ague and gout. The Dandelion, by bringing good health, chased away many ailments. For health, Dandelion root has been chewed. Bartram said it cured the infirm bladder. Hecate was said to have served dandelion greens to Theseus, who was a Sun hero. Fernie called dandelions a great cure for kidney problems. Dandelions clear sight.

The Marigold, which tracked the Sun, was called the emblem of the Sun. And it opened in response to the Sun's brightness. As it had the special blessing of Helius, it had a special power as a love charm. For strengthening love bonds, marigolds were planted where a lover's shadow had fallen. To keep a love from straying, soil was dug from under a lover's footprint, put in a pot, and marigold seeds set on it. Marigold was put in potions designed to create lust. In some potions, it was mixed with rosemary. To keep milk from being stolen by fairies, wreaths of marigolds were put around the necks of the cows. Also, marigolds were used to detect thieves, as Leyel has said. Marigolds gathered in Leo and wrapped, each with a dog's tooth, in bay leaves; if a thing had been stolen from the man with the dog tooth charm, he had but to put the charm under his pillow and sleep on it to see the thief. Put in a sacred place, if a woman untrue to her mate had entered, she would not have been able to leave until the charm had permitted her to depart. The charm would have kept the bearer from being spoken ill of unless the speaker was speaking words of peace.

Marigolds, by facing the Sun, gained power from their lord. They cleared the air of ailments and promoted sleep. It was said, to look at marigolds would draw malicious humors out of the head and strengthen eyesight. The aroma from them would have cured sores and skin disorders. And marigolds eased fevers and guarded against the evil eye. As a lotion, marigold was used for ailing eyes and to ease fevers, it was rubbed over the heart, and it was used to relieve swellings. Marigolds were used to treat headache, jaundice and ague, and to strengthen the heart. Some agues were treated by, each day, taking seven marigold seeds with wine. In soup, marigolds brought good health and vigour.

Marigolds have been used in predicting the weather. If they were open in the morning, they predicted the weather would stay dry. If they had remained closed, it was said, one should have expected rain.

At night, marigolds would have been seen flashing in the dark, lit with their own lights.

The Columbine was an herb favoured by Jupiter. It was the saucy harlequin who inspired infidelity. A man finding a columbine might have suspected infidelity of his mate. The Lion and the Eagle favoured it and it was called food of the Lion. The Columbine had a virtue of bringing women in labour a speedy childbirth. Also, as an opener of ways, it opened obstructions in the liver and helped those with stones in the kidneys. It was used to treat sores in the mouth and throat and to treat jaundice. It was, to get courage, rubbed on the hands. That, from Apuleius Platonicus.

A dangerous herb of the Time of the Lion was Sun Spurge, also called Churnstaff. It was called the Sun Gazer, and it was used to drive away fistulaes, carbuncles and warts. It was sometimes used as a purge; but, being violent, that often caused injury. Apollonius of Tyana listed it as one of the herbs used in magic.

Pausanias said that sacrifices to Zeus were burned with white poplar. White Poplar was favoured by Zeus.

The stone of the Time of the Lion would be the Diamond, the King of Stones. It represented the Sun, and the head of the shaft of the Sun. It was a Thunderstone. Relating to lightning, it gave strength and fearlessness to its wearer, but, even to its wearer, it could be deadly. In a diamond, a red spot brought death and often, it was death to its wearer. The Diamond drove away night spirits and guarded against insanity. Its strength was enhanced when it was set in gold, as gold is the royal metal. Gold was a gift from the Sun.

For the Time of the Lion; the Lion, the Spirit of Fire, would move onto the stage with heat. In that time, Furina held a special place: the first festival of the Time of the Lion. As she, as Goddess of the Furies, was named patroness of one of the Twelve Roman Orders of Priests, she was honoured with a feast: July twentyfifth, Furrinalia. This day, as a request for rain, magistrates wearing no official robes or insignia, went to a spring, poured water on a flint. Perhaps Furina was a fire being who watched for wrong doers. For libations to the Goddess of the Furies; these, said Callimachus, should be something other than wine.

August first was the celebration of the wedding of Lugus, Lord of the Sun, to the Lady of the Land. This was the high point and glory of the Summer and everyone who was able was expected to take part in the celebration. It was a custom for people to go to the places where the lords of the lands were holding their courts. For the celebration, it was a custom to be well dressed and anyone who had borrowed a thing which the lender might have needed for the celebration, good manners required that it be returned in time for the lender to be able to fit it into his celebration plans. Craftsmen displayed their best work and entertainers, musicians and bards, planned to be in best form. Dramas displaying acts of the deities were presented, King Goat was crowned and a feast held in his honour. Feasts symbolized, and were considered, gifts of the deities. Laws and official business was given consideration it was due and there was a King's Peace: all persons were required to be respecting it. At night, sacred fires were built on high hills and the first fruits of harvest, which represented the Harvest Goddess; in some areas, known as Tailtu; was given to Lugus.

August second, called Lammas Morrow, would feature the funeral games for the Harvest Goddess. First fruits of the harvest were made into loaves and eaten in rituals honouring the Goddess. Lamas, the Lion Spirit of Fire, would have been the chief force honoured. The Spirit of Fire would also have been known as Leo the Lion.

The Games were a sacred ritual and well done, they would have increased the yield of grain, fish, fruit and milk. With the Games, there were sales tents and entertainments; some, bawdy, as the mighty Lugus' copulation was a major event. And the Games would have inspired and lent strength to Lugus in copulation as in all else. Copulation related to heat and to fire. It produced heat. Lugus, as dramas illustrated, on rays of light, came down from the Sky in a silver boat to copulate with the Lady of the Land. In drama and song, it was not forgotten that Lugus entered every gate because he was the master of all crafts.

The Lamas festivals highlighted the importance of leaders and laws, the glory and durability at the top. The festivals demonstrated that quality was recognized and that a place was made for it. It was pointed out that other leaders insisted that Lugus take his rightful place at the top.

Kings, it was thought, were favoured by deities and deities let it be known to the public that the Kings were favoured and then, when they were not. Giraldus said that as the deities favoured Julius Caesar, they were quick to inform the citizens of his victories. Then, after the leader's deaths, as they had been by the deities selected to lead, they were, by many, expected to continue to supply leadership. Said Nettleship, after Julius Caesar's death, prayers to him continued to be said and people still expected him to supply leadership. Julius Caesar had dreamed he was up among the stars, the clouds beneath his feet. Apelles showed Alexander the Great, after Alexander's death, conferring with the gods. When he was emperor, Alexander celebrated the Lammas Festival at the City of

Lyons. Skene said that King Dathi, after he had been slain, was carried to battle after battle and as a dead body, was said to have won nineteen of them.

Another deity honoured at the Lammas Festivals was the horned god. He certainly would have represented a defeated Sun God. Murray said that there was no suggestion that he was ever a sacrificed divine king. He was a King God, or King Puck. Puck would equate with Bog. In the religion of the old peoples, such as were in Tuscany and Sumaria, there was a rivalry between the Lion Deity and a Horned Deity. It could be found in backwoods areas where the more primitive deities could never die out. In urban areas the old deities persisted, but became demonic. The Chimaera had the head of a lion and the head of a goat, plus the head of a snake.

At Lammas, King Puck was crowned and rode at the head of a parade, and during the festival, he was treated like a king. At the end of the festival, he was returned to the wilds. The horned deity belonged to more primitive times, but horns continued to be respected as a sign of divinity. They related to the Otherworld and, goats especially, were friends of the Fairy Kingdom. King Pucks' parade suggested Fairyland. King Puck was asked to bestow blessings and was given credit for many good outcomes and that included military victories.

During the festival, omens were looked for. A goose carrying a straw was said to have predicted late summer storms. A fog would have meant a cold and snowy winter. A red Moon would have predicted coming wind; a pale Moon, coming rain.

August thirteenth was called Nemoralia and, according to Cooper, honoured not only Diana, but the Sun Gods, as there was a parade featuring two huge Sun Giants; one on a black horse; the other, on a white. There were vegetation rituals and, at night, for women, torchlight marches to Diana's groves where there were hair washing rituals and other ceremonies. Diana related to the bright Moon, the dark Night Sky, and the darkness of witchcraft. She regulated Circles of the Moon and Great Circles of Life.

August nineteenth was Vinalia Rustica, which was also called Vinaliurum. The festival especially honoured Jupiter, Venus and Bacchus; but, said Macrobius, it was more a sacred feast for Jupiter than for the others, as this was his high season and he was the Great Spirit of the Sky that inspired all living things.

Grapes were the fruit especially related to Venus; so, on this day, especially, she was asked for blessing and rituals were done to encourage the Grape. Venus, the Spirit of Love, was a protectress of vegetation and, especially, of gardens. Another fruit related particularly to Venus was the Apple. The Apple sits on the way to the Otherworld and holds within it, the Sacred Pentacle, the symbol for Mankind, and especially, the Female. It was the sacred symbol of Athene, of Ariadne and of all other Star Goddesses. The five pointed star represented the five organs of sense and the five organs of action, which are the foot, the hand, the tongue, the genitals and the anus. The Apple, which held the Sacred Star, was the key to the Underworld. Venus' sacred number was fifteen and at times she was represented by the number, Fifteen. Rising through the Water Veil, she would have held three apples, or been blessed with the spirit of three apples, as they would have been the Three Spirits which form Life.

The Star, or Pentacle, represented the head, legs and arms of the human: the female more than the male, because, to get the male, there would be an addition. In biology, the generic human is female. Before birth, an addition would be made to get the male. The Star represented the Goddess of Death and was a window to the Underworld.

As five, as a number, is odd, it would have the male stability which other odd numbers would have. Female numbers beyond two would hold the abyss in their centers.

Jupiter held the stability of the male and the organization of numbers. His oracle was at the zero spot where neither man nor animal cast a shadow, according to Pausanias. According to Iamblichos, Pythagoras held that the eternal essence of number was the providential principle of the Universe. As all was an organization of numbers, Pythagoras was able to know many secrets of past and future. The element of Fire held the logic of number and Jupiter at times appeared as a symbol of Fire.

The celebration of Vinalia was joyful and bawdy and designed to fill the five senses with pleasure. As wine had fiery spirits in it, Jupiter took a special interest. And during the festival, the deities gave gifts beyond what people seemed to be able to wisely use. On logs of poplar, sacrifices were made to Jupiter, and on the fires, for sacrifices to the deities, flowers were given so that the air was perfumed. One list of flowers chosen had on it, chervil, thyme, fennel, chamomile, pennyroyal, geranium and rue.

Rituals were done for many deities. To the Goat Goddess, offerings were made so that she would continue to be a protective deity, and that she herself would not disturb the vines.

August twentieth, Zakynthos, celebrated the death of Bacchus, God of the Vine, – and of vegetation in general. Bacchus brought joy and freedom from toil. At its peak, this was the destructive and deadly frenzy. One might have romanticized and wished to be part of the love; related, as it was, to the mad death; but one would have paid a price if one had been put on that path. The force of Bacchus gave instant pleasure, unfettered love and freedom. But the price for this was often pain and death. Bacchus inspired dream and his oracles gave prophetic dream. Iamblichos said, Bacchus served under Saturn. Bacchus was associated with the Thyrsus, a staff wound with ivy and grape vine and topped with a pine cone, and it related, said Pausanias, to rebirth.

The celebration of Zakynthos included the selection of the animal, a goat or a bull, to take on the Spirit of Bacchus, then to be sacrificed. The selection of the animal was made by priests who were directed by Bacchus himself, as the animal was to become himself.

The selection the Animal, which was Bacchus, was given a procession to the Temple of Bacchus, which Pausanias said might be little more than a circle of crude stones. A Bacchus' procession has been described by Westrupp: priests marched in phallus hats; and these, followed by marchers with ivy wrapped, phallus tipped poles; then, thyrsus bearers, marchers with winnowing fans, torch bearers, flute players; then, marchers carrying baskets of fruit, jugs of wine, baskets of flowers. Bacchus was said to favour roses and black bryony and white bryony.

Nutt said that processions to honour Bacchus were a big part of his celebration. Nutt had the procession led by a piper; the piper, followed by singing women, each, with a puppet which had a huge phallus; these, followed by men with jugs of wine or baskets of fruit; these, decorated with ivy and violets. Behind these were men with the goat, then a man riding an ass.

The remade Bacchus would have been in bright ribbons with, as Tibullus pictured him, clusters of grapes hanging from his horns.

In the procession, the Phallus had a place of honour. Iamblichos said that the representation of a phallus, consecrated, came near to being a deity.

In the temple, the sacrificial Bacchus would have been given a wreath, which it was the custom of Bacchus to wear: grape vine and ivy with the beautiful, but poisonous, black bryony woven through it; as favoured by

Venus, it attracted love. The bowls used in the temple would have been of plane tree wood, as Bacchus favoured the Plane Tree.

In death, Halliday said that the animal should have been happy, and it would have been thought unlucky if the animal had fought against being sacrificed. If the sacrifice had predicted good fortune, Halliday said that the entrals would often have been eaten along with the other portions. To pay for the killing, selected women would have been whipped, said Pausanias.

At the festival, among the rites given Bacchus, were dramatizations, said Aristophanes. On these, much effort was made to have them worthy of Bacchus, so that the Spirit of Bacchus would continue as an active constituent of people's lives. Aristophanes said that Bacchus was thought to favour and enjoy obscene burlesques.

The Spirit of Bacchus was said to relate to the mystic frenzy of untamed nature. Lucanus said Bacchus might be represented by mountains. Bacchus has appeared as a symbol for Fire.

After the more structured rituals for Bacchus had been completed, the celebrating would have become rowdy. Along with Bacchus, Semele then would have been celebrated. She was a deadly Goddess of Dark Earth who delighted in killing so that she could bring forth new growth, and she was said to have been one of the mothers of Bacchus. Hislop said another was said to have been a snake. At the celebrations, Opsopaus said the followers of Bacchus would carry snakes.

Women, at this time, held rites at alters of Bacchus and at those of Semele. At the rites, they went into frenzies, drank and engaged in orgies, and ran in wild hunts. Any beast or human in their way would likely have been torn apart, perhaps eaten, even if it had been a son or mate of one of the mad women.

At the end of the Time of the Lion, August twentythird, was the celebration for Vulcan, God of Fire. Also, he was Vulcan the Smith, God of Craft, and his celebration was called Vulcanalia. At Vulcanalia, the streets were illuminated by torches and lanterns and there were torch races to hilltops where the torches were given to Vulcan. In fires for Vulcan, heads of families sacrificed fish.

Vulcan was considered, a master of the secrets of life. He was a healer, and for curing snake bites, his aid has often been sought. Paracelsus called him an artist and an alchemist. Windle said that King Alfred called him wise. People thought of Vulcan as being near at hand. Catullus spoke of taking poetry to him.

Nemesis, at this time, was honoured also. A shape changer, she protected homes, antiquities, reliques, families and the reputations of the dead. She was much feared. She was also thought to regulate seasonal change. She favoured the huge, ghostly Plane Tree. It was a plane tree which guarded her sacred well.

Card V: In the center would be Lamasthu, the Spirit of Fire, the Guardian of the Time under the Lion. Naked, she stands on ground covered with marigolds and dandelions and in her right hand she holds a red rose. It was the powerful and magical symbol of blooming things. Blooming relates to flame. The marigolds at her feet are, according to Lucius Apuleius, flowers sacred to the Sun. Dandelions restore and enhance fertility. In the Time of the Lion, the focus is more on the flowers than on the leaves, as the flowers show honour to the Sun and these, and especially the bright golden flowers, would provide a symbol for the Sun. Lactantius said that the golden flower holds the purest essence of gold and is recognized by the dreamer as a thing of true value. At the card's sides: columbine, and chamomile.

Lamasthu has been called a form of the Sun, but she is more than that: she is the Spirit of Fire, the pure Spirit of the cleansing element. This lion headed goddess has been called Lampetia, Daughter of the Sun, who acted as cowherd for the Sun's cattle. She was plagued by Hera because she presented a threat. It was thought, she had once been a ruler, but had been replaced by other deities; so, angered, she struck those who neglected to honour her. She was said to bring fevers, eat the flesh off people, and suck their blood. Women would hang tokens of Lamasthu, so that the goddess would see she was honoured and take her anger to some other place. On Card V, out of her mouth would shoot a tongue of flame.

Lamasthu is associated with the Lamiae: destructive demons said to suckle pigs and dogs and to steal babies. Marcus Aurelius said that these were female monsters whom people used when those people wanted to scare children.

To the right rear of the Lion Goddess, on a post, would be the Eagle King with, in a claw, a sheaf of lightning bolts. The Crowned Eagle, said Lactantius, represents the Spirit Ascending, the Winged Sun.

The tall Spear of Ash, standing along the left of the card, would represent the Great Force of the bright royal days of high summer: Jupiter. His lightning let people know he was looking out for injustice. Pater said that the place where a farm worker was struck by lightning was considered sacred and a monument was placed there. Stones found where lightning had struck were called thunderstones. They were said to fall with a great noise. Solinus said that they protected from lightning, gave victory in battle and in courts and induced sleep.

It was a spear of ash which Cheiron gave Achilles and with which Achilles slew Hector.

Fairbanks said that more than any other, Jupiter deserved the name of God the final arbiter. In the center of every month Jupiter is honoured. At this time, worshippers look up to where his statues rise up from behind high alters, rise up so that thought rises to his tall skies, and worshippers feel his presence. Jupiter represents the will to take charge and be responsible.

In the skies, when Jupiter is with the Lion, he is bringing riches. When he, with Saturn, is with the Lion, he and Saturn would be bringing even more riches.

The Ash Spear would also be the Spirit of Lugus.

At the top of the card, reaching out from the right, would be a limb of the Ash. The Ash is the Chief who directs. It represents strength and knowledge, and its strength protects. It has a role in transformation and in movement, and movement might be a huge and sudden change and this, even to an Astral World. The Ash is associated with elves and wood spirits. It is said, the Ash is favoured by gnomes. Ash smoke is said to chase snakes and demons.

The Diamond, King of Stones, would be at the bottom of the card. The Diamond represents the Sun, which is the Royal Seat of Fire. The Diamond protects against insanity; but, in general, it is concerned with power and death, and not so much, with healing. It suggests weddings.

To the rear of the card, left of center, would be a hill, on top of which would be a bonfire. In the fire, unseen, there might well be an honourable man's genitals and chamomile. The gift of the genitals was to aid fertility in cattle.

Fire is the energizing spirit of life, said Benedictus. It matures and purifies in man: in the material and in the Astral body.

Said Hartmann, there is essential and hidden fire in all things.

Fire makes the house sacred, said Hocart. According to Villinganus, Pythagoras said he could not, without a light, think of worshiping a deity.

The Time of the Lion is the Time of Lugus Longspeare. His symbol is the Spear which slays all which is before it. Superhot it is, so when not carried, must stand with its tip in a sacred cauldron. The Spear is of ash. The Ash is a tree which, in August, revealed the meanings of linear forms. The forms hold meanings behind meanings and these might be cryptic and mysterious.

The Time of the Lion is a time for bright love, for daring and for death. The Lion influence would be toward power, purity, clear thinking and courage. It would give inventiveness. The Lions influence, at its powerful center, is toward the one track mind, toward self sacrifice and toward the death which purifies the spirit. The influence at this time might b toward selfishness, self centeredness and pride. With this influence, one might grab property and power and this, with little regard for the rights or welfare of others. Good health would be encouraged, but chiefly as an aid in gaining influence and power. And there would be a drive to rebel, which might generate mass madness and cruelty.

The Time of the Lion is a time of abundance and generosity, of taking charge and of being responsible, of seeing to the welfare of a community, of observing justice and of enforcing the law. Solon felt, said Snell, that the power of a free state founded on righteousness would be guaranteed by Zeus.

The focus in this time is on the Element of Fire. Said Lactantius, Prometheus anointed men with Fire.

VI ~ Reaper

The sixth time section, The Reaper, is much about Ceres in her mature, giving phase. This is the time of Virgo, who was widely known to be Ceres; who, as Aratus saw her, sailed the night sky brandishing a sheaf of grain. Edward Davies called her the ancient Sow Goddess known as Ceres plus a number of variations of that name, but identified as the same goddess by the consistency of her ways, such as the use of the Sickle Moon for her Boat. Harrison called her a protector of pigs and of crops. She favoured swineherds and was sometimes found in their company. When her daughter, Proserpine, was carried into the Underworld, a swineherd and some pigs got swept with her through the open gate, and this indicated the close relationship of Ceres and Proserpine to pigs, and to pigs' association with the Underworld and so, with Underworld magics. Swineherds were often thought to read the future. Ellis tells of a hero who, to learn of the future, slept in a pigsty.

Ceres was said to have, at times, taken horse form, and while in that form, been fucked by Poseidon, who had taken the form of a stallion. The result of that copulation was said to have been twins: Pluto, Underworld God of Wealth, and Proserpine. One account of a happening was that Pluto swept his sister into the Underworld, which caused Ceres so much grief that she would not supply what the World needed from her until an agreement was reached by which Proserpine would spend part of her time in the World of the Living; part, in the Underworld. It was said, Proserpine swallowed six pomegranate seeds while in the Underworld, so needed each year to be in the Underworld, a month for each seed.

It was realized, however, that Proserpine, as Mate of Hades and Queen of the Underworld, would have had many reasons for trips to the Underworld and, at times, these would not have been directly related to Ceres. As Seymour has said, Ceres' mother-daughter relationship with Proserpine was thought, a spiritual tie and not a physical relationship.

Rituals, as Nagy has said, were a dominant feature of the personality of Ceres. The rituals for Ceres were widespread; especially, where she was generous and appreciated. And many have felt a need to understand and controle the forces growing things. Snell said that there were, in rural areas, programs for showing respect in which all in a community were expected to take part; and most, took pleasure in being part of the community, but each person would have needed to be in harmony with the others.

The worship of Ceres, as much of it was in areas which had little communication with rulers of the lands, had a power beyond that which was generally realized. The religion, as Pater said, was more of objects than of philosophy. People did what made Nature work.

Ceres relates to the cycle of the year. Many of Ceres' rituals which were performed, related to the vegetation's stage of development. A ritual for birth called for grain to be planted on a grave so that Ceres would call life from death. The Cycle of the Year was related to the Cycle of Life, which was divided into seven stages. Ceres' initiatory rituals were done in seven stages to relate to that cycle. In initiatory rituals, as Ceres herself was sometimes in sow form, the sacred pig had his place to represent Man. From temples, initiates carried pigs to the water, washed themselves and the pigs, then returned with the pigs and the pigs were sacrificed to Ceres in order, as Eisner has said, to reinforce a belief in the afterlife, and to cause new birth.

In a spring ritual, leaping dances were done to encourage the growth of grain; as, with Ceres, grain represented life in general.

In spring, for Ceres, there was a festival held so that she would give blessings and especially, those of light and purification. In this, torches were tied to the tails of foxes. Then cheered on by crowds and directed by Ceres, the foxes would have run to where fire and light was most needed for health and for purification.

In the Time of the Reaper, the influence of Ceres was seen throughout. Vertumnus, honoured on August twentythird, regulated seasonal change in vegetation. By Ovidius, he was called a protector of vegetation, of growing things.

August twentyfourth, called Mania, honoured the manes, the ghosts of ancestors. And these influence and protect households with which they are associated. On this day, passageways to the Underworld were opened; also, tombs of the dead. This was one of the three times when the gates were opened. The other two being October fifth and November eighth. Ceres, related to the Underworld, was associated with the Mania. At times, she was called Chthonia, a chief of the Chthonic deities. For Ceres' priestesses, in initiation, their last trial was to go to the Underworld, then return. But what their trip to the Underworld involved, said van Gennep, has been kept secret.

Mania was celebrated with carnivals, and if the day was fair and clear, a prosperous autumn was expected. August twentyfifth, called Opiconsivia, honoured Ops and Consus. Rites were done which gave to life as well as took from it. Ops is Goddess of Sowing and Reaping. She was looked to for good harvests and other gifts. She was a gift giver. For mates, she had Saturn and Consus. On this day, women held rites at which men were excluded. For these, they sat with bare bottoms on the ground. Ops was called Ops the Beautiful. The words, optimism, opulent and optimal would relate to her characteristics. She gives; also, takes items of this world to her realm. She is a Goddess of Death. Items she takes include people.

Another force which focused on this time was Consus, an Earth God who was a law giver; especially, in the field of conservation. He was a regulator of gifts which Earth gave. He was the Horse God who presided over the Festival of Consualia, held about the twentyfirst of August. In Consus' honour, mule races were held and mules, decorated with ribbons. There was merrymaking and a procession, priests and authorities wearing white robes and wreaths of flowers, to an alter of Ceres. At the rear of the procession would have been men leading one or more heifers by ropes. At the alter, with a sickle used for cutting the heifers' throats, would have been the priestess. If more than one heifer was sacrificed, it was thought important that they would all fall in the same direction. Only women were permitted in the area around the alter. These rites were celebrated at underground alters, the ways to which were, each year, opened only on this day.

On this day, at alters, corn was sacrificed to Ceres and new wine to Liber and until this was done, no one was permitted to eat or drink. The alters of Consus; underground in dark, mysterious, labyrinthine ways; suggested ways to the Underworld; the dark, dreadful realm of Chthonian Unknown; and this balanced the bright Sun and life giving fruit of the Time of the Reaper.

Also, at this time, sacrifices were made at the alters of Hercules. And this was the day for honouring Camulus, God of the Hazel. Camulus had a mighty sword and was called, by Windle and others, a God of War. He was called protector of the Sow Goddess in the Vale of Mysteries and championed the Goddess against the Forces of the Sky, and he was a mate to the Sow Goddess, selected by her because of his wisdom and his abilities as a bard.

Camulus brought the Sow Goddess from the Underworld, and the Sow Goddess brought the Bee and gifts of grain. At the same time the Sow Goddess brought the Bee; she brought, also, a cat monster, a monster wolf and a monster bird. In a book by Collingwood, there is a reproduction of an ancient picture of a figure with a three pronged staff, and beside him, a pig.

Bees, said Edward Davies, were considered to be Priestesses of the Goddess. The Bee, said Plinius, was the chief of insects. Bees, he said, had government with collective leadership, a code of manners and individual enterprise. He said that they mourned the deaths of kings and when in mourning, if they had not been taken food, as the bees would not have then been gathering food, they might have starved to death.

Bees were much valued by the deities, Jupiter was said to have been nourished by honey brought to him by bees. Nagy said Apollo had Bee Maidens who, when fed honey, would speak prophecy. Of master poets, it was said when they slept, bees put honey on their lips. Bulfinch said bees were called Messengers of the Gods. It was said, according to Wallace, bees had seven senses. Halliday said, bees were said to have brought, from the Underworld, elements of life's material needed for rebirth. As it was thought some of the material was in honey, honey was fed to the newborn, the rebirth of the life force.

As bees were born of warmth, they represented rebirth. The hive was said to stay the warmth of the blood of life. The hive was the spiritual continuation of the community. The spiritual consciousness of the bee led to the social life of the bee hive being a spiritual community.

When a family had beehives, it was often the bees were considered, members of the family. If there was family news, said Trevelyan, the bees were informed. If there was a celebration, the hives were decorated. If there was a death in the family, the head of the family, dressed for a funeral, would have informed the bees. In some areas, the hives would have been dressed for the funeral. If one did not share joys and sorrows with his bees, it was thought, his hives would likely wither away. If one neglected to tell bees of an important event, said Kightly, the bees might have been annoyed and left the hive. It was thought, bees leaving a family would bring misfortune or death. Bulfinch said, when because of some misdeed, the bees left the country; the priests, to save the country, needed advice from Proteus as to how to get the bees back. A sacrifice was made.

Herodotus said that when bees made a nest in the cut off head of Commander Onesilus, that caused the head to be honoured and to be looked to for advise.

Bees' wax was considered, a sacred substance. It was used for ritual candles.

On this day, the Ash was honoured for revealing the meanings in forms called Runes. Shape, as that found in the bark of trees; has, and communicates, meaning. From an understanding of the meanings, shapes were used to produce magical results.

The revelation of the meanings found in Ash was announced by the North Europe God, Wotan, who was associated with Mercury.

It was in late August, said Howard, that a horn dance was held. This featured six dancers with stag horns. The horn dancers would have had the support of other personalities and musicians. Howard and Trent both list the fool as being there at the horn dance. Trent lists Robin Hood as being there with archers. Howard lists a hobby horse and a triangle player as being there. Stag horns, triangle and Fool would have had Underworld associations. Jackson has a Horned Guardian of the portal between the worlds. He represents, said Jackson, the terror of death.

August thirtieth, Charisteria, is a thanks giving day.

September thirteenth, Lectisternia, honoured Jupiter, Juno and Minerva; then, other deities would have been celebrated also. The celebration included a procession with these three major deities being borne in decorated cars and these, followed by musicians, dancers, athletes, craftsmen whose work was, during the celebration, to be judged; then, entertainers and clowns. After the procession, white oxen would have been sacrificed to Jupiter; lambs, to Minerva. White oxen were raised especially for sacrifice and would never have worked. The parades and entertainments became very splendid. Cars were often works of art. Entertainment included dramas, displays and contests.

Mid month was thought, the correct time for honouring Jupiter and mid September, for celebrating the blessings he had given throughout the year and that would have included Ceres' harvest.

A feast for Venus was held at this Time and she would have had her representation, beside a representation of Mars, displayed on a decorated couch.

Shrines and alters for Ceres were decorated and, throughout the farmlands, there were special thanks giving rituals for Ceres and other deities who cared for farms and harvests. Collingwood has pictured a row of three seated goddesses: one holding a sheaf of grain; a second, apples and a third, grapes. Pomona, Goddess of Apples, was honoured especially at this Time.

Festivals for Ceres were held at the Equinox. It was the Time of the Festival of Demetria, at which Ceres was honoured with carnivals and fairs.

The harvest festival was preceded by many rituals for Ceres and by many customs relating to Ceres. Ridgeway said that milkstone, sacred to Ceres, was worn, by plowmen, on the left arm so Ceres would bless the grain. Candles, as plow lights, were put in the fields for harvest deities. Gomme said these promoted respectful and lawful community life.

A big factor in the celebration of the harvest was the Spirit of Corn. When harvesting, a custom was to leave a few sheaves standing. In some cases, as harvesters neared the last sheaves, there was humour and ribald joking about the identity and activity of those sheaves. The Last Sheaves were usually the Corn Doll and she was thought to be the Spirit of the Corn. She held the Spirit of Ceres, the Spirit of the Corn Mother, Demeter. The Spirit of the Corn was sometimes thought to have had the Spirit Form of a Rabbit. Frazer has harvesters jumping around so that the Rabbit would not escape. He said they would have shouted such things as...

"Don't let the hare out."

"Don't let it bite you."

The Spirit in the last sheaves might have been called the Nick; or, as Howard called it, the Neck.

The last sheaves, the Spirit of the Corn, was most often, in spite of any jokes, held in awe and treated with respect. Although the trepidation might have seemed foolish and could be joked about, there was a sinister nature to the Sheaves, which inspired a dread which couldn't be laughed away.

The job of cutting the Last Sheaves was sometimes assigned. There was sometimes competition to be first to get to those Last Sheaves. Sometimes, the harvesters would have taken turns throwing sickles at the last sheaves; each, trying for the honour of having cut them down. Often, the Last Sheaves would have, first, been bound together.

There was the thought, he who cut the Last Sheaves would have been related to the Spirit of the Corn. Often, the Sheaves would have been made into a doll, the Corn Doll. The harvester would likely have been called the Mate of the Corn Doll, or the Son of the Corn Doll. There were portents attached to the Corn Doll and to the Mate of the Corn Doll. If the one called the Mate would have been a single man; it was thought, he was soon to be married.

In spite of the joking and foolishness, of which the Corn Doll was the center, there was an atmosphere of terror and dread attached to her. She was spooky. As Iamblichos said of another representation, the representation came near to having the status of a deity. Likely, the atmosphere of the Underworld would have been with her. The dead were sometimes called Demeter's people.

The Corn Doll had many customs attached to her, as she was thought to have powers which should be given careful consideration. People attempted to be correct and respectful in their treatment of the Corn Doll.

There was a custom to place the Corn Doll on an alter of Ceres. To the Corn Doll, thanks would have been given and she would have been requested for blessings. Often, she was given an honoured place at a feast. Then, to give protection, she might have been placed over a door. To inspire growth in crops, she might have been placed in fields. Where there were a number of farming areas, one of the Corn Dolls might have been selected to rule over the group of areas. Some activities would have been done because it would have been felt that the Corn Doll desired them. Manners might have been observed because the Corn Doll would have been pleased.

There was often much made of the person who had cut the last sheaves. He was likely considered King of the Harvest. Often, there would have been rituals involving his being chased and captured. He might have been locked in a barn from which he would have needed to break out. Sometimes, he was shut out of his house, so needed to break in. He was sometimes dressed in straw and grain. He, with the Corn Doll, was sometimes put in a decorated wagon and, with laughter, shouting, banging of pans and vulgar words and actions, driven through the town. The ride through town might have been a wild ride.

The harvest festival, sometimes called Demetria, was often held September twentyfirst; however, many times, other dates have been selected for the festival. Many customs had the Corn Doll and her mate, at the festivals, featured in various ways. The Corn Doll, often placed on a shrine to Ceres, would have been, of the festival, the Spirit Director. Her spirit would have permeated the festival's activities and functions. She might have been called on to be a physical part in some of them. She might have been represented by a person, a person who might have been called Corn Queen, and the Corn Queen might have had a big role in rituals and contests. Trent mentioned a Corn Doll pole and said that around it, the Corn Queen led the dance. At the festival, featured activities might have centered around the Corn Doll's Mate. He might have been dressed in grain and placed among other honoured farm products and implements. He was sometimes dressed and treated like a baby, with the thought that he would someday be the powerful Lord of Grain. He might have been required to eat a man made from the last grain harvested. After that, he might have been anointed and crowned. Then, likely, he would have gained some authority at the festival and beyond.

Beyond Demetria, the Corn Doll might have become too unsettling to have been kept as a physical presence. There was often a ritual for returning the goddess to the soil. After praises and prayers, the Corn Doll might have been danced around; then, by the men, pissed on. Should any outsider person have come to where the ritual was being done, he would have been in danger of being caught, knocked down, pissed on and, perhaps, had serious damage done to him. The Corn Doll might then have been buried in the fields.

At the festival there have been many harvest related games and contests, displays, and entertainments by music, acrobatics and clowns. Fortune tellings were usual festival activities. Ceres would have been the center of many decorations and activities. A feature given by Chadwick was the harvest festival wagon carrying the representation of Ceres crowned with flowers and carrying a sheaf of corn and a sickle. The wagon was filled with cheering farmers. Pulling the wagon were horses covered with white sheets.

At harvest festivals, a number of deities and their alters were given places. Liber was often represented and, at some of his alters, men had their genitals blessed. Bacchus would have been honoured, as the festival was much about food, eating and drinking. For Ceres, grain represented life. Full jars and full chests of grain represented abundance and were used in celebrations to encourage abundance and to indicate appreciation. Jars and vases played a big role in celebrations for Ceres. Manilius said Ceres had been represented with a vase and a jar of corn.

The vase had a double meaning. It held food, but also suggested a funeral urn. Baskets, which were used in the celebrations, also suggested the generosity of Ceres. Aristophanes said that women, on their heads, in baskets, carried the sacred implements of Ceres. Newly weds called on Ceres for productiveness. People have thrown grain on the newly weds so Ceres would bless them with children.

It was thought, if Ceres had been made unhappy, much other unhappiness would have resulted from it. Ovidius reported that a stolen statue of Ceres led to a crop failure. In another time when Ceres was unhappy, when a woodman had felled an oak and a dryad had complained to Ceres about it, Ceres caused the woodman to die from not being able to stop eating.

Ovidius said that Jupiter would likely have punished the woodman for felling the oak, but gave Ceres, because of the dryad, a chance to express her anger.

When Ceres was brought to a stillness by the sadness of Proserpine going to the Underworld, vegetation stopped growing and the joy of growing didn't return until Proserpine was returned and the spell of sadness was broken by Baubo, Goddess of Sex, making Ceres laugh.

In celebrations for Ceres, it was thought, Ceres would be in charge, would be directing the activities. As Ceres was in controle of rituals, in the sacrifice of animals, the parts cut off and given to her were assumed to be the parts which she, at that time, had taken a liking to. As Ceres gave raw materials, it was thought that these were what she would think it proper to be given. She was given fireless sacrifices of materials in their natural state: honey in the comb, unspun wool, uncooked grain, unpressed grapes.

For the good harvest, Ops also would have received thanks. Ops, as the ground itself, gave blessings. To connect with Ops, women had rituals in which their fundaments were placed bare on the ground. Ritual grounding was a way of getting health and protection from the Goddess of the Underground. Ground absorbed destructive energies and gave support and strengthening. The ground, Ops, provided a comfortable center from which spiritual support could be expected. From the released tension and freedom from worry, given by the grounded center, the woman could organize her energies, direct her thought, plan action.

As Ceres and Ops related to the Underworld, they were looked to for knowledge of the future. It was thought, a way to contact these goddesses and through them, the dead, was through holes in the ground.

Putnam said that to communicate with the dead, one needed a crack in Earth. These cracks and holes, called oracles, have been used from most ancient times, and most of them have been under the authority of ancient underground or Underworld deities. Some of the oracles were stumbled upon, seemingly, by accident. The Oracle of Demonaeus, said Diodorus, was found by a goat. In one of her temples, Ceres had an oracle. With this oracle, there was a mirror which was used for gaining knowledge.

In the Time of the Reaper, the major force focused on would be Ceres. She is a protector of growing things. Then, with her sickle, she brings death in order to make growing things edible and to give room for more birth. Ceres is a teacher who educates, especially in areas associated with agriculture. She is a law giver. She has been said to reward thoughtfulness shown to her by bestowing blessings and learnings. She was said to observe the conduct of individual farmers, to reward virtue with good crops. When, because of a poor crop, a statue of Ceres was thrown into the sea, Ceres brought down her wrath upon that land. People, following instructions of the Delphic Oracle, returned the statue to its place and showed it special honours. Ceres then permitted the land to again be blessed with crops.

Ceres and other deities with whom she is associated would have interests in homes and the related concerns, as property, family, heritage and ancestors. Land itself was thought to be valued by the deities. Pausanias said that if land was taken from a location, the depleted location would suffer.

Ceres relates to the cycle of the year and so, to the Underworld with its positive and negative aspects. She would have a concern for ghosts.

A flower favoured by Ceres would be the Red Poppy, which is the Flower of sleep. The Poppy is also favoured by Spes, Goddess of Hope. When Ceres was sad over her missing daughter, Somnus, God of Sleep, sent her the Poppy, and they sprang up about her to ease her sorrow, and they continued to spring up in her fields. Poppies grew on the banks of the Lethe, the river of forgetfulness, which bordered on the Land of the Dead. Poppies were given to the dead, who, sometimes, wore them; sometimes, as crowns. Poppies would grow to mark the place where blood had flowed, where warriors had died. Frazer said, it was said they had grown from the spilled blood of gods. Poppies have been called thundercups, as to pick one was said to invite thunderstorms. Poppies brought sleep and were said to bring fantastic dreams. Helen put poppy into Ulysses wine. Looking long at poppies, said Apuleius Platonicus, would cause blindness. The Poppy related to fertility, and to the dead, so were used in prediction. Lovers slapped the petals between their hands. If the petals held together, the love would be true. Glaucus, after eating poppy, was drawn to a life in the Sea. Poppies were used to cool frenzies, to relieve gout and inflammations and to cure sore throat and stomachache. The seeds brought good health. Poppy would summon demons.

The Poppy is the Flower form of the Goddess Parthenos. The flower is the symbol of blood, sleep and death. It was thought best to plant poppies under the Dark Moon. Knowledge of the poppies was taught by Morpheus.

Ceres favoured flowers which bees favoured: Lavender, Baum, Poppy and Pennyroyal.

Pennyroyal was much favoured by bees. Put on a hive, it was said to keep bees from forsaking the hive. It was said to have the power to bring drowned bees back to life. It was associated with rebirth, was used in birthing initiations and it has been used for expelling dead babies and afterbirths. It provoked menstrual flow. It was said, when pennyroyal was mixed with stone from a lapwing's nest, then rubbed on the belly of a female, the female would give birth to a dark baby: this, from Albertus.

Pennyroyal was used for cleanings, purifications and empowerments. It was used for purifying water and it was especially useful for pearls. Insects that had drowned, if rolled in pennyroyal ashes, would come back to life.

Pennyroyal was used for chasing demons, especially, malicious water beings. In gardens, it was valued for chasing pests and aiding other plants, and it protected against bites and stings.

Pennyroyal was a flower of dream and inspiration. It was a flower loved by Juno, Venus, Selene, Diana and cats. It was much used in charms and valued as an aid in birthings. Dioscorides listed it as a cure for ailing genitals. Pennyroyal relates to reincarnation.

Pennyroyal was used for treating gout, cramps, dropsy, lethargy, toothache, stomachache, ulcers and disorders of the bladder and of the kidneys. It was used to purify the blood and to cool the itch. As an antiseptic, it was valued as a treatment for sores and wounds. Garlands of pennyroyal were worn for chasing headaches.

Another flower which was favoured by the bees was Lavender. Vergilius suggested planting it for the pleasure of bees. Corrigan called it an herb of mystery and said that it added strength and permanence to magical workings. It was said to bring luck and to confuse malicious spirits and malicious beings. It has served as an aid to poets, and was used for cleaning and purifying and especially, as it related to the Underworld, purifying the dead. Tools were cleaned with lavender and sacred areas, sprinkled with water from off stalks of lavender. For protection, and for a safe trip to the Underworld, people put clippings of their hair around lavender plants. Lavender was used to bless homes and to protect birthings. As lavender attracted good fortune, lavender honey was much valued.

As it had a calming influence, lavender was used to calm and clear nerves, relieve anxiety and bring serenity. It quickened the senses and balanced spiritual energies. It eased pain and melancholy. As it related to the dead, it was put in dream pillows for prophetic dreams. It was used for disinfecting wounds, for driving away moths and for keeping linen fresh. When lavender seeds were planted, charms have been said and rituals done that the lavender might protect from spells, attract love and aid persons in obtaining longevity. Lavender was put under the beds of those with whom one wished to copulate. To be free from headache, one method was to rub the head with bacon, wrap the bacon in ash leaves, then bury it under a lavender plant. Also, to avoid headaches, people put lavender in their hats. The fragrance of lavender was used to bring sedation, cure headache, aid the circulatory system, relieve pain, and to treat inflammations, colds, epilepsy, dropsy and palsy. Ophichus favoured the Lavender. Lavender was planted and gathered under the Dark Moon.

In the Time of the Reaper, a most valued herb was Balm, and one of its values: it especially was favoured by bees. In its most powerful form, it played a part in a drink made to give everlasting good health. Paracelsus claimed that balm would completely revivify a person, relieve a languishing nature and renew youth. Balm would strengthen mental power and memory. Balm drove away age. Rulandus said that balm had the power to cure all ills and to awaken the dead.

A chief value of balm was that bees delighted in it. Dioscorides called it Bee Leaf. It was said, hives rubbed with balm made bees stick to them and guided bees to them and helped bees find their way back to them. And it caused bees to keep together.

Said Gerard, balm drove away melancholy vapors and brought joy. It took away heaviness of the mind and sharpened wit and understanding. It lifted the spirits and balanced emotions. It was taken to correct ailments which were due to a disordered state of the nervous system. Balm brought an increase of spirituality. Balm was calming. The scent of balm was said to calm the heart.

To attract love, balm was carried and used in charms. It was used in baths for gaining romance. Balm had a close relationship with Venus. For attracting love, sprigs of balm were soaked for several hours in wine. The drink would not only attract love, but bring rejuvenation. Balm brought alertness and insight.

Balm inspired good health, and some of its cures seemed quite magical. Fernie said balm leaves worked magical cures for consumption, and that balm juice closed green wounds and kept them free from inflammation. Plinius said balm, if tied to a sword that made the cut, would stop the bleeding. Balm was used to combat rabies. It cured gastrointestinal ailments and diseases of the throat and lungs. Balm promoted menstruation and regulated the menstrual cycle. Balm aided in childbirth.

Balm cured by fragrance, lotion and tonic. It cured bites and stings of beasts and insects, cured muscle pains and spasms, brought relaxation and rest; it cleared skin problems and cured gout. It aided respiration, brought sleep and banished nightmares. Balm was used in cleanings and purifications.

Crosswort was favoured by bees. Put on a hive, it would keep the bees from being stolen.

Meadowsweet is a mysterious and dangerous plant of the Time of the Reaper. It was said, if one were to sleep under a Meadowsweet, one might well sleep forever; or wake, have many nightmares.

Meadowsweet was held by the deities to be most sacred and was much favoured by bees. It was a flower of the Underworld, related to the Owl and sacred to Minerva. It was called, Queen of the Meadow. A characteristic of Meadowsweet was its heady aroma. It made the heart merry and joyful; but, in delighting the senses, it tended to draw one into lands of fantasy. Brides often included meadowsweet in their bouquets. Meadowsweet was used in magic. Midsummer, it was collected so that it might reveal thieves. Meadowsweet, put into a pond, would point to the thief. Meadowsweet sinking, the thief would be a man; floating, a woman. Meadowsweet flowers were carried as they brought joy and happiness to relationships. Also, the flowers were put in beer and wine so that the benefits could be gotten by drinking the blessings of joy. And the drink renewed tissues and systems throughout the body. Meadowsweet was used to treat dropsy, digestive problems, rheumatism, and sores and wounds, to bring down fevers and to clean the blood. Meadowsweet flowers, brought into the house were said to invite Death.

A flower of the Reaper, Periwinkle was also a flower of the Underworld. To pick one off a grave was to invite Death. Periwinkle was called the Sorcerer's Violet, as it was associated with magic, darkness and death. It was called, also, a flower of the dead. Wreaths of periwinkle were put on coffins. Periwinkle was placed on dead children to be lowered with them into the ground. It was a custom to make offerings of periwinkle to the dead. It was used as a charm to bring peace and joy to the dead.

Periwinkle was much used in charms and potions and many of these related to love. Put in amulets, powdered periwinkle was carried to attract love. For producing love, powdered periwinkle flowers were put in philters. A boy and a girl, to bind love, in some cases, would share a periwinkle leaf. Albertus has said that periwinkle was the most powerful flower for producing love. He said that powdered periwinkle, wrapped with earthworm and put with stonecrop, brought love between a man and a woman – if it was put in their mead. And he said that the mix put in the mouths of some beasts would make the beasts break in half. To bring safe births, periwinkle was tied high up around a woman's thigh. Periwinkle was used in charms for eliminating negative energy, and it chased demons and nightmares.

As periwinkle related to the Moon, it affected menstrual flow. And periwinkle was called a fairy flower. It held memories of the past. And if one had kept periwinkle with him, it was thought, periwinkle would have brought him wealth and the good opinion of others, so that he should have seemed ever acceptable. Periwinkle was said to expel snakes, wild beasts and toxins and ailments caused by demons. It was used in exorcisms.

Periwinkle was used to combat hysteria, fits, scurvy, dysentery, sore throat, stomachache, piles and nerve disorders. To ease cramps, it was bound around the muscles. It cured inflammations. It brought down tension and anxiety and protected against magic spells. Pitman listed it as giving a sense of inner clarity. It gave a person an ability to conduct himself with grace.

Periwinkle was used in purifications and consecrations. It took shaded plots of land and most of the other flowers on that plot, it sent to the Underworld, said Apuleius Platonicus.

Periwinkle was gathered in the first night, the ninth night, the eleventh night, or the thirteenth night after the New Moon. To gather periwinkle, a person should be clean and be wearing clean clothes. Sometimes a person said a charm as he gathered it.

Periwinkle stands as a symbol for lasting friendship and for ever lasting life.

Wheat, Oats, Barley and Rye represent the abundance of Ceres and Ops. In Ceres honour wheat and barley were planted on graves where justice was maintained. The grains were a gift from the deities. For justice, it needed to have rites which gave to Nature as well as took from it.

Grain, as it was brought from the Underworld, related to prophecy. One way it was used was to put it on a hearth. For the answer to a question of future abundance, if the corn had jumped toward the fire, grain was going to be dear.

Black Bryony, an herb of the Time of the Reaper, was thought to be somewhat demonic. It was found growing near crossroads and under gallows, and pulled from the ground, was said to scream, and the person who pulled it, to die within a year. Injured, it was said to groan, and the person who injured it, to die groaning. As black bryony was dangerous, people would pay attention to what seemed to be its demands. It was reported, an old horse got locked out of his barn, so wandered to where there was bryony on a rope which was tied to a bell. The horse reached for the bryony and so, rang the bell. People went to see the cause of the bell's ringing, saw the bryony with the horse under it, so thought that they had been summoned by the bryony. They took the horse home and said they understood the bryony demanded it.

Black bryony was used as a medication, but was known to be dangerous. As an ointment, mixed with hog grease, it was used for paralysis, rheumatism and gout. Taken by mouth, it often caused pain and death and it was thought, that use should have been avoided by all but master herbalists. For some ailments, it was given mixed with honey. Bryony was used in witchcraft.

White Bryony was dangerous. The whole plant was magical and, especially, the root was used in witchcraft. Often, it would have been demon like in form. These roots were thought, able to cast spells. A wreath of white bryony was worn by Augustus Caesar for protection from lightning.

Bryony was a dangerous medication which would have often caused death, but herbalists considered it to have medical value. It was used by Dioscorides and by Galienus. It was used for sciatica, rheumatism, pneumonia, pleurisy, lumbago and gout.

The tree representing the Reaper would have been the Hazel, the Tree form of the God, Camulus.

The Hazel had the Nut of Knowledge and these fell into a sacred pool. There they were eaten by the ancient Salmon who held knowledge of all things.

The Hazel was Lord of the Five Senses. His nuts falling into the Sacred Spring made a music as beautiful as any in the World, and from the spring flowed the Five Streams of the Five Senses. The Hazel was Lord of Music and Poetry. There was strong magic in songs of the Hazel.

The Hazel was Lord of Fertility. Women gave sacks of hazel nuts to new brides, trusting that the new brides would become mothers.

The Hazel was the Tree of Law. Law courts were protected by the Hazel.

The Hazel held strong magic of protection. For protection, a person would, with a hazel rod, inscribe a circle around himself. If the rod had been cut Midsummer Eve, it could have been made to whip a person, had he been ever so far away. The rod could also have been used for driving malicious spirits out of cattle and for securing crops. That hazel rod could have traced a triangle, then put a demon into it, so that it would have become his gaol. Cut at midnight, Midsummer Eve, hazel twigs would give protection. The twigs, carried with a person, would protect, even from falls. Put in the harness of a horse, the twigs would have protected the horse from spells. Three hazel pegs, cut Midsummer Eve and put in the beams of a house would have protected the house from fire. The magical hazel wand could have been used for summoning demons and for exorcising demons, and it gave protection, especially, from fire, lightning, enchantments and other aggressions. Hazel also guards against shipwrecks. Hazel rods were used for stirring raw milk to keep it from being disturbed by fairies. To protect against malicious beings, hazel, with burdock and mugwort was hung over doors.

Rago said that for binding a fairy, hazel rods were used. The fairy would have been bound in a crystal. Three Wednesdays in a row, the crystal would have been dipped in the blood of a white hen, washed in spring water, then purified with hyssop smoke. Three peeled hazel rods were then buried under a mound. On a Wednesday, while facing East, the fairy would have been called three times; then facing East, the next Friday, the fairy would have been called, bound into the crystal.

Divining rods, made from hazel, were used for discovering water and other treasures. The rods were cut under the New Moon and from the East side of the tree, and rods selected for divining rods were usually forked. Beside water, they were used for finding minerals and lost items. Standing stones beaten by hazel were said to bring rain. For magic trips, wishing caps were made from hazel twigs.

Vibrations from hazel wood, according to Maple, were used to take pain away from ague.

Hazel nuts were said to be much favoured by Goblins. As Cob was Lord over Goblins, the nuts were sometimes called Cob Nuts.

Hazel nuts were sacred and to pick them when they were green was said to bring misfortune.

The Hazel was the ninth tree, so was at the Gate to the Underworld. Then, as he was Master of Poetry, Wisdom and Song, the Goddess of Earth took him for a mate.

The Hazel inspired creativity, love of beauty, love of country and of the deities. He taught skills in magics, such as in vocalizations and in the use of symbols. He gave skills in arbitration. Hazel brought wealth, but it was thought, the gifts from Hazel were involved with sacrifice.

Peridot was a stone favoured by Ceres. It suggested ripening grain and gold. It could foreshow the future, give protection from enchantment and bring spiritual awareness. It inspired eloquence, brought health, increased friendship, strengthened memory and encouraged honesty. To chase demons, it was tied to the left arm by the hair of an ass. Put under the tongue, it could give a look at the future. To augment its power, it was set in gold. Peridot discouraged envy.

At that time of the Reaper, a big factor was the wide ground. Aeschylus spoke of Earth's great generative power. He said that the forces of the Bright Sky loved to penetrate Earth and Earth aspired to that union. Also, Eugenius said Mother Earth copulated not only with the plow, but with stars and planets, and the shafts expressing their love were many. And the Earth Mother was a powerful healer. Her energy was received through grounding. Also, according to Theophrastus, ground was put into useful healing mixes. Also, minerals, said Valentinus, draw strength from Earth.

The Wide Land took energy which would have been an overload, or have been otherwise damaging. Especially at the opening of gates to the

Underworld, there was a give and take of energies. Lands became better adjusted. People, by grounding and especially, at that time, took advantage of the benefit which the ground gave; picked up strength, tranquility and other virtues; rid themselves of confusions, stress and other negativity. The Earth, Ops, supplied a center of comfort from which spirituality could be expected, balance could flow. From released tension, freedom from worry, given by the grounding, there might have been given a chance to organize energies, direct thought; an opportunity to plan action.

Over the ground, the wide expanse of grain would represent Ceres, her power and goodness. Grains were sacred plants brought from the Underworld. Hole has told us, poultry, for protection, was given blessed wheat. It was considered risky, at harvest time, to pick flowers which were blooming among the grain.

In the center of the field of grain would be Ceres as she has appeared as Virgo, in a hooded cloak, in her right hand, a sickle; in her left, a sheaf of wheat in which would be mixed a small number of poppies: perhaps, three.

The sickle, which Ceres holds, would show Ceres bringing death in order to make life edible and to give room for more birth.

Especially, where the environment favoured agriculture, Ceres was given many honours.

On the lower left might be seen the beehive. The Bee gave blessings and withdrew fortune. Said Steiner, the Bee was the symbol of spirituality that knew no mortality.

To the right rear would be the Sow. The Sow and the Bee, coming from the Underworld, would have been looked to for predictions. As they associated with pigs, swineherds were often looked to for predictions. And pigs, if their tails were hanging straight, were forecasting rain.

And right rear would be the Hazel. To the left rear would be a stack of wheat, harvested fruits, as apples and plums, to the front of it – and nuts.

At the bottom right and bottom left corners, three peridots set in gold in each corner. They represent the wealth from the Underworld and, also, the number of the card: six. Six relates to life and death. As two triangles, it would have life force coming into this World and going from it. Six relates to sex and to the female. It has male triangles, but there would be the dark center, the abyss of the female, which would draw items into it. It might be the Horn of Plenty which pulls life into the World of the Dead, the solitude of the Spirit World. Six gives death; but, also, life, love, beauty and fruits of the Harvest.

VII ~ Scale

The Seventh Time is the Time of the Scale. The Scale holds the key to knowledge of past, present and future, as all things go on the Scale which enforces balance. A key to telling what a thing would do would be the knowledge of what the balance would be. The Scale would form order out of chaos. The attraction to balance is a force which is needed in order for form to exist.

In the Time of the Scale, a major force would have been Europa, the Wide Eyed Mother Goddess who was the Rising Dawn; then, the Flooding Darkness; who Rode the Moon. She might have been called Eurynome, whose dancing gave birth to the Serpent Wind, the beast whom she threw into the Underworld. Her authority expanded over the vastness, so she was called the Wide Ruling one. As were other deities related to the Wind, she was said to have been related to the Spirit of the Snake. She was a Great Expanse of Existence and wide sections of it, people experienced without awareness. She was a body of subconscious and unconscious. She was a body of information known without the realization of knowing. She balanced the focused information authority puts forward. It is, as Jung said, the Female Unconscious to balance the Male Conscious. It is an attraction of opposites to fit on the triangle Scale. To get a balance, what was in the unconscious would have been incorporated into total picture.

Europa was a powerful force. She rode over her wide domain with her unstoppable spear, rode over subconscious, unconscious and the little bits known without realizations. She was the Spirit of Sacredness which filled farmlands to the Moon filled sky: her form, at times, would have seemed bovine; at times, in human form, the great Queen Mother. Under her, the chickens were fed, the cows were milked, little rituals were respected: out of chaos, order was maintained.

Nemesis, also, was a force of the Scale. She was a shape changer who, as an awful monster, rushed down on persons to enforce justice. She kept the orderly continuity of civilization, saw that a harmony was maintained between past, present and future. She enforced the observance of traditions of respect. She was said to have been raped by Jupiter and so, laid an egg from which Helen, the symbol of beauty, was born.

A third force of the Time of the Scale was Minos, Chief Judge of the Underworld. Minos held the Underworld Aspects of The Moon. He was the Minotaur, the ox headed Darkness at the center of the Maze. As Zacharias said, he was called Asterios, and that would relate him to the Corona Borealis, the Star Castle of the Dead.

Minos, as a King Judge, was known for his characteristic of judicial exactness. Pausanias said, in illustrating his character of being just; when a woman, thinking to please Minos, betrayed her people; Minos ordered birds to rip her apart and throw her into the Sea.

Minos represented, when he was center stage, the power of the female centered law. He was the Ox God and in one form, the Sacred Ox. But going from an age which favoured intuition to an age which favoured logic, he was out of place. As Reckford said, he was a creative force which transcended Hellenistic limits. So he self destructed, as Worthen said. Jupiter ordered Minos to slay the Sacred Bull, and Minos was the Sacred Bull. Campbell suggested that the Sword within the Maze of Death might have been the Age running out of energy and dying out.

Others from the Age of the Ox evolved from being great kings to being judges. According to Ovidius, Rhadamanthus and Aeacus were great kings who became judges in the Underworld.

The stars regulated justice. Astraea, a Star Goddess, according to Valerius, had a devotion to justice so great that, at the end of the Golden Age, she was the last goddess, the last deity, to take a physical presence from this World. She represented Astral laws, and these were from the Astral Plane, which was a shadow universe with its own framework of law. Astraea ever demands justice. Justice is a way of forming balance.

Venus, a Star Force who related to the Time of the Scale, related also to justice. Venus, in her personality, held love and care and a reverent approach to life. She cared for gardens and protected that which she favoured, and brought retributions. Lucius Apuleius called Venus the Spirit of Vegetation who bound as slaves, bodies to her. Also, she was the Personification of Love. She removed it, as a Spirit Force, from the mundane. Venus ruled over the enrichment of society, of substances, of reproduction, of the formation of tissue and she related to hidden intelligence. Venus caused the expulsion, according to Lucretius, of harmful things as well as pleasurable things. Venus was said to enjoy jokes and other humour, and to enjoy sensual pleasure; so, cared for gardens.

Grapes, Apples, Violets, Pears and Red Roses, especially, were associated with her. And Venus promoted music. She expected bloodless sacrifices at quiet, rustic alters.

Trees and flowers have spirit powers and often make judgements. A patch of onions or a single daisy might say, "yes," with so strong a voice that one would not question it. The Linden, the Oak, the Hawthorn, the Beech and the Plane have all been associated with justice, and have demanded such respect that libations have often been poured out to them.

The tree that would most represent the Time of the Scale would have been the Apple. Graves said the Apple was a tree sacred to Venus and Selene. It was the tree under which the Unicorn slept. The Apple Tree is one of the trees most likely to give its surplus spiritual energy to Man.

The Apple is the major key to the Underworld and it is a Guard at the Gate to the Underworld. Apples form a barrier between life and death. For keeping young and in good health, apples were eaten.

The Apple, in its center, held the Sacred Pentacle, which is the symbol representing Woman. And, as the Woman is the generic human, it is also the symbol representing Mankind. And it is the symbol which represents fertility. And the Apple promotes fertility, love and health. It is used in love and in fertility potions. And it is said, "An apple a day keeps the doctor away."

And a person could gain aura health by going to an apple which had more energy than it needed, then perhaps trading a gift for a gift.

The Apple, as it travelled between worlds, was looked to for knowledge and, especially, for knowledge of the future. A number of ways have been used for getting apples to reveal their secrets. One: a single person might peel an apple so that the skin would come off in a single spiral. The first person who would come and see the spiral would have a clue concerning the identity of the future mate of the peeler. Another method: a person might take an apple seed in the left hand, cover it with the right hand, shake the seed while saying a charm: then, look at the seed. The seed should point to where true love is. Rhys said the apple seeds might have been floated, each with a name. If they had held the names of the possible future husband, the husband would have had the name which had been held by the seed which had floated the longest.

The Apple was selected to be part of a judgement, the judgement of Paris. Paris, by selecting Aphrodite over Hera and Athene, was given, for a mate, Helen; who was, in human form, Bright Moonlight, and the

Spirit of the Apple Tree. Her apple which caused the judgement was called the Apple of Discord. Another case when Aphrodite was involved with the magic of the Apple: Aphrodite gave three apples to the warrior, Hippomenes, and by them, in a race, he was able to defeat the Goddess, Atalanta.

The Apple held the magic of Life Force. Lud, from an account told by Ingersoll, threw the apple into the dragon's mouth and so, slew the dragon. At times, the Magic Apple would be the Sun. Lud was Lugus.

The Plane Tree, sacred to Europa and to Nemesis, is a stout guardian. It symbolizes protection, genius, magnificence, shelter and friendship. It guards shrines and sacred wells.

The Time of the Scale was a time when a focus was on spiritual values and people committed body and spirit to them. Values, however, would vary, individual to individual, place to place. The Spirit of Justice would make, of the same situation, different calls. But the Time of the Scale would be a time of spiritual power, so that efforts would have been made by persons; each, to follow his concepts of the dictates of Justice. And each person had given to him, rules presented by his environment, and others presented by his Spirit World and the image of himself in it.

September twentyfourth, Deities of Justice were honoured. Respects were shown to Nemesis. To honour her, women spit on their breasts.

Europa, as a great queen, was celebrated with flowers. Theocritus pictured her with her maidens, the maidens adorned with hyacinths and daffodils. In some places, the day was Nemesis Fest.

September twentyeight was a celebration called The Braderie, which honoured, especially, the goddess whom, according to Collingwood, the Romans called The Nymph Brigantia. There were fairs filled with song and dance and flowers and many of the songs particularly honoured Brigantia. Geese were sacrificed to the deities and current cakes were served, as they were thought to bring good fortune. Flowers and bunches of carrots were handed out. The carrots were thought to inspire love and to bring reproduction.

The flower most favoured was the Queen Anne's Lace. Beside Brigantia, it was favoured by Apollo and Venus. It related to Wind. At the Braderie, to inspire fertility and to give good fortune, bunches of Queen Anne's Lace roots were given out and songs, which asked the flower for aid in reproduction, were sung. In some places, as the flower was associated with Venus, it was called Love in the mist. The root held purifying agents and improved eyesight and, especially, night vision. They were used, also, to preserve and restore wind in horses.

Queen Anne's Lace was used in treating jaundice, dropsy, dysentery, gout and ailments of the bladder and kidneys. It was also used for ulcers.

In Queen Anne's Lace, there was, near the center of its flowery head, a small, purple flower, and this was, according to Fernie, used for driving off the demons of epilepsy.

A second flower seen at the Braderie fairs was Goldenrod. It was said, as a friend of Venus, to bring good fortune. It was said to protect lost beauty and to make things whole. The message from Goldenrod was, "Be careful."

Bartram called Goldenrod a most effective cure for kidney ailments. It also had other virtues. It was used to combat the stone and other obstructions. It was used for treating dropsy, headache, skin ailments and digestive problems. Also, for men and animals, it would cure sores and ulcers.

Caraway, an herb of the Scale, was an herb used at fairs and festivals. As it was favoured by Mercury and Venus, it was used at weddings and put in wedding cakes. Caraway cakes would keep doves from straying from their homes. Caraway had an ability to hold things together, to keep things where they belonged. Grieve said that it was thought to prevent the theft of anything which contained it and to hold a thief within an invaded house.

Caraway was used to treat earaches and gastrointestinal problems and, especially, those where the problem was one which involved air.

Corydalis was used for magical cures. Corydalis smoke was used for driving away demons and malicious spirits. It was created by smoke which rose from the Underworld.

In the night after the Fair Day, courts were held on dark hills, and the custom was to conduct them with great dignity and quietness; for, overhead, the Wild Hunt rode, with all they swept up, to the World of the Dead. Through the sky, flights of geese also collected people and took them to the World of the Dead.

At the courts, not only numbers of the living, but also, some of the dead, were called up to stand before the court. Voices were kept down because of the awful nature of the supervising deities, and because of the demons and spirits which might have been near.

In the night, Nick and other demons were said to have pissed on the

Blackberries, so the berries became property of the Underworld; so, were not to be eaten.

October first was called Tigillum Sororium, or Fides Day. Fides, God of Faithfulness, and Janus, the two faced God of Doors, were honoured and ritualists wrapped their hands in white linen.

At the Time of the Scale, people would be careful to pay attention to the Underworld: to watch for omens, to honour ancestors and to decorate graves.

The White Campion is a flower of Death and picking it was said to bring death to the picker's mother and the chance the picker would be killed by lightning. It was visited by night flying moths.

The Evening Lychnis opened to welcome the Evening Star. It had a calming effect on man and beast. It was used for treating wounds, sores and ulcers. It was favoured by moths.

The Forgetmenot was favoured by Venus, as it promoted love and music. Related to lust, it encouraged copulation and brought reproduction. To bring lust, the root was boiled in wine and this, as the only breakfast, served as an opener of ways. Forgetmenot was an opener of doors. It brought prosperity. It was a finder of hidden treasure. As a medication, as it related to air, it was found useful in pulmonary afflictions. Boiled in wine Gerard said it was found useful in treating the venoms of scorpions and snakes, and it was a valued treatment for ailments of the left lung. It was said to have the power to harden metals; especially, those to be used for weapons. As an opener of ways; it is said, it would open the way to the Underworld. It was said, a musician was gathering herbs and, about to enter a cave, heard a voice,

> "Don't forget me."
> He looked around, saw the little blue flower.
> "You must have a use," said he.

He picked the flower, walked into the cave. While in the cave, rocks fell and blocked the way out. The little blue flower opened a door in the cave wall and the musician went through it.

Forgetmenots express doubt. As a gift, they might have asked a question.

In the Time of the Scale, Vervain was an herb of importance. It was included in the Cauldron as an herb selected for the brew of inspiration. It was used for parting the veils to the Underworld.

Vervain was an herb which inspired mental journeying and was useful in divination. An order of priests once carried it in important rituals. To drive off malicious spirits, rooms were sprinkled with water from stalks of vervain. As a just arbiter, it was used for casting lots. The aroma of vervain would have banished worry over injustice. The vervain flowers were often put on alters.

Vervain was a sacred herb of Mercury, and of Diana and was used when petitioning Diana. To purge away demons, it was put in purification baths. Banquet tables were sprinkled with water off its leaves and stalks of vervain were used for sweeping sacred areas, and sacred tools were consecrated with vervain smoke. In some areas, priests wore crowns of vervain when working exorcisms. Warriors have carried vervain with them into battle and administrators, into difficult negotiations; as in negotiations, it influenced in favour of success and peace. And poets, to gain inspiration and increased skill, wore it when making presentations. Children were encouraged to bear vervain root so that they would have been easier to teach, and have been influenced toward joy.

Vervain had power in the Spirit World. It gave power to witchcraft and could cause spirits and demons to materialize. It could bring spirits from the Underworld. As vervain reached into the Underworld, it could bring psychic awakening, lead a person to love, or drift a person into dream. Leyel said that it was sometimes hung around the neck to keep dreams away. It would drive away malicious forces and counter harmful spells, including forces and spells from the Underworld. For that protection, people have used vervain for forming protective circles.

Vervain was an herb of copulation and passion. It was often carried by brides and was put under the pillow for success in love. It assisted in copulation and brought success in reproduction. Favoured by Venus, it was much used in love potions. Lucius Apuleius listed it as an herb favoured by doves.

Vervain was valued as a health giving herb. Glandstar said that vervain was used to normalize and balance the body systems. It was used to open obstructions. Vervain tea was used for relieving stress and for altering consciousness. It brought enthusiasm and inspired idealism. Bartram called it a hypnotic and relaxing sedative and it was used to fight the demons of epilepsy. Gerard said it was used to fight fevers. For liver pains, Apuleius Platonicus said one should mix, Midsummer, five spoons of vervain in wine. For dog bites, Apuleius said vervain should be mixed with wheat and that, put on the bite. The wheat would then be fed to chickens.

Vervain was used, also, for jaundice, dropsy and gout. Albertus said if vervain was put in fertile ground, in eight weeks, it would produce worms which would kill the people they touched. If the worms, said Albertus, had been put on a dove house, the doves in the area would have gathered around that house. The worms taken to where people were, he said the worms would make them quarrel. If put in the Sun, the worms would have made the Sun seem blue. Smiths sharpened knives with vervain.

Vervain was planted in gardens and taken into houses so that it would bring health and abundance. Plinius said if a banquet hall was sprinkled by vervain before a banquet, the guests would certainly be merrier.

A time for gathering vervain was at the rising of Sirona, Queen of Stars. A correct way to dig it was with the left hand. Then it was waved over the head and a libation of honey poured. The roots and the tops of the plants were kept in separate places. In storing it, one tradition was to put it on wheat or barley. For collecting it, the best time was considered to be from the twentythird of the Waning Moon to the New Moon. It was a custom, while collecting it, to state some worthwhile use, as a sorrow to be eased, to which the vervain was to be put. At that time, no Moon should have been visible. The vervain was dried in a dark place.

Vervain balanced and harmonized, in women, periods of bleeding and milk production. Also, Lavender balanced energies and this relieved anxiety and encouraged serenity and calm.

A stone of influence in the Time of the Scale was the Amethyst. Amethyst was a nymph whom Bacchus had a tiger slay because she had a greater love for Diana than for him. Diana turned the slain nymph into a pure white stone. Bacchus poured wine over her giving her a lasting colour.

Amethyst would have had an influence toward a melancholy mood, and it might have caused with some, a drift toward insanity; but it purified and clarified thought, so was an influence toward gaining understanding, and abilities in problem solving. It quelled strong passion, eschewed drunkenness and led toward peace of mind. It brought spiritual mastery. Engraved with the Sun and the Moon, it repelled sorcery. It gave protection from disease and injury and gave the warrior the ability to overcome aggression. It was seen to contain no fire, which related it to the Spirit World and to Death. It was an influence toward psychic ability and self assurance and gave abilities used in gaining hidden knowledge. Its colour, purple, related to mourning, aided imagination, brought inspiration and peace. It related to spirituality and intuition. It was a step toward invisibility, toward the Spirit World. It was the royal colour, so would have influenced leaders.

The Amethyst was favoured by Mercury. It was an aid to hunters.

The number of the Time of the Scale, seven, related to a move to another grouping: seven days before another week, seven notes before another octave. The octave relates to balance, to judgement. Philostratus the Elder said Apollo had seven strings to his lyre, and they balanced the seven gates to his wall in the East. Pythagoras said seven was the most appropriate number to be used in rites. Solon divided the life of Man into ten seven year periods. Isidorus said seven was the symbol of the Seven Fold Completeness, which gathered the many into one and trampled on all errors of impiety. Seven symbolizes completeness. It relates to the Spirit World, as it is a boundary. It is a path for messages from the Underworld. It inspires spirituality and attention to detail. It represents Life balanced by Death.

The Scale relates to judgement, to balance, to change. Balance forces justice, so that what is just is insistent even when it is reluctant. In rituals, there was felt a need to get justice right, even if it meant having an axe stand in judgement for being part of a ritual which it was obvious it could not avoid. The instinct to have justice, the need to do what is honourable would be moved forward by the example of the Scale itself. One would see, as Zimmer has said, life pushed along the path by antagonistic opposites. The resolution of opposites is a function of Time. At some point, each force would become one with a counter force. As a rule, the deities would not have been promoting this balance, but would have fit into the necessity of the interplay to form balance. The Ram, as Manilius said, would have been against balance, but he would have met a force, equally against, pulling against him. The Scale would have functioned, as Dionysius said, because of the irreversible coherence of all that exists.

Justice is a way of having balance. The Chief Judge regulated balance. When a segment of Time was long enough, his axe cut it. The Chief Judge holds the Scale which measures each movement, tips at the point when it needs to balance. It forces changes.

The Time of the Scale focused on changes: the autumn leaf, the purple sunset. There would have been an honouring of grandparents, a look at their step into the Underworld. The Time of the Scale would have focused on contracts, on legal agreements. Ghosts were part of the picture in the

Time of the Scale: they did not escape the Scale.

In the center of Card Seven is the ox headed Minos in his purple robe. He is the Great Judge from the Underworld. As Pythagoras has, through an insight, seen: in his left hand would be the Scale. In his right hand, he would hold his double headed axe, the axe which gives sacred segments. Minos is not much concerned with wickedness or good; but when, for a segment, its time has run out. His axe held magical power.

At the left of the card would stand a spear, the Symbol of Europa. To the right rear is the Apple Tree. Around it is wound the Snake. At the right would stand a sword. Below the sword and spear, Queenanne's lace. Around Minos would be a circle of vervain, which protects, brings love and enforces a spiritual attitude on those who approach the Scale. The robe would inspire reverence. At the bottom of the card, the Amethyst, and in the distance, purple hills.

The Scale brings judgement. Said Boethius, Judgement is the best of all the gifts gods bring: it holds the ends.

The Scale could be the secret behind the Life Force and the key to understanding the Paths.

A factor in balance: it was thought, the deities would usually approve of fair play; as, if one took, one should give. Hunters, when seeking fortune, through ritual, in the hunt; also had rites directed toward the welfare of the hunted. This would have been an effort to have harmony. The deities would be thought to have approved.

With The Scale, it seems the great that have the great falls. Callimachus said, the gods give small gifts to small men.

Nemesis, said Pausanias, was the most implacable of deities. However, she would not have been unjust. Women exorcised Nemesis by spitting on their breasts, said Callimachus.

VIII ~ Demon

The Time of the Demon, the eighth section of time, is much concerned with the Otherworld. The chief deity of this time would be Hekate, Goddess of the Dark Moon. By human standards, Hekate would seem grotesque. Her hair is snake like and her facial features seem animalistic: at times, horse like; at times, dog like. She walks the roads followed by the barks and howls of dogs. Where ways fork, because Hekate favours three ways, people leave offerings for her. Hekate is a teacher of witchcraft and a giver of gifts. Black lambs and black people were sacrificed to her. As a Queen of Death, Hekate can pass between this world and the Otherworld. In this world, she walks through nights. She governs a host of spirits and demons. She is remote and ancient and one of the few deities free to give gifts outside the authority of Jupiter. At times she gives wealth and honour and often aids those who in contests call for her aid. She often gives good fortune to fishermen, and also gives blessings to women in childbirth. Hekate supports farmers and gives food and other help to beggars and to others who walk the roads. Ceres, in her search for Proserpine, went to Hekate for help. People put images of Hekate in their houses so that they would be recognized as worshipers of Hekate and would not be troubled by demons, by dogs of this world or the Otherworld, or by other beings who honour that goddess.

Hekate is a Goddess of Regeneration and a guardian of roads to the Underworld. She favours solitude, so shrines built for her are, as a rule, hidden deep in forests. The ends of months are sacred to her.

A day celebrated during the Time of the Demon is Kourotis, held October twentyfirst in honour of Ursula, Bear Goddess of the Moon. Another is Halloween, October thirtyfirst. This is one of the two times when the veils between this world and the Otherworld are considered to be the thinnest. Beings from the Otherworld might, at times, rise through the waterveil and trouble This World. Or those in the Otherworld might send messages; perhaps, through dreams or omens; to this world. Also, from this world, people might contact the Otherworld. For Halloween, people decorate their homes using Otherworld and harvest themes. Orange and black are the colours of the day, but many colours are used in the decorations. On Halloween, Dead Suppers are a tradition. Places are set for honoured dead and the meal is eaten in silence. Often, a bell marks the start and end of the meal. After supper, people in costume wander through the night, attend parties where games, many of them relating to the Otherworld, are played. Bobbing for apples might be biting the heads of floating witches. Apples, as at their center is a 5 point star, would represent people. Apples are often, especially on Halloween, used in forecasting. Also for forecasting, nuts are put by Halloween fires. For decorations, cauldrons, brooms, scythes, skeletons, Jackolanterns, witches' hats, corn stalks and corn are found useful. These are also used in Halloween rituals. Bats, black cats, crows and owls are made part of Halloween celebrations. These are sometimes the forms taken by witches. There is, through the night, dancing and other ritual around bonfires. Some people cover their bodies with flying ointment, which was an ointment made with herbs and other ingredients, such as soot and pork fat, which held needed powers. Herbs that have been often selected are smallage, monkshood, black nightshade, yarrow, parsley, cinquefoil, poplar, and rue. Some ointment was said to be powerful enough to permit one to rise aloft and disappear from sight. The ointment was also useful in trance dancing around the bonfire, during which the dancers take on aspects of animals. Masks would have been worn for protection as they were said to confuse demons.

The bonfire was an important part of Halloween, which is also Samhain. And hearth fires were lit also, and they would burn away impurities. And the bonfire was a bone fire, in that it burned the bones of animals, and this related to sacrifice. It honoured the hunted animals who had gone to the Underworld. There was often a cauldron which related to rebirth. Edward Davies told of a frantic ritual dance, around a sacred cauldron, done to the clashing of shields. One sacred cauldron was said to have come from a land under the sea. As the cauldron related to the sea, it was said, a storm could be raised by emptying a cauldron of water into the sea.

The Samhain dancing could give the feeling of being caught up in the Maze of the Spider Goddess, the Goddess of Death. One might have felt himself merging with the Spirit World as he was swept into the Maze. This is a time for gaining knowledge from the Underworld. This knowledge might be obtained by observing shadows from the fires. At this time, eating an apple could give foresight. At midnight, according to Ferguson, on Samhain, combing hair while eating an apple, while standing in front of a mirror in a darkened room; one might see a lover over his or her left shoulder. Apple seeds put on a hearth, if they pop and fly: good omen. If the seeds had both popped close to the same time, that predicted that the lovers would stay together. If a beech chip had stayed dry on Halloween, coming warm weather was predicted, said Ferguson.

The day after Halloween, Samhain, was a time for honouring the dead. Candles and decorations were put on graves. One custom: buns on which the names of persons who had recently died were taken house to house.

November tenth, Nincnevin, Diana was honoured and it was said, she and her company rode through the Sky. And there was the Wild Hunt: Underworld hunters, with their dogs, rode through the Sky to pick up those headed for the Underworld. Geese also flew through the Sky to escort people to the Underworld.

November eleventh: Heroes were honoured with music, decorations, parades and speeches. Cooper said that Harvest Gods were thanked and folk dances, games and athletic contests were held. Oxen were sacrificed, Bacchus honoured and wine, enjoyed.

November eleventh, the Blackthorn was honoured along with Lunantishees, who were the elven brings who kept it company and gave it protection. The Blackthorn, called the Tree of Death, or The Tree of Misfortune, is a Tree of the Underworld. It is a favourite of Diana and Selene and relates to the Divine Sow; and it serves as the home of the Lunantishees: Moon fairies whose influence is toward receptivity, imagination and the mysterious.

In governing, the Blackthorn has been found, useful. Blackthorn wands are considered to be powerful and are valued especially for gaining protection. Blackthorn clubs were used by officers of the law. The thorns were used for sticking into dolls, or into black candles, which represented, and had been made part of, living people. For getting rid of warts, a toad was rubbed on each wart, then impaled on a thorn of a blackthorn. The Blackthorn is a tree of witchcraft: as Blamires said, a tree for secret magics. Blackthorn flowers are said to be unlucky in the house, as the tree is aggressive and dangerous, and called quick to fight. It has been called the Blasting Rod. It stands for strife, for authority and for punishment. It would controle destructive forces. Blackthorn plums are used for treating colic and for breaking the stone. And they take away injury and bring fresh health. It is said, if it is fair during the flowering of the Blackthorn; then come May, there would be winds and long cold showers. If Blackthorn first flowers on a sunny day, then May would get the winds and cold showers.

November sixteenth is a special day for Hekate. Piles of stones, or crude columns, to honour her, were built at road forks, and on the night of the sixteenth, offerings were put on these piles; then, to honour Hekate, somber feasts were held. For her, black lambs, black dogs and black humans were sacrificed at her alters, which, Ovidius said, were hidden deep in the forests. Aristophanes said that Hekate gave wealth and honour to those who called on her for aid, she often gave it, said Nagy; and especially, if it was for aid in athletic contests. At crossroads, to be rid of warts, a person would bury a wart with half a bean, then say a prayer to Hekate.

Hekate is Queen of Witchcraft and, said Monaghan, she shared knowledge with those who worshipped her. Hekate, in the night, walked the roads carrying her torch and was followed by dogs and by the barking of dogs she had passed by.

Witches played a big part in the Time of the Demon and especially, at Samhain, when the veils between the worlds were at their thinnest. Witches were those who had super powers in abilities to make magical changes. At times, these were, in some way, quite different looking than most other people. Robbins told of some people who could be spotted as magicians because of having two pupils in each eye. An eye might be the thing which identified the witch. The strange looking eye was sometimes called the evil eye, as it might have caused disasters to have come to persons. There were counter powers which people used against the evil eye. Westropp said that amber beads, sacred to the Sun, have been used to take away the eye's power, and that bright objects have been used to distract it. Also, eggs have been used for defending against the evil eye.

Some witches, said Nicholas Remigius, could generate so much toxic energy that a person who touched the witch who had that energy, if he had not been in the witch's good wishes, he would die.

It was thought, witches often had powers over winds, said Murray. It is said, storms were raised by tying the joints of dead men to the feet of cats; then, throwing the cats into the sea. Witches would sometimes cause winds by sucking eggs dry. Sometimes, said Trevelyan, witches captured winds, then sealed them in empty egg shells; then, let them out as needed. Some witches could call up winds by whistling. Birds were thought to whistle up winds, said Frazer.

From ancient times, witches have had their basic systems of magic tied to the Moon and to circles related to the Moon. They developed, said Lindholm, methods of controlling powers of the Astral World.

The Time of the Demon honours a number of classes of demonic beings who have in common an appreciation of energy coming from the Underworld. This time is filled with, beside witches, elves, goblins and many unusual beings and which of them would be demons would be a question of semantics. Kittredge said some classed demons as elementals. Some demons, then, might be much like Lars, which Plautus said guarded estates and were much like the dwarf of the Norse. Some of the beings would seem more animal than human, as the goblin like being Spicer pictured, which was covered with matted, course hair, and the dwarf with goose feet.

Often, demonic beings are workers for their own communities or helpers in this World's societies. Small, brown beings, said Hodson of one type, were usually seen to be hard at work on one project or another. However, demons were often problems, as Tertullianus has said. He spoke of malicious winged demons with godlike powers. Disastrous tempests were said to have been stirred up by demons, and the demons had the power to bind men's minds, said Remigius. Some demons were said to make furniture jump around and many of the demons were carnal and passionate, said Nevius. A demon copulated with Emperor Justinian's mother, said Procopius, so that Justinian could put himself, or parts of himself, into the Otherworld when he wished to do so. And he could appear to be a lump of clay.

Lactantius mentioned a demon which he called a Demogorgone, which he said was particularly dangerous.

Demons all had this in common: they could move from one dimension to the other. An elf, said Keightley, had just purchased a horse when the elf, or fairy, suddenly vanished.

The fairies, Giraldus said, had the gates to their lands guarded by dogs.

The other dimension would seem to have different areas; each, with its own characteristics. The lands of nymphs and elves seems very different from Hades' Realm. The lands of elves were seemingly more like Outer World except, according to Giraldus, they were vegetarian, and in their lands, truth was a must.

Relations with demons and Otherworld beings were complex, as Otherworlds had their own rules. Apollonius Rhodius said that Peraebius lived in poverty because his father, the father of Peraebius, ignored the plea of a Hamadryad.

Spells have been used for getting demons to be of service. E M Butler has given an example of a witches spell. The spell caster bound a demon, Luridan, with her own blood; then said Luridan three times, and this bound the demon to one year of service. This demon in that time could have destroyed enemies or served in the home.

Jacob Grimm gave a spell for gaining service of gnomes. In this, a table was set with milk and honey. Then, a black pullet was killed over the food; half of it, thrown east; half, west. This was said to have gotten the service of two gnomes.

Nevius said that Athenians were remarkable for their worship of demons, and that the Spartan King, Agesilaus worshipped demons.

It was thought, animals could touch the Otherworld more than humans, and numbers of animals, it was thought, were demons who, for mysterious reasons, have served as animals in this World. At times, it was important that they be kept away from water.

If a demon was desired, another way to obtain one was to sacrifice a cock and for it, hold a funeral. The cock, except for the intestines, was then burnt. The intestines, along with burnt human bone, pith from an elder, soil from a grave, water off a toad, a black spider, a crooked pin, candle wax, hair from a dead man, hog's dung, henbane, bistort, black hellebore, black bryony, black nightshade, from a grave, yarrow picked at New Moon, black bean, basil, monkshood, sage and eggshells are mixed into clay. From the mix, a demon is sculptured, put into a hole which had been dug for it, then pissed on. The hole is then covered over. A demon is sometimes summoned from the smoke of a mix of herbs. One such mix contains henbane, hemp, hemlock, poppy, parsley, black hellebore, fennel and coriander. The demon would take shape within the smoke. Another mix for calling demons lists hemlock, henbane, fennel, black poppy, parsley and coriander; and these, collected in the last quarter of the Moon. Another mix has walnut, broom, blackthorn, chestnut, meadowsweet, hawthorn and oak, and these, mixed with nine stalks of fern. The mix is burnt.

A wheel of symbols was sometimes used for calling up a demon. One would sit in a circle; the circle, formed by what were called Negative Symbols of Wholeness. On the circle was a six point star; the points; each, lying outside the circle; were topped by crosses.

A demon was sometimes called by a circle of summoners; each summoner, holding a lamp. A charm was repeated by the summoners until a demon entered the circle.

A witch might have conjured up a demon through a series of ritualistic actions. The seven days before a New Moon would have been spent in purification. The seventh day, she would have risen at sunrise, taken a white cock to a body of water, cut off the head of the cock, drunk his blood. His head was then thrown into the water. A demon might then have been formed of periwinkle covered with a mix of earthworm and leek. The blood of the sacrifice would have nourished the substance of the demon.

In a way given by Rose, a witch might have taken a virgin hen to a crossroad and, at midnight, drawn a circle with a cypress stick nine and one half inches long; the circle, seven feet across. The witch would have stood in the circle facing East, torn the hen in half and commanded the demon to come.

She might have summoned the demon by burning parsley root and hemlock.

Some witches conjured up demons with which they rode through the night sky; sometimes, in company with other witches, and this might have included Goddess Diana. There would have been a variety of demonic beings. A gourd carved into a jackolantern would be apt to pick up demonic, goblinish qualities.

When demons were a problem, there were ways by which they could be cleared out. A sigil, said Villinganus, was used by some to send unwanted beings to the Otherworld. Sigils also have been used for protecting objects or areas. Some items, for their protection, were each marked with a cross.

Birds and animals, as they are more easily than humans touched by Otherworld influence; are, as a rule, affected by the thinness of the veil at the Time of the Demon. Some animals and birds are affected more than others. Dogs, cats, goats, bats, crows, owls and toads would be among those most affected, and through them, people expected to gain Underworld knowledge. Flapping bats were thought to predict weddings. Trevelyan said bats by flying around peoples heads have predicted misfortunes.

Some witches took animal or bird form. Forms often selected were the forms of cat, rabbit, owl and toad. Cats are mysterious beasts with strange ways and they have often been seen seated on a broom, behind a witch, on night rides. Hyginus said that Diana took the form of a cat in order to hide from the monster, Typhon. The Witch Goddess Mara also would take cat form.

Cats and deities who favour cats have a great fondness for catnip. Catnip is associated with witchcraft. It is said to have been found useful for shape shifting and for working illusion. It was used for concealments and for workings relating to dream. Catnip root was used to generate, in persons, ferociousness and anger. According to Fox, chewing on catnip root would make a person cross. Turneiserius told of a hangman who needed to chew this root so that he could perform his duties.

Catnip gives strength. It brings conception and aids birthing. It chases snakes and rats.

Catnip has been used for treating fevers, colds, headache, urinary problems and nerve disorders. As a lotion, it has proved useful for bites and stings and, as a compress over the eyes, for headache. As an enema, it has been used for gastrointestinal problems, headache, nerve disorders, purifications, convulsions, fevers, spasms, piles and to chase worms.

Selene, Hekate, Venus and Diana favour Catnip.

Cats were also fond of Pennyroyal. For women, it provoked the courses and aided delivery. According to Theophrastus, its aroma chased away ailments. And it chased away fleas.

The Plant Kingdom was especially in focus during the Time of the Demon; as, being a step closer to the Underworld than is the Animal Kingdom. Much communication with the Underworld, which was especially relevant during this time, was done through the Plant Kingdom. Many plants; such as, parsley, basil, monkshood and mint; were very close to the Underworld. It was reported that young children could take advantage of the Underworld relationships of plants, as they could hear the talk and music of the plants.

Some communion with plants was done with the aid of the Sun or the Moon. Infusions of herbs were put in glass jars, and the jars, put where the Sun's, or the Moon's, beams would strike them. If inviting the Moon's beams, it was said, the jar should be left open; if the Suns, it was said, it should be left closed. The infusions of celandine, energized by the Sun's beams, would bring joy and brighten the night. For communion with the Underworld, an infusion empowered by the Moon would have been one more usually selected. A person desiring communication with a deity might have selected an infusion of catnip, basil, periwinkle or mint, had it empowered, then, sprinkled on the supplicant with a willow switch.

Vervain, which had been collected with September dew still on it, might have been selected. The weaving of plants might have summoned deities. Curses or charms given by a deity might have been woven into a string of flax. Sage, during the Time of the Demon, might have been used for communion with the Underworld. At midnight, Heroes' Eve, a person, by stripping the leaves of a stalk of sage, might have seen a vision.

Basil was favoured by Hekate and Underworld deities. It was called the King of Herbs and was related to Death. Associated with witchcraft and basilisks, it was considered, a dangerous herb. Leyel said, put in horsedung, basil was said to breed venomous beasts. It was said that rubbed between two stones, basil would produce scorpions, and used as a perfume, it would grow scorpions in the head. Scorpions were said to grow in rotting basil. With basil smoke, people have invoked salamanders, basilisks, scorpions and dragons.

A powerful herb, basil chased away harmful and negative forces. Planted on graves, it gave courage and protection to persons in this World, and to the dead, who were on the road to the next. Planted on gardens, it gave protection, except to gardens where there was rue. For rue demanded purity and basil was considered, impure, as it related to bastards and basilisks: things of unnatural birth. And it related to malformations, copulations, toxins, hatreds, ghosts and venoms. In a garden together, basil and rue did not do well.

As basil related to venom, it was used to draw venom out of bites and stings. Basil had a power to repel. Secretly put under a dish of fish, it would keep a woman from taking any. Basil was used to drive away scorpions. It would expel births and afterbirths. It banished warts. For protection, areas were sprinkled with water off stalks of basil.

Said to attract love, basil has been used as a symbol of love. To attract love, it was carried and put in dream pillows. Basil was put in love potions. It was said, if a girl accepted a sprig of basil from a lover, she would have love for him. With love, basil harmonizes the sexual with the spiritual. It promoted fertility. And as it has been used as a symbol of mourning, it was said to represent love with tears. It was used at funerals, used in funeral rituals, and drunk by persons wishing to contact the dead.

By scent, lotion and drink, basil promoted a calm, alert mind. It cleaned and purified and, picked while in bloom, was said to attract wealth. It cleared the mind and stimulated memory. It was carried by people who wanted support in a new or unusual venture. For gaining wealth; it was sometimes entwined with marjoram; sometimes, tied to red or green candles. Wreaths of basil were said to give protection.

Women used basil for increasing menstrual flow. The aroma from basil brought sleep and fantastic dreams. Basil was used for treating ailing kidneys, rheumatism, digestion problems and colds. Basil root was put in pigs' feed to keep the pigs free from disease.

It was said, basil was rejuvenated by the touch of a handsome woman. Bees favoured basil; however, as a monster, basil was, by custom, abused. When sowing basil, it was a custom to face East and curse.

Albertus said Basil related to the Time of the Demon.

Black nightshade was an herb of the Demon which could be deadly. Associated with sleep, trance, fantasy and death; nightshade was one of the herbs used for summoning demons. One method which was used: the nightshade was burned; then, a demon was called through the smoke. Also, Black nightshade was used for gaining a view into the Underworld. From nightshade, one would get prophetic dreams. A nightshade might have taken the form of a beautiful, but deadly, woman.

Black nightshade attracts love. For this, it was put in potions and men wore black nightshade to attract love and to increase their ability in copulation. A correct way to obtain it was to go out naked, stand on one foot and to pick it while the dew was still on it. Nightshade juice was drunk to increase the chance of success in scrying. To prevent blotches, nightshade root was carried. It chased spells from animals.

Black nightshade, an antispasmodic, was used in treating rheumatism, dropsy and gout and to take away pain. It was put on the scrotum to treat problems with the genitals. Nightshade leaves, said Gerard, were soaked in wine and put on the temples to banish headaches. Nightshade was used for gaining protection from scarlet fever. It aided hearing and neuralgia. Animals called it food.

Henbane was an herb of gloom and gloomy places and often, it was found growing among ruins. When growing around the doors of homes, it protected against curses and drove away malicious beings and malicious spirits. Henbane was a grave, gloomy herb. It was worn for communication with the Underworld. Some people of the Underworld were crowned with it. Apollonius Tyana listed it as an herb used in magic. Mixed with realgar and snakeshead iris, then with the blood of a rabbit and put in the rabbit's skin, it would have caused many of the area's rabbits to congregate around it. Henbane was used for summoning ghosts and for bringing beings from the Spirit Realm. It was used as an aid to flying and sometimes, to flying to fantastic lands. An herb of darkness, it was used in dark rituals. Henbane had strange ways, as it was given to mad persons in order to make them sane; but for a sane person, to eat it was to invite insanity. Henbane root, as a charm against malicious forces, was hung from the neck. Also, henbane was worn to gain clairvoyance and insight and to attract love. Smelling henbane flowers, or washing the feet in henbane lotion, induced sleep, but it was likely, an unquiet sleep. The sleep might have been filled with restless and disturbing images and adventures. To eat any henbane might have brought strange frenzy and hallucination. Eating too much henbane, or going to sleep where henbane was growing, it was likely to have caused that person to have slept forever.

As a medication, henbane reduced swellings, cooled inflammations and improved hearing. It eased pain. Apuleius Platonicus claimed that, rubbed on sore teats, it would take away pain. Henbane leaves were put on the head to reduce fever and take away inflammation. Henbane would drive off demons of epilepsy and of convulsion through the aroma of its flowers. Henbane leaves were used to treat gout, sciatica and pains in the joints and to calm nerves.

As henbane was an herb of darkness. Chickens, which were birds of the Sun, were troubled by it. Hekate included it among the flowers in her garden. Saturn favoured henbane.

Monkshood gave a view into the Underworld and this, at times, was a close look from which the viewer failed to return. The views induced by monkshood, however, were often prophetic. Cerberus brought forth Monkshood from the Underworld and planted it in Hekate's garden. And from it, Hekate fashioned saliva for Cerberus. And Monkshood became the poison of the deities. Some of it fell on a marble floor and turned the floor to dust. Medea tried to poison Theseus with monkshood. Cheiron was wounded by a weapon poisoned with monkshood. However, monkshood combats other toxins and protects against venomous creatures. If a venomous creature had threatened a person and he had thrown monkshood at it, the monkshood would have formed a protective barrier.

Monkshood was used to purify, to consecrate, and to poison weapons. Sacrifices to Hades were sometimes treated to monkshood. In ointments which gave flying ability, monkshood was often included. Bees, especially bumble bees, favour monkshood. In heart and lung sickness, it has served as a life saving medication.

It was said, Black Bryony and White Bryony were somewhat demonic. The root of the white bryony was sometimes, as a person, consecrated.

A major deity in the Time of the Demon would have been Styx, Goddess of Underworld Waters. She was associated with darkness, with dark waters and with the terrors of Death; and with Goddesses of Strength, of Valour; with Nike, a Goddess of Victory, and with Charon, Ferryman of the Dead.

Minthe, Queen of the Underworld, was a force of the Time of the Demon. She was beautiful and cold and had a form in the Plant Kingdom: Spearmint. Minthe cleaned Jupiter's table before his dinner was served. People, to honour Jupiter and his table, wore crowns of spearmint when they dined.

Spearmint was used in herb baths as it aided memory and inspired love and copulation. It was used in cleanings and purifications. Spearmint tea cured headaches, strengthened nerves and toned muscles. Gastrointestinal problems were cured by spearmint. Spearmint eased pain by tonic, lotion and aroma.

Near the Sacred Spring, spearmint would have often been found and there, it would have filled the air with its scent, and this would have awakened mental alertness, spiritual awareness and given insight.

Spearmint was favoured by Venus, and bees took much pleasure in it. Spearmint related to Water and Water was a promoter of change. Water deities frequently changed form. Tethys was known for changing shape. And from Pomponius Mela, there were the nine Witches of the Sacred Spring who read the future, controlled winds and the Sea, were healers and changed shape.

Water not only relates to change of form, but to change from birth to death, from death to birth. The relation of water to life, said Ussher, has been known from times most ancient.

The Blue Spinel would represent the Sacred Well, and the Time of the Demon, so would be a dark Veil to the Underworld. At the bottom of Card Eight, the Veil is represented by a dark pool, the margin of which is seen, and out of the pool has crawled a scorpion, a symbol of darkness and death.

The Spinel, a dark blue stone favoured by Selene, would be in the bottom left corner of the card.

In the lower left of the card is a cauldron. A goblin is to the right of the cauldron. He would certainly be a type of demon. Often, it was felt important to know with which demon one was dealing. If the demon with which one was communicating had an interest in a particular part of the body; it would be well, said Leyel, if that person was aware of it.

From the bottom of the card, a path leads to a fork of the way. And from the fork; paths lead, one toward the right, one toward the left; toward distant hills. Forked ways to the Underworld, said Rutherford, are in ancient mystery religions and were well known to the Pythagoreans. These were represented by horned beasts. Horned beings relate to this fork. The fork is represented by the wishbone of a chicken, a somewhat sinister token which gives answers when it is pulled apart, as this would give it an Underworld connection. At Samhain, said Kightly, it was baked in a pudding and the person to whom it was given got luck.

The Fork, according to Pythagoras, symbolized life. It represented an important choice one must make: a choice which would put one toward one type of life, or toward another. In the Time of the Demon, at a fork in a road, at midnight, a person might sit on a three legged stool in order to hear secrets, such as of a person who would be near to death.

By the fork, a pile of stones would hold an offering for Hekate, the great Goddess of Witchcraft. On either side of the fork, a dark dog would be howling at the dark sky. Dogs howl when Hekate is near. Hekate gives food and help to beggars and to those who walk the road. Hekate gives aid to women in childbirth. She gives help to farmers and fishermen. People hung tokens of Hekate in their houses so they would be recognized as followers and would not be troubled by dogs in this World or the next.

Below a Sickle Moon, a witch on her broomstick rides through the dark sky, and riding on the broom straws, her black cat. The witch is in a gown and she wears a conical hat.

Witches powers cover a wide range. The witch, Meroe could, it was said, bend rivers, put out stars, lower the sky, draw down the Moon, send gods to the Underworld and return the dead to life. When Meroe needed blood for her magic, she took it from people and so, caused their death.

Witches, it was said, have blasted crops and raised storms, but much of what they have done was said to be helpful.

The broom would represent the witch's tools. These would not likely be exotic works of art, but friends and companions of her daily living, that helped with her chores, with what ever needed doing. They would have extended the reach of her physical and spiritual self. Her broom would sweep, her stick would be stout, her knife would cut. The powers of the tools would extend beyond the physical.

The broom would have many abilities. In sweeping, it would not only rid an area of dust, but would sweep away negative energies. And it is used for sweeping sacred circles. The broom would have Underworld connections and would have powers even a witch might take care with. Sweeping the house in May might sweep the head of the house away, and if there are blooms on the broom, to sweep with it could be deadly. As a tool, a broom can blast or give fertility. It can give aid in flying. It has the power to clean and give purification and the power to calm storms. A broom is put by the front door so that a visitor would be forced to leave. If a woman were looking for a husband, or selling beer, she would hang her broom outside her door. Spence said that a woman, if she stepped over a broom, it was thought, she would have a baby before she had a husband.

Broom has provided a valued medication. It was valued as a treatment for dropsy, and Culpeper listed it as a treatment for ague, gout and sciatica. Bartram said it is a diuretic which increases the power of the heart.

The best way to establish the best relations with the broom, it was thought, would be to gather the materials for it in a ritual way, a way that would be pleasing to members of the Plant Kingdom, and an appreciation should be shown to Mother Earth. The shaft, Nomolos thought it best if it were Ash, Willow or Hazel, and if it were hand hewn. Each of these would have values which for them would be peculiar. Linneaus said that his hazel staff had a marvelous ability for finding money. Grieve said that a broom, by having a great quantity of bloom, indicated the coming of riches.

Nomolos said that Helen was said to have put her jewels on a broom and sent the broom out of Troy.

In the sky near the witch, a few bats fly.

In the lower right of the card, in a patch of weeds, a jackolantern is falling apart, returning to the Underworld. The ragged, scraggy weeds would be difficult to identify; however, catnip and nightshade should be among them. Catnip would please the cat, as cats love to roll in it. It is found useful in shape shifting, especially, that relating to the forms and personalities of cats. Catnip chases nightmares and works magical cures related to cats, and promotes fertility. Catnip smoke drives away negative thought.

A gnarled, twisted blackthorn, on the left, is in front of distant hills.

The Time of the Demon is a dangerous time. It relates to conception and death and, especially, to the death of old people. Its number, eight, relates to the Wheel, which is the Wheel of Life, the Wheel of the Year, and all other cycles. At the center of eight, as with other even numbers past two, is a black pit. Pull away the points on the spokes and all falls into the abyss. One might feel himself merging with the Spirit World as he is drawn into, or falls into, the darkness. Eight is the eight step octave and the eighth step. It is the jump off into the unknown.

Strange shapes might seem to lurk in a shadowy world, now vaguely seen. This relates to the Water Veil, between life and death. One influence is a one toward maliciousness. Petronius said that assassins and poisoners would be likely to be born under the Sign of Scorpio, which would be in the Time of the Demon.

In the Time of the Demon there is joy, and there is pain.

Goblins dance in the crossroads, said Skene.

IX ~ Archer

The Time of the Archer is the Time of the Old Suns, the Long Haired Suns. These are thought to have been great lords of this World, but are now wise and judicial lords in the Underworld. A mighty Old Sun is Hyperion. He was known over a wide area and, as he was known in many places, there are many variations of his name. He is the ancient Yew Tree Sun, the giver of gifts, of blessings and of clemency to wrong doers. He went to the Underworld to defend the Earth Mother and became lord over her lands. In some places according to Callimachus, asses were sacrificed to Hyperion.

Another team of horses which headed for the barn is that which pulled the chariot of the Sun, Helios. Helios was a mighty, wise, all seeing god. At times, his size seemed nearly that of Jupiter's, but his permitting Phaeton to drive his chariot seemed to lessen his stature and to indicate that even though it was Phaeton who had fallen, Helios was on a downward slide, was to be spending less time riding in his chariot across the sky. And when, according to Fiske, the dangerous Cacus stole sheep from Helios, it took Jupiter to slay Cacus and get the sheep back.

Sheep, said Ovidius, as they have associations with dying Suns, have Underworld relations.

But Helios is considered, a Great Sun around whom things revolve. Gold light flashes from the eyes of women descended from Helios. Lucius Apuleius told of a ritual where the initiates were crowned as representations of Helios.

Among the earliest of Suns would be Horse Suns and Sun Horsemen. Related to these would be Cheiron, the Centaur. He was Lord over a Host of Centaurs, all of whom had the chest, arms and head of a man and the four legs of a horse. As the horse was considered a most noble beast, Centaurs, even among gods, were considered noble. Cheiron had been the Sun.

Cheiron was an archer, a healer and Teacher of Medical Arts, a musician and Teacher of Music, and a Lord of great wisdom and justice, and he was thought to have a knowledge of the future, and men and gods valued his friendship. He was said to have taught medicine to Aesculapius, the

Snake Doctor. When Achilles needed aid, he came down from the Stars to give it.

As Sun Gods often had conflicts with other Sun Gods, Cheiron, in this tradition, had conflicts with Hercules, who is a Solar Hero, former Sun. Cheiron was also, for Hercules, a friend and teacher. The conflict between Hercules and the Centaurs led to Cheiron being wounded in the foot; and so, placed in the Night Sky.

An ancient philosopher said that what Cheiron represented, as part man, part horse, was a spiritual representation. If one needed a physical representation, Cheiron would probably be more like a wooded mountain top than either a man, or a horse, or that combination of both.

For Cheiron, as with other Centaurs, the bow would be the major weapon, but an important other weapon would be the single blade stone axe. The Club, the Spear and the Thunderstone were weapons used by Deities of the Sun.

The Time of the Archer is a time of sacrifice and reflection. Honours are paid to age and wisdom. With November birth, there is a tendency to second sight.

The introductory celebration for this time was the feast of the Yew Trees. With the celebration there would have been beautiful music, and this is held November twentysecond. At the end of the day, Vulcan bolted shut the gates to the Time of the Demon, to the malicious, the mischievous, the sinister, the humourous, the outlandish, the deceitful forces which would have smudged the purity of the coming time. On the twentythird, a feast was held in honour of Vulcan the Smith. Thanks were given to Vulcan, and to the deities of the harvest, and to deities who had given blessings during the past seasons. It was the time to wear fine clothes and to display awards.

The ancient, mysterious Yew is the Tree of the Archer. It was the Bow which sent sacred shafts from the skies. The Yew is the tree which completes the wheel. It relates to death and rebirth.

The Yew is a form which Sun Gods take. One ancient yew, it was said, had been in salmon, eagle and human forms. These are forms which oppose the Snake, which meets the Yew in the area of darkness, death, loss and transformation.

The Yew is a tree which gives protection. To guard the dead, it is planted in graveyards and usually, the northern part, for that would be the part closest to the Underworld. Branches of yew are carried in funeral processions, put on coffins and put in graves, so that the dead might be protected. It is planted at springs where it guards the ways to the Underworld. Yews are planted on boundaries to guard and to judge the justice of the boundary and people were taken to those trees to be chastised.

Yews are thought to guard, judge and give wisdom. Apuleius Platonicus said that they protected against ghosts. Chiefs and others have gone to yews and sat under them to gain wisdom and inspiration in order to make wise judgements. Under venerable yews, yew sticks are cast and symbols, which had been placed on them, examined so that wisdom might be obtained. Of the Yew's knowledge, it was said, the Yew represented the sum of all that had gone before it; so, in the presence of a yew; humility, is a virtue.

People wanting fertility and birth, walk around a yew.

For wands, yew is the wood many magicians prefer, and some have felt they needed to obtain that wood during a lunar eclipse.

Staffs of yew are put behind doors in order that they give protection. These are expected to protect, especially, from lightning and from archers. Yew is the wood for bows, and some of these give magical protection. In ancient times, magical spears were said to have been made of yew.

Yew is toxic. Eating yew can kill men and beasts, but when a cure is needed and other cures have failed, as with cancer, sometimes yew will work a magical cure. As a rule, yew wood is not burned, but for some magic, a yew fire is thought to be needed.

With yews, there is an element of danger. Linnaeus said yews have been felt to endanger those sleeping under them, and Apuleius Platonicus said, sleeping in the shade of a grim yew could be fatal.

Said Apuleius, the yews are somber trees which attract mists and vapors.

Yews have formed silent groves of ancient trees. Yew groves are dark, gloomy and haunted: groves where reality might shift among shifting shadows. The air off yew leaves gives eerie, sometimes otherworldly, trips. The Yew is a bringer of dream, as it rests partly in Dream World. In some dreams, the shadowy dead would be seen. A person might climb a yew, become invisible.

Said Apuleius, goblins and mist fairies live among yew branches. Nightmares nest in yew branches. Pale spirits, called Green Ladies, reach out pale hands, give dreadful chills. Should anyone harm a yew, these ladies would haunt him. Historian Lucanius said that no Sylvan Priest would enter a yew grove after dark. Life energy under yews would be at a low ebb. Yews, said Ovidius, shade the road which leads to the River Styx.

The Yew was considered the sacred tree of the Archer, and records indicate that it was considered so in times most ancient. Sir George Trevelyan said that many of the yews were planted by the Druids thousands of years ago – in places sacred to the Sun, as most ancient Suns would have had a yew tree form; a form, one with a Yew Bow which sent Earthward, shafts of light. Readers of ancient rock markings have seen pictured, the Yew Sun with his Bow of Yew. As ancient Suns have gone to the Underworld, the Yew would be partly in the Underworld, so would inspire some dread.

The Yew is an upholder of the law. It suggests justice, charity and wisdom. The Yew seems to go on and on through Time. Of the Yew, an ancient saying was, "Root and branch shall change places and the newness shall seem a miracle."

Archers and bows would be spiritually linked. The ancient archer might have been buried with his bow. At times, yew wands were bent like a bow. Yew wands and yew symbols can be used to draw power from all worlds. The wand can be used to establish sacred space and quiet space for trance, ritual, or communion with ancestors.

The Yew suggests gloom, melancholy, change, transformation and loss. The big change is suggested: death. The Yew suggests that which is ancient and venerable. The Yew represents birth and death. The Yew gives wisdom and patience, which might be used in working with change.

Sophia, Goddess of Wisdom, is honoured November twentyeighth.

December first, the philosopher, Pythagoras, was sent to the Underworld.

December seventh, Haloia, honoured Ceres. Ceres is represented garlanded with wheat. Eating and drinking, even to intoxication, is said to honour Ceres. Before the feast, hands are washed and purified in running water and freshly cleaned clothes are put on. Oxen are crowned with decorations and given feasts in the mangers and, as signs of prosperity, stick houses are built on hearths, and this is from an account given by Tibullus.

Sun Gods are master healers and, especially Cheiron, aided others in becoming gifted healers.

Cheiron taught communication with plants. He taught the reading of signs given by plants, so the plants could more easily help the people who need the aid. A number of plants, at giving help, would be at their best in the Time of the Archer. One of these, the Red Centaury, is favoured by Cheiron.

Called the Center of the Sun, the Red Centaury opens in bright sunlight. It is the herb to which Cheiron gave his own name, as it was the herb which cured him when he was struck by a shaft which had been poisoned with the blood of the Hydra.

The Centaury has strong magic and can work fantastic effects. Albertus said witches would have been able to join centaury with the blood of a female lapwing, or a black plover; and this mix, put in an oil of a lamp, when the lamp was lit, all the people in that light would have believed themselves to be in a company of witches; each, with her head among the stars and her feet planted in the ground. If that mix, under the stars, had been put in a fire, it would have appeared that the stars ran against one another and fought. If the mix had been put up a man's nose, Albertus said, he would have run away.

Witches have used Centaury in potions designed to increase psychic powers. Centaury has been carried to ward off malicious spirits. It drives away malicious energies, counters unwelcome magics and gives courage, aggressiveness and muscle tone. In the house, it serves to ward off illness and to bring good fortune.

As a tonic, centaury purifies the blood and clears the liver and spleen. And it is used to treat kidney trouble, gastrointestinal problems, dropsy, gout, rheumatism and ulcers. It is used to combat toxins and venoms and to kill worms. As a lotion, it is used for healing sores and wounds. It is used for relieving mental pressures, and it is given, said R M Lucas, to expel timidity. The smoke of centaury is used for spirit workings and trance. Centaury drives away snakes. It is favoured by Mars.

Valerian is an herb sacred to Vulcan and has been used in the celebration of Vulcanalia, August twentythird. Beside Vulcan, it is favoured by Venus, so is useful for love charms and charms for fertility. Women use valerian for adjusting menstrual flow. As a love charm, one method used was to hide it in the room of the intended. Valerian was considered one of the more important magical herbs. One list of nine magical herbs included Valerian and Centaury. Valerian represents purity and courage, and it promotes peace. Water is sprinkled from valerian stalks in order to protect and purify areas. Valerian tonic was said to restore peace between man and his wife. To attract love, women put valerian in their underclothes. Animals are charmed by it, and especially, cats; and these, go crazy over it. To be rid of rats, rats were said to have been led away by valerian.

Valerian inspires courage. For this, it is carried by warriors. It gives feelings of confidence and well being. It is sprinkled in areas to stop strife and bring peace. It has the power to stop men from quarreling, even if by potions they have been set to the conflict. To attract money, it is put in a cotton bag; the bag, put under the pillow.

Valerian is used in cleanings and purifications. As a tonic, it is taken for coughs, colic, hysteria, heart problems, bladder trouble, epilepsy, headache, muscular and joint pain, neurosis and to bring sleep. Valerian counters toxins and combats bites and stings. It relaxes, calms and brings tranquility. It is used to sedate. It is made into calming, healing baths. As a lotion, it heals sores and wounds. It gives protection from the plague. Valerian is added to many other medications so that the healing ability of the other medications would be increased. R. M. Lucas lists one valued combination: valerian combined with vervain and mistletoe.

Sage is an herb of the Archer with great power and range. She is a nymph favoured not only by Cheiron, but by Jupiter and Mars, and she is generally honoured. Lucius Apuleius referred to the friendly relations Mars had with Sage.

A marvelous thing was reported of Sage; that if Sage is put in a glass bowl and covered with cow dung, that it will give birth to a worm which will have the tail of a bird. If a man, and this from Albertus, is touched on the chest with the blood of that worm, he will lose the sense of touch for fifteen days or more. If the worm, in a fire, is burned to ashes, there will be a rainbow and with that, thunder. If the worm's ashes are mixed with the oil in a lamp, then the lamp lit, the whole area around the lamp will seem to be filled with snakes.

In potions to bring nightmare cats, sage is mixed with semen, menstrual blood, hog dung and hypericum.

There were Romans who felt that a way to prolong life was to have sage in a garden. And sage is said to do best in gardens which, it is admitted, are under the rule of a woman. In a garden, it is said, if the sage is doing well, the owners of the garden likely will be doing well. Sage is thought, an indicator of fortune.

Sage has the ability to extend life. A saying is: "Eat sage in May and live for aye."

Sage, as Skinner has said, is associated with far seeing wisdom and so, is much favoured by Consus, who promoted the wise regulation of farming. Sage relates to ascetic living, sacrifice, safety and calm. It is used for the restoration and enhancement of reproductive powers and for looking into the future and especially, when it concerns romance. Sage aids memory, gives energy, combats lethargy and quickens the senses. For procuring blessings of the deities, gaining good health and longevity and for getting wishes granted, the smoke from sage smudge sticks is used. Sage chases vertigo and depression said Bartram. Sage encourages mental balance. It brings euphoria.

Sage cleans and cures ulcers, provokes urine, brings relief to tired muscles, gives strength, conditions the blood, expels ague and kills worms. And it is useful in treating epilepsy, itch, stitch, arthritic conditions, palsy and liver conditions. As food, sage aids the digestive system.

Sage stalks are used for sweeping away unwanted energies and for sprinkling purifying waters. Sage is used in wedding wreaths as it promotes domestic peace.

In gardens, sage aids other plants in developing useful properties. It drives away harmful insects. Toads are fond of sitting under sage.

Women use sage to bring down their courses and to regulate their milk flow.

Rue approves of sage and the two grow well together.

When gathering sage, nothing having any iron on it should be used. A harvesting ritual used: sage is gathered barefoot, in a white dress and with a silver knife. And libations are given.

Rose lists a meaning of sage as being esteem.

The Wood Pink, important at this time, houses spirits of the dead so that these spirits can quickly return when the time comes for their rebirth. A princess was in danger of being slain by rivals, so got a witch to turn her into a wood pink so she could not be found. When the danger was gone, she became again a human.

The Wood Pink is favoured by Jupiter and by deities of the Underworld. As a flower which inspires love, it has been found useful for love potions. It is of interest to butterflies and to moths; however, not so much to bees. Bees, as a rule, have little interest in the Pinks.

The Pink serves as a symbol for boldness.

The Pinks are protectors of spirits, and of ghosts, and many Pinks serve as houses for the dead. A mighty warrior hid in a red campion.

The Corn Cockle, a mysterious member of the Pink family, would often house the dead. Sometimes called the Demons Eye, it is thought to portend ill fortune. Its seeds can cause illness. Corn cockle is used for treating dropsy, jaundice, tension, gastritis and in some cases, paralysis.

Bouncing Bet, of the Pink family, serves to provide houses for the dead. It is used in cleaning and purifying. With the body, it cleans both inside and out. It is used as a cure for the itch. Bouncing Bet is favoured by Jupiter and Venus.

With the Pinks, it would be certain to bring disaster if a person should pick a flower housing a dead person. Bees avoid disturbing the slumbering dead.

The Yellow Gentian, an herb of witchcraft, was one used by Medea, the witch who slew the children of Jason. It is a flower used to chase depression and self doubt. As a tonic, it is restorative. It brings energy and vigour. It repairs the digestive system and cures fevers.

In the Gentian family, Felwort, called Dead Men's Mittens, combats venoms and expels worms. As its purple colour suggests, it relates to the Underworld. As a tonic, it fortifies the gastrointestinal system and purifies the blood and is used for treating gout, liver ailments, scrofula, fevers and colds. As a lotion, it removes aches from muscles and joints and refreshes the body. It heals wounds and sores. Felwort prevents swoonings and strengthens the spirit. From its root, a refreshing drink is made.

Coltsfoot serves as a symbol of healing. Its early grey hairs remind us of autumn. Its leaves are used for starting fires and its smoke is therapeutic. The smoke is considered usually most effective when the leaves are burned on cypress coals. It is used for curing headaches, coughs and pulmonary problems. Coltsfoot tea is used for treating colds, sore throats, agues, consumption, asthma and to bring general good health. To treat neuralgia, it is used as a lotion and this, put on the back and genitals. Birds put coltsfoot leaves in their nests. Women, before dawn on Fridays, in order to attract husbands, sow coltsfoot seeds while saying a charm. Fernie said, if the seed puffs fly away with no wind, it means coming rain. Herbalists put pictures of the horse hoof shaped coltsfoot leaves on signs to advertise to the public that the shop fights disease, and the sign suggests, especially, fighting colds.

Masterwort is favoured by Hercules and by Jupiter. It was said to protect against malicious spirits and witchcraft, and Gerard said that it was carried for that reason.

Masterwort was revealed in a dream as a way to fight plague. It is used as an aromatic stimulant and as an antispasmodic. It is used to combat toxins and venoms and to heal wounds. A tonic made from the root is used for treating dropsy, palsy, epilepsy, dyspepsia and gout. It corrects menstrual disorders, and heals ulcers. It is used to take away headaches. An ointment from the root is used for treating gout, and swellings.

The bright golden flowers of Arnica bring energy of the Sun. It brings the disoriented personality back together. It is used to condition the feet and to treat fevers and paralytic afflictions. As a lotion, it is used on sprains and bruises and to stimulate hair growth and to grow hair where it is wanted. It kills pain. In small quantities, said Grieve, it has been used to combat epilepsy. It is a toxin and its methods of healing should be considered magical. It is included in some lists of nine magical herbs. It rejuvenates the systems of the body.

Yellow Dock is a healing herb used as a blood purifier. As a pot herb, it gives strength and readjusts the body systems. It has been found useful in treating hepatitis, jaundice, cancer, gastrointestinal problems, scrofula, ulcers, rheumatism, lymph glands, problems with the spleen and coughs. As a lotion, it aids sore muscles; cures rashes, itches and sprains, and heals burns and blisters. It cures skin ailments not only in people, but in animals also. It is used for treating sores on horses. Dock cures boils and infections. It is effective in countering bites and stings and especially, nettle stings. A charm used with Dock is, "Dock in, nettle out."

Dock is an herb of power. Witches use dock stalks to strike down their enemies.

Colewort and dock are used in making an ointment used on swollen testicles.

Shepherds Purse is an herb favoured by Cheiron. And chickens, as they are birds of the Sun, favour Shepherds Purse. It is an herb of warriors. As Marion Davies has said, it grows where men fight their battles. There, it is needed for stopping bleeding; first, for wounds; then, for piles, lungs, kidneys, throat, intestines and other parts of the body in which bleeding is a problem. Put on the pelvic area, it checks excessive menstrual flow. It is used for healing bruises and for treating rheumatism, dropsy, dysentery, inflammations and jaundice. For jaundice, one method of cure: it was tied to the wrists and feet.

When shepherds purse is needed, it is most always found fresh and ready to use. It is always, said Father Young, to be found someplace in bloom. It serves as an aid to Earth and also is an aid to other herbs. For spells, witches find shepherds purse useful.

Woad heals wounds and gives protection. It gave a protective covering to some of the warriors who went into battle, as many warriors did, as was recorded by Diodorus and Tacitus, unclothed. Many warriors, for power and protection, painted on themselves with woad, magical symbols. Woad is not an herb much favoured by bees.

Spiny Cocklebur gives a yellow dye. As a healing herb, it is valued for curing mad dog bites.

Dusty Miller, Centaurea Cineraria, honours age. It is used for ailing eyes.

A stone relating to the Time of the Archer is the Topaz, which is golden yellow like the setting Sun. It is called the Emblem of Friendship. It encourages kindness and affection and banishes malicious demons and spells. It checks lust and insanity, discourages greed and calms anger. Topaz brings beauty, strength, courage, knowledge, enlightenment and loyalty. It aids the heart. It was said, according to Fernie, to pale when toxins come near it. Topaz holds a radiance which dispels darkness and brightens wit, according to Fernie. As it carries energy of the Sun, Topaz is seen to shine at night. Topaz was used by seamen in directing a ships course.

For added power, the Topaz is set in gold, as gold carries the quickening, life giving power of the Sun. The Sun is the soul of Gold.

To purify and energize topaz, a recommended herb is spearmint.

For the power to put demons of darkness to flight and to banish dark spirits, a topaz is, by hair of an ass, tied to the left arm.

The Topaz represented Gods of the Sun. By holding a noble topaz, one might learn of its past. And by holding it one would gain Sun energy. Topaz is called the Stone of November.

The golden colour of the Topaz relates to healing. It relates to the healing touch of the hands of royal lords.

The number of the Time of the Archer is nine. It is the number of segments between this World and the Otherworld. There are nine Moons which measure the time from the Otherworld to this World. Nine Waves rise between the Otherworld and birth in this World. There are nine Walls between this World and the Otherworld Castle of Earth. It takes nine jumps for the Wind Horse to get to the Otherworld. Walpurga ran nine days to get from this World to the Otherworld.

Nine relates to dragons. The Lambton Worm was one of the dragons which coiled nine times around a hilltop. Because Lambton slew it, for nine generations, the Lords Lambton were slain. Whewell lists nine relative concepts: difference, identity, beginning, majority, minority, equality, middle, contrariety and end. He lists nine absolute concepts: majesty, virtue, truth, will, wisdom, duration, goodness, greatness, power. Whewell also lists nine questions.

In the Sky, the Longhaired Sun is sinking toward purple hills. This Sun is an important judge and would influence the great expanse of existence, including the stars. To avert harm, people tell threatening dreams to the sinking Sun, then go wash in the clear water of brooks, as the water is a way out of this World. The Old Sun was said to have crossed water on bones of the dead.

The Longhaired Suns relate to wisdom and learning. It was thought, they would approve of a person gaining a knowledge of history, as this knowledge would be an influence toward establishing order.

High in the Sky is the Archer, Cheiron, an Old Sun. Like Old Suns, he is a bold warrior and fine musician. It has been said, his music likely moves at a good gallop. His bow is an ancient weapon used by Man in the Stone Age. The Bow, said Frobenius, is associated with the Winter Sun. And this would have been the Longhaired Suns.

The Archer would have had also, the Single Blade Axe and the blade would have been of stone.

The Archer Horse Man represents the Sun and suggests that it had more than one form. The Yew Tree and Yew bow were thought to be part, or forms of, the Sun. And gods other than Cheiron were thought to be part horse. Mark had the ears of a horse and Sylvanus had the ears of an ass. And there were ancient coronation ceremonies in which the lord was required to be a horse, walk on all fours and have relations with a sacred mare. Armstrong said that in some rituals, he was required to eat a mare's flesh.

In a field of tall weeds, right of center of the field, there would have been an old, gnarled yew. On the left, in the Sky, would be a single blade axe. On the right, a harp. The harp sometimes represented an instrument of torture.

Among the tall weeds, sage and centaury might be recognized; perhaps corn cockle.

In the sky, far off near the purple hills, there would be three ravens.

These were messengers of the Suns and they flew into the Otherworld.

At the bottom of the card, a strip of dark gold held, in the right corner, a topaz; and, in the left corner, a coltsfoot leaf.

The Archer represents wisdom, purity, courage. With Card Nine and Card Ten there would usually be harmony. The Archer favours the Goat.

The sinking of the Sun is a worry to some philosophers: can one know the Sun will always return?

For the general public, said Fiske, this is not a worry. A major teaching and gift of the Sun: it shows the way to the Underworld.

X ~ Horned Piper

The Time of the Horned Piper is a time of darkness and mystery. There would be respect, disrespect, sacredness and celebration. The time goes from disorder and chaos into wild, mad celebration. Celebration would be hilarious, crude, vulgar, sense pleasing and frightening. All this, while outside, nature is cold and dark and the Sun is going to the Underworld. Malicious and deadly forces roam through the darkness. Then there is the sacredness of the new birth of the Sun. Through the expanse of bare, bleak cold, a spark of light. This light, signaling new birth, would be represented by the Holly, which shines brightly through the dark forest.

On the card, there is little to represent graphically the bleak, icy landscape or darkness which lingers in the cold forests. However, beneath the concealing frost, there is a spark of new life which red holly berries indicate.

At the center of the card is the hearth, as this is considered the alter of the Earth Goddess. On the hearth burns the Oak Yule Log, and this represents the death of the Old Sun. On a platter, in front of the hearth, would be a roast boar. He would be the Old Sun who sacrificed himself to be food for his people and went to the Underworld to be renewed. The apple in his mouth is the key to passing between worlds; so, coming back into this world. This is a time of sacrifice. The Holly is a tree of sacrifice and represents the sacrifice of the harvest god and the Old Sun.

Above the Yule Log is the mantle from which hang stockings filled with gifts. Deities of Earth are gift givers and Old Nick, the Transporter of the Dead, in the sacred season, when he is prohibited from being malicious, has time to deliver them.

On Lord Boar, where he was, in front of the hearth, were honoured members of the Plant Kingdom: Rosemary, Thyme and Bay Laurel; and these would add their personalities to this environment. And bowls of fruits and nuts would be near the Lord Boar.

To the left of the hearth would be the decorated Pine, decorated with balls and topped with a five point star, and this would represent the Kingdom of Death and would act as a charm to protect against malicious beings. Some decorations on the tree are sacrifices to Saturn and Hades, who are, in this season, shown honour. Dolls were offered to Saturn and masks, to Hades. It is said that Hercules said that those deities would prefer these to bodies and heads.

Below the tree would be decorated gifts. It is said, gifts and decorations bring blessings from the deities, bring magical blessings.

Fir and juniper would be in vases over the hearth and to the right of the hearth would be an evergreen wreath, and candles. Evergreen acts as a charm against malicious beings. The lit candle would show the sacredness of the place. The sacred circle of the wreath would relate to the circle of the year. The holiday being celebrated honours the completion of the circle of the year. One name for it is Yule, which means circle. The number of the card, X, relates to the circle. It is the sum of the first four numbers, all of which are sacred.

Across the top of the card would be Holly and Ivy from which would be hung bells. The sound of the bells would purify the air. From the center of the greens would hang Mistletoe. It was the Mistletoe which slew the Old Sun. This was done with the force of two deities: Loki and Hodur. This caused the Queen Goddess, Frigg, to stand under the Mistletoe and, to show she bore no ill will for the Mistletoe, under the Mistletoe, she had the other deities kiss her. The Mistletoe is a magical herb, so is collected in a magical way. It is called the lofty herb and the herb of dignity; however, it is often classed with the trees. For sacred use, it is seldom gathered from any tree other than the Oak. A correct time for gathering it would be the dark of night. The Moon would be a New Moon or a Sickle Moon – when the Moon is not seen. For collecting it, a stone knife or a golden sickle would be used, and when cut, it should fall on a pure white linen cloth. The cloth would add virtues to the Mistletoe. It would promote purity and give psychic power.

The Mistletoe should not be permitted to touch the ground, and compensation would be made to the Oak for the gift. Libations would certainly be made, and at times, greater payments were made and these have included numbers of oxen, which have been considered to be of much value.

Mistletoe inspires copulation and instigates birth. It is put in coffins to bring rebirth. The first cow that calves after the New Year is at times given mistletoe so that the whole herd will have good health. Mistletoe promotes good harvests and a good crop of mistletoe predicts good harvests. It has the power to open locks, to expel ill humours, to protect from lightning and is carried, to ward off epilepsy. It will cure many ailments of the body and mind and will chase sinister spirits. However, mistletoe can be toxic.

Mistletoe will bring harm if it is in a house at any time other than the Yuletide Season and the Midsummer Season. January fifth is the day, after the Yule, when it should be taken out of the house – along with the other evergreens.

In the bottom left and right corners would be tourmalines. Tourmalines are of a shiny blackness and through the blackness glimmer sparkles of red and green. Favoured by Saturn, it is called a stone of ill luck and is said to be aglow with malignant fire.

A horned flute player would be on the card's far left, and this might be Pan. On the far right would be an old, ass eared deity, Sylvanus, and he would be holding a mug of wine. To the right of the hearth would be Nick with his sack and broom and wearing cloak with the hood with the pointy top.

Pan and Sylvanus are ancient gods of the wild, untamed woodlands. Pan is the Crude Stone Dancing God who, along with sprites and other nature forces, lingers in the darkness and shadow of rugged, out of the way places; and he can strike panic or terror in people who find themselves wandering in the wilds. It is thought that Pan, along with other unfamiliar nature forces, is more likely to inflict harm than to give good. However, when trouble comes to a land, the support of Pan can be relied on. Also, along with other beings of the wild, Pan is associated with the beauties of wild places. His is the instrument of pipes out of which beautiful music comes. And a wild, strange music it is. Pan sponsors the reproduction of flora and fauna, so causes men to lust. Pan comes in dreams to bring instruction, and in other ways, he might bring helpful knowledge and prophecy. And Pan might bring sudden mysterious, seemingly groundless fears. Torch races are held in his honour. Pan favours the Holly and the Pine. He helps drive out invading warriors.

Sylvanus is thought of as being jovial, hairy and balding, and often inebriated. He is sometimes shown on an ass attended by Satyrs who keep him from falling off. Sylvanus is sometimes seen wearing a crown of pine and he might be carrying pipes or a pruning knife. An Ass God, he is thought possessed of wisdom, absurdity, folly and prophetic powers, and he is thought to have served as a teacher to Bacchus. He is a guardian of forests, fields, herds and flocks and is sometimes a protector of homes and a friend to hunters. In spite of his jolly, cheerful look, he will often be frightening and dangerous and his laughter, seem sardonic. In a forest, he might seem more tree than human. He is associated with the forest at sunset and is sometimes said to be the Man in the Moon. He is thought, dangerous after dark and, to stay in his good graces, people make appropriate sacrifices to him. He is thought to appreciate milk, wine, grapes, pigs and wheat ears. In sunny summer fields, Sylvanus might be seen on his ass, somewhat drunk and aimlessly wandering. Often, he would seem to be sleepy. It is thought, if bound with chains of flowers, he would give prophecy. Trees he favours: pine and ivy.

The Ass, on which Sylvanus is often pictured as riding, was not only sacred to Sylvanus, but to Saturn as well. Agrippa calls the Ass saturnian, and it is associated with the Yuletide Fool.

At this season, Earth is celebrated, so a most important force, at this time, would be Gaea. Gaea is a gift giver and she holds knowledge of the future. There are holes in Earth at a number of locations which are held to be sacred to Gaea. And at these holes, people hope to gain knowledge from Gaea. At times, at the cracks and holes, people hear whispers, gain knowledge. At the cracks and holes people leave gifts for Gaea: often, cakes and honey. Gaea is praised for her many gifts and especially, for crops. Tools sacred to her are the sickle and the plow, and the sickle, she fashioned for a weapon. In her honour, plows are carried in procession and it is often to Gaea, the most sacred oaths are sworn. The sacred Hearth is her alter.

The Time of the Horned Piper would, in spirit, begin December sixth, the Faunus Festival. Ancient philosophers said, Pan and the Satyrs were the first to become aware that there was a problem with the King of the Sky. There should be a torch parade and sacrifice to Pan. At this time, the Earth Spirit, Nick, is honoured and, by some, at this time, expected to give gifts. He relates to Water.

The Horned Piper is a major deity in two sections of time. The first: the few days which are between the time when the Time of the Twelve Signs of the Zodiac end and when the New Sun is born. The second: the Sun's birth to Aquarius. The first, the few days on the Snake's tail, is a time when the order of the Sun's Year is at an end and before new order is established. The old, the ancient order ruled by Saturn, comes in to keep Earth from spinning into complete chaos. The pipes of the Piper add to the largely unstructured joy, to the wild dance. Then, under the new sun, the Piper is the Spirit of the silent, mysterious dark places. He is Lord of Beasts, and these come and go at his command. His is the music of pipes, and this, we have from Dionysius, which is played for libations, brings a feeling of tranquility. There is a sudden shift from sense overload: bright light, loud wild music, roaring laughter, heavy aromas, stimulating food and drink, physical exertion and sexual stimulation: to darkness and silence; from a shouting swirling mob, to an alone feeling, to an empty, barren, cold place. The drop from one to the other, as one might learn from Aldous Huxley, would put the mind in a different place. One might hear, see, understand a thing which would be beyond normal human range. One might get a look into an Otherworld.

As the Old Sun moves toward darkness, ancient powers with a seeming randomness of structure, move in to fill the void. One of these is the ancient Earth Goddess, Ops. She, the all seeing, great gift giver, is honoured, at this season; especially, on December nineteenth. December nineteenth is called Ophalia.

December twentyfirst, called Angeronalia, honours Angerona, Goddess of Winter and Death. She expresses the need for respectful silence in the sacred hours and quiet torch lit, or candle lit, processions are made on the eve before her day and dreams that eve are thought, especially prophetic.

December twentysecond, December twentythird is the Saturnalia. December twentyfourth is called Children's Saturnalia. It is also Yule Eve. The Saturnalia brings Saturn back as Lord, and he proclaims a King's Peace, and he has nothing to do with the old social order; so, all members of society are treated as equal. They dine and socialize together. Jokes and games can be made at the expense of the old order. Representing Saturn, fool kings are appointed, and people are masked to represent other deities who, in spirit, surely would be present. The malicious beings, under the spell of greenery and other charms, would join in the pleasures of the celebrations. The pine is up and decorated. Games of chance and other activities, which might not be permitted under the old order, are freely enjoyed at Saturnalia.

The Yule is filled with feasting, light and song. Rituals are done to harness the power of the changing Time. Wreaths relate to the magic Wheel of the Year. It is a custom, as Hole relates, to have, on a pole, a wheel of wheat for the birds. The Boar's Head Feast is magical, as the death of the Boar represents the sacrifice of the Old Sun. The Boar is crowned with a wreath of rosemary, thyme and bay and he has an apple in his mouth, which acts as a key to open the way from one world to another. The liver of Lord Boar would be inspected and predictions made from it; then, as it is considered sacred, it is important that it be eaten and especially, if it had predicted good fortune. All discarded insides would be respectfully burnt.

At Boarshead Feasts, sprigs of rosemary, thyme and laurel are tied with red string and handed out. Dipped in wine, they bring happiness. The Laurel, called Bay, is the Goddess Daphne and she, a Goddess of Inspiration, is favoured by Apollo.

The Yule Log also represents the Old Sun in his going to the Underworld. It is a most ancient representation. The ritual of obtaining the Yule Log would give respect to the tree. In cutting it, the woodman would take care to spit on his hands before taking hold of his axe, as this petitions a spirit of Water to go between him and harm done to the tree.

When the Yule Log is cut, there are rituals for taking it from the wood to the hearth, and these would often include the singing of carols, sung as charms. Often, it would be the same songs sung year after year.

When the Yule Log gets to the hearth, there would be rituals. Some people put, beside the Yule Log, a piece of turf from their fields. Some, have a blindfolded boy beat the Log while requesting favours to be granted during the coming year. It is certain, some person would be designated to pour a libation on the Yule Log. Often, a bit of last year's Yule Log is included in this year's Yule fire.

Yule Log ashes are considered to have powers. One custom is to put some in a sieve and shake them from the sieve onto the hearth. From these ashes, predictions are made. The ashes under the Yule Log, according to Harrison, are thought to have, if disturbed, a harmful effect on ancestors. After Yule, for protection and blessings, Yule ashes are taken out and spread on the fields.

Smoke carries information to deities; especially, to those of spirit and Air; so, Yule wishes, especially, those of children, are written out and burned on the Yule Log so that Santa, who is Nick, transporter of Dead to the Underworld, might read them in the smoke.

Often, to keep a sacred atmosphere around the Yule Log, squint eyed and other unwholesome people are not permitted in front of it.

To collect gifts from the Underworld, stockings are hung from the mantle over the hearth, the hearth with its tools.

Yule morning comes with an air filled with pure joy. Many bells ring to cleanse the air of all impurities. Through the day, joy and laughter builds into whirling colours: greens, reds, silvers, golds. There are whirling dances and circle games and other ritual games, as Blindman's Bluff, and in these, often people are dropped out are ritually sent to the Otherworld. Gambling is done, often for nuts, as nuts are sacred to the gods and can be used in predicting. He who had been made Fool King would carry a club of the Holly, which is the tree of sacrifice, and would promote bawdiness. A horse god would be represented and would often be constructed from a horse's skull and a man under a sheet. Often, one or more horned deities are represented. Maskers make their rounds and these entertainers take part in song, dramas and other rituals. The rituals would serve to benefit the farm's animals and trees. For fruit and nut trees, there are sung or spoken charms, libations and swattings with a staff. With nut trees, the swattings are thought to be quite important. And as charms with the animals, there are gifts and libations. If the gift of a cake is put on the horns of an ox; then the gift of wassail thrown in the face of the ox; fortune might be told from the way the cake falls.

Maskers become carnations of what they represent. The ancient animal spirits would be here. With in the buffoonery and laughter, there is the sense and realization that the spirit goes to the Underworld. The absurd dramas confirm it. And all, mixed with the mad swirling of song, dance and clowning – and the flashing of light and colour; especially, the Underworld colours of red, green, gold and silver. Little has changed since the way it was described by Tacitus many centuries ago. He had many naked dancers flinging themselves madly among the sharp points of swords and spears.

At the end of Yule, the Fool King, as Saturn, is sacrificed and sent to the Otherworld.

December twentysixth, Boxing Day, is a sacred honouring of the Sun. On this day, the Sun breaks out of the Underworld, breaks past Belenus, the Ox Lord, who is Guardian of the Gate. Gifts are given, on this day, to the unmoneyed. As the day is sacred, it is the day given to a number of activities felt to be important. As a custom, bleeding horses is done on this day. Often, fox hunts are held on Boxing Day.

December thirtyfirst, the end of the year is celebrated and the day is called Hogmanay. It honours the ancient Sun God, Ogmios, or Ogmagog, and the Sun's return to strength. Ogmios, a god of great strength, taught the craft of writing.

Hogmanay is a time for loud parties and these might overflow into loud processions through the night. At midnight, a roar of noise welcomes in the New Year.

What one does New Year's Day would have a bearing on the coming year's activities. The first visitor of the year to a home is felt to have great influence. In many areas, this visitor needs to be a man and there are customs dictating what he should bring and what he should do, and that he be physically acceptable; as, not a flat footed or squint eyed person. One thought is, that he should enter every room of the house; another, that he should stir the ashes in the fireplace; another, that he should make a fire. Gifts it is hoped he will bring are, in some areas, a lump of coal, bread and salt. In some areas, the gifts, which serve as magical charms, will be a silver coin, an apple and whisky. Sometimes, he brings a branch of evergreen and with it, sprinkles all those within the house. Then, the visitor would certainly be given food and drink. Often, the family would keep silent until the first visitor got there.

There are other New Years customs which are felt to be important. Often, gifts for elementals are put in places where the elementals would find them. Many people feel that they need to wear something new. Other customs: houses are cleaned, doorposts anointed. Pork and beans are often eaten New Years Day, as they relate to the Underworld, as New Years Day relates to the Underworld, to ancestors. And Janus, who, with two faces, looks both forward and backward, is especially honoured New Years Day. And Janus and the Underworld relate to prophecy. At this time, for prophetic knowledge, one might walk into a room, throw a shoe over the left shoulder, then say, "Bat, Bat, come under my hat."

Activities done New Years Day would affect activities throughout the year. People avoid hanging a new calendar, New Years Day, before Sun's rise; as, hanging the calendar too early would invite disaster. Washing clothes New Years Day would invite a year of hard work and likely washing clothes would be part of it. Sewing on New Years Day, during the coming year there would be sewing for a funeral. In some areas, a cake is thrown against the front door so that, through the year, the home will be free from hunger. There are, on New Years Day, physical contests; the winner, representing the New Year, would give energy to the coming year.

On New Years Day, people use weather in making predictions. No wind would predict a dry summer; hard winds, a flood. Breezes would bring rains.

Many people will wear at least one new thing on New Years Day. It is thought, dangerous to give anyone fire on New Years Day. Fires are made on New Years Day for the protection of crops through the year ahead.

On New Years Day, water is drawn from wells and springs as it brings health, wards off malicious spirits and, when given to cows, increases their milk. In some places, with branches of evergreen, the water is sprinkled in houses and on the people in them. After drawing the water, a gift of herbs would be given and wells and springs are dressed with herbs and bay.

Part of the blessing, at this time, would come from the Goat Goddess, Amalthea. She cares for the new born Sun, and she supplies care and milk to Jupiter, to the Sun and to the people of her lands.

January fifth, Koreion, or Epiphany Eve, the Yule Tree and all Yuletide greens need to be taken out of the house. Holly, Ivy and Mistletoe, especially, are dangerous if in the house at times other than Yuletide and the days of the Midsummer Season. They would be given to the fire. From the smoke, people get predictions as to how the crops will do in the coming season. Often, masking is done around the fires and often there are maskers representing Bacchus, Sylvanus, Pan, Belenus, and Cernunos and there are witches with booms. There is noise, dance, vulgarity, music, and pranks are played; as, binding boys and girls together with cords. In some areas, there are noisy, disorderly processions through the countryside in order to scare away malicious beings. From the fires, torches are lit and taken to orchards and fields so that crops will get virtues from the fires. The mad running to and fro is done to wild music and songs with nonsense lyrics, as wisdom of the Snake's Tail is still being felt. As Jackson says, the masks worn evoke the powers of the Otherworld. They relate to the Snake.

This is a time, also, for blessing plows. According to Chadwick, the plow is carried around a fire. Then in the night, the Goddess would carry a golden plow over the fields.

January sixth, Epiphany is a time for purification. Shrines are cleaned and purified and statues of deities washed. Some are carried seven times around the shrines before being returned to their places.

As Apollo, according to Macrobius, rises from the Land of the Dead, a ritual of purification is a custom. There would be music and ritual washing; sometimes, washing a representation of Apollo. Sometimes, the representation is taken to a body of water and washed. One custom is to have music by a Star Choir. Members would wear stars on their heads and the leader, have a star on the end of his staff. Some of the songs sung would be Star Songs blessing the Waters.

At the top of the card, the Holly relates to chaos and to the Otherworld. It is a tree favoured by Sylvanus, the Ass and the Green Man and is a tree favoured by Saturn. The Fool King would wear sprigs of Holly. Holly stands for justice and retribution. As a tree of protection, it gives protection from lightning, witchcraft and malicious spirits. Relating to the Wheel; it is associated with the Wheel of the Year and in keeping with this relationship, holly is used for axles. Holly repels poison and other sources of injury. A stick of holly thrown at an animal would cause that animal to lie down. Holly is used in dream magic and in attracting woman.

The Holly King, as a Green Man, went to the Underworld. To send him there, one had to strike each of his twentyfour horses with a stick of holly charcoal.

Holly flowers will cause water to freeze.

Holly relates to balance. As male to female, it balances with Ivy. From Grieve: "Christmastide comes in like a bride With Holly and Ivy clad."

Holly also acts as a balance with the Oak.

Holly is used to treat jaundice, colic, pleurisy, rheumatism, smallpox, dropsy and fevers and to mend broken bones.

Ivy is sacred to the Moon, Saturn, Bacchus and Pan and can prevent the entering of malicious beings. It is an emblem of immortality. Ivy wreaths represent the Circle of the Yule and symbolize life, death and rebirth. Corn dolls are often bound to the Ivy wreaths. Ivy protects against injuries and other disasters and inspires the development of durability, tenacity, harmonies, knowledge, wisdom and transformations needed for achieving goals. As a charm, it is used in gaining love, fertility and other good things. Ivy flowers, in their late blooming, are much valued by the sacred bees. From Gerard: a lotion made from ivy leaves is a cure for ailing eyes.

Adding their magics to the Time of the Horned Piper would be powerful herbs, rosemary and thyme, and the Bay. These herbs would crown and dress the head of the Boar and decorate both sides of the card.

Thyme is held sacred, as it is favoured by Mars and Venus. It grew where Helen's tears fell as she was being taken to Troy. It is an herb used for communicating with fairies. By thyme, in June, fairies are inspired to dance. Thyme was said to grow in the garden of the Fairy Queen. Bees favour thyme. It chases malicious spirits from graves.

Thyme is an herb of protection and relates to the Otherworld, so aids women in having a safe and speedy childbirth. And it is used in communicating with the dead, and in gaining prophecy; especially, where love and romance are concerned. Thyme is worn to attract love. In potions, it is used for wild times and copulation. To please fairies, it is put in fairy rings and grown around beehives. Blooming near hives, it is thought to indicate a fine year for honey. Thyme is put in coffins and planted on graves. It is worn to inspire courage and action. It is strengthening and energizing and it banishes shyness and melancholy. And thyme chases nightmares, and renews spirits.

Thyme is used for cleaning and purifying sacred temples, and it is burned on alters.

Thyme keeps thunder from curdling milk. Eating thyme improves eyesight and strengthens the lungs and chases worms from the body. It keeps the mind and body balanced and regulated, and brings joy to foods.

Thyme is used to clean and heal wounds and sores, to heal burns and to treat rheumatism, arthritis, gastrointestinal ailments, gout, colds, and coughs. And Culpeper adds gall stone, pains in the spleen, pain in the liver, the sciatica and pulmonary problems to the list.

Thyme is used for preserving linen. As it gives strength and courage, warriors wear it into battle. And it puts to flight venomous creatures. It promotes general good health and long life and is valued for Yuletide rituals and decorations.

Rosemary is used in cleaning, purifying and protecting. As it us used at weddings and funerals, it is called the Flower of Birth and Death. At funerals, as it protects the corpse, it is carried by mourners. And it is put on coffins as they are lowered into the graves. With yew and juniper, it is put along the way the corpse is to travel. At some funerals, it is burned as an incense. Rosemary has been thought of as a symbol of the funeral. Rosemary is an emblem of constancy and fidelity and is used to insure that the person missing will be remembered. It is especially helpful in aiding the memory of love.

Rosemary is beneficial in weddings as it inspires love. It is often included among the flowers in the bridal bouquet and it is a custom for betrothed couples to exchange wreaths of rosemary. It promotes purity and an extended youthfulness.

Rosemary wreaths are crowns for deities. The living and the dead are preserved by the smell of rosemary. Sprigs of rosemary are hung in houses to purify and freshen the air, to banish spells and to chase away harmful spirits. Rosemary is put in docks in courts of justice to drive away disease. Rosemary smoke purifies flocks. It is magical and has been used to provide escapes from gaols and from other confinements. It is used to disinfect after plagues.

Rosemary is favoured by Apollo and Deities of the Sea and is associated with the Olympic Games. It is associated with rebirth. Sleeping Beauty was awakened by having rosemary rubbed on her forehead. Keightley said that the Sleeping Beauty was bathed in rosemary flowers. To increase beauty, women wash their faces with water off rosemary leaves.

Rosemary is used in many rituals, and these would include Moon rituals. As rosemary gives purification and promotes wisdom, courage and loyalty, among other virtues, sacred areas are often sprinkled with water off rosemary leaves. And rosemary is often included among the herbs used in ritual baths. It is put in beds and in dream pillows to chase away bad dreams and to bring good dreams, memory, love, and sleep. Spoons made of rosemary wood increase the health giving qualities of food and improve food flavours. It is said, a rosemary wood box would keep a person young. Bread baked with rosemary wood would keep a person in good health.

In gardens, rosemary banishes harmful insects. Fairies enjoy being in rosemary and bees love it. Perfume from the flowers will chase away harmful spirits, purify the air, quicken the senses, relieve fatigue, take away headache and bring elevated mental activity and sweet dreams. In the garden, rosemary grows best where women rule, and it is said, it should be sown in the Dark of the Moon.

Rosemary is used in charms. Powdered rosemary tied to the right arm in a linen cloth makes one light and merry. A love charm is to put rosemary in a cup at each of the four points of the compass, then pour wine over them while requesting aid in love. Another love charm: rosemary is wrapped in linen and buried. Three days later, it is dug up and burned. The ashes would then be put in the intended lover's wine. People use a laurel, rosemary and thyme bath for bringing love.

Rosemary is put in books for their preservation. Rosemary leaves, to keep ale fresh, are put in the ale. Rosemary is put with linen to preserve the linen and to keep pests away from it. Sprigs of rosemary dipped in wine are given as a token of fidelity and that they might bring happiness.

Rosemary is used as a lotion and as a tonic. As a lotion, rosemary cures wounds, and put on the entire body, it brings health. With linen, it cures gout, and it strengthens the eyes, and rubbed on the eyes, it strengthens the senses. As a lotion made with white wine, rosemary makes the face fair.

Rosemary, as a tonic, is used to treat coughs, colic, kidney trouble, liver problems, stomach ailments and dropsy. Rosemary, said Buchman, is used to treat hysterical depression. Rosemary tonic is said to be a good tonic for the heart and nerve disorders, and it drives out worms from the intestines. Kloss lists it used it to cure mental disturbance, nervous conditions and the headaches of which they are the cause. Among other ailments, Kloss lists it as a treatment for sore throats. Rosemary aids digestion.

Worn around the neck, rosemary is said to stimulate blood flow, increase the flow of urine, and to give protection from disease and malicious spells, to bring clarity to the mind and to balance the emotions.

Rosemary is said to have the power to shape a climate of thought, to hold an experience of Spirit World motions and to give ability in memory, so that it has been symbolic of memory. Rosemary sends the message, "Remember me."

Rosemary, Thyme and Laurel form a wreath given to the Boar, which is the carnation of the Sun God, for his trip to the Underworld. And rosemary is used in Yuletide decorations.

Rosemary inspires loving memories. It is planted on graves and is an emblem of eternity.

On graves, one might find rosemary and thyme: rosemary means memory and the meaning of thyme is valour.

Holly is the tree of the highest profile in the Time of the Horned Piper. It represents the time at the end of twelve Moons, then its influence and visibility carries on. First, it is in the house until January fifth. Then, there is the bright memory of the outrageous, outlandish Fool and his sacrifice, and the memory would often be slow to fade. But the Tree of the Fool King is the Tree of the Time of the Fool; so, the Tree of the Fool. But as Janus looks out on frozen January, his tree of that time would be the Birch. However, the Birch takes charge of the Fool, educates the Fool and gives the Fool first gifts. The influence of Saturn and Horned Pipers linger through the Time of the First Moon, and the Holly is sacred to them.

The Birch is the tree at the Gates to the Underworld, and it stands on the banks of the Styx. It is associated with birth and beginnings, which would include the birth of the New Year. At birth, the Birch takes possession in the name of this World. It gives care to those who are newly born, and gives protection from the Underworld. Birch is used to sweep away malicious spirits. As a switch, it takes possession, brings people to awareness and gives perception. It represents, and brings, law and purity. The Birch gives knowledge, and it inspires copulation. The Birch is often the tree selected for the Maypole.

Birch represents authority. To represent authority, birch rods are bound around an axe. The Sybilline Tablets of Tarquin were written on birchbark. Ghosts are said to be given birch, which would insure that they would be prompt to return to the Underworld. Birch protects the newly born from being snatched back into the Underworld. It protects against the evil eye.

Birch, seen pale and slender in the forest, is called a beautiful nymph, and the Lady of the Woods. She can be dangerous. A grove of birch can lure a person into the Underworld. The Birch can also save a person from going to the Underworld.

Birch is used in love charms. One of these is to take a stick of birch, write on it in red, "Bring me true love." Then, with rosemary and thyme, burn the stick – while saying a love charm to Venus and Mars.

Birch is used for treating stone in the kidney and stone in the bladder, for treating rheumatism, dropsy and gout. It cures sores in the mouth and drives out worms. It cures dysentery and protects women against barrenness. As a lotion, it heals sores and wounds and corrects skin problems. Birch protects from lightning, but if honoured by lightning from Donar, the wood is considered a sacred gift from the Birch.

The Birch gives aid in communication.

In dark forest, on icy ground, a pale, slender trunk of a birch would be seen: the First Moon's Tree.

January twenty, as Signs of the Zodiac are shifting, is a time for predictions. At this time, to dream of a lover, it is a custom for a woman to put thyme in one of her shoes, rosemary in the other; then, put one shoe on one side of her bed, the other shoe on the other.

The Mistletoe, hanging below the Holly and Ivy, would be hanging above the hearth, the alter of the Earth Goddess. This, the lofty herb, the herb of dignity, promotes the well being of populations.

There would always be an open way to the alter of the Earth Goddess. So, said Hawthorne, in any home, if a witch had a way to the hearth, she had a way out and, likely, it would be up the chimney on a broomstick. The broom is a magical tool and one of its uses is for sweeping away impurities from the dead before they are taken to the Underworld. Nick, who is basically malicious; so, would often find his way into a house blocked by charms; would enter a house by the same road by which a witch might wish to leave it. As Yule Season is sacred, malicious acts prohibited, Nick is hindered from doing his usual activities; so, he is put to work carrying gifts.

Especially at Yule, other somewhat malicious beings enter homes by Gaea's road: goblins, elves, brownies, bogarts, bogies, kobolds and many others. And the misrule at Yule is much to their pleasure. They join in the mad, wild celebrations and aid the disorder of the dances. And Gaea would certainly join the dance. From Gladstar: "She dances in the night skies."

Gladstar calls Gaea, the Spirit of Longevity.

To the right of the hearth, and above, is a wreath, and to the right, over some greens, a candle. Candles are gifts of the Sacred Bee, and the Bee was brought from the Underworld by Gaea.

Card X has much to do with prediction. It has major boundaries within its scope, and boundaries are doors to the Underworld, which hold knowledge of the Future. Card X holds a number of other relationships to the Underworld. One is the doorway of the hearth. And Card X has the sudden switch from flashing light and frantic movement to cold, dark, lonely, still, silent areas and not only is the change at a boundary, but the shock of sense switch gives a flash of ability to intuition.

Card X holds many charms and relates to much giving. Animals are given gifts of food and cakes are for fruit trees left in the tree's crotches. Card X holds, also, a time of sacrifice. Card X is also the still, silent expanse of nature where the music is a quiet song of peace. Card X, the Dragon would gobble up a force which had become too decadent to move forward. It would eat the Old Sun to make room for that which would bring new energy. Then the New Sun would break free from the Dragon of Darkness. Light would fall on a bare winter landscape to give a look beyond the chaotic and the structured, to new beginnings, to freedom to make changes. However, darkness still lingers in the cold forests.

In the light of the First Moon, the tree at the start of things is a glimmer of white in the darkness. In the year, the first time the cattle are driven to the fields they are driven with birch switches. It is said, dead girls dance in the moonlight among the birches. It is a beautiful dance, but a dance of death, for any who see the dance soon die.

The card number is X, the sum of the first four sacred numbers. It represents the Circle and is a female number, which relates to sex. It has no solid center, but at its center is a dark abyss.

The Time of the Horned Piper combines chaotic ends with primitive beginnings. Ends would relate to the Golden Age, the age when bizarre and incredible things were said to have happened on Earth, when deities were said to have physically walked on Earth. Customs revert to, and personalities active at this time, reflect an earlier age. Basic instinct and animal energy inspires new directions. And there is a music of flutes which brings messages from the Gods.

This is a shadowy card. In a dark corner, a shadowy pine; then, from the flickering light, wavery shadows would fall.

XI ~ Cup Bearer

In the early season, Nature is a problem and the reliability of the deities, a question. The Sun is back: not considered strong, but back. This is a time of a bleak, cold landscape, and a purity with the bleakness.

In center of Card XI is a deity, on one knee, pouring water on Earth below, and he pours from a large cup. This would be Phaenon, Cup Bearer for the Sky God, Uranus. Phaenon's gift of water attracted attention when it was what put out the fires which had been set by the Sun God, Phaeton.

In the Classical World, the ancient and obscure Phaeton had little chance of rising in the East and being recognized as the Sun. Helios rode the Sun Car as he had day in and day out ever since Hyperion had gone to Selene's house in the Underworld. Phaeton went to Helios' golden house and told Helios that he, Phaeton, was his son; so, he, Phaeton, should have a share in riding the Sun Car. Helios was adamant in his objection to this request, but he did agree to let Phaeton drive the car one time, so that Phaeton could show to all that he was indeed a Sun. With a few instructions from Helios, Phaeton stepped into the car. However, it had been ages since Phaeton had made a round through the sky. Much had changed. Monsters had changed positions and he had no rapport with the ones which were close to the way which he wanted to take. He drove up and down, this way and that, frantically trying to get out of their way. Jupiter, Zeus Pater, saw the strange sight, the Sun gone mad. He saw wide areas of fires; other areas, freezing. Jupiter hit the Sun Car with a bolt of lightning, knocked Phaeton out into the stars. Jupiter then had a talk with Helios, expressed his displeasure at the lack of wisdom in letting Phaeton drive the Sun Car. Helios had become very big, but his stature was to become lessened. Gods grow great, then fade. As classic writers have said, the gods don't know everything; but Helios, who is far seeing, might have suspected all was not in harmony. If the Sun Car was going to have trouble, it would be best for Helios if he were not in it. He wasn't. A stand in Sun God, a Fool King, was.

The failure of the sun reflected, to some extent, on the deities in general. Jupiter was having trouble extinguishing the fires caused by

Phaeton; so, Uranus sent his Cup Bearer, Phaenon, to put out the fires. It was thought, this disturbed Jupiter that Phaenon had a power which he, Jupiter, seemed not to have. Phaenon might represent powers of Nature which are beyond the Pantheon of the gods; represent hidden things in the great expanse of Nature. Jupiter was looking to destroy Phaenon, but Uranus had his Cup Bearer hidden away in the grey folds of his cloak, and Uranus gave Judgement that Phaenon couldn't be destroyed. Phaenon became a star, a bright one.

The balance in the Pantheon was changing. Apollo was gaining in strength. In the background, in Uranus, the Great Grey Sky Ox, there would be very little change. And nature, of which Uranus seemed, in a way, a part, would be moving in its way. The Great Wheels of the seasons keep turning, causing rain when the Wheels of Nature demand that it be there; rain, beyond the power of great gods to entirely regulate, coming when the turning Wheels of Time call for it to come.

At this turning, important points in the progress of Nature are honoured, and lesser deities, deities in which all peoples hopes are not hitched. An early point would be February second, Candlemas. These honour, one, time of first milk of the ewes. The deity chiefly honoured at this time has not always been widely known throughout the Classical World. However, she is a major force in many areas and is known as Bridget, Goddess of Dawn. As she is Goddess of Light, she is Goddess of Enlightenment. She is related to all the basic elements. With Water, she protects sacred wells. With Fire, she rules smithing and, also, the soft light of candles, gifts from the sacred Bee. Relating to Earth and Air, she is a healer with a special love for animals. Imbolc, Bridget comes out of darkness to bring light – and renewal. And she brings beauty and song. She gives protection, especially, to the young; especially, to sheep and cows. As a Goddess of Dawn, Bridget is said to hang her clothes on the Sun's first rays. Out of human form, Monaghan suggests, she would have been thought of as the power of Hills, or of Rushing Rivers. Bridget is a warrior goddess who protects her lands. She might be seen dressed in white, wearing fruits of Apple, and of Rowan.

At Imbolc, to welcome Bridget, in one tradition, fresh rushes are put on the floors and women wear sprigs of alehoof when they go to do their milking. Cribs for Bridget are put on hearths, a club and a candle beside it. Often, a cloth is put near Bridget's crib in hope that Bridget will touch it so that ever after, it would have healing power. The club is put there so that Bridget would chase off malicious beings. Charms, made of grain stalks woven into crosses, are put on walls or ceilings. One custom, we have from Ferguson, has Bridget welcomed with,

"Come Bridget, thy bed is ready."
This, said three times.

During the day, a custom has hoops of rope carried from house to house for people to climb through in order to gain, from Bridget, good health. Straw doll representations of Bridget are carried around also and, to bring luck, given out. In the evening, there would be programs featuring poetry and music.

February second, Festum Candelarum, or Candlemas, hearths are looked at to see if there is an imprint of Bridget's club in the ashes. An imprint would indicate that there would be a good harvest.

Juno is honoured also, and, for her, there is a tradition of the Februa procession: a candle lit procession for purity. Bears and other wild animals are honoured. Hibernating animals are thought to be weather predictors. A bright day, the animal would object to it, go back to sleep. This would predict a long period of cold weather. No Sun at mid day, warm weather would be on the way and spring soon come. Rain on Candlemas is said to wash winter away. The awakening of hibernating animals relates to rebirth. There is a search, at this time, for suggestions of birth. Ritual preparations are invocations: the bath, the use of the broom, the unwinding Spiral Dance, the going masked from house to house with the Bridget Oat Sheaf Doll, the Bridget Crib. People clean, purify, prepare for births.

With the Feast of Candlemas, candles relate to spirituality and purity. White wine, oat cakes and milk are thought appropriate foods.

Girls at Candlemas throw lumps of Earth at crows in order to gain predictions of what kind of man they would marry. It the crow did not fly, the girl might have sspected she would not marry.

Festum Candelarum is one of the four celebrations, one every three months, which honour turning points of the life cycle of Earth. Each of the Four has a goddess as a central force driving the cycle. The Earth Cycle has, as part of it, the agricultural cycle. The place on the agricultural cycle would be the place of birth.

February twelfth is a day for honouring the Bear Goddess, Artemis, the warrior goddess who slew the great giant, Tityos. Her priestesses, Bear Virgins, are deadly. At times, on this day, men, their feet ritually painted black with soot, are sacrificed to the goddess.

February fourteenth, February fifteenth; Valentines Day, Lupercalia; lesser Sun deities are honoured with boisterous rituals intended to inspire reproduction. The customs of Valentines Day inspire romance and mating. Birds are said to mate on Valentines Day.

As Love has a relationship with the Sun, deities of Love; Aphrodite, Eros and Venus; are honoured with those of the Sun; Granus and Vali. Pennick lists Vali as a god honoured on this day, but in the Classical World, that god might have been called by some variation of that name. Juno is also honoured at this time.

Eros, in a Sun God aspect, shoots copulating arrows into the hearts of lovers.

Gaily decorated greeting cards, letters and tokens which, on this day, are passed between men and women, go by the name of valentines. Colours used on these are usually white for purity and red for passion.

On Valentines Day, under red and white decorations, romantic dances are held and confections, flowers and other presents given. A tradition has Granus Fires, on the hills, lit; and, at some of these; boys, out of a box, draw the names of girls who, for the evening, are to be their partners. At the fires and at the dances, romance related games are played. Sometimes, at the evening's close, girls put five Bay leaves; the leaves, sacred to the Sun; under their pillows in order to get prophetic love dreams.

At this time, a Valentine love madness will infect people and other animals. A calf born Valentines Day is thought to be of little practical value. At Valentines, some think it unwise to set hens. A Valentines Day birth is a way to get infected.

The fifteenth, Lupercalia, honours Lupercus and Pan. The she wolf who gave first milk to the first children of Rome is also honoured. Lupercus is the cannibalistic Sun God whom Jupiter turned into a wolf. On Lupercalia, cakes are made from the first fruits of the last year's harvest. First fruits, because that is when the harvest is young and strong. The Spirit of the sacrificed young, strong harvest goes into the men. A widely practiced Lupercalia ritual: men divide into two parties: the Wolf Party, representing Lupercus, and the Goat Party, representing Pan. The purpose of the ritual is to insure fertility and purity in women and, especially, in the land.

After the sacrifices, the men wash themselves in milk; then, in their separate parties, smear themselves with blood and milk; then drink wine, howl, laugh loudly, and act like animals. The men put on goatskin belts, drink more wine; then, when insanity reaches a peak, the men of each party take goatskin straps, called Februas, and race each other to the towns where, with the straps, they whip the women they catch up with to make these women pure and fertile. Some people they catch, they paint black streaks on them to indicate that these are sacrifices.

A love charm used on Lupercalia is to run three times around a graveyard while throwing hemp seeds and shouting,

> "I sow hemp seed, hemp seed I sow.
> Come, my true love, the hemp to mow."

February twentyfirst, Feralia, or Biiken Fire Day, is a day for celebrating the return of the Sun God, Eborc, Ipor, or Hyperion; and for carrying gifts to the graves of the dead. Also, food is set out of doors for ghosts, but by the use of Buckthorn and hemp ropes, certain areas are of ghosts kept free. It is mostly ghosts connected to one's family with which one would be concerned. Care might be taken to keep from having an unharmonious mix of ghosts. On this day, dinner would be eaten in silence while each one present would be thinking of his responsibility to the Otherworld. At the table, the dinner is commenced and terminated by the ringing of a bell. Often, new wine is served from a pitcher from which spirits are thought to rise. The pitcher is thought, related to a burial urn and from it, libations are poured to Ceres, Mercury and Proserpine.

After dinner, there is the solemn march to the cemetery and these parades would be an empowering dance. Marchers carry wine, milk and flowers to put on the graves.

After dark, fires are lit on the hilltops in celebrating the return of the Sun God, and torches from the fires are run down into the dark fields for blessings, encouragement and so the Young Sun will grant requests. "The deities," said Ausonius, "are reasonable, so if one keeps requests in reason, he will usually find a sympathetic ear."

February twentysecond, Eboracum, is a day for joy, for flags and patriotic music in honour of the Sun God, the Yew Tree and the country. Places are decorated in bright colours. Red candies, in the shape of the single blade axe of the Sun, are handed out. Cakes are with cherries decorated, so represent the fruit of the Yew, which tree is a Sun form and is also the Bow of the Sun. General George Washington, the Father of a Nation, is honoured on this day.

February twentythird, Terminalia, borders are honoured. They are doors to the Underworld so are sacred and are sometimes protected by ghosts. On Terminalia, asses are sacrificed to the Sun.

The Time of the Cup Bearer brings birth and fertility, brings the shaping of matter to compliment the spirit. It brings purity and clarity and this aids looks into the Otherworld. At this time, the Young Sun is honoured and some of the somewhat obscure deities and some of these have solar connections. The shafts of Eros and Aphrodite bring usually, not death or deadly fire, but Love; however, they relate to the Sun. Gods in early, animal form are honoured and there is a suggestion of chaos. There is an unease with deities and a search for a controlling force, or spirit, or, for the many forces in nature. Attention is paid to rocks, trees and wells.

This is a time of Air. The Great Sky is important. The Great Moving Force of the Cup Bearer is Uranus, the Great Grey Sky. As E. O. James says, he personified Nature before creation and independent of particularity. He is a God of Formless Sky, of Crude Stone. He gave a spiritual need to form. As matter takes shape, as Whewell points out, spiritual meanings can be realized in the properties of number and figure. The properties would produce states of mind and sensual relations. Uranus is the Great Grey Judge. He created form. He inspired the honouring of Crude Stone.

A major force on card XI is Latona, the Dark Sky. She seems more a part of nature than do many of the deities who are more thought of as doing things. Latona is considered to have given birth to light. Apollo, in one aspect, is Light of the Sun and Artemis, in one aspect, Light of the Moon. Hera, the Light of Day, is jealous and chases Latona away. But that the Dark Sky is to be respected is made clear by the example of what happened to Niobe. Because of a slight done to Latona, Niobe's children were, by Apollo and Artemis, shot through with arrows and Niobe, turned to stone. And this is the Time of Latona, the Light, not of heat, but of Enlightenment, of Spirituality, of Beauty: the sacred light of the candle, Latona is called the Beautiful Dark Lady and this needs no physical rendering. The Beautiful Venus at Laussel is certainly different from that at Willendorf. Beauty is one's mental picture.

Card XI, on the right, is a branch of the Rowan, called the Quicken, as it breaks through the frost to awaken life, and to bring new birth. It is a tree of beginnings and of enlightenment. It inspires prophecy. The Rowan is used for contacting spirits, some of which give knowledge of the future.

The Rowan instigates prosperity, brings courage, inspires quick production and protects against witchcraft, drowning, snakes and demons. It is used in healing wounds. To drive away spells, horse whips are made of rowan and rowan is put over barn doors and in chicken houses. Rowan charms are made by the sticks, to form a cross, being tied together with red wool, or by seven notches being cut in the sticks. For protection, rowan is used for milk pails. To gain the good will of fairies, children carry rowan berries. Rowan is planted in cemeteries to keep unwelcome spirits away and in yards to bring luck. People use rowan smoke for confusing enemies. For protection, rowan is tied to the tails of cattle and is put on ships. For giving courage, rowan rings are put around the legs of cocks.

Rowan is associated with the Sun. Its branches are cut after the first rays of the Sun have touched them. If the branches are to be used for aiding cow's udders, they are not permitted to touch the ground. The Rowan is the Raven's tree.

An herb associated with the Cup Bearer is Alehoof. Alehoof protects against witchcraft and gives a person an ability to recognize witches. It is used for purification and has been found useful in treating lung complaints, headaches, kidney ailments, sore throats, liver complaints, sore eyes and indigestion and in purifying the blood. Alehoof is an ingredient in some beers.

The Garnet reflects the fruits of the Rowan and the Yew and holds the spark of courage and of procreation. It promotes devotion, sincerity and loyalty.

The Bear is important in the Time of the Cup Bearer. Not only is it a powerful goddess, but a god who protects and gives valuable gifts. The god is Arthur, the Dark Bear. He supervised the distribution of grain and honey and defended his people at such places as Badon Hill, where, we learn from Nennius, Arthur slew ninehundredsixty warriors.

In the upper center of Card XI, brought in by the Great Wind, is Phaenon, on one knee, pouring from a great cup. Running water is life giving. It would awaken life in the frosty land. The turned down cup refreshes. It is a libation. It returns life to Earth; so, is slaying. It is the cup seen on ancient grave markers.

On the card, at the lower right, is a branch of the Rowan. At the lower left is a Dark Bear. Bear's claws are considered, instruments of sorcery. At the bottom of the card, in each corner, is a garnet, and between these, a few small Alehoof plants.

Card XI holds insight and inspiration. It also holds doubt, worry, speculation and risk taking, hesitation and unsettled purpose. One is likely to make tentative moves; fearful, yet enthusiastic. There is a freshness about this time.

XII ~ Wave

The major image of Card XII would be the Wave. This is Water, all of its aspects, all of its deities. One, the Wave is the seemingly boundless Sea, the great body of Water. The great body of Water, the veil between the worlds, between life and death; should one be out on the deep, might bring a bottomless feeling of lostness; and so, cause panic. It might inspire vision and dream, might give discoveries, give knowledge, give insight, give other gifts.

The great Sea can be calm, sleepy, playful; then suddenly rise up, an awful monster causing terror; sometimes, death. Out in the deep, it might develop mists, causing one to drift away, lost in its darkness; or, float away trapped in its dreamworlds.

The Great Sea is beautiful in its vastness, is awe inspiring, is breathe taking.

Going to Sea might be done as a ritual, as an initiation, The Sea might be invoked through ritual. A trance trip to Sea might bring the Sea's gifts, might bring terrors from the Sea.

The Sea is seen as a great god: Neptune, Poseidon or Lear; as a sea goddess: Doris, or shape shifting Tethys. Deities of the Sea often change shape. They often take the form of a horse. Poseidon, was in horse form when he seduced Earth. Neptune is not only the element beyond the ports, he is Water everywhere, lakes to rain puddles. He is the mysterious element in the sacred chalice, which might be drifting in his mysterious waves.

A big influence on the Sea is the Moon and the many deities of the Moon. Of the first of these is Juno. As Juno has first, a New Moon form, she is an important Goddess of Birth who leads the way to light. As March 1 is often considered the birth of the year, she is honoured at this time. In her honour, Vesta's fire is lit and the day is called Matronalia.

Also, on this day, Mars is honoured and his shrines, decorated with fresh boughs of bay. The shields of Mars are moved and priests put on war paint, dance, clash spears against shields and chant invocations to Mars.

Whuppity Stourie, an elemental lady healer, is honoured and for her, the day is sometimes called Whuppity Stourie Day. Her healing of pigs associates her with the Sacred Sow. A Sow is a form which Earth takes. At a spring ritual for Ceres, pigs are washed.

The day is also called Davids Day, as it is the day Dofyd came to conquer Avagddu, the Dark Sky. The Onion is his sacred herb and the sacred herb of Uther, the Dragon King, and of Arthur. Uther, when going into battle, wore an onion on his helm. March 1, to honour Uther, Arthur and Dofyd, and to assist the new born Sun; onions are worn. Often, it is the leek type of onions that are worn. Onions are often worn into battle as they protect from weapons, fire and lightning – and the evil eye.

The Onion relates not only to the Dragon King, but to snakes in general. Onions, like snakes, shed their skins and are born again. Onion skins are weather predictors. When onion skins are thin, a mild winter is said to be coming.

As the Onion has a relationship with the Snake, it is called upon to counter problems with snakes. Onions are used for curing snake bites and for banishing worms from the intestines. Albertus said that garlic, of the onion family, gives protection from snakes.

As the Onion relates to rebirth, onions are valued for treating problems relating to conception. They are used for increasing sperm production and for providing correct functioning of women's sex organs. For love attraction, Albertus names leek and periwinkle; together, wrapped in powdered earthworm; as a charm. As with snakes, onions are thought, magical. They are worn for protection from vampires and witchcraft. They are said to drive away moles. In the first hours of March 1, one might look into the future, obtain a vision of a future mate, by walking three times around a leek bed.

As the Snake is a healer, the Onion is valued for working cures. It is used as a cure for earache, lethargy, ulcers, dropsy, colds, coughs and gravel. Garlic cures epilepsy and rheumatism and protects cattle from anthrax. Onion cleans the blood.

The Onion has an ogre form. As an ogre, he mints coins, and this would indicate a relationship with the Moon. Deities of the Moon favour snakes. Juno sent the great snake, Python, to torment Letona. Snakes relate to the Wave. The Snake of the Sea swallows the Sun.

The Onion is a powerful spirit which can be dangerous. It was said, "Above the field, the Norse beheld the stern aspect of the god. And on his helm did weep to see the Onion's dreadful nod."

As March 1 has a relation to birth, it relates to the Underworld, to its dark knowledge. On this day, knowledge might be obtained by one throwing a shoe over his head. If the toe of the shoe had landed pointed out, that would have predicted moving or death. Related to the Underworld, corpse candles would appear March 1 when someone was soon to die. They are thought, related to the dead Sun.

March 1 is a time for cleaning and purification. Spring water is sprinkled in the rooms of the house; then, with the broom, enchantments are swept out of the house.

March 2, Sacred Wells are honoured and the day is called, after a god of Sacred Wells, Chads Day, or Ceaddas Day. As Ceadda is a healer, many springs and wells have healing powers. Wells and springs can also be used for looking into the future. At one well, with a skull, 3 times water was dipped, sipped and the remainder thrown over the head in order to gain a vision of the future. Another method of using well, or spring, water for predicting: a wooden tub is put by the ill person's bed, the tub filled with the sacred water, then a wooden bowl is put on the water. Sunwise motion of the bowl indicates the road to recovery; widdershins motion, the reverse. From some pools, wells or springs; a stone, or stones, are taken and these, used in predicting the future. For this use, gifts are given to the spring or well. March 1, libations of milk are made at some sacred springs and wells. Some of these springs and wells are handsomely decorated.

March 2 is a day when sacred waters have special healing powers. At some springs and wells, for the special powers; it is thought the water needs to be quaffed before sunrise. The sacred water has other uses. A person away from home, if his socks are boiled in the sacred water, it could require him to go home. Some springs inspire musical ability. Also, physical beauty can be given by springs and wells. And these gifts can be taken away of withheld. And springs and wells can cause storms and other troubles. During an eclipse, wells and springs are covered to keep their waters from being contaminated.

March 3 is Lear's Day, the day for the Sea. The Lord of the Sea brews life giving apple beer. The Sea relates to fertility. Avoid travel.

March 7 honours the Moon and the coming of Spring. Called Junonalia, or Marzana, it celebrates Selene, Juno, the Goddess of Winter Earth and the coming of the deities of Spring. At the front of a parade, the Goddess of Winter is taken to a river or brook so that she washes away. It is a custom to give gifts to bodies of water. People and dolls representing people have been given to the rivers. Men, before marrying, have put locks of their intended's hair into rivers so that the river ladies would have first claim. If a girl died unwed, a pitcher of the water was put on her grave. Girls, before they wed, have a custom of each giving a lock of hair to a river to offer themselves first, to a river god. As rivers are forked, they hold a relationship to horned beasts. As the horned, dark goddess, Selene, favours bald men and horned beings. This puts the river gods in her favour. River gods sometimes battle the Sea.

March 14 is a day for the Horse and especially, the War Horse. The day, Equirria, also honours Mars and Earth God, Consus, as Consus is a protector of horses: And their shrines, on this day, are decorated. On Equirria, there are horse races. Neptune is a lover of horses and patron of horse races: this, from Bulfinch.

The Horse comes from the Sea. Some horses, feeling this kinship, return to Water. The Sea gave the horses which pull the Sun, and the Sun itself has, at times, Horse form. The Horse is sacred and magical. Horse's skulls, as charms to ward off witchcraft, are nailed above barn doors. Horseshoes, to secure good luck, are nailed, open end up, over doors. Before sunrise, in a barn, among horses, standing an hour, is considered a way to cure consumption. Horses are believed, able to see Otherworld beings and some are, it is thought, beings of the Otherworld. Some people, if they see what they suspect is an Otherworld horse, they will spit at it to put a water barrier between it and them. Otherworld horses are certainly dangerous. Many, called Water Horses, will turn into water if they contact a brook or river.

March 15, the death of Julius Caesar is remembered.

The Clover represents life rising from water. It represents 3 factors unified, coming forth as life. Its petals represent, in one aspect, spirit, mind and body. In people, these aspects relate to faith, wisdom and valour. The coming together of 3 forces to make life is represented, beside in the clover, in Neptune's trident and in the staff of Mercury. The Clover, the coming together of the 3 forces, is a key to the Underworld. It is an opener of ways. As an opener of ways, it is worn to inspire prophetic dreams. Also, its frequent use as an expectorant relates to its being an opener of ways. The 3 leaf clover is carried to break witchcraft spells – and to serve as a charm against malicious actions which might be directed toward the person carrying it. The Goddess of Hope, Spes, is seen holding a clover leaf.

Clover is used in foretelling fortunes in love. Finding a 2 leaf clover indicates binding love. Red clover is sometimes given as a request for fidelity and white clover, as a pledge of fidelity. Snakes avoid clover.

The 4 leaf clover is the sacred cross. It is the resolution of conflicts, the balance of the 4 elements. It is said to spring up where fairies leave their footprints, to be under the protection of the fairies and to be magical. It gives an ability to see through magics and to break spells. Women put 4 leaf clovers in their right shoes in order to attract mates. It is sometimes put under the pillow to bring in dream a future mate. And the 4 leaf clover brings good luck, and a look into the Underworld.

Clover is a major visual theme, used in many decorations, for Agonium Martiale, March 17. As it opposes snakes, snakes are said to keep out of clumps of clover. People use it to cure snakebites and people drink clover juice to gain protection from snakes. Clover has a gift of healing. It is used in treating wounds, respiratory problems, coughs, ulcers, tissue repair, gastrointestinal problems, gout, spasms, swellings, syphilis, skin eruptions, inflammations, heart problems, eye problems, gout and cancer. It inspires cheerfulness. It is used in cleaning and energizing copper and sacred tools. Clover is best gathered under a Full Moon.

Cress is an herb of the Wave. Cress takes different forms as, sometimes, it is water cress, which relates closely to the Spirit of Water; but a usual cress is bitter cress. Cress is favoured by Selene and Ceridwen. Ceridwen included the Cress in her cauldron when she brewed her potion of inspiration. As a healer, cress is used as a lotion and as a tonic to treat respiratory ailments and it is eaten to clear the mind.

Delphinium, or Larkspur, an herb of the Wave, is said to have been created by Neptune. He is said, at the request of a dolphin who wished to honour the fisherman, to have turned the fisherman into the herb. From most ancient times, the Delphinium has been known as a sacred herb and has been put on graves and has decorated shrines. It is a poison, but has value in healing. It is used in treating colic and piles. For blessings, it is put under sheets.

The Dolphin who called for the Delphinium is sacred to Apollo, as Apollo at times takes dolphin form. Lovers of music, dolphins saved the life of harper Arion when the harper was threatened by enemies. Arion is the musical quality of the Sea. Dolphins act as a community to solve problems.

From Gerard: Delphinium, as a medication, was said to have been used by larks.

The tree of the Wave is the Elder. The Elder can be seen as the guardian of a spring which, Heselton has said, in some places would be called a rag well. The name, from rags tied to the guardian tree, perhaps, in hope that some wish might be granted.

It is thought, the Elder is rooted in the Underworld and is able to send the living there. It is said, if one should walk over a fallen elder, he is doomed to die within the year. It is thought, dangerous to take elder into a house. Those who do, take a chance of being pulled away by ghosts. To burn elder, and especially, in the house, is said to bring demons or death. Beds made of elder are said to be dangerous. Should a cradle be made of elder, the Lady of the Elder, it is said, would be likely to choke, steal or otherwise harm any baby that was in it. To go to sleep under an elder could be deadly. And one should be careful what one uses elder for. A child or an animal switched with elder might wither away.

Elders are attracted to witchcraft, to the darker powers. Pith from elder sticks put on water, would likely float toward a witch, if one be present. Elder is used for the dangerous practice of looking into the Underworld. On a dark Midsummer Eve, standing under an elder, one might see beings in the Underworld. One might plant an elder in a cemetery so that when it bloomed, the dead buried there could communicate their pleasure. Musical instruments made from elder wood can seem magical, as they are pleasing to ghosts and ghosts can add to the effects of the music. Branches of elder are taken to funerals so the Muses can weave song into them. Elder is used for the handles of the whips used by many of the hearse drivers. From Fernie: Elder is buried with the dead to keep them safe from witches. If the elder had been blessed by the muses, it would cheer the dead with the blessings of music.

Elders like lonesome wild places, lonely cemeteries, and often grow where blood has been spilled; especially, from the blood of slaughtered warriors. To drink from a bowl made of elder would make men's hands grow out of the ground.

Around elders, circles of power can be felt. The Spirit of the Elder is a lady who can be scary. She could seem, though ghostly, beautiful: then, suddenly, an awful shell of a person; scary even to those whom she protects. For prophecy, some women hold a branch of elder, then say,

> "Sweet Elder, I shake, I shake,
> Where is the love I wake?"

They then would listen for a dog to bark. The direction from which the bark would come would signal the direction in which a lover would be.

The Elder eschews the element of Fire. Those dear to the Sun are likely not well liked by the Elder. Elders are usually protective of farms and farm animals. However, they dislike chickens, which are birds of the Sun, and, at times, will injure or slay them. The pleasure which elders take in music is most often greater where the elders are not disturbed by chickens. For musical instruments, the wood should be gotten from elders which have never been disturbed by the crowing of a rooster. Elders favour geese. Cows enjoy the company of elders. Horses do not.

Amulets made of elder wood are best kept out of sunlight. As elders dislike the Sun, these amulets, which are looked to for protection and cures, would lack power if the wood from which they had been made had been struck by the light of the Sun.

Many other tools are made of elder wood and these, for the most part, are best kept out of sunlight. Elder is used for beams for the hangman, reels for the angler, skewers for the butcher, combs for the groom, shoe trees for the cobbler and shuttles for weaver.

Farmers use fence poles of elder in order to keep out unwanted beings, and these include mice and moles.

Elder sticks and staffs are of use to the healer. Elder sticks, chewed, get rid of toothaches. To get rid of fevers, elder sticks are pounded into the ground. Elder sticks are carried for protection from robbers, insects, worms and snakes. Taken to weddings, they bring good fortune. From Aburrow: horsemen carry them to keep from getting sores from the saddles. Worn around the neck, if the stick has never touched sunlight, it would fend off erysipelas and other ailments.

Elder sticks and staffs are best gathered on Epiphany. Before collecting any part of an elder, one must first obtain permission. It is a custom to go to the Elder uncovered. As Father Young relates, many have made it a habit to uncover when walking past, or, especially, when standing before, an elder. Uncovered, one asks politely to have some of the elder, explains what one wants it for; then, listens to see if the elder is willing to give the gift. Permission given, one makes a compensatory gift; then, for a stick, or staff, one spits three times before making the first cut.

For the healer, the entire elder is found to be of value. The roots and bark are used to cleanse the gastrointestinal system. From the bark, a lotion is made for treating rheumatism, stings, wounds, muscle aches, sores, skin disorders and bites. To get the bark, the sticks should be peeled toward the trunk. From the leaves, a tea is made. It is used in treating quinsy, dropsy, influenza, colds, erysipelas, sciatica, syphilis, rheumatism and gout. For warts, the leaves are rubbed on the wart, then buried under wet mud, so that as they rot, the wart will fade. Leaves are best gathered Midsummer morning after the dew has dried. From elder blooms, a tea is made and used in treating headache, fevers, ulcers, influenza, colds, scrofula, asthma, pleurisy, urinary problems, epilepsy, palsy, kidney and liver problems and impure blood. A lotion from the flowers is used for headache, burns, bruises and sprains. One method used for headaches: the hair is washed in a bowl of lotion, then combed; then, tallow run through the comb, into the bowl. The contents of the bowl is poured onto the base of an elder. Flowers are best gathered when in full bloom.

Elderberry juice and elderberry wine bring good health and long life. The wine is used to quiet the nerves and to aid the heart and circulatory system. Elder lotions are put on plants to ward off harmful insects and aphids. Sheep eat elder, Fernie said, to cure themselves from foot disease. Elder trees give protections from lightning.

Wonderful as they are, the cures the Elder gives could be painful or deadly. They are treated with respect, handled with care.

The Elder is a Tree of Judgement. It is a custom to give judgement while standing under an elder. To use a weapon which had a handle of elder wood was to invite judgement upon oneself. King William Rufus was sacrificed by a bowman who was standing under an elder. Many beings, including werewolves, come under the authority of the Elder Lady.

Some springs are guarded by elders and at some of these, Undines are found. Gomme said that some of these were sacred wells held waters of life which were guarded by fish. To gain blessings, pins were thrown into wells. If one drank, he threw three handfuls of water on Earth or a stone.

Mother Shipton, a powerful witch, is said to have turned herself into an elder tree. This, from Ferguson.

The Elder has been called the Tree of Music, the Tree of Sorrow, the Tree of Sacrifice, the Tree of Doom. The Elder is an emblem of sorrow and death.

The wave relates to music. Ocean Deities are gifted in music. This, from Philostratus the Elder.

A music of the Sea would be that of the shell, as the one which Triton is shown to be blowing. In some representations, he seems to be blowing up a storm. Many statues of Triton represent him, with a trident, blowing a conch shell as if, said historian Sitwell, sounding a burglar alarm. The shell is said to give warning, to give protection and to controle the weather. Also it is said to inspire a good harvest.

A characteristic of the Sea: its changeability. The Sea God, Proteus, said Dionysius, could change shape, either actual or by deception, making viewers think they see him in what ways he chose. It is said, Proteus, while being held, changed from one monster to another. Bound with flowers, he would give knowledge of the future.

The Spirit of the Sea is seen as Tethys and Doris, shape shifting goddesses of the ever changing Sea. The Sea merges the one with the all. It instigates a loss of the personal self. One takes in the collective unconscious, becomes merged into the Great Sea. The blue Sea gives spiritual inspiration, opens blocked communication, inspires calm and peace.

The Sea Waters everywhere would be the Great Wave. The Great Wave is the Spirit of Neptune, the Lord of Water. Water is life giving. Especially from running water, people get strength and health. In clear brooks, people wash away the effects of bad dreams. People who have offended the deities, wash to purify themselves, but in doing so, sometimes offend the deity of the brook so that she withholds virtues.

Water, as the veil between the worlds, is looked for to give knowledge of the future. For this knowledge, people often go to springs and wells. On the sea, sailors will often gain intuitions about coming events. They might get from Orion signs as to how a voyage will go. Rain might provide knowledge. Its coming might be announced by oxen gazing heavenward. It might indicate its coming by a double or triple ring around the Moon, or by the gathering and squawking of crows. It is said that Gaius Cornelius might have learned of a great battle by observing a thunderstorm.

Water is associated with birth. The Ninth Wave brings birth. As the Spirit of Water is, in a big part, female; birth is one of its functions. Waves, as horses, rise out of the Sea. Forces of Water include generation, creativeness.

Neptune is the Great Giant Sea, the boundless Sea; primal, basic Water. It cleanses. It wipes the slate clean. It is the veil between life and death. The Sea gives and takes away, discovers and conceals; a giant of hidden powers and hidden shifting moods. One can find oneself out at sea, lost, out of one's depth; perhaps, on a spiritual search where there is insecurity, mystery, confusion, fright, illusion and, perhaps discovery. The Sea is rich. It gives gifts. It holds rich Otherworlds from which come gold and gems.

The Time of the Wave holds an influence toward confusion and seeming lack of direction, toward instinct, creativity, wisdom and appreciation of art and music.

Aquamarine is a gem which relates to the Sea. It holds a power of the Sea, a creative force. It aids the eyes.

Related to the Wave, the Onion. From Bett: the Spirit of the Onion is a rich giant who mints money and throws it about. He is a lusty lord who inspires copulation. Related to the Wave, Clover brings luck and inspires cheerfulness. Delphiniums are related to the Wave. Put in front of snakes and harmful beasts, delphiniums take their power away. They protect against venoms and scorpions, as they hold the spirit of the sacred Dolphin: Gerard. Neptune, a lusty god, holds the spirit of The Wave.

The Wave tends to reflect other cards. If a Lion is across from it, it might show some lion qualities. Much of the time, it is a sympathetic card.

XIV ~ Craftsman

In the center of Card XIV would be the Lame Smith, Vulcan, with his hammer, at his anvil. The Smith has been called an artist and an alchemist. He uses magical tools and makes magical tools. Horseshoes, plowshares and swords are magical, as they are made by smiths.

Vulcan is a God of Fire. He is especially thought of in connection with Earthly Fire, but his fire was considered, as bright and hot as that of the sky. In one description, it lept and ran like golden sunshine.

Vulcan, as Fire, is a purifying agent and ashes, left by fire, relate to purity, sterility and death. Ashes are pure. It is a custom to swear by the ashes of one's father. This relates Vulcan to Justice and to the Underworld. He is called arbiter of the purifying process. This relates Vulcan to medicine, to the supervision of the making of medicines. They would be made under his authority. Healing is a property of Vulcan. Vulcan is a god of many magics. His Fire creates the magic of smithing and of many other magical crafts. Vulcan creates many magical objects, magical even in the eyes of other deities. He made gates with locks which demons and deities couldn't open. One of these is the door to Hera's chamber. He made golden shoes which could travel as fast as lightning, travel over any surface. He made magical tripods and magical chariots. He made a magical scepter for Agamemnon and many magical weapons. Some of his artifacts could be dangerous. He made a chair which Hera, having sat in, couldn't get out of until he released her. He made thunderbolts used by other deities. He made, in the field of protections, the Temple of the Sun and other temples. He made a net in which he trapped Mars. Hades is a friend of Mars, God of War; so he traded with Vulcan, the net for Underworld privileges and set Mars free. This gives an explanation for Vulcan's relationship to the Underworld.

The God of Craft, Vulcan, expands over numberless endeavours, over all construction. A number of other powerful deities are deities over craft. Minerva, Athene and Lugus are deities of huge influence, huge authority, with special interest in crafts. The chief focus of Minerva is on spinning. Lugus is a smith, but he is certainly more often thought of as a cobbler.

Lugus, like Vulcan, represents Fire.

Fire, though hard working, is thought of as an expression of anger. Vulcan can be an expression of anger, can flood a hill with flame, but he is usually well mannered – and helpful. He has a gentlemanly respect for ladies. When he was told that Thetis, the Sea Goddess, was coming to see him, he washed and put on a clean tunic. The Smith is considered to be hard working and unpretentious, but his workaday projects are thought to have caused great turnings in the realms of the deities and so, on Earth. Vulcan, it is said, rose before dawn to complete a bit of drudgery, a shield for Aeneas. That was an unromantic but important part in a huge cycle of Earth shaking events.

Vulcan is thought of as a lusty, good hearted God who enjoys drink, good drink and companionship, and if he flies into a rage, his fits of anger are likely soon over and he isn't likely to hold grudges. When he had Hera stuck in a chair, Bacchus took him out drinking and after some good drinks and a few laughs, he released Hera. Among his good hearted judgements, after Orion had been blinded by a goddess, Vulcan had a messenger conduct the lusty Orion to the Palace of the Sun to get cured by Aurora.

Vulcan is associated with Earth. The Craftsman seems less remote than many other deities, seems more closely related to common men. He is spoken of as having down to Earth common sense. People believe his forges to be under local volcanoes, or in nearby caves. His magical tools have been found in ancient forts.

There are different versions of the telling of how Vulcan came to Earth. One explanation is, Vulcan took Hera's side in a dispute she was having with Jupiter and Jupiter, in anger, threw him out of the Sky. In the fall he damaged a leg, so became one of a number of lame gods. The magical Smith might be lamed to keep him from running off, or from leading warriors into battle. He might be showing a down hill slide toward the Underworld.

Less remote than many other deities, the Craftsman has seemed most ready to give help. In some places, he is considered the chief deity. In some places, he is a friendly deity that is close to the people and is much like the working people. He likes horses and if he sees one that needs a shoe, he'll likely put one on; then, if a rider, noticing the horse has been shoed and passing a cave, hut, or stones that might be the god's smithy; leaves a coin, he is pleased. But he lets it be known, he is not pleased if he is left more for his work than would be given the local smith. Vulcan might have the horse become difficult, so the rider would know his displeasure. When really angry, Vulcan has cut off peoples heads and made the skulls into fancy drinking cups.

Vulcan is a healer; especially, he is called upon to cure snake bites.

Many crafts and artifacts contain more or less of an element of magic. Smiths, as a rule, hammer magics into the things they make. Women, at their wheels, twist magic into the threads of their cloth.

Vulcan is honoured at 2 celebrations: August 23, Volcanalia, and November 23, Vulcan Fest. Volcanalia, torch races are held in honour of Vulcan and for him, sacrifices are made. By the heads of families; fish, and other animals also, are thrown into the sacred fire. Black dogs are often included among the sacrificed animals. Streets are illuminated. To win the torch race, the runner's torch needed to stay lit.

November 23, Vulcan is honoured for blocking way against malicious beings, so, keeping the coming season pure.

The Horse is favoured by Vulcan. The Boar and the Black Dog are other animals to which he relates. Pigs are a source of Underworld energy.

The chestnut is the Tree of the Craftsman. Chestnuts have a relationship to the Underworld. Chestnut wood is used for carpentry, and this would include the temples, which thrust upward into eternal life. Chestnut flowers were among those used in making the woman who sent a Sun God to the Underworld. The Chestnut tree is a favourite tree of the Divine Sow, and ghosts favour the Chestnut. Chestnut sticks can give a knowledge of the future. Chestnut wands have been used for acts of theft and chestnuts are used in charms for gaining copulation. Chestnut tea is used in treating coughs and fevers. The scent from chestnut flowers takes away despair and gives the ability to correct errors.

Chestnuts are served as part of the Hero Day, November eleventh, fest.

Valerian is an herb favoured by Vulcan. It is used in the celebration of Volcanalia.

Vervain is a favoured flower. Fennel also is favoured.

On the hand, the thumb represents Vulcan.

On Card Fourteen, the Smith, Vulcan, would stand in front of a smithy, its entrance, shaded by a bough of a chestnut tree, would stand in front of an anvil, would hold his hammer.

The sound of the hammer on the anvil relates to the crafting of music. Pythagoras discovered a value in music, said Cassiodorus, from the sound of hammers on anvils.

On either side of the anvil, clumps of blooming valerian would extend to the sides of the card. Valerian adds power to blessings.

Behind the Smith would be a fiery forge.

Wisps of smoke would rise from a hill to the right rear of the smithy; the smoke, from a fire perhaps caused by Vulcan.

According to Philostratus of Nervianus, the fire of Vulcan, like golden sunshine, would leap and run over the plain: the Spirit of Vulcan.

In each corner of the card, a horseshoe would be holding luck; so, the open end, up.

For holding luck, horseshoes are often nailed above doors. Spence said that it has been thought best if the horseshoe was nailed with its own nails. The best horseshoes, some have said, were from the left hind foot of a grey mare. A horseshoe found along a road would likely have been lucky. The Horseshoe has a relationship with the Moon: this, from Spence.

The Smith: as custom dictates, at a feast, he is served the first drink.

The Great Smith, Vulcan, Paracelsus declared to be an artist.

XV ~ Tower

The Tower is a focal point of protective force. One instinct which material things have in common: the effort to survive. The Tower represents this effort. It is a defense against Chaos, the Snake which eats all matter. As the Tower would be intended to give spiritual as well as physical protection, its construction would be done as a ritual. All buildings have about them some aspects of the Tower, but if the basic reason for the construction is for mundane use, ritual might well be limited. If, however, the reason for constructing the building is to supply protection, ritual would want to be carefully done, the spiritual and physical needs of the Tower carefully considered. Location of the Tower would be most important. Often, the selection of the location would have been done by spiritual forces before the builders found the need to do the construction. Then builders, through the subconscious, would discover an energy force field, a spiritual tower, which is a temple. Before men built temples for deities, deities themselves would have established temples on Earth: stones, mounds or trees which thrust into the spirit world and give shelter to spirits. Ancient images of deities are to be found on Standing Stones. Stones themselves have been thought to contain the spirits of deities: to give justice, cures and other blessings. For some stones, torch lit rituals have been held and offerings given.

In selecting a location for a sacred tower, many people would feel the energy of places which deities had used for sacred purposes and would recognize the rightness of these places for towers. If people's selections of locations were not ones which the deities had selected, the deities would, at times, cause corrections to be made. Stone walls might be taken down and the stones, moved to the correct location. People have witnessed pigs moving the stones, and one time; it was doves they saw moving them. At times, the deities themselves moved the stones. They sometimes told builders to move them.

One thing all towers would have in common: their basic energy fields would have the same shape. The Universe is said to be constructed of triangles and circles and each energy field would conform with the basic construction of the Universe. Triangles and circles are themselves said to hold magical force. The Circle is the Pictish symbol of protection and is known as a basic element of magic. The triangle forms and focuses fields of force and extended, these fields become pyramids and cones of power. The power of these energy fields has been seen to preserve food, to sharpen knives, to give healing power to water and to bestow special powers on herbs: tests recorded by Flanagan.

Pyramids and cones are the triangle lines of force formed by triads of circles of energy. And the place where a pyramid's triad of three circles intersects is known as the pyramid's eye. And the eye is called a place of special powers. Through that magical eye, one looks to see into the Spirit World. The point of a pyramid would extend into this magical space. Some temples have never taken more of a material form than that of an energy flow. There are rituals for building these towers of force, towers constructed of energy fields. The rituals might include the use of visualization, charms, magical tools or dance. With dance; dancers, as they dance, might leave trails, threads of energy. In the dance, the threads of energy, woven together, might be given added power by sound and thought, using such tools as chant, visualization or the formation of magical forms such as runic shapes. As the dancers dance, the threads peak above them to form an energy cone. The threads, in part, are formed by the auras of the dancers. The chants might, beside the magic of their spoken charms, add to their power by a magical blending of tones. Some dances are done with a rhythmic, simultaneous step and while dancing, a visualizing of an assortment of symbols. The symbols, visualized in unison, would relate to, and combine with, auric energy, and this provide material for the temple. A temple would be strengthened when people, over a period of time; by sound, visualization, motion and emotion; add to the original temple form. This temple would certainly last longer than the group of people who thought to create it. It would be a connection with the divine, would be a place to which people could spiritually relate, regardless of where these people might be in the physical world. Any number of ways of relating to the temple: the use of ritual, visualization, chant or magical tools: would provide a key for getting back into its sacred space, so permit a continued contact with the deities. The Temple connects worlds enabling spirits to return to specific locations so that contact can be kept.

With rituals, changes would be made in the spiritual and so, physical reality. What would be built would depend on the needs of the sacred space. What had been there would be a determining factor. An object's energy flow has a shape, has a shape which would forecast that object's future shape. A flower seed would hold an energy shape of a mature flower. So, a tower would form in a way it was ordained to be shaped.

Some towers, built from sacred formulas and divine calculations, would have followed the lines of the energy flow, become pyramids. The spiritual pyramid is a projection of lines from the Astral Triad. It is a form sacred to Jupiter. Sacred numbers found in its measurement are found to relate to those of life energy, basic numbers found in all living organisms, humans to pine cones. The basic colour of the energy flow would be green, the colour of renewing and of rebirth, of expansion and growth. It is the colour produced by the pyramid.

At the center of the pyramid, energy tends to rise and this flow of energy has been called the pyramid's sacred fire, as it is an energy which is thought as moving toward the Spirit World, as the pyramid would extend indefinitely upward. As energy would flow upward, the pyramid would be expected to attract and pull energy downward. For this reason, Ross Hamilton has called the pyramid a spiritual magnet. That sacred flow in the center of the pyramid would be a place for sacred tools. The peak of the pyramid would provide a conduit for divine knowledge. The tripod of the Sibyl represents the Triadic Spirit. The Sibyl, at the peak, gazed through the Eye of Knowledge.

Even though every tower would have an energy flow of a pyramid shape, many a tower would find another material form more appropriate to its need. The building of a tower has been considered a sacred ritual. Careful mathematical and astrological calculations have been observed, along with the many other needs of each particular tower. There would certainly have been ceremonies where blessings and often sacrifices would have been a part. Sometimes, foundations were bathed in human blood. In some cases, a person was buried alive at each corner of a tower, so that the deaths would occur below the tower, ghosts of the dead serve as its protectors. It was recorded by Nennius, that for a temple's construction, one of its walls needed to be sprinkled with human blood if the temple were to stand. Often, an evergreen tree is placed, with ceremony, at the top of a tower being constructed. At the building of some towers, one or more animals, or sometimes, a deity, were said to have given physical help with the building's construction.

As a tower is a focal point of power, there is often competition for the use of it. At one tower, there was a controversy between Athene and Poseidon as to who should be considered its chief deity, as that was to indicate which of them was to rule over a great area of land. Poseidon had given the tower a pool and Athene, an olive tree. Then, warriors invaded the land, drained the pool and burnt the olive tree. But the olive tree immediately grew back. The warriors seeing that, fled in terror. The tower was awarded to Athene.

The tower is the tool from which a deity generates power over a land, so powers over nature are concentrated at towers, the houses of the deities. Towers are built in order that deities might protect the land. The builders give a promise of concern for the deity and make a declaration that the values represented by that deity will be observed. Power is given by the towers to the deities and the towers give them authority and link the power of the land to that of the deities; each tower, to the deity, or deities, whom the tower serves. Some of the deities seem to prefer to be worshipped at crude, rustic or rudimentary towers; perhaps, stones or shrines. Many deities, however, are thought to appreciate splendid, or great, towers.

A mighty center of protection is the Parthenon in Athens, a temple of Athene's. The power of Athene is reflected in her temples, and the temples increase her power. As Athene was considered to appreciate art, care was given to make her temples beautiful and so, to obtain her blessings.

The Parthenon, called Athene's greatest temple and the epitome of classic beauty; is thought that among temples, it best represents the culmination of classic form. Athene stands with gentle grace, in severe contemplation, in classic simplicity, in the exact center of the temple.

The force of Athene, with her power and beauty, is evinced in others of Athene's temples. At the Temple of Aegina, in the middle of fighting warriors, stands Athene holding, with ease and grace, her spear and aegis. Her grace is accented by the angular power and vigour of the warriors. The movement of the statue of Athene at Samothrace is accented by the motion of the lithe, athletic body counter to that of the flowing, transparent, stone clothes.

Athene's temples were built with such grace and grandeur, have given such a feeling of purity to those who have visited them, that they are said to have, through the ages, affected architecture. The uplifting space, which seems to be held in those temples, seems to create a movement into the Otherworld. The feeling of quietness generated by the great spaces compelled a hush and a respect for Athene and the other deities who might have an interest in the temples, a respect often inspiring ritualistic gesture.

That a temple did not terminate at its solid material walls is a fact which builders were aware of. In the Temple of Athena Nike, the off balance movement of the statue of Athene seems to move space. Athene, on the alter of the Temple of Zeus at Pergamon, fighting the giant son of Nertha, gives a feeling of moving space – as she floats in the temple's mysterious inner space. The Temple of Fortuna Virgilis in Rome also gives the impression of connecting Earth with the Otherworld. The temple is high off the ground and is reached by a long flight of stairs. Tall, slender columns, topped by graceful Ionian capitals, supports triangular gables. The temple seems to float on the shadows and air between the columns. In its airy aloofness, it takes charge of the surrounding area, hovering protectively over the lands below it. In some of the temples, the great domes give a feeling of lightness; the arches and pillars, leading to darkness, connect to invisible space, give an impression of huge space and richness. As Eiseley has said, hidden within a temple's tensions is the upward surge of space. Stone arches, he called, "space bows," as they seem to drive space upward; and there, space hovers without limits. Temples are said to reflect and reverberate harmonies of musical tones; connected, as they are, with the stars.

A study of the construction of sacred temples is thought to reveal knowledge, not only of the past, but of things to come, and the knowledge temples give is an element of their gift of protection.

In the Otherworld, great temples are important. One of the major temples is the Castle of the Northern Crown, Ariadne's revolving tower for the dead. Another, the stronghold of Mother Earth, protected by 9 concentric rings of walls. Another is the Tower of the Sun, a magnificent palace built by Vulcan. Bees constructed a tower for Apollo. Manannan had, for the dead, a tower shaped like a beehive. Dead Suns sleep in the Temple of the Moon, which is constructed of elm with a roof of ivywood. The word, "temple," comes from a word meaning wood.

An Otherworld tower, Connings Tower, is also a place for the dead. The tower is in the Sea. When warriors approach, they get swallowed by monster waves who integrate themselves and the warriors into a chain. The dead were also domiciled in a castle which is described by Spence as revolving and with sides like glass. Similar castles were served, according to Hodson, by servers who were shining, shimmering and silent.

In constructing a temple, the structure should be made in harmony with its energy pyramid. As Flanagan has said, energy has shape. Blockages of the energy could cause trouble. The Pyramid, said Campbell, is the fundamental temple: opposites culminating in unity. Jupiter, according to Herodotus, considered the Pyramid to be sacred. To bring good fortune, Gomme said that there were pyramids built of horses' heads.

Jupiter was known to have beautiful temples, but in most part, these would not have been physical pyramids. But they would have conformed to the needs of the energy pyramid. And the temple would have fit other needs which Jupiter would have had. Vitruvius said Jupiter's alters would have faced East. And they would have been high, with representations of Jupiter over these, so the viewer would have looked up to the gods who would have been high above. Vitruvius said alters of Vesta and Ertha would be built low to the ground. Diana's temples had tall, slender columns to fit the personality of the goddess.

In gathering materials, even if the temple is to be but a stone circle, the materials should seem to offer themselves. If materials are important stones, offerings might be needed on the ground from which they were removed. Proper rituals and libations, while building, would be observed. In constructing, each builder would put a material part of himself in the building. With some temples, the building is done all or in part in magical ways. Some temples are set to be in harmony with Otherworld temples. Some great stones have been moved through the air, set on sacred spots and in the correct way. Temples would be built, Wendell said, where star and Earth forms form natural harmonies. Often these places would have had a history of attracting sacred rituals and spirit temples. Leland said that if Otherworld beings are called into a temple by ritual, they tend to remain. This would keep the temple strong.

A perverse builder could make errors when building, and this could cause disasters. Gomme said that a mason put a piece of tombstone in a tower wall and people died because of it.

A magic temple was said to have been built by Vergilius which was built on a foundation of eggs.

The chief deity representing Card Fifteen would be Athene, a protector of the Universe. Athene threw the Great Serpent, Draco, into the Sky to guard the Apple Tree, which holds the fruit all things need in order to continue existence, and to guard the hole where the Apple Tree had been, so that no destroying force would come out of it.

Athene relates to the Dawn, to Rocky Cliffs and the rocky ground. At times, she has been seen as owl eyed and Gorgon faced. Her round shield is protection for her followers. Athene is a defender of cities and a protector of homes, hearths and sacred places, an extractor of due punishments and a blessings giver. She rules winds and storms. She has been prayed to for protection in childbirth. She is a wise and mighty warrior said to have once defeated Mars. She is a Goddess of Craftsmanship and Invention and a patron of smiths, spinners and weavers. Sacred to her are the pot, the loom, the spindle and the distaff. Her sacred number is Five.

Athene's big celebration is Panathenaea, July eleventh. She is also honoured, Lucarium, the Festival of the Sacred Groves, held March eighteenth.

For the Panathenaea, Athene is honoured with parades and with rituals at her shrines. One tradition is to carry the garment of Athene at the front of the parade. The garment, a white sleeveless dress trimmed with gold, would have been woven by Athene's temple virgins. In the tradition, behind the garment bearers would walk elders with olive branches and behind these, armed men attended by men who carry small boats. These are followed by women who carry water pots. Next come men crowned with millet and these, sing hymns to Athene. These are followed by maidens who wear wreaths of figs on their heads and carry baskets containing sacred tools. The maidens are attended by women who carry stools. Men in festival coats walk to the rear of the procession. In some of the parades, at the front, a ship is carried. It is usual for the procession to proceed to a location where a newly washed statue of Athene is dressed in her new dress and put on a bed of flowers. The processions are a part of the festivals and are often followed by torch races, gymnastic contests and poetry and music contests. It is usual to award the winners crowns of olive and jugs of olive oil.

At Lucarium, Athene is honoured as protector of sacred groves. As Athene represents purity; at her festivals, clothes worn and items presented to her would be newly cleaned. At Lucarium, there is a custom for men to wear, on their breasts, charms as protection against the evil eye.

Athene represents harmony. She once refused to aid Ulysses because the aid would have displeased Poseidon and so, caused disharmony. And, according to Seymour, Poseidon refused to help Ulysses because he thought Athene would be displeased.

A second protector of the Tower would be Rhea, a personification of the Mountain and a bringer of crops. She wears a castle shaped helm and she carries a double bladed axe. Purity is important to Rhea. Iamblichos said Priests of Rhea, by song and sacrifice, purged away impurity and animosity so that they could receive messages.

Rhea's milk, supporting creation, was said to have left a trail across the Sky. Nennius called Rhea the most holy queen. Processions, loud with cymbals, pipes and drums, are held in her honour. The noise of percussion instruments in Earth rituals, said Lucretius, was to protect the Earth Mother from the attacks of Saturn.

Often, the processions led to places where there were orgies.

Rhea's helm would represent a protection for places which would need fortification.

A third protector of the Tower would be Pallas, Goddess of Dawn. A warrior goddess, she is a protector of lands and, especially, cattle and sheep. She is often pictured with a sword and shield. Pallas is said to be a friend of Hercules.

A protecting tree would be the Plane Tree, the tree which gave shelter to Europa. The tree represents strength. It relates to cattle and has a five section leaf. This relates it to the Goddess and to mankind, especially, the female. The Plane Tree gives protection to sacred springs.

The Olive, the sacred tree of Athene, is also a protecting tree relating to The Tower. It is a sponsor of good health, order and purity.

The Fig is also sacred to Athene and it is also a sponsor of good health.

Protecting animals would be the Ram, the Owl, the Cock, the Ox and the Bee. The Cock and the Ram represent the power of the Dawn. The Owl, Callimachus called the Messenger of Athene. It was also called Athene's thunderbird, as it carries her thunderbolts. Wisdom is an element of protection and the Owl, one of the wisest of animals, was gone to for instruction.

The Bee would be a protector of The Tower. Bees bring knowledge and blessings. Beehives have been afforded much respect and it is thought an ill omen should its bees leave it. Bees have been kept informed on the news of the house, and in the case of a death, formal clothes were worn when that news was given to the bees and the hive, dressed for the funeral. Bees give advice and withhold blessings. In a Roman war, when a general fighting against Rome was slain, his body wasn't honoured until bees settled on it to indicate that it should be. The Romans, directed by the bees, honoured it.

The Tower is a center of spiritual force, a center where spirit might connect with deities. Although for The Tower, the basic force lines would be the same, each tower would be an individual, would contain countless variations in order to conform to many spiritual desires or needs. Hercules had a tower which at its peak, for its eye, had a crystal globe and this was an eye from which Hercules gazed out upon the World. For Diana, a tower was made with tall, slender columns, as these would represent the personality of the deity; so, give a path by which her worshipers share her feelings.

The Tower, as a focal point, would attract the lightning. Lightning is a destructive force and, also, a generative and creative force. It would represent the will of Jupiter expressed as an electrical force. Lightning might destroy The Tower; or make major changes, but leave the Tower standing. It might dislodge stones, might burn the inside of the Tower, might make changes in the whole World. It might provide the light and force which would inspire change.

Lightning creates balance. It sends energy to that which lacks sufficient energy. As a creator of balance, it enforces justice. One highly praised Roman general, after his most impressive victory, was struck by lightning; so, creating a balance between punishments and rewards. King Dathi was also, after a major victory, struck by lightning and this, on the place where another victorious king, King Niall, had been struck by lightning. King Laoghaire was struck by lightning after he had broken an oath.

Lightning might destroy one thing in order to make room for a new thing and the new thing might be a thing of which the World is in need.

In the center of Card Fifteen is The Tower. Towers do rise and fall. All things do have births and deaths. But while Towers stand, they usually offer protection; sometimes, highly valued protection. The Tower is also a creative force. It inspires and forces creativity.

Lightning would be striking the Tower. The lightning might represent a spiritual stroke of energy; a stroke, perhaps to destroy a concept and so, make way for a spiritual awakening. The stroke might represent a needed purifying or cleansing. It might create a new awareness.

The Tower is the Great Penis. Lightning striking the Tower, a Great Orgasm. This might represent a major birthing. Perhaps what would seem a minor creation or destruction would prove to be, later, considered major.

The number of The Tower, fifteen, would be the total of the sacred numbers of each of the three goddesses, each being five.

The Tower would represent more than a physical tower. It could be a concept, and this might relate to a tradition, a government, or a person. Mental towers might be created, and these might reach toward unreachable goals, might reach toward the stars. Some goals might be reached in sacred time, which, as Eiseley has said, is of a higher dimension than secular time. A goal might be reached in dream time. And Eiseley said that it is the nature of Man to have dreams which go past our reach. Such a tower one might see in the lines of Coleridge: "Could I revive within me her symphony and song, to such a deep delight 'twould win me, that music loud and long, I would build that dome in air, that sunny dome! Those caves of ice: And all who heard should see them there, and all should cry, Beware! Beware! His flashing eyes, his floating hair! Weave a circle round him thrice, and close your eyes with holy dread, for he on honeydew hath fed, and drunk the milk of paradise." – S T Coleridge.

A Real tower, but one with no physical place.

For a protecting physical tower, Wendell said the best are natural temples where the locations call us to them.

To protect towers, there is the spirit force of trees.

At the bottom right of the card is an olive wreath. At the bottom left, a switch with leaves of the Plane Tree. These counter witchcraft.

And the Tower protects itself. It has its own magic. Tacitus said that there was a timidity about molesting people in sacred places. Lucius Apuleius said that when he entered a sacred place, he made some sign of respect.

The top window in the Tower would be the Eye.

And the beginning of the Tower is Dream.

Some towers are quite magical. The towers of Thebes, it was said, were built of song.

A word from the Tower might be, Courage.

              Courage.

XVI ~ Gaoler

In the center of the Underworld sits Hades, the ram horned, faceless god; holding, in his left hand, his two pronged pitchfork. The prongs represent the dual aspects which are in all things: top and bottom, day and night, light and dark, living and dead, countless others.

Hades is the ruler of the shamanic Underworld, the realm of the Path of Choice, the forked path. The forked way in that shamanic place is spoken of by the Pythagoreans, as Pythagoras communicated with the dead and gave secrets to his followers.

The way not only represents the choice from which there is no return, but a choice by which some option had to die. It represents a balance between action and reaction, between helpful and harmful and the need to have some living, some dead. In one shamantic trip, two fields of cows were seen: one field, of white; the other field, of black cows. Any cow which changed fields, changed colour. And the number of cows in one field remained balanced against the number of cows in the other, as cows moved to fill vacant spaces.

Hades keeps the balance between worlds. When the Snake Doctor was curing too many, Hades went to Olympus and demanded that Jupiter restore the balance. Jupiter banished the Snake Doctor. Hades, Lord over Man and Animal, is seen seated over the Snake.

The Snake, related to the 4 elements, is the beast of birth and death. It is the beast which swallowed the Sun – and suffered death so that the Sun could be reborn. The Snake could represent the trip between death and rebirth. The Snake means darkness with all of its ramifications. Snakes have great powers for taking the living into the darkness of death. They are set as guards at gates to the Underworld. Also, snakes are gifted in curing the living, in keeping them out of the Underworld. Snake doctors, in the World of the Living, are known for their skill. Snake eggs and snake oil are known for working miraculous cures. Adder stones are put into water to gain healing infusions. An adder stone set in a ring has been credited with healing. For the living, adder stones have other virtues also. Besides healing, they protect against demons and encourage prosperity. As like attracts like, the beasts related to the Snake can draw poisons from infections and illness. Dried tadpoles are, in this way, used for cures.

A deity of the Underworld is Semele. Monaghan has her the ancient deity of the dark ground. She has a lust for producing life and throwing it up to the World, and a gluttonous urge to gobble it back into death. She was a Mother of Bacchus and at bacchanals, is celebrated with exuberant frenzy. In her honour, there is madness and drunken orgy and vigourous activity as in running and copulation and randomly met with men and beasts were ripped apart by the female mobs and offered to Semele.

And Hyacenthos is an Underworld Gaoler. He demanded life be sent to him, and he rejoiced when blood soaked the ground, and sent up flowers. Joyful feasts and other celebrations accompanied the sending of fine gifts to Hyacenthos. The gifts: often fine young women.

Natosuelta is a deity who relates to the Underworld. She is the Raven Goddess who creates and destroys. She creates, then drops the creations out of life. Propertius has the Crow singing the death song. In old times, there was little distinction made between ravens and crows. The Crow, called a bird of the Underworld, is used by deities as a messenger to the Underworld because of its relationship to that region. Because it eats corn; so, the Spirit of the Corn, it is recognized as the Bird of Death. As the Bird of Death, the Crow symbolizes Time flying toward the West. This relates to the Circle of Time and so, to Cronus. And this makes it fearful.

Eiseley said that to know time is to fear it.

Charon's landing point in the Underworld has been called Crow Station.

Korax, a Crow God, is a God of Death. Apollo sent him to slay the warrior poet, Archilochus. For that act, Korax had to go the Underworld, as Archilochus was considered, a sacred deity.

Witches were said to ride on crows.

Another bird with Underworld connections is the Lapwing. Rhys said it is the keeper of Underworld secrets. Pausanias said that hounds were keepers of Otherworld secrets. As they were thought, most valiant of animals, they were sacrificed to Mars, and as hounds related to the Underworld, the sacrifices were made at night. Giraldus said hounds were thought to guard gates to the Underworld. And they hunt the skies to collect the dead. Hocart said that to get eaten by dogs was thought to harm the dead.

Corpses are said to gain Underworld powers. They are looked to for prophecy and feared for their dark powers, so are carefully treated.

Propertius said, if an animal crossed over a corpse, the animal was killed, as it would have gathered dark powers off the corpse.

From the corpse, body parts have been taken so that prophecy or other powers could be gained. For prophecy, the liver might have been removed and inspected. At times, the intestines, for prophecy, would have been inspected. The head, genitals and feet were thought to hold heavy powers; so these might well have been returned to the deities; the penis, at times honoured by being wrapped in ivy and violets. Heads were given places of honour in shrines. After battles, warriors have decked themselves in wreaths of heads. Halliday said that horses' skulls were put in gardens as charms to ward off witchcraft.

Teeth and hair, especially, of hanged men, have been valued for use in charms and potions. Hands and fingers have been found to be powerful tools. A tool called the Hand of Glory was made by cutting off the hand of a hanged man, soaking the hand in a brine mix of salt and salt peter, parching it under the Sun; then preserving it in vervain and fern. The hand was sometimes made to hold a candle; sometimes, the fingers supplied the light. The light caused people to sleep, so that the person holding the light could go about unobserved.

Dalyell said that moles' teeth and mice's bones were considered instruments of sorcery.

Rulandus said spiritual water for magical use was collected from off the ashes of dead bodies.

Underworld influence is mysterious and can be strong. It can prepare the mind and set the mood for death. A cold shudder down the spine was said to foretell of a death. Corpse candles, which are phantom candles which appear to mark the path a funeral would be going to take, and mock funerals, are sent from the Underworld to prepare a community for a death. Strange horses and cattle, sent from the Underworld, can foretell disaster. In some areas, said Trevelyan, if one saw a strange white horse, he would spit to quickly put water between himself and it and so, prevent trouble, which might have been coming to him from the Underworld.

It is usual for corpses to be sent respectfully to the Underworld, assisted by magics and proper rituals. In times past, when corpses of humans were given to Earth; they were, in some traditions, sent with companion corpses of dogs, or horses, or dogs and horses. Sometimes men of wood went to the Underworld with the corpses; sometimes, representations of deities. Weapons and tools have also been sent to the Underworld with corpses; and these, according to Windle, would have been broken and so, killed, so that they would have become part of the Underworld.

A water and milk bath was used, said Spence, for expelling spirits of the Underworld and cleaning off Underworld influences.

It is thought, risky to disturb the dead after they have been given rest or to otherwise disturb the Underworld. Keightley said that properties stolen from the Otherworld were thought dangerous and it was thought, they could cause disasters. Even Ulysses considered calling up Underworld powers a risk. It was said, he dug a trench, poured blood of a sacrificed sheep into it; poured honey, wine and water around it and scattered meal over it; then, summoned a spirit. Then from that place he hurried away quickly in case Proserpine should send more to that place than was wanted.

Many thought that after death, a person was swished up on spread sails, as Propertius said, to the stars and from there, he suspected that we did not return once Charon had been paid and the Gate, shut. It has been said, if a person is permitted to return from the Otherworld, his visit is usually cut short. Breaking some rule, as touching iron, might be the thing which would drop him back with the dead. A Sybil led Aeneas into Hades' Realm and protected him against spirits, so his return was made possible. Marcus Bach was of the opinion that the dead were returned to the World of the Living to amend the shortcomings of previous births. But what the Realm of Hades is remains a mystery. Ordericus said, knowing that people die, or when they will die, is not knowing about death. Ordericus described the impressive funeral procession of a sacrificed king and thought this might have an effect on the Underworld: the grandness of the procession and the gift of a king. Suggestions of some of the feeling of the Realm of Hades might sometimes get to the World of the Living. Lindholm tells of forces releasing hidden spiritualities that had never become part of our collective subconscious. Wendell spoke of the Death Energy. She said it should be savored slowly like a fine wine. She described it as a sentient and responsive shadow which, to get a full experience of it, one should become shadow like, become veiled in a garment of shadow.

Gems are related to the Underworld. Huxley said that an intense looking at a gem could be a way to get a vision of the Otherworld.

The World of the Dead has its awful aspect and there is a feeling of dread that comes with the mention of its name. Keightley told of an Elf woman who was living among humans until when someone mentioned

Death, she vanished.

Said Ovidius, the Underworld is feared because it is unknown.

The Plant Kingdom gives those of this World a tie to the Underworld. Some members of the Plant Kingdom have special relationships to the Underworld, relationships which can have a meaning to people in the World of the Living.

A Tree of the Underworld is the Walnut. It is favoured by Jupiter as it supplies food for the deities. The Walnut Tree is the Goddess Carya, Goddess of Darkness and Witchcraft. She is favoured by Diana, and the followers of Diana often hold rituals under walnut trees. The Walnut is a link breaker. It gives the freedom to change and the strength for moving up new roads.

Walnuts are magical. They bring fertility, strength and longevity and inspire copulation. The Walnut is considered a symbol of fertility, and for an increase in fertility, couples eat walnuts together. A witch might use walnuts in spells. Put under a person's chair, the person would be unable to rise until the walnut is removed. Women obtained sterility by, before marrying, roasting walnuts; then, after the wedding, planting the roasted walnuts. A sack of walnuts would make dreams come true.

Gods sent out prophecy, said Ellis, which was read in walnut twigs. Twigs were cut, peeled and marked. After a petition to the gods, they were cast; then three twigs selected to be read.

Walnuts are carried to strengthen the heart and to protect against rheumatism. To cure fevers, walnuts are split, each half rubbed on the ill person; then the halves are put together, wrapped in wool, then buried. The fragrance of walnut, said Edward Bach, protects against unwanted influence. Father Young listed walnuts as improving mental abilities. Walnut leaves are used for treating snake bites, sore throats, ulcers and other problems of the digestive system. From walnut husks, a potion is made for expelling worms from the intestines. According to Gerard, spiders were put in walnut shells to work charms against ailments.

The Walnut counters thunder strikes, fevers and spells. It promotes magic, copulation, fertility and gives inspiration, strength, danger, misfortune and dream. It is a melancholy tree and goblins and demons hover in the darkness of its branches. It is a custom to beat walnut trees in order to improve their productivity.

Flowers related to the Underworld are the Daffodil, the Violet, the Monkshood, the Henbane, the Poppy, the Yarrow, the Mint and the Black

Nightshade. And the Elder relates to the Underworld.

The Spirit of Mint is Queen of the Underworld. Mint promotes love and copulation. It is favoured by Venus.

Daffodils are planted near tombstones so that they might provide food for the dead. The fumes from daffodils cause sleep, dream and death, and a nod by a daffodil toward a person predicts death.

The death of loved ones causes one's violets to wither. Violets are a symbol of faithfulness. Coffins have, by their magic, held an aroma of violets.

Underworld life relates to, and draws from, life in the World of the Living. Hades receives images from the living. Patroclos' ghost, said Lucretius, got its energy from the living Patroclos. And, said Marcus Bach, it would not be wiser than was the living individual.

The Underworld is not only a place where one puts the dead, but a place which shapes matter into life. Beasts in a transitional stage, as tadpoles, relate to the Underworld. In another way, toads would be beasts in transition; so, relate to the Underworld.

In the center of the Underworld is Hades, a ram horned figure with only darkness where his face would be. He is seated on a crude stone and below the stone is a snake. In his left hand, Hades holds a two pronged pitchfork. In the lower left corner is a severed hand. At the top right stands a two pronged branch of the Walnut, a tree of melancholy and gloom. The card is dark and shadowy. In dark walls, goblin like life would seem to be forming. In the upper left corner of the card is a crow. In the lower right corner is the Dog, a guardian of the gate to the Underworld.

XVII ~ Star

The Star is a protecting, caring point of brightness, a point toward which one reaches. The Star is the selected Star in a field of many stars. As one rises toward the Star, one enters a maze, becomes merged into the Spirit World, an Astral Plane, a shadow universe with its own laws. There would be great space, solitude, a place where astral forms are given birth.

Enduring as it seems, even the most fixed star is part of the life death cycle. In the North, single stars seem fixed in the night sky. Among these, the Castle of the Star Goddess, Ariadne. The Star Goddess is a directing focal point around which the Astral Creations turn and change.

In the night, one sees great fields of stars sail overhead, and in the night sky, one sees that the stars have formed patterns. To many of the patterns, names have been given and these are called constellations. These constellations are seldom recognized from visible conformations relating to their name, as the conformations as outlined by their stars seldom have a resemblance to the figures which they represent. The constellations have their names from the need the heavens have to have a particular force in a particular place. At one stable point, Ariadne, the directing goddess, sends out lines of force. She, like the magician in his small wheel, seems to be turning the big wheel, but her want conforms to the need of all creation.

Philosophers named the forces as they were identified and many of these were outlined as constellations. The philosophers realized that much learning could be gained from the study of the constellations and other stars. They recognized 7 moveable forces, 2 of these, seldom, if ever seen, which unite, and trigger the actions of, other forces of the Heavens. And these moveable forces, they called the Wandering Stars.

There is a need to understand the Heavens because of the great energies which they hold, as their energy is all of it tied into Earth's energy. Man is said to have 2 bodies: one composed of Earth elements; the other, of energy, or spirit, from the stars. Each has an effect on the other. And all Earth's matter is reflected in the Heavens. As Franz Hartmann has said, "Celestial forces affect all matter. Matter is the battleground for all astral influences."

One charts the constellations and other stars for ways to solve even the most complex of problems. Even a look at the stars might give valued information. Orion is said to warn sailors of coming trouble. It is thought best to question the stars on clear nights.

Most stars swing in and out of sight, but the ones in the far North seem stable and so, would be expected to be there when they are needed. Some of the lovely stars would be known to us in a different size from that in which they are usually seen. Humans draw stars to them. The stars come down in the size which is needed.

In the Far North is the castle of the Star which could represent all stars: Ariadne, Queen of Death and Goddess of Doors. The Star Queen is unclothed, as Naked Truth causes veils to vanish. The place of the Goddess of Death is her Castle of Stars, the Northern Crown, the Corona Borealis, a revolving castle with force lines which draw all life to its center. These lines tie in and harmonize with the force lines throughout the Heavens.

The center of the star castle, invisible, is the Star. The Star contains the perfect mathematical proportions which are found in the growth patterns of all living things: She represents the perfect math from which all things come and to which all things return.

Ariadne, as she is Star Goddess, is a Goddess of Dawn, of Dusk and of the Sea. Her abode was sometimes called the Sea Castle and she was in danger from Gods of Day, as Rhys has said.

It was once by many people thought that the Star provided an example of stability, that it would provide the stable center around which all else would turn, would go from their places, then to their places return. Then it was discovered that stars shift and fall, that the Star did not guarantee that the bodies would return to their places. Stars seemed to blink out and be forever lost. It was thought that perhaps all stars would fall. It was suspected that the Star in the Star Castle of the Dead was a fallen star, was dead. The Star which had served as an axle for all things, which had covered the Door to the Underworld, had moved, leaving a hole. A monster had come out of the hole and had threatened to destroy deities and their system. The monster was turned back and a dragon, put in the sky to guard the hole and Apple Tree which had moved from where it had covered the hole and added its projection to the shaft of starlight. But the Dragon has proved not entirely reliable, so there can never be a going back to the time when there was a feeling of complete stability.

But the Castle of the Dead, the Corona Borealis, remains in the northern sky, a place which is there for the dead. Ariadne is there, a beautiful waif, to love and copulate with those who have the love and dedication to ask it of her. Gazing upon her, one might clothe his flesh with starshine, sail up worthy of beauty and wonder in the great stillness. The Star Castle must be the place from where one hears the great harmonies of the Heavens, sees the pure light: a music beyond music, a light beyond light. At its center is Ariadne, the Star Spider Goddess who inspires those who do the Crane Dance to come to the center of her maze. But she is dead. She has died many times. Bacchus slew her. Artemis slew her. She made her magic too large, split her castle and fell into the abyss. And she died in childbirth. In spite of this, the Star is felt to represent hope, the blind faith in the turnings of the Universe. The Star is a Goddess of Death, but also a goddess of many other things. She is a Goddess of Birth.

To demonstrate that life returns, Ariadne brought Theseus, the Sun Hero, out of her deadly web and if he showed lack of appreciation for her charms, he knew her but briefly and he had nothing to do in her strange land and in his busy life, he forgot. So the separation has been explained. As Ariadne is a Spider Goddess, she might be a difficult companion for one filled with sunlight. Spiders carry a toxin which clashes with things which are pure. It attracts that which is impure. Elias Ashmole, the wizard, hung three spiders around his neck to draw the ague away from him. Spiders hold Underworld knowledge. If a river is going to flood, they will build their webs high up. If they expect rain, they will build many webs. Gomme said that spiders bring good luck to a house and that killing one brings misfortune. An especially honoured spider is the Cross Spider, a spider which has a cross on it, and it is bad fortune to harm it or its web. A stone in this spider repels harmful things.

Ariadne was the weaver who was the equal of Athene and so, was belittled by Athene. Her web was a maze which revolved around her Castle of Death. All creation joins the dance through her maze, dances to the Music of the Stars. Kepler spoke of the harmonies of the stars as music. Steiner said it was a music which, with practice, a person could hear.

The dance was called the Crane Dance and, under a number of names, is done as a ritual; as knowledge from the deities, as Hocart has said, is maintained through ritual.

The stars in that Maze in the Sky are a wonder to behold and each might be thought a minor deity, and each would represent purity, truth and beauty; but few of them, as individuals, are known. Sirona was called a Star Princess. Astraea was, from the center of stars, said to have come to Earth to see that the rules of Justice were complied with. She was said to have been the last of the old deities who had a physical presence in Europe, and she was likely the beautiful Star Goddess who turned herself into a quail in order to get away from Jupiter, and she seems to have looked like a Nymph.

This goddess was also called Asteria. And the male form of that name, Asterios, was the name given to the Minotaur, who was, by Zacharias, called the Darkness at the center of the Maze. Asteria might have been dark, as some stars fell and became dark.

Some stars have a wider area of influence, and a weightier influence, than nearly all the others of that great host in the heavens. Among the most influential stars are the Wandering Stars. Wandering Stars, said Kepler, were considered major deities. Pythagoras put their number at seven. These influence the Sun, the Moon and, to a greater or lesser extent, all else. Their influence is especially noticed when they are in the angle between the Sun and the Moon. The narrower the angle, said Lyndoe, the greater would be the influence of the Wandering Stars within that angle. Symbols representing the Wandering Stars have been put on sacred tools and also otherwise used as charms.

The wide starry heavens are a picture of the way things are: each star, representing truth. Tiberius said, the stars are governed by inflexible necessity.

Iamblichos said that learning from the stars is logical, mathematical and in keeping with what the Wind Snake would teach, and to gain that knowledge, one did not need to draw down the deities.

Ovidius said that the most honoured form of forecasting has been a study of the starry heavens.

Benedictus said that all natural art and wisdom is given to man by the stars. The reasoning mind has an attraction to the stars. They are the lawful instructors of Man.

Lindholm said that even for small decisions, with a great many, the stars needed to be consulted. Ogilvie said successful battle leaders, as is known, have been guided by the stars. Said Anneaus Lucanus, as falling stars were seen before Pompeius' battle, he should have expected defeat.

A star falling and becoming dark would have been a grief in the heavens; and this, it is said, would have had a balancing grief on Earth. The energies of the stars were said to reflect energies on Earth. Also, energies are said to come from the stars. The celestial influx, said Rulandus, can give power and virtue. Also, he said, illusory bodies, at times, are made visible by force from the stars. Swords and knives made in line with star energies are said to have great cutting power.

In the silent still center of the ever turning heavens is the dark castle, the Castle of Death. It is seen in the North where the cold air has frozen life, which, said Hartmann, is equated with death. Ariadne is there. Propertius saw her as slender, pale, lovely and asleep. Mistress of Minos, she sat serene over the vast abyss. To quell conflicts, she threw rainbows, deadly rainbows. She holds the thread of life. When an activity, an age, an individual, runs out of energy, she breaks the thread. When Theseus ended the life of an age; with her string, she led him out of the Maze. The Maze was called Ariadne's Dancing floor. Ariadne sits in her mysterious castle which has been called, Castle of the Strong Door. It holds, said Spence, a shadowy radiance, a brilliant twilight where silvery light mingled with jet darkness. Ariadne was dead: slain by Bacchus, slain by Athene and destroyed by the force of her own magic, a magic which split her castle and dropped her into the dark abyss.

The Goddess of Death, as a female, held the Abyss of Emptiness into which all creation must fall; but as a deity, she held the stability of a number, Number Five, which represented the indestructibility of number, and of divine nature.

Aratus said that Bacchus gave the slain Ariadne a crown, as bacchic frenzy would have led one to her castle. Bulfinch said that the crown was silver. Silver relates to the Underworld. Silver relates to love. Ariadne is said to give complete love to all, who are worthy, who ask it of her.

An animal associated with Ariadne is the Bear. The Slain Bear is a Guardian of the World of the Dead. It had been slain by Artemis. Propertius has the dead, in the barge of Charon, setting sail and ending at the Star of Callisto, the beautiful Bear Goddess.

The tree of the Star would be the Silver Fir. Winter and Summer it points to the Land of the Dead. Jupiter made the Fir Spirit into a tree and he favours it and considers it sacred. The Fir is protected by its spirit. It holds knowledge from the Underworld, so is useful in forecasting. A person can predict his fate from the way the light from a fir causes his shadow to fall.

The Fir relates to birth, and is associated with witchcraft. A custom is to carry a lit fir torch around a new born's crib. The Fir protects against lightning and witchcraft. To protect against nightmares, a branch of fir is put across the bed. In forests, as a guide it has been seen to shine with light.

The Fir, according to W E Butler, has an aura usually containing more energy than its needs call for; so, a person in need of aural energy can usually get it as a gift from a fir. From the Fir, new insights might be gained. There might be an urge, in new ventures, to jump ahead too fast and too quickly. A stick of fir not quite burned through protects from lightning. Fir cones are carried as charms to bring fertility. Among other gifts, firs will sometimes give silver, but the silver given might be associated with demons. Porteous said elves were said to live in firs. Firs are said to be guardians of birds and animals. As protection against malicious spirits, it is hung over barn doors.

Firs represent inner strength and calm. They are trees of shadow, darkness, demise, silence, winter and birth.

Silver is the metal which relates to Astral Energies and so, to telepathy, intuition and dreams. It relates to the Spider and to toxins.

This Star is Ariadne, and she is always on her path to her fall. Some said she might have escaped from her position as Queen of Death if Theseus had been true to her, but Philostratus the Elder said Theseus was not to blame. He took her because of appreciation, but he knew little of her personality, and she likely did not offer a day of lively fun and he being Theseus, he could not spend a life doing nothing but feasting on love. He needed to be doing Theseus type things. So he was gone and Bacchus killed her. And there was no way for her not to be, first and last, the Goddess of Death.

The Star represents love, beauty and trust.

The Star loves and protects flowers. Favourites are the Fern, which grants invisibility, and the Chicory, which has a root which can give invisibility. But herbs in general, "Know and watch for their loving star," said Father Young.

In healing, it is said, a star will complete the work of a medical herb.

In the physical World, there is no place for the Castle of the Dead. If a bird were to fly toward where the Castle of the Dead is thought to be, she would never get there by flying. There is no physical direction by which one could get there, as that castle rests within another dimension. The castle could as easily be seen by looking down below a cemetery, or by looking in the direction the Ship of Stone, with its dead passenger, is to take. One sees the Corona Borealis in the North because one expects to see it there, there where the dead would be still and frozen with the cold. And the still spot in the Sky might point to going forever into empty space. But these represent other darkness. One assigns it to the North.

On the card, at the bottom, would be the dark silhouettes of the tops of firs against a dark night sky. Firs are often put at the beginnings of things.

In the Sky, in the upper right, would be a small ring of lights. In the Sky, left center, the Star, Ariadne, would be falling. She is spread, unclothed on her five points, falling. Every star is a falling star. Every star is a Star of Wonder, Star of Light, Star of Royal Beauty. Many who love the Star, appeal to it:

> "Star light, Star bright, first star I've seen
> tonight; I wish I may, I wish I might,
> have the wish I wish tonight."

XVIII ~ Sun

Card 18 is the Sun. The Sun has come to be called Apollo. Apollo, as a god, appears more versatile than other gods whose duties he assumed, as the more versatile gods have tended to replace the less versatile. Also, Apollo is handsome. As Man has become more civilized, more urban, his gods have become less crude, less grotesque. The versatile Apollo has come to rule as the Sun, bringing to his rule so many attributes that he is sometimes thought of as Attributes of the Sun, so that the Sun itself might be Helios, or Hyperion. Among Apollo's strengths are his masteries of prophecy, healing, poetry, mathmatics, archery, beauty, athletics, music, art and logic.

Apollo's temples are known to have been especially lovely, as under his influence, art is closely tied to beauty.

Music is a discipline under his rule and he inspires a system of harmonies throughout the celestial realms and as Pathagoras recognized, the harmonies in music relate to visual harmonies. They also relate to geometry, to arithmetic, to architecture. They relate to pyramids and so, to prophecy. As the movements of all things are connected, these harmonies would relate to astrology.

Apollo, as a musician, enjoys playing the flute, but more attention, it seems, he gives to his harp. His harp has 7 strings. It is said, each string honours one of the 7 Muses. They also equal the 7 rays of colour in the rainbow. The strings are the number of steps to the next octave, so the harp might sing a memorial to death. As a symbol, the harp might represent an instrument of torture. The harp might symbolize beauty.

For prophecy, Apollo established oracles for giving advice and foreknowledge. The Delphic Oracle, he is said to have taken from Themis. The Oracle became relied on. Talbot said Cicero thought that the oracle could not have received so many fine gifts if it did not give accurate forecasts. It was at Delphi, said Euripides, that Orestes learned he was to go to the Taurian citadel for the statue of Artemis.

For the oracles, Apollo brought the tripod, a powerful pyramid which revealed secrets by solar logic, in which the past and the future fit together in a coherent design. Apollo based his logic on exact number. Iamblichos said all things are assimilated to number. It is the ruler of forms and ideas and the cause of gods. And many prophets gave Apollo, as the Master of Number, credit for their divine inspiration.

Apollo authorized women, the Sibyls, to read the messages of the oracle, and he supervised the Sibyls' behavior. When a Sibyl wouldn't tell what she had learned, Apollo filled her with fire so that fire shot from her mouth. She shit fire. Then she gave the message which she needed to give. The Sibyls gave messages from Apollo which kept harmony and peace in the ancient world. They withheld knowledge from the public and gave it to wise leaders who used it for keeping a harmonious society. Apollo had many other ways of giving this knowledge. Pausanias said he had an oracle well at Cyaneae where he showed the future in water. It was suggested, by Marcus Lucanus, Apollo might have informed Gaius Cornelius of a battle by the Sun dimming.

Ovidius said that Gaea was displeased with Apollo for taking the Delphic Oracle and with his fancy ways of giving out knowledge, so she made ways to give free knowledge and so, lessen the pile of expensive gifts to Apollo.

Apollo became recognized, though focused on a bright globe, as the total light, including its source and extending into all its powers and attributes. The light gives eloquence and virtues of courage and honour and it gives knowledge in math, astronomy and logic. Plotinus said all that streams from the Sun will be some form of light.

People picture Apollo as representing the epitome of clear thinking. Eisner said he brings order out of chaos; but added, he does little to excite the imagination.

In the speculations of Martianus Minneius; Mercury, who is known to have a brilliant mind, went to Apollo for advice. The advice he got came in the form of a mathematical solution. Mercury wished to know who would be the best choice in the selection of a mate for himself. Apollo said that since Mercury related to the number three, his mate should have a basic number of four; so together, as seven, they could complete a system and work together as a perfect program. According to Martianus, Venus did not approve of the mathematical solution which Apollo gave. The solution also displeased Hera.

Apollo did not have good fortune with females. With a number of his chosen women he found trouble in the relationship. Apollo liked best those who tended to reflect his own beauty. He admires his own traits, his youthful body. He favours the young over the old. Apollo likes perfection; as, new, sharp knives more than old.

Apollo is honoured for his athletic ability. He excels at jumping and is said to be faster than Mercury. He might give to favoured athletes, great strength. Laurel crowns, representing honours from Apollo, are awarded to winners of athletic contests.

Apollo is one of the deities most looked to for healing. The ailing often went to temples of Apollo. Apollo is a master of herbs and for their master, the herbs do much healing. Some of those he favours are chamomile, delphiniums, daisies, dandelions, marigolds, celandines, beets and the bitter rue. He enjoys the bright blooms. The Marigold brings joy and energy. It drives away the evil eye and ill winds. If its petals are parallel to the ground before 9 in the morning, it is announcing the coming of good weather. The Dandelion is a great aid to healers and gains cheers of gratitude for removing kidney stones and for working other dramatic cures. It holds psychic power and, gathered at Beltane, protects against malicious witchcraft. The Rue guards against the invasions of malicious demons. The Chamomile gives help to humans, animals and other plants. The Bee favours the Chamomile. The Daisy, in the field of love, reveals secrets. The Beet is honoured to be on tables set for Apollo. It repels snakes and other venomous creatures, and it opens obstructions in the liver and spleen, removes headaches, improves eyesight and cures jaundice, skin problems and earache.

Bright flowers, especially, bright yellow flowers, are favoured by the Sun.

Apollo is Lord of the Apple, of the Land of the Apple; however his emblematic tree is the laurel, also called the Bay. The Laurel is the Nymph, Daphne. As the nymphs dance unclad, they asked Apollo to watch for Peeping Toms. While watching, Apollo was struck by the beauty of Daphne. When he ran to capture her, to save herself from his embrace, she turned herself into a laurel tree. So to honour her, Apollo put a wreath of laurel on his head, and he made the laurel ever green. Wreaths of laurel have been given to winners of athletic contests and to persons who have made outstanding contributions in poetry, music and learning, so that the memory of their achievements would be ever lasting. Daphne is called the daughter of the River God Peneus.

The Sibyls honoured the Laurel and chewed laurel leaves as part of their ritual of giving knowledge, and mediums, through the ages, have chewed laurel leaves to gain inspiration.

Laurel relates to lords and monarchs. It is said, if the laurels wither, the monarch who rules the land where the laurels are would be expected to die. One custom has poets holding laurel while reciting.

March first, the Temples of Vesta are decked with laurel. Laurel is used for cleaning and purification. The aroma of laurel cleans and purifies the air. At Yule, Laurel is among the sacred greens and especially, among those which crown the Lord Boar.

Laurel relates to love. To attract love, laurel is given to sacred fires; or, to attract love, laurel oil is put on a beeswax candle and love meditated on while the candle burns. To dream of love, of a future lover, a method given by Aborrow is to pin a laurel leaf on each corner of a pillow, then one in the center of the pillow, then sleep on the pillow. Laurel leaves put under the pillow, then slept on, brings the gift of ability in poetry.

The laurel gives protection from malicious forces and from lightning. Laurel tea fosters learning and brings good health. In a bath, or used as a lotion, laurel cures sore muscles, rheumatism, sprains and bruises. Laurel chases off epilepsy and the plague.

At New Year, sprigs of laurel were given as gifts. It was a good omen, during a feast of Apollo, if there was a happy crackling of laurel leaves. Apollo, as the Sun, had many followers, and these, worshipped Apollo in a great variety of ways. In country areas, Apollo was a folk hero. Tacitus said men and boys, in honour of Apollo, danced naked, sunwise around a fire. Then, around the fire, all joined the dance. While musicians played, a scarecrow King Death was sacrificed; the burnt remains, scattered on the fields.

Apollo had well attended festivals in farming areas, but in well populated urban areas, he became better known for his beautiful, splendid, impressive temples. People admired them; but the temples did not inspire and instigate the masses into emotional frenzies. The christenings and other rituals were artistically and correctly done, and were appreciated, but they were not exciting. They tied into magical formulas which only a small number of the population were allowed link into in a complete way. One ritual, which Iamblichos gives an account of, linked with the divine inspiration from the sacred vibration of Apollo. This was achieved, by a person otherwise worthy, by drinking the blood of a lamb which had been sacrificed to Apollo.

Apollo was thought of as caretaker of sheep, said Callimachus, and this would include even the sheep on Earth. He said, by Apollo's look, herds and flocks are blessed with health, milk and increase. And people expecting long life and happy marriage should make glad sounds with harp and voice for Apollo. But only those who are worthy should go to his alter. Pausanias said sheep related to the Sea and that Apollo's sheep were herded by Nereids. Porteous said the sea nymphs were called Meliades which took care of Apollo's sheep. Ovidius said, as Suns go to the Underworld, sheep have Underworld connections. Halliday said that black sheep, for prophecy, were sacrificed head downward so the blood of the sheep would give the dead the power to speak. He said that the place of sacrifice would have been selected by the sheep. Sheep entrails would have been inspected.

Apollo has a flock of sheep which, it is said, he is most fond. Shepherds often benefit by the favour of Apollo.

But Apollo was in a movement away from flesh and blood deities and toward gods constructed of numbers, and Pythagoras had said that in truth, deities are composed of numbers. And the force of the Sun more than that of other deities would seem numerical.

Ausonius said that the placement and regulation of the force areas in the heavens is under the direction of the Sun, and these are the ancient signs which early philosophers, from times most ancient, have recognized as areas of force. And these signs would controle actions on Earth. And the Sun, said Vetruvius, influences the actions of the Wandering Stars.

The Sun was, from ancient times, considered to be a teacher. Even more important than helping the harvest, said Frobenius, which the Sun did; was being shown, by the Sun, the road to and from the Underworld. Apollo would have been an important person in the Underworld, said Frobenius.

The Sun, as Light, contains reason and logic, and this leads to individuality and away from group functions and, certainly, mass actions. Apollo is known to have the characteristic of individuality, of uniqueness, and this fosters aloofness, fosters aloneness. Apollo has been called the God of Solitude. And this, as Ure has said, relates the Sun to aloof and alone birds: birds of solitude: the hawk and the swan. At dawn, the Swan is said to welcome the Sun into the Sky.

To get away from Typhon, Hyginus said that Apollo turned himself into a bird.

Callimachus said swans and crows were sacred to Apollo; however, for birds held sacred, crows seemed often quite ill treated. As messengers, Apollo found them useful. Crows and ravens were considered to be the same type of bird. As messengers, they got, at times, poor pay for their service. Apollo, according to Gubernatis, sent the crow off to find lustral water for a sacrifice to Jupiter. Then he turned the crow black for bringing back bad news. Armstrong called it a raven, the bird which brought back to Apollo the news of the unfaithfulness of Koronus.

Pausanias said Apollo sent Korax, the Crow Death God, to slay Archilochus, the Poetry God. Apollo felt poetry was so sacred a gift that it needed to be balanced by blindness or death. Then Korax needed to be punished for killing a sacred poet.

Chickens are sacred birds of the Sun. With chickens, the Hen lays the Golden Egg. The Rooster announces the Sun. The crow of the rooster breaks spells and expels spirits and demons. Minucius said Apollo's sacred chickens gave portents. As they were sacred, a general's blasphemous remarks about them caused him disaster.

Dolphins are favoured by Apollo, as Apollo is, at times, in Dolphin form. Dolphins were known to live in a cooperative and just society. As are many of Ocean's citizens, they are lovers of music. Arion, a harper who made magical music, was rescued by a dolphin. The rescue so pleased Neptune that he turned the dolphin into a flower and this is called the Delphinium. A feast day was designated for honouring the Dolphin and Apollo. After Apollo killed the great snake, Python, he took this day for cleansing himself. On this day, others follow Apollo's example and, in pure waters, cleanse themselves. The Feast of Delphinia is held April sixth. On this day, shrines and homes are decorated with laurel and delphiniums, areas are made clean and there are purification rituals and music programs.

Apollo slew Python, daughter of Gaea, in order to controle the point where the lines of force meet, so that at that center of force fields he could rule. By slaying Python, he came to be considered, Ruler of Snakes.

Apollo, it is said, would be present at all holidays which honour the Sun, and he can share in the sacrifices; as, if donkeys are sacrificed to Hyperion, Apollo can share. Some holidays honour other aspects of being, but also honour the Sun. Apollo then would be getting a share of those celebrations.

Apollo, as the Sun, has been called the Soul of Gold, which is the metal of purity. The Sun's Gold, according to Albertus, has healing power, and this power is extended to the gold of the fur of the Lion. Gold holds the quickening, life giving power of the Sun. Gold in Apollo's temples is minted into coins and Apollo protects the integrity of each coin, as it is from the Sun that showers of gold come.

Apollo demands honesty. Dealings done under his watchful eye had best be honest. Apollo is not always friendly, but he himself deals honestly. Apollo, it was said, was faithful to his contracts.

Apollo insists that deities be respected. He can be malicious to a person if that person, or a member of that person's family, is guilty of disrespect to a deity, or to a shrine. It was said, Apollo put an arrow in each of Niobe's sons because Niobe showed disrespect to Latona. In Apollo's feeling about the rightness of balance, he thought a poet the recipient of too much praise, so Apollo slew him.

When Apollo slew a Cyclops, he displeased Jupiter, so Jupiter gave him extra duties.

Apollo displeased Hera; but, said Ridgeway, Athene and Jupiter refused to take sides in the case.

Apollo ruled by force, said Eisner. Followers he sometimes got by kidnapping them.

Pausanias said Apollo sometimes took the form of a wolf.

Apollo brings order out of Chaos. He inspires striving for perfection. Things done on Sunday would often show his influence. The time to sharpen swords would be on Sunday. Apollo's advice seems to be, "Follow the wisdom of the gods and be safe." He has a strict moral code and those who do not live in harmony with his code are advised to avoid his alters.

Apollo inspires a general clear thinking, a rise in self awareness, a birth into spiritual awakening and a recognition of thinkers.

Apollo likes solitude, which he has much of the time. When he is in the sky, he is the only Sun. Then, his number is one. The other numbers to which he relates fall away when he becomes the Sun, the Eye of Day.

Yellow flowers, by some, are thought to hold a finer gold than the metal: the golden sunlight of the Sun. These would break through and clear away fantasy and false information, aid learning, bring happiness, inspire promotion, bring health and the confidence and feeling of correctness of the path to those who should rule. In the yellow sunlight is logic, and problem solving, and power.

The Card of the Sun would hold the voyage of the Sun: nine sweeps to get to the Underworld, nine waves to bring his return to the World of the Living: to complete the Circle. Apollo is represented by the ring finger.

XIX ~ Moon

Section 19 is the Moon. To the Moon, a sacred number would be 19, as the concurrence of lunar time and solar time takes place every 19 years. As the Moon, Selene is said to sail through the sky in her silver car pulled by the white oxen, which Pan had given her.

Selene is seen as a beautiful, veiled lady wearing a long white robe and known as the Peaceful Moonlight on the fields. Over the fields, she is sometimes pictured riding an ass: this, from Pausanias.

Selene gave her love to a shepherd, Endymion. That love caused Selene to leave her place in the sky and spend time laying with her shepherd lover, so Jupiter transported Endymion to the Underworld and put him to sleep so Selene would always find him on her trips there. And Selene took over the care of Endymion's sheep. But her worries over Endymion cause her to fade and grow pale. Also, Selene loves and cares for Suns who have fallen into the Underworld. She has them sleep in her temple of elm with its ivy roof.

Selene inspires interpretations of events and gives power in intuitive and visionary work; however, there is a large variation in power which she gives. The Sign of the Crab is called the House of the Moon, and the influence of Selene would be strong during the time under that sign. Selene would have her exaltation in the Sign of Taurus and would exert, usually, her strongest influence at this time. When her gibbous phase is in the Bull's face, she fills the imaginative faculty with fantasies. Philosophers such as Johannes Kepler have thought that many of those fantasies would contain within them much that is in agreement with reality. Selene, at the Full, would be expected to give power in intuitive and visionary thinking. For discovery of occult knowledge, Selene seems most help when in conjunction with Saturn. It seems, one's best time for intuition is on one's lunar birthday and most success would come when one has not asked for the intuition he would get.

People born under a Full Moon would often have ability in visionary and intuitive work. Birth under a Waning Moon would aid work in healing. But what Selene would give would depend, at any given time, on her own mood. If she would be feeling strong, she might give splendid dream time, fine time for love, time for working strong and lasting spells, strong energy for charging magical tools, top power to healing herbs.

There may be some lack of controle of Selene's full power. If one is to perform surgery, one might avoid Selene at Full. For surgery, Selene seems most help one week before or one week after the New Moon. Sometimes, when there are other forces one is working with, one stays away from Selene's heavy hand. Most healing herbs are gathered at New Moon and that would be the best time for cutting hair and nails. For a rewarding relationship with Selene, a person might look for her in his Sun Sign. For work using imagination, intuition or dream, Selene is most help when she is at the Full. As a rule, that is the time when spirits are most easily contacted.

Selene has an interest in farming activities. When at the Full, she inspires the harvesting of grains and mushrooms, and of root crops when these are being harvested for seed. She has bread set to rise when she is at the Full. As animals would relate to Selene most when she is at the Full, they might well be most difficult to handle at this time. Carpenters often avoid trees which fall when Selene is Full. Selene waxing, shear sheep.

When Selene is New and in a water sign, the chickens born in that time would usually keep healthy and be good layers. Apples, olives, pears and vines planted at that time might well be expected to prosper. It seems best to plant potatoes when Selene is nearly dark. When Dark, Selene rests; then, waxing, gains and gives power and often, pleasure. Waxing, she gives protection and virility. That seems a good time for planting. Butchering hogs at that time, the bacon would likely be fat and rich. The hogs butchered under the waning, the bacon from these would likely be lean. When Selene is waxing and, best, close to Full, that would be a good time to shear sheep. Selene, as a Waxing Moon, is a help to annuals which produce their yield above ground if they are planted during this phase. She seems most helpful to asparagus, cabbage, celery, cress, lettuce and parsley if they are planted under a young Waxing Moon; most helpful to beans, peas and cucumbers if planted under an old Waxing Moon.

When waning, Selene is often in the mood to influence, and to lend energy toward cleansing, healing and purification. Usually, when Selene is waning, she is most help to winter wheat and other biennial crops, and to bulb and root vegetables. It has seemed best to plant potatoes when Selene is nearly dark, has seemed best to cut trees when Selene is waning, if the trees are to be used in carpentry.

Selene's placement in the sky would affect the type of influence she would be. One type of change would be in the part of the body she would be the most focused on. It is thought best not to have surgery on the part of the body which Selene it focused on. In Pisces, Selene would be focused on the feet; in Aries, the head; in Taurus, the neck; in Gemini, the arms; in Cancer, the breast; in Virgo, the belly; in Libra, the reins; in Scorpio, the crotch; in Sagittarius, the thighs; in Capricorn, the knees; in Aquarius, the legs. When Selene is in Leo, surgery usually should be avoided. When Selene is in a person's birth sign, it is usually wise for that person to avoid surgery.

Cultivating is thought most effective when Selene, as a Waning Moon, is in a barren sign: Gemini, Aquarius, Leo or Aries. Selene in Virgo is a good time for cultivating.

Lettuce, cabbage and root crops are planted when Selene is in Taurus; most others, when Selene is in a water sign. Onions are planted when Selene is in Sagittarius; vines, when she is in Libra.

Selene might aid in the acquisition of wealth. How much help she would be at a given time might be predicted from what angle she was in with Leo. For speculating, what a person's Sun Sign is would determine where he would want Selene. An Aquarius person might want her in Libra. A Scorpio person, Pisces; a Gemini person, Capricorn; and Aries person, Leo; a Virgo person, Taurus; a Taurus person, Libra or Capricorn; a Pisces person, Cancer; a Libra person, Taurus or Aries; a Cancer person, Scorpio; a Leo person, Leo; a Sagittarius person, Libra; a Capricorn person, Virgo.

One reason Selene generates the power she does is the characteristic she has of moving quickly from position to position. Her quick changes have caused her to be called the Impeller of the Zodiac. The quickly shifting aspects have seemed to cause many observed events which have seemed to wait on such a force to be a starter for the happening. The waters of this World and otherworlds, including those in the bodies of the living and the dead, are sensitive to Selene's changes. Female bodies are particularly sensitive to Selene's changes. The moods of the vast seas, its deep mysteries, sudden discoveries, and frightening disorientations, all relate to Selene. There might be feelings of being lost, or out of one's depth, or of flowing away with the Moon and the waters; or there might be a sudden clearing of mist and a revelation: all these would relate to aspects of Selene. As Selene influences the seas, sailors give much attention to her.

They get from her, reports of coming weather. Selene waxing, slender and clear on the third day, she heralds calm; but on that day, if she seems thick and blunted, rain and South Wind would be expected. If she curls either tip, wind would be expected from the West. On that third day, if her halo blushes red, a storm would be expected. When Full, or at either quarter, if clear and bright, good weather would be expected; if ruddy, wind: if dark with dark spots, rain. A broken ring around Selene would indicate coming wind; a double or triple ring, rain.

Rudhyar said that objectivity and clear consciousness would be fed by the Full Moon. This would lead to seeing things which had before been suggested. The Full Moon is thought of as giving fulfillment.

In the first quarter, Rudhyar said that lack of flexibility and forcing issues can cause problems. The Waning Moon, he said, causes people to want to display learning and perspectives and to instigate causes and false causes. A third quarter tendency is a trouble in decision making in directions in thinking. The balsamic Moon would be an end product of a past; perhaps, prophetic of the future; perhaps, a ruin from which a future would be made.

Selene's movements can cause great harm. There can be savage storms. Once in the past, when the Moon vanished from a clear sky, crops failed and many lords died.

At times, by conflicts with the Sun, Selene brings misfortunes. An eclipse would show such a conflict. It was after an eclipse, the City of London burned. After another eclipse, King Erkenbert died and his death was followed by a number of plaques. Ovidius said that the bad effects from an eclipse usually overbalance the good; that it is a custom to make noise to counter the evil cause of the eclipse. There is a custom, after an eclipse, of washing in a flowing brook to wash away impurities and ill luck.

It was thought, said Kittredge, that washing new clothes under a New Moon would be likely to bring an accident.

Selene, as a Crescent holding her old form, predicts bad weather. Selene, coming from New Moon, it is thought, ill luck to see her first through tree branches. Should this occur, to avoid ill luck, one might take a silver coin, spit on both sides of it and conceal it.

It has been thought, said A van Gennep, that the Moon phases affect the movement of celestial bodies and the circulation of the blood.

Menstruating women relate to Selene. As they are toxic, they can cause Selene to bring harm. The Moon covered with blood would bring disaster.

She is reported to have been covered with blood before Queen Matilda and Earl Robert died. Menstruation is regulated by Selene. Blood from a first menstruation, if collected during an eclipse, would have magical powers. Menstruating women, by going near grape vines, by going near mares, might cause the grape vines to wither, might cause the mares to miscarry: this, under the authority of Selene.

For countering negative energies, blackberries are gathered under a Waxing Moon when the Waxing Moon and Venus are in opposition to Mars.

Corrigan said that the best time for an herb bath is under the Waxing Moon. A single candle is used and on ending the bath, it is extinguished in the bath water.

Selene relates to pools, springs, mirrors, crystals and glass. To see her face reversed in a glass is a sign of death. It is not good to see Selene through glass and especially, if one is seeing her for the first time in her new cycle as she is coming from the dark.

As mirrors relate to Selene, it is thought, they should be respected. To break a mirror is thought to bring seven years of bad luck.

The Pool can be, according to Heselton, a more perfect mirror than that which is made by man. A still pool could be seen as truly the entrance to the depths of Earth. Said Heselton, into the depths of Earth and into the depths of the person who would be looking into it.

Cups and cauldrons are symbolic of the Sacred Pool and The Cup and The Cauldron are thought to be owned by the Moon. Lactantius said drink from the Chalice and gain knowledge. The sacred Chalice at times was made from the sacrificed person who would have represented the king, and the drink from it, said W G Gray, would have been sunshine and rain, blessings from the blood of the sacrifice.

Crystals, especially, crystal globes are favoured by Selene, and a favoured stone is the Moonstone. Moonstones, according to Sylvaticus, wax and wane with the Moon. Kunz said that they arouse feelings of love, and that they permit lovers to look into the future. To see into the future, the lover, when the Moon is Full, would hold a moonstone in his, or her, mouth.

Selene gives knowledge through crystals and stones as well as through mirrors and pools. And under her authority, crystals and stones have other powers also. A person skilled in the use of a crystal might bend others to her, or his, will. To arouse passion, a moonstone might be wrapped in a yellow cloth.

Libanius said that the Moon gives prophecy by vision, omens and dreams. Tacitus said that if one slept by an oracle, one would be likely to get prophetic dreams. Libanius said that the dreams would be likely to be brought by the Dioscuri, who served Selene. Pausanias said that in the Temple of Pasiphae and Ino there was a Fountain of the Moon by which, if one slept, that person would likely have prophetic dreams.

The Moon gives knowledge much of the time through intuition and omens. Much knowledge revealed by Selene would be knowledge from the Underworld. At either Quarter Moon, if a person stood on a threshold, barefoot, a hand on each door jam, eyes closed; when that person opened his, or her, eyes; he, or she, would be able to read the future in the first animal seen.

It is said that Selene, in the gloaming, might take energy from the Sun.

Selene respects age. Often bald men are by her shown favour.

Beside Selene, other deities take Moon form. Diana is the Spirit of the Dark Sky and has the Moon as her central focus. She is the youthful Huntress, but a Guardian of the Wilds. In one aspect, she is the gracious and powerful Mother Goddess pictured by the ancients: the Moon Mother. Diana is the bringer of pregnancy and the bringer of death. As Leland has said, she encouraged woman followers. The message from Diana to the seekers was said to be, when the Full Moon is on the fields, gather in a secret place for learning.

Diana is an enchantress who clouds herself in fabulous illusion and dream. She is a protector of women, a supervisor of birthings and a patroness of women's activities. Kings rule at her pleasure.

Zimmer called Diana, Goddess of Lake and Grove. Rulandus told of a pool called Diana's Bath. It was, said Rulandus, adorned only by the beauties of nature. The bath, in a grove, was a beautiful pool formed of soft pumice stone. Under the trees, said Macaulay, there was a custom to offer Diana human sacrifices. In her grove, Diana was served by other female deities. Two listed by Frazer are Ergeria and Virbius. Of trees, Diana favours the Beech, as Skinner has said, and prophecy was given through the murmur of its leaves. The Walnut is also a tree she favours. Diana met gatherings of witches in the tree's shade.

Diana is Queen of the Fairies and a chief Goddess of Witches and as such, rides through the sky with witches. And Diana has a link with elementals. Some fairies, Children of Diana, are said to be formed of

Moon Rays. Like Diana, fairies are said to favour odd numbers. As Diana relates to water, Junius said, she rides a sea monster.

August thirteenth is a day for Diana. At this time, women go to her temples and to her shrines in the sacred groves. In the groves, for Diana, there was ritual hair washing, then dancing and feasting. With Diana, there was Lunar mysticism. And at times, a dionystic frenzy.

As magical charms, Diana is said to give stones with holes through their centers. It is said, there are chalices which come from Fairyland, and these would relate to Diana and to the Moon.

Artemis is a powerful huntress who takes Moon form. Gomme called her the savage Bear Goddess of the Dark Sky and said that she had ruled supreme. Harrison said that in times past, she was a chief goddess who took bear form. Pausanias said she was a Goddess of Battle and was often pictured in armour. Artemis was said to also have been seen as a tree and as a mermaid.

Artemis is a Goddess of Birth and Death, and relating to birth, Patroness of Childbirth. The newborn are under her protection, so she is given a part in naming and blessing rituals, and these are sometimes incorporated into Moon rituals. Many christenings are performed in beautiful temples of Artemis. Artemis also had a part in birthing rituals. The Moon, as Case has said, relates to knots, as they bind and separate segments. In birthing rituals, all knots in the areas of the birthings, said Gray, were untied.

As Artemis is a lover of wild places, it was said, she would only visit a city when called by a woman for aid in childbirth.

Artemis is an Elemental Force, a ruler of nymphs and a regulator of life in the wilds. She enforces balance, slays animals where they threaten balance. She runs naked and wild as do animals, but slays men who happen upon her, and she, running naked and wild.

Bulfinch tells of Actaeon, who came upon Artemis when she was naked, and, because of it, was turned into a stag and was eaten by his own dogs.

Artemis inspires natural instinct over society imposed structures. At her woodland revels, to which women went to worship her, there was instinct to the point of madness: wild music, wild naked dancing, frenzy, violence, drink. Sometimes grotesque, sometimes beautiful, at the moonlight revels, Artemis often inspired packs of women to drink and dance naked; then rush through the wilds stripping, copulating with, ripping apart, eating raw: any or all of these, any animal or man they came across. And usually a protector of animals, Artemis would run with the Moon mad pack slaying what she would come across.

Artemis, as a Goddess of the Amazons, is a warrior and battle leader. Clothed in willow branches, she watched women do stomping war dances to inspire battle. The women dance, clash shields for Artemis, then ready themselves for battle.

Artemis is quick to anger, quick to slay. She killed Bear Goddess Callisto, River God Cenchrias and the monster, Tityus. When she felt Niobe had not shown proper respect to Latona, she shot many of Niobe's daughters with her bow, which was her weapon of choice.

Artemis is a Goddess of Justice. When there was fighting in front of one of her alters, she brought a plague down upon the area served by the alter. To atone for the blasphemous fighting, a Priestess of Artemis had the young men of the city whipped in front of Artemis' alters; each man, whipped to Artemis' satisfaction, as the priestess interpreted it.

Usually Artemis is looked to for help and understanding. Especially, women look for aid from Artemis. However, Artemis sometimes shows kindness to men. Sailors and travelers, male and female, seek aid from Artemis. Maidens seek help in finding a mate. Often, after making a request, maidens sacrifice hair to Artemis. Rituals for Artemis are nearly always women's rituals. To serve in Artemis' Temple, men were castrated.

Artemis is looked to for purification and for healing; especially looked to for healing snake bites.

Artemis loves and inspires the arts. Her temples are known for their beauty and beautiful music is featured at her celebrations.

Artemis, the Bear Goddess, is known as a Sickle Moon and as a Wood Nymph, wild and free with limitless dreams, a Waxing Moon: This is the way she is seen by Gladstar.

She is pictured with a horned deer, which Ridgeway identifies as a horned doe.

Artemis is celebrated February twelfth and April twentyseventh. Manas said that objects sacred to Artemis were carried in procession, and in the procession, in front of the objects, there was acrobatic dancing. The procession led to where there would be a sacrifice and before the sacrifice, music and dancing.

April eighth, Artemis and Moon Goddess Iphigenia are honoured.

The Full and Dark Moons are often celebrated and rituals held. Some groups try to have rituals every Full Moon and some, every Dark Moon.

In one ritual, at Full Moon, after a sacred space has been established, virtues from Moonbeams might be captured. The circle would be around a stone alter on which would be a cup of spring water and a wreath of vervain and rue. The priestess in the center would carry the wreath three times around the alter, return it to its place; then, take a cord made from a yellow, a green and a blue string; the strings, braided together; would make a loop in the cord. The priestess would then look, through the loop, at the Full Moon to catch a Moonbeam. While holding the Moonbeam, a desire might be put into a well stated charm, then the loop tied into three knots. Fruit would then be put on the alter for the Full Moon.

A ritual used for blessing the vines would be done with the Sickle Waxing Moon. The sacred circle would be established. The priestess would then lift the wine filled horn and say that by the sung charms and blessings of Diana, the wine would be Diana's sacred blood to be the sacred drink so that it would flow into and bless the vines. An offering of fruit would be given to Diana.

This, said Leland, would relate the Horned Diana to Bacchus. Callimachus wrote of an alter built entirely of Horns of Diana, and these would be Horns of Plenty, and these would relate Diana to Bacchus and to celebrations of Bacchus.

Moon journeys are sometimes taken, and these would sometimes be through rituals done under the Dark Moon. A sacred circle would be established and, under the Dark Moon, on the alter, a single flame would be lit. In the circle, one might go through the veils, through the ghostly light, between worlds. There, a totem animal might be met. A person might be led into strange landscapes and there, might gain insight, might experience magic. From the journey, the traveler might become encumbered with taboos and obligations.

The journey might be made in Moonlight. Mindpower might take the traveler through Moonlit veils.

At Full Moon, after a sacred circle has been established, a circle of power might be developed. For this, dancers would form a circle, move around the circle in a dance, dance faster and faster, blending auras so that the colours become white. The air would become light; then all the dancers would ground their bodies; with their hands, draw pentacles.

The dance is sometimes more complex, sometimes a woven fabric and often, the priestess would be dancing in the spinning circle.

The Moon might then be drawn down. This is an ancient ritual.

Aristophanes said women drew down the Moon in order to gain its powers.

A priestess in the center of the circle might raise her arms to form a vee and into the vortex of power, with strong desire and strong words, call down the Moon.

She at the center of power might be the Moon carnate.

Or, the Moon might be on her, on a circle, as Spirit Light.

The wedding is a ritual that would be related to the Moon. The wedding should be under the Waxing Moon and best, close to Full.

As many goddesses take Moon form, the Moon has a range of personalities and each, with many moods. The mood of Selene might depend on whether or not she is worried at that time about Endymion.

Beside Forms thought of as major, the Moon might be in a number of other Forms. Included would be Andromeda, Phaedra, Pasiphae, Io and Iphigenia.

Andromeda was threatened by the Sea's dark forms, threatened by a dragon from the Sea, but was rescued by the Sun.

Phaedra had a conflict with the Sun. She slew a Sun Horse.

Pasiphae had a passion for, and copulated with, a White Ox, who is a God of Darkness and Justice.

Io is the beautiful Moon, often in the form of a Wandering Cow. Io would be a wanderer. Perhaps in the gloaming she would be seen as troubled and insecure. Because Jupiter favoured her, Hera tormented her. A flower Io favours is the Violet.

Iphigenia sadly accepts the blood of men sacrificed, then flees through the Sea's Dark Blue Gate. She is Goddess of Dream. Dreams come from her place in the fiery Sky. Iphigenia is honoured especially April eight, Mounichia.

The Moon Goddesses have many things in common, so the Moon can be looked to for consistent characteristics. The Moon is looked to for dream and fantasy. She also harbours melancholy and haunting terrors. Strange, fantastic visions might come from the Moon. When Full, the goddesses would usually have overflowing energy and a person born at this time would likely be full of vigour, be difficult to regulate, to controle. A child who cut a tooth under the Full Moon would be rewarded. If the beams of the Full Moon would fall on a sleeping person, that person would likely become insane. The Crescent Moon, if the horns would be pointed up, would be carrying blessings to Earth. Waxing, the Crescent Moon would bring good fortune to travelers and to lovers. For spirit from the Moon, a stone shaped like a Crescent Moon has been carried. Areas of influence, Junius lists rhythms, instincts, reflections, motherings, fertility, and heritage. A general rule said of the moon is, waxing, she aids love: waning, prediction.

The Moon causes a desire for the mysterious and she inspires breaking away from fetters and running free with the Night Wind. A flock of birds flying over a Full Moon predicts travel.

The Moon relates to the ancient past. It preserves ties to societies' heritage.

The Moon is a mover of waters, a cool shifter of tides. Boethius spoke of the Moon's cold and watery ways.

The Moon rules Monday. It is thought, best not to borrow or lend on Monday, best to pay for purchases. One might expect a child born on Monday to be fair of face. The Moon encourages and bequeaths beauty. The index finger, it is said, is the finger which most relates to the Moon.

It is thought best to treat the Moon with respect. Some have felt it proper to go outside and greet the first New Moon after the New Year. An angry crowd came near to slaying Anaxagoras, said Fiske, for calling the Moon, dead matter.

As Rhys has said, cattle are often associated with the Moon. The Car of Selene was pulled by white oxen and the Moon herself would take the form of a horned beast. There are sacred herds of cattle related to the Underworld and guarded by the Moon.

Cats relate to the Moon and to the Underworld. Diana, Hyginus said, to hide from the snake monster, Typhon, took Cat form. Ceram said that the relation of cats to magic has long been known; as, if a black cat had crossed a person's path, that person would, from very ancient days, likely have expected ill fortune. Drowning a cat has been said to stir up a storm. Cats were kept, said Murray, because of their ability to work magic. For reward, said Murray, they were given a bit of their owner's blood.

Dogs are favoured by the Moon and were often companions of Diana and Hekate. Dogs followed Hekate as she walked the roads. At Diana's Groves, hunting dogs were welcomed at her rituals.

The Rabbit is the sacred magical animal favoured by the Moon. It is a special animal of Selene, and it is looked to for divine guidance. It served as a direction finder for Queen Boudicca. Said Gubernatis, the Rabbit drew the Lion Sun into a golden net. And, said Gubernatis, the

Moon told her followers to build in the grove which they would see the Rabbit go into. There was a custom, before a hunter killed a rabbit, he got permission from the Moon Goddess. A custom was, said Lethbridge, before the hunter killed the rabbit, he made a sacrifice to the Moon.

Sextus Placitus said that to get a male child, a rabbit's belly would be dried, sliced, put in wine and drunk by a man and his woman. For scorpion stings, Sextus said that a rabbit's rennet in wine should be drunk.

Armstrong said that a rabbit crossing in front of a person would bring him good fortune; crossing behind, ill luck. A rabbit running ahead would predict a victory.

The left hind foot of a rabbit is thought, especially magical, and is worn as a charm.

First of trees sacred to the Moon would be the Elm. Selene's temple in the Underworld is formed of elm with a roof of ivy. Elm is used as a totem tree. It is the tree of Morpheus, which protected Orpheus. The Elm is the tree of Selene and, sacred to Morpheus, God of Sleep, it brings sleep. Dreams hover in elm branches ready to flood onto any person sleeping or lingering below them. In elm branches nightmares hide. Some of the elm dreams would be prophetic.

The Elm is a melancholy tree. It is said to grieve. Orpheus went under elms because of the elms' feeling for melancholy. As the elms were lovers of music, they danced to the music of Orpheus. As elms favour and inspire musicians, they are called, trees of song.

Elms grieve for fallen elms. The death of elms relates to the death of persons of stature in the lands where the fallen elms had been. The fall of an elm could cause the death of a person, or the ruin of a community.

Elms are comfortable in cemeteries. They bless funerals and give sympathy to mourners.

The Elm is a gift from Hades. Nymphs planted elms around the tomb of the father of Andromache, as Andromache was held sacred by the Moon. The Elm is the sacred tree of elves, and elves have made elms their home.

Establishing communication with an elm can open ways of communicating with many herbs and with the Fairy Kingdom. And an elm can give encouragement and inner strength to rise above adversity, and if a person would have a faded spirit, the elm might gift aural energy. However, some persons have found elms difficult. Some, have felt elms to be unfriendly, have felt themselves to be attacked. An elm might take energy, might take from an aura, or might drop a branch on a person.

Meditation with an elm can provide peace, intuition, foresight, relaxation and understanding. For a look into the future, an elm leaf might be pricked, put under the pillow and slept on. Women use elm for easing menstrual cycles and for aiding their reproductive systems. A lotion from the elm can make the skin fair and beautiful. The Elm cures wounds, sores, ulcers, sore eyes, bladder and kidney troubles and problems in the gastrointestinal system. A bough of elm hung over a doorway would protect a house.

Hekate and Saturn favour the Elm and Venus would favour it. Elms, from early days, as Macaulay said, have supported the grape vines.

For the Moon, a second sacred tree is the Ivy. Selene has it cover the roof of her Underworld Temple. In graveyards, it inhibits ghosts from straying out of the Underworld. At celebrations for Artemis, women carry staffs wrapped in ivy. For Diana, women wear ivy crowns. Ivywood cups are used for protection from intoxication. The cups give protection, also, from whooping cough. At rituals for Artemis, ivy leaves are chewed, and this would sometimes produce prophetic visions. An ivy leaf put under the pillow and slept on would give prophetic vision or prophetic dreams. For inspired vision, poets are sometimes given ivy crowns. As ivy inspires fidelity, crowns of ivy are sometimes given to newlyweds.

Ivy might be seen along the mystical path to the Underworld.

Ivy is used for treating jaundice and, mixed with oil, sunburn. If the ivy on a person's house dies suddenly, it predicts death.

Ivy is a sacred tree of Bacchus, Sylvanus, Ariadne, Saturn and Pan.

The Moon has other favourite trees: Elder, Willow, Beech, Walnut and Blackthorn.

To be rid of an illness, a person would go to an elder, stand in Moonlight and ask to be cured.

The Willow is often found at boundaries, found where land meets water. Boundaries are gates to the Underworld and water has the Waterveil, which is a way to the Underworld. This would relate the Willow to the Dark Moon; and so, to witchcraft, wisdom, withering, wit, whisk and whip. And the Willow relates to subtlety, insight, intuition, flexibility, deception and cunning. Willow wands are found useful. They are used for finding the correct places for holding funerals, for finding water, for chasing away malicious spirits and for getting rid of spells. As a whip, it is thought, a child whipped with a willow stick would have his growth stunted, or would wither away.

The Willow is a dangerous tree. At night, a willow might come out of the ground and take a person to the Underworld. And willow is used in rituals of sacrifice. Offerings have been sent to the Underworld in willow baskets. In flying, willow baskets have been used. With willow, one flies from trauma.

Willow is used in healing eyes and for relieving pain and sadness, and for relieving sadness, it is used at funerals.

The Blackthorn is a tree of protection. It is used for wands, staffs and clubs. The wands have special abilities in blasting. From the blackthorn comes health giving wine.

Toads and snakes are favoured by Goddesses of the Moon.

Goddesses of the Moon like flowers; especially, pale flowers, those which are pale in colour. Large green leaves, also, are pleasing to the goddesses. Juno and Diana consider the White Lily emblematic. Hyssop, Chervil, Mugwort, Vervain, Violet, Daisy and mallow meet with favour. Mint and Catnip meet with favour and Burdock is favoured by the Bear.

The number for the Moon is Nineteen: Nine, the usual number of Moons, conception to birth; plus ten, the number of the Circle. The Moon regulates circles: high to low, light to dark, death to birth, among others.

In the Sky is the Full Moon. A bow and arrow is near the bottom of an elm, a dangerous tree which might steal energy, strike with a falling limb or call in a malicious ghost. In the shadows, on the far left, is a rabbit. The rabbit represents eternity. White flowers might be seen in the darkness near the bottom of the card.

In the center, on the ground, is a circle of light. In the center of the circle, the naked, drawn down moon, standing, her arms raised to form a vee.

Lady Moon gives fantasy, gives dream and, certainly, Lady Moon gives love. In a flood, the emotion of love sweeps over Earth from all phases of the Moon. For gaining love, one kisses the hand to the New Sickle Moon. The Full Moon might inspire the naked dance, but the Sickle Moon brings the pure, gentle love to lonely places.

"Lady Moon, Lady Moon
where are you sailing?"
"Over the sea. Over the sea."
"Lady Moon, Lady Moon

whom are you loving?"
"All that love me. All that love me."

Monday's Child is fair of face.

XX ~ Teacher

Card twenty is the Teacher. The Chief Teacher is Minerva. She has been called Goddess of a Thousand Works. As that name implies, Minerva has a wide range of areas of interest. At her festivals; teachers, scholars and craftsmen skilled in a great variety of crafts are honoured. Minerva integrated the fields of philosophy and other learning. She is known as a music master and she integrates music with mathmatics. Education is important to her and one reason, it relates to the cause and effect movements of all things, including the deities.

Minerva directed education to seven forms of learning and it was taught that mastery of the seven forms would make one wise, would make one free from being ignorant, so the forms are called the Liberalizing Arts. Arithmetic, Music, Astronomy and Geometry are four of the forms and these study scientific calculation. The other three forms: Didactic, Grammar and Rhetoric: use philosophical reasoning. Autissiodorensis said that the first four, being most pure, relate to the upper air, and the other three, to the lower air, the air near Earth. The forms are tied together in numerical formulas which bind together all matter and, as all matter has its spiritual aspect, it is all tied together and to the deities.

Minerva directed an understanding that the different cycles of matter, when understood, permit one to predict. As Minerva instructed, it was learned, all bodies have waves of force which radiate from them and so, bodies connect and influence one another: These may be sympathetic, or antipathetic, to one another, depending on their characteristics or on their positions. Observations of what bodies, especially, the celestial, are doing, is a way of determining what deities are up to.

A human has been called a microcosmos; so, it was taught, what the heavens do would be mirrored in Man. The understandings of these relationships were important in spiritual regeneration and in the development of strengths, including those which have been called divine powers. It was taught, the heavenly bodies are examined because their pure rings of vibrations, more than the more muddied rings of the bodies on the lower level, permit a person to accurately measure influences such as sensations and emotions.

Perception was taught and thinkers were trained in the development of a receptive state of mind. Rings of colour and of music were observed. It was explained, some are perceptible only through feeling that they are there, or through seeing them with the mind. It was observed, the rings have this in common: that they group themselves in units of sevens: that the holy number, seven, as Isidorus said, forms natural divisions in its manifestations.

Beside the natures of individual bodies, relationships were considered, one body to others. It was shown, the angles formed by the bodies are important, as some qualities might do well at a wide angle, but not at a sharp angle; others, the reverse. It was seen, the paths between the bodies form triangles and it became understood, triangles and circles form the heavens. They have been called the building blocks of the Universe. Each triangle holds the force waves of three other triangles; so, as Eugenius has said, knowledge is gained by the observing of the rotation of time through triangles. And the triangles might be in a magical location.

As the Universe and its relationships were studied, the importance of balance became understood. Even a person's health was seen to depend on balance. It was taught, there was wisdom in creating symmetry from the study of time, as it went through the window provided by the forces. In persons of much wisdom, the knowledge picked up in the bright light of the conscious was balanced by that picked up through the unconscious. As Hulme has said, a thing might be picked from the unconscious by music and art before the conscious, even in a bright light, is aware of it. One watched the balance of forces. The form of an action, and an environment and its movement; as Vetruvius has said, would depend on the varying degrees of attraction, or repulsion, in the elements acting at a time on a space. It might be the forces to shape a temple, or a war. The knowledge of what the shape would be would come from discovering the point where the four elements balance, one against the other: the center of the cross.

As bodies were studied, their complex vibrations observed, an appreciation for each individual was developed. Persons were led to understandings; to becoming self aware, self conscious; to develop individual critical, analytic and creative thought. Thinkers, under the force of Minerva, were becoming part of what Curtius called, a great mysterious movement in western self consciousness.

The learning developed understandings which led to persons acting in wise ways, and to speaking wisely. It was realized, said Lucretius, World was not created for the pleasure of only mankind, but for the well being of all things in nature.

One took individual responsibility. He did not let the masses do his thinking for him. He admired individual achievement without feeling the need to be a blind follower of the one he admired. He did not waste his time with foolishness. As Marcus Aurelius said, the wise man did not waste anger on dead things. He led a just and sensible existence. It was said, a wise man spoke to men as if the gods were listening, and to the gods as if men were listening.

The wise man belonged to a religious group, a religion, with a membership of one: himself.

Minerva appreciates those who teach and those who learn. As she relates to the thread of existence, she appreciates history and those who teach history. It was said, fortunate is he who has a knowledge of history.

Minerva appreciates achievement, but will draw the line at vanity. When she got word of a woman who had bragged of being a better spinner than herself, Minerva went to where the woman was and demanded competition. Minerva won the contest, rose up in anger and turned the woman into a spider.

Minerva has authority in music. She is concerned with music productions and with the making and the playing of musical instruments.

Healing is an area in which Minerva has an interest and much healing is done under her supervision.

Minerva is a deadly warrior. Her chief weapons are a sword and shield and thunderbolts, which she made and had an owl carry.

Minerva is associated with the Wheel, its arts and magics. The Circle is a way to learning. Much knowledge can be gained from the window where three circles intersect. And the Circle protects. It is a symbol of protection. Minerva carries a circular shield. At maturity, it was a custom to present a young man with a soldier's magical shield.

Minerva is honoured with a number of festivals. The festival of Quinquatrus, March nineteenth, would be the one where she is most visible. At this joyful festival, she is honoured with feast, song, poetry and dramatic presentations. In her name, teachers, actors and craftsmen are honoured. As Minerva favours rope sellers, these are given special attention. Warriors, feasting, give praise to Mars and Minerva, and they get bawdy, as Minerva promotes copulation. In Minerva's name, teachers, for the gift of learning, are given gifts of silver. Also, gifts of silver are given to Minerva, said Livius.

March twentythird, Tubilustrum, is a second festival in which Minerva shares honours with Mars. In their honour, war trumpets are cleaned and there are parades featuring the trumpets.

September thirteenth, Lectisternia, Jupiter, Juno and Minerva are the chief deities honoured. Crafts are displayed and, under the authority of Minerva, judged. There are Harvest Festival contests and games and a parade in which Jupiter, in his glory, is represented. Banners which picture lions, eagles and bright lightning would be held high, and, in the parade, there would be bright military gear. Decorations would include branches of oak and walnut, and hangings would picture geese and owls. Large flint stones, which, when struck together, bring rain, would be displayed. The Corn Doll would have a place of honour. Entertainments would include acrobats, puppet shows and athletic contests, and there would be loud music. It was thought proper to sacrifice one or more oxen to Jupiter. A shrine for Ceres would have been freshly decorated.

A second teacher would be Bellona, a Snake Goddess and Goddess of War who carries a whip and will whip the masses into a frenzy when she sees that a situation calls for it. From her temple, Bellona Calls for the start of wars and she directs negotiations which end wars. She is the educator in situations where there are conflicts. She is a dark faced goddess with snaky hair.

Brigantia is a highly honoured leader and teacher. Brigantia brings light out of darkness. She brings enlightenment, instructs in the arts, in poetry and song. She is a healer, a teacher in herb craft. She teaches crafts; especially, smithcraft, and acts as a sponsor for goldsmiths. For animals, especially cows and sheep, she is a care giver, and she favours shepherds and milkmaids. She owns a cauldron and from it comes the drink of enlightenment. A warrior goddess, she defends her interests with a mighty club. She has been known as, according to Collingwood, the Nymph Brigantia. She was a beautiful Goddess of the Dawn. One would start new adventures under Brigantia.

The tree of the Teacher is the Beech. It is an Underworld tree related to darkness, yet it brings enlightenment, and so, light. It represents learning and justice. And it supports the harvest. It is a friend to other herbs and trees and supports their growth. It radiates energy, energy which numbers of persons might find helpful.

The Beech holds learning. The meaning of beech is book. Aborrow called the Beech, the birth of mysteries and the holder of hard facts. And the Beech gives knowledge through the whispering of its leaves. The wind through beech leaves opens the doors to perception, gives hidden knowledge, reveals secrets. The wood and the bark of the Beech are used for giving knowledge by symbols and signs.

The Beech forms sacred groves, patronized by owls, where the primitive forces, the unstructured things, the ever changing winds, make their home. Elves favour beech groves with their gatherings. Beeches serve as homes for dryads. Beeches can be spooky, said Heselton. They relate, he said, to Samhain. The Beech is the sacred tree of Minerva, and of Diana. To honour Diana, winners of the Pythean Games were crowned with beech. The Beech is a tree favoured by Saturn. It supplies wood used in the Yule fires. Bacchus' drinking bowl is made of beech. Beech is a wood used for bowls used in ritual, and a wood often chosen for use in casting lots. It is a wood on which sacred symbols are often put. The Beech promotes honour and good judgement. The Beech is favoured by Pan.

From beech tar, a lotion is made which cures sores and skin ailments. Beech tonic is used to cure bronchitis. Pigs, deer and goats are fond of beech. Horses are not.

The Oak and the Hazel are trees held to be of great value by the Teacher. The Ash is also considered, by the Teacher, to be of great value, and it is one of the four trees listed by Ovidius as being sacred. The other three, being the Beech, the Elm and the Ivy. The Beech, said Skene, related to the Teacher, to the Moon and to the Scale.

Trees in general act as teachers. At the fore front among them are the Birch, the Chestnut, the Willow, the Oak, the Poplar, the Elder and the Yew.

Many herbs would be associated with the Teacher. Minerva's sacred herb would be the Flax. Other favoured herbs would be Bitter Cress, Balm, Alehoof, Valerian, Vervain, Pennyroyal, Yarrow, Catnip, Mint, Sage and Rue.

In the Plant World, Minerva favours Blue Flax. Blue Flax is the pure herb which produces the pure linen used in making sacred clothes. According to Pythagoras, flax gains the virtue of purity by growing among sacred fruit trees. Blue flax represents not only purity, but creativity, calm, wisdom and spirituality. It gives the faculty of intuition and ability in communication.

Flax expels still births and afterbirths. It heals burns and rashes and cleans and cures sores and ulcers. It is used to treat liver problems, dropsy and gastrointestinal trouble. Grieve said that children, in their seventh year, to become beautiful, dance in fields of flax.

Alehoof, Bitter Cress, Vervain and Valerian are favoured by Brigantia. Bitter Cress and Vervain went into the Cauldron and became part of the magical brew which gave inspiration.

Associated with the Teacher are the Snake and the Owl. The Owl is the ancient bird of wisdom which communicated with the Underworld. According to Plinius, the Owl dislikes Bacchus. He said that when a person, for three days, drinks owl eggs in wine, he will lose his desire for wine. Philostratus Nervianus said that when a person eats an owl egg, he takes a dislike for wine before having tried it.

For the teacher, Tuesday would often be a good day. Trevelyan said that it is considered lucky to meet a stranger on Tuesday. It is said, Tuesday's child is full of grace.

In the center of Card Twenty would be Minerva, a Goddess of Darkness. A stately goddess in a dark robe, she would be holding a spear and a round shield and to her right rear would be a spinning wheel. To the right front would be a distaff. At the top left would be an owl holding thunderbolts. The Owl is emblematic of Minerva. It gives knowledge of the future. To hear an owl hoot three times portends death. Witches relate to owls and, at times, take owl form. Owls are messengers of Minerva.

Along the right side of the card rises the trunk of a beech. The beech spreads branches into the sky. Flax blooms in the bottom corners of the card.

XXI ~ Hanged Man

Twentyone is the Hanged Man. One might turn from the Hanged Man, look at the moving crowd. There will be a person going against the flow. If the crowd is turning with the Sun, he is going widdershins. If the crowd is going counter to the Sun, he is going Sunwise. The Hanged Man might be thought the mirror image of that person going counter to the crowd: the Going Person. He invites a look into deep waters, waters which are dark and pure.

The Hanged Man represents a person who had been standing on the shifting sands of what a person ought to do. That certainly is what he would have been doing. Certainly, as he walked through the field of traps: customs, laws, taboos, climates of opinion: one of these would have caught him up and hanged him. He might have a feeling that he needs to be hanging to satisfy his need for truth; so, to the end, he wears his mask of who he ought to be, what he ought to do; except that his mask is his entirely exposed self. The self behind the mask is the many things his unformed self might have formed. The form he selected might be the balance to some direction, the other side of the story. It might be a left over opinion by one who missed the boat, the ship of change; but even that ship might have been a ship of fools; or, it might have been a step toward a coming trend, but made a bit too early. Even then, it might be a spark which causes the trend to come; the very spark which ignites the beacon which will guide the masses into a new way. Even as he hangs, he might think himself the mirrored image in the waters below which shows a leap for joy. He might have physical pain, but the compensation might be the spiritual truth which he thinks he sees. The Hanged Man might be a shaman who has discarded this world and is working in his Otherworld. He might be a willing sacrifice to his mask which without, he would feel he no longer had purpose for being. A person walks on the limited geography of what he sees as spiritual reality. Outside of that, he might see little meaning. The hanging might itself lead to spiritual rebirth. The trap might have been in the Grove of Mysteries from which he got a peek at another existence.

A trap might be the inability to select a path, to make the choice of one system over another: a white system over a black, an eastern over a western. One person might go step by step up the white system only to discover that as he has become better and better by one scale, he has gone to the bottom of the other scale. He might get a feeling that the second is the more true scale. A person who has become the top banker might see himself the least valued person among social activists and entertainment stars. He might want to find a new feeling of self worth where a former status would no longer be recognized and that, even by himself. He might be ready to tune in, turn on and drop out, but not able to function as a drop out. Or, the Sword Bridge to his new path might be too narrow. He must realize his choice is really, which path to take toward the Land of Death and the choice might be complicated by the fact that the purpose of death might not be able to be truly understood without dying. And at the point when he would have that understanding, he is again in a Land of the Living.

The Hanged Man hangs by his left foot, tied by a rope to a limb of a linden. His posture is impromptu. He is astonished to be caught and suddenly hanged. He is unclothed.

Lindens are usually helpful. They are planted to guard homes. They offer shade as a relief from summer heat. And tea from the flowers is used to correct stomach and nerve disorders, to relieve tension, to banish depression, to fight colds and to encourage sleep. Linden tonic assists heart action and improves the circulatory system, cures coughs and chases spasms. Linden charcoal is made into ointment for use on sores and burns. Linden flower baths release emotional blocks, aid communication of feelings, calm hysteria and ease shoulder and back pains. Bees favour the Linden and from its flowers make a fine honey.

But the Linden is a tree which has peculiar ways. Often it is the tree which snares the person who is reaching too high. It was the Linden which, by a leaf, put a spot on Seigfried, which was a weak spot, which caused the death of the seemingly indestructible hero. If one were to fall asleep beneath a linden, he might be spirited away to the Otherworld. The strong flowers of the linden can bring unsettled states and fantastic visions. They can bring a sudden change of fortune. They chase malicious spirits and demons, as demons of epilepsy and demons of convulsions. Linden flowers increase abilities in spirit travel and communication and they tie loving relationships.

The Linden protects against lightning. As a tree favoured by the deities, petitions and offerings are left with it. Of those who come to it, the Linden requires quality work. The Linden is called the Tree of Judgement. And judges have often sat under lindens to hear cases and pass judgements. And fortune tellers make use of lindens. For looking into the future, some of them twine linden around their fingers. Birds who build nests in lindens would give prophecy.

Fairies love lindens. Lindens are also associated with dwarfs. Keightley tells of a dwarf lady seated at the base of a linden, casting out rune spells to trap knights.

The Linden is the Goddess Phylyra, who is called the Mother of Cheiron. Apollonius said Cronus, in Horse form, fucked Phylyra, so caused her shame, so she took the Form of the Linden. Her special friends include Jupiter and Venus. Jupiter gave Baucis, a hospitable housewife, Linden Form.

Lindens are favoured by snakes and some of the snakes associated with lindens have been awful dragons; some of them, called Lindworms.

The Linden is a Tree of Sacrifice. It can be treacherous. It put the soft place on the hero's back which permitted the spear to enter. In the judgement of the tree, the hero had lived long enough. From the limbs of lindens, persons were offered to the deities. A custom was to give wreaths of linden to heroes.

Linden trees themselves foretell the future. It is said, if a linden withers, the area over which it extends its influence will fall on hard times.

The chief herb of the Hanged Man would be the Mandrake. Mandrakes were known for growing under gallows and it was thought, these were the most magical. As hanged men ejaculate, ejaculate as they hang, mandrakes would be growing from ejaculations, so would be looked to for aid in reproductions and conceptions. The tears fallen from the hanged men are thought to have effects on mandrakes. And it is thought, said Gerard, that the flesh that falls from those that are hanged causes the mandrakes to grow into human shape, and so, to have some human characteristics. As they are thought to resemble either male or female, the mandrakes would have personalities which would be influenced by the one sex or the other, so dealings with mandrakes would likely take sex into consideration.

Mandrakes grow not only under gallos, but at crossroads and over graves, and especially, those of suicides. Mandrakes from those places are thought, the most magical, but they grow in other places also. It was said, the mandrake first grew on Medusa's grave and has grown on many a grave since. Circe, Hekate and Hades favour the Mandrake.

Mandrakes were thought to be difficult and dangerous to gather. The obtaining of a mandrake, in past times, was likely to have been dramatic, as mandrakes were said to emit a death dealing scream when pulled from the ground. There was a custom, explained by Marion Davies and others, of using a dog to pull up the mandrake. To gather the mandrake, the soil around the root would be spaded; then, a cord tied to the mandrake and to a dog. Food would be put down for the dog, then some, beyond the reach of the cord. The scream of the mandrake would likely have killed the dog, but the humans would have been out of the area. Any human who had been close to the scream would likely have died or gone insane.

When a mandrake had been pulled up, it would certainly have been handled with care. A custom was, to make symbols over it, then put it in a black bag. It was treated with care and respect. Kept in a sacred place in a home, it would expel malicious atmospheres. It was thought by many, it should be kept wrapped in white cloth; so, give protection from robbers.

The Mandrake is an herb of much power and it is involved in mysterious ways. It is used to reverse spells, said Clusius. It can produce dream effects, can bring nightmares and can cause barrenness. To give knowledge, de Givry said that it was reputed to nod its head, yes; or, shake its head, no. It was thought, it would predict the future. The mandrake was expected to make sudden changes, but was known to be unpredictable. In courts of law, for favourable turns, mandrakes were worn under the left armpit. For the mandrake to bring babies, women wore it on their crotch.

Mandrakes would drive away demons and spirits which would torment a person or cause illness. They might calm persons troubled with frenzie. They might reveal secrets.

As a medication, mandrake soothes the system, but might chill it to a dangerous degree. It can banish pain and bring sleep, and sleep might come from the smell of its flowers or fruit. It is used as a flying ointment and is listed as an aphrodisiac. If a coin stolen from a poor widow is put under it, it would, it is said, draw money from other people's pockets.

It is said, a mandrake is hard to get rid of, as it keeps coming back. If one bought it, he should sell it and be certain to receive less than he paid for it, or so it has been said.

In rituals, and workings, with Hekate or Hades, mandrakes might be used.

At times, it was said, pulling up a mandrake caused the ground to crack and people to fall into the crack. At times, demons or elves have been under the mandrake which was pulled. And these also screamed, so that the effects of the scream was spread over a greater area.

The Hanged Man would be associated with the Snake, and with its non critical judgement. The Snake might find him guilty of being in the wrong place at the wrong time. He might find himself associated with the Snake Goddess, Eurydice. She was a beautiful queen, a dark phantom, who was the Judgement of Death. She was a Spirit in the Underworld to whom men were sacrificed. Eurydice would have been the goddess, pictured by Blair, who was holding a snake in each hand. As Blair said, she holds life, death and regeneration in her hands. She has power and grace, but brought toward this World by the God of Song, she became a fading phantom. For her, the God of Song was sacrificed. The Snake Goddess relates to communication. She is a messenger. Her Snake form would be the Blacksnake, which is the emblem of Total Darkness. Blacksnakes are hanged headless, by the tail, so that the Wind Gods will send rain. Death causes change. Wind Gods relate to birth and death. Wind Gods are lusty. They are said to snatch maidens, wrap them in dark cloud and seduce them. Dancing maidens are most at risk since dance relates to copulation. Birth and death relate snakes to the octave. Relating to the octave, Boreas has a 7 chambered cave. His snake form relates him also.

The octave is the system which makes 7 steps, then changes to a mirror image of itself. Life and Death, Day and Night, are major systems which form octaves. The Snake relates to these: it eats the Sun, the bright light of those systems.

The Snake shapes the octave. It guards against change and it causes change. The Wind Snake could be the Wind of Change. The change could be a sudden move into the next octave.

In the Life Death octave, the Snake can cause sudden death. Its bite can be suddenly fatal. The Snake might also strike with dragon fire. At times, the fire takes out that which is at top power. Often, dragon fire burns useless things to ash. Dragon fire can destroy: it can also create. The flash of fire can be copulation. The Snake can represent birth. Birth is, at times, represented by the Serpent Egg bound by the coils of the Serpent. In holding birth and that which is potential, there is similarity to the Fool.

The Serpent not only creates and destroys; it regulates and guards creation. It is a guardian against change. It is a guardian of secrets and a protector of laws. It heals and repairs, working and providing sometimes marvelous cures. It guards lands and treasure. It controles spirits. In this, it can be called on to trap and bind spirits into vessels. When they are needed, it can deliver messages, even to the Underworld. It guards the Gate to the Underworld.

In causing or protecting form; and so, regulating, change; the Serpent Path would be regulated by the Stars. The Path might be a sudden move from point to point to work miraculous change, and this path of dragon power, spiritual or physical force, might be predicted from the placement of fire symbols.

The number 21 is 3 octaves, each of 7 steps leading to a new octave, a different reality, the top of one becoming the bottom of the next; as day does to night, then night, to day; as a coin displays a head, then, a tails. Which one is best, who can say? "Treason never prospers, and this the reason: For if it prosper, who dare call it treason?"

The Hanged Man presents a question. One does not know why he is hanging. He himself might not know. One, certainly, has more questions than answers. One can be certain, in going into a new octave, some will have lept too soon; some, left behind. With a year as an octave, the Hemp might have snared the March Hare, come out so early as to seem mad, seem part of the madness of early March. Mad dream might have lured him away from being down to Earth.

One can be certain, however, that the Hanged Man is a man of value to the total picture. At times a skater; perhaps, out of style in dress; perhaps, one who would be the only one skating widdershins, against the law or custom for the ice; so, he might be on a dangerous path, but be the one holding the picture together, the one supplying the needed excitement. His bit of red threading in and out of the spinning greens might keep the picture from wearying through boredom, might save a community from collapse.

As can be seen, hanging is not what would usually be thought of as fun. It can cause pain, can cause death. But it can have its rewards. As one looks at the Hanged Man, one might feel the great joy beyond the obvious suffering and pain. And disgrace. The Hanged Man hangs by his left foot, as he relates to the left, to the Bend Sinister, to contrary actions, to wicked actions. This does not concern the Hanged Man. The Hanged Man is between worlds. He is taking himself to a different place.

The Hanged Man might be, as Case pictures him, the mute, dark mirror of substance, which would have each individual as a wave in the Great Sea of all substance.

Waite believed the Hanged Man expressed an aspect of the relations between the Universe and the Divine; or, one might say, the Spirit of Divinity.

These philosophical profundities might not have occurred to the Hanged Man. He might be giving thought to the relationship between a man, his mask and death. His question might be, did he make a poor choice. But the Great Sea might hold something of his inner life, and will hold him with all that will be born. He might accept the Spirit of it. He might be thinking, Wednesday's Child is full of woe.

As a custom, those sacrificed to the Wind God are hanged from lindens. The lindens would connect them with the Astral World.

In the Sky, dark clouds would be somewhat snakelike. At the bottom of the card, a snake. The coils of the snake hold within them, the fiery creative force. On the ground would be mandrakes: perhaps, seven.

XXII ~ Strong

A symbol of strength would be Hercules. Armed with his oaken club, he is a match for nearly everything he meets. Hercules displayed marvelous strength from an early age. It was said, Juno disliked Hercules' mother, so to attack her, sent two what have been called Snakes of Darkness. Hercules, a young child, strangled both of them.

Hercules left home, then along the road met two goddesses, one of whom offered him a life of pleasure; the other, of duty. He chose duty, began serving mankind.

Spoken of as a clever, eloquent, bright bearded giant, Hercules is said to have been the slayer of many tyrannous kings. Lands were said to have been ruled by his wise legislation. It was reported, when envoys came to collect tribute from a city which he had under his protection, he cut off their noses.

Graves said that Hercules had a reputation of being a skillful teacher; especially, in seamanship and in agriculture. Sailors sought his advise. He was said to be a caretaker of nature, was looked to for bringing rain. And he provided charms against nightmares.

Among women, Hercules had a reputation of being good at copulation. Pausanias said that in one night, Hercules fucked fifty maidens, had a son by each of them and by the eldest and the youngest, had twins. But Hercules was known first as a strong warrior. When Daphnis got captured by the King of Phrygia, Hercules went to her aid, cut off the King's head and threw it into a river.

Hercules married the beautiful Megaera and took on the duties of a lord, but then it was, Juno's Full Moon, whose light has the power to make men mad, fell on Hercules as he slept.

At a dinner, Hercules declared the wine lacked quality, punched the cup bearer and the cup bearer died. Then, said Pausanias, Hercules went to study music with the Music Master, Linus, but when the master tried to make suggestions, Hercules hit him with a musical instrument and the master died.

Hercules killed others in fits of temper. Then, he and his friend Iphitus were drinking high up in a tower. The two got into an argument and

Hercules threw Iphitus out of the tower.

Queen Omphale was visiting the land and Juno made her a visit and Hercules was sold as a slave. Juno went to Hercules and said that because of the unjust slaying of Iphitus, she had sold him to Omphale, Queen of Cloudlands.

Next he knew, Hercules was in the queen's hall, and in the hall were many fine looking warriors, more of them, women than men. Queen Omphale was a great warrior. She defeated kingdoms, made the kings and champions, her slaves and in wrestling, defeated them all.

First, Queen Omphale dressed Hercules in her nearly transparent purple gown, set him in her garden and to spinning at her wheel, and if he made a mistake, she would spank his ass with her golden slipper. Hercules became her favourite champion and they enjoyed wrestling together, and Hercules went out and won battles for her. He killed the murderous tyrant, King Syleus, killed a dangerous dragon, captured the champion, Itoni. In the time with Queen Omphale, they had a number of children, at least four of whom became well respected champions.

Then, the queen became troubled by a host of thievish, grotesque goblins called the Cercopes. Hercules drove them away and in doing it, captured two of them. These, he strung up. As they hung there, the two continued to shout insults at Hercules and the queen and this, to the amusement of all in the court. Hercules tired of the noise and let them go.

Soon after that, Queen Omphale gave Hercules his bow and arrows and his club and wished him a good trip home.

At home, Hercules was restless. What he left to find, when he bid Omphale farewell, was adventure, not home life. Then, he missed the ring of champions that were his fellows at the queens' halls. And Megaera just was not fun, as Omphale had been. And Megaera became angry and jealous. Hercules hit her and she died. Hercules, in grief, realized he had been defeated by his own strength, so took himself to Delphi to purify himself. Hercules went to a healing river to wash his mind of wrong thinking, but the river would not help. Pausanias said the River did not clean Hercules, but Hercules' failings gave the River a bad smell.

Hercules' mind, burdened by his mad act, he went to the Delphic Oracle to find out what he needed to do to make amends and so, balance the scale. When the Pythoness would not answer his question, he took her tripod, which is itself alive and moves in keeping with its own thinking. Apollo, angered by that outrage, went to Delphi and brought reason to the situation.

Juno took herself to Delphi and confronted Hercules and expressed her anger that he had not honoured his wife, been true to her, but killed her. Juno, for punishment, sent Hercules to work for King Eurystheus so that Hercules would be kept busy for a long time.

King Eurystheus was thought of as The Great Head, as the force of his head expanded over a wide area. He said, first, Hercules must slay the Nemean Lion. The Nemean Lion was dangerous to the general population. She moved in from the East spreading fire over the hills, and she brought with her a host of monsters who tormented people with sores and fevers.

Hercules tracked the Nemean Lion to her den and as her hide served as an armour, needed to strangle her to bring about her demise. Hercules ripped off her hide and had a garment made out of it, so that, as told by Zimmer, the fierce lion looked out over his own face, so that people fled in terror from what seemed, the combined force.

When Hercules returned to King Eurystheus, the king said, for the next task, he had to slay the Hydra, the many headed female monster whom Hera had as a guard of the gate to the Underworld at Lerna. The Hydra had nine heads that to Hercules, would have seemed like nine striking snakes. Every time Hercules knocked off a head, one or more new heads would grow out to take its place; and Hera, angry that her guard was being attacked, sent King Crab to bite Hercules to keep him from killing the Hydra. Hercules then set all the heads on fire except the one he determined to be the master head. This, he knocked off before the others had a chance to grow back. He had slain the Hydra by cutting off the master head, and, under a rock, he buried it.

Hercules next had to capture the Wild Arcadian Horses, and these were guarded by the Centaurs. Hercules, after defeating the Centaurs, was able to capture the horses.

For his next task, Hercules had to capture the brazen hoofed, golden horned Deer of Cerynea. This capture, as Ridgeway observed, took an alert mind and shrewd planning. And Hercules showed that he could be diplomatic, as diplomacy was needed, because the deer he was to capture was a roe sacred to the Moon and a special friend to Artemis.

Hercules next duty was to slay the vicious birds which had hovered over the stagnant waters of Lake Stymphalis terrorizing the local population. These birds, with his bow and arrows, he shot.

Hercules next, had to clean the Augean Stables. He needed to clean, in a day, stables which had housed the threethousand oxen of King Augeas. Hercules, by his inventiveness, channeled two rivers so that they would flow through the stables and so, get them clean.

For Hercules next job, he must subdue the Cretan Bull and ride it across the sea to Mycenae.

The next job given Hercules was that of delivering Diomedes' flesh eating horses to King Eurystheus. The problem was, with out having eaten flesh, they couldn't be driven. To solve that problem, Hercules threw Diomedes to the horses, then drove them to King Eurystheus. The horses had eaten Diomedes, as they could not have been driven otherwise.

For the next job for Hercules, King Eurystheus wanted Queen Hippolyta's girdle for his daughter.

Hercules went to the land of the Amazons to capture the girdle, and, said Epicharmus, Peleus went with him and he also had hopes of winning the girdle. To defend her queen, Warrior Amazon Aella rushed at Hercules and was slain, but Hercules won the girdle from Hippolyta. He took it to King Eurystheus.

Then King Eurystheus wanted Hercules to get for him, Geryon's purple cows. Geryon was a three headed, many armed fire breathing monster favoured by Juno.

Hercules hied to the land of Geryon and there, met the savage guard dog, Othrus. The guard dog he slew, then was attacked by two champions, Erythones and Ithnos. Hercules slew the champions, then attacked a great serpent whom Juno had sent to guard the rain cows, as the cows were sacred to the Moon. Angry at Hercules for his attack on the snake, Juno sent King Crab to bite him and so, try to prevent him from slaying the snake. But Hercules slew the snake.

Hercules then located Geryon and in the course of his struggles with the giant, managed to pull his plug so that the giant's fire bled away and the giant died. Hercules drove off the cows.

As he was driving the cows, the giant Bergion, son of Poseidon, tried to steal the cows from him. Hercules slew the giant. Then, as onward he drove the cows, he was attacked by the giant, Albion. He slew Albion.

Then, driving the cows, Hercules did not notice he had several cows missing until he heard them mooing down in a cave. He went to the cave and saw that Cacus, a three headed fire breathing, Lord of Fire, had them by the tails. Hercules, with his club, beat the giant until Cacus roared with pain. Hercules drove off his cattle. With the cows together, Hercules drove the purple rain cows to the palace of King Eurystheus.

King Eurystheus next would have Apples of the Hesperides, which were on a tree guarded by a fiery dragon. The apples were keys to the Underworld and were at the distant top of creation from where the hole went into the Underworld.

Hercules, wearing the garment made from the lion's skin, set out with his mighty club. Long he walked toward the place from where the Sun sank toward the Underworld. Hercules walked for a long time. He got to the sea and came upon some nymphs, as the story has been told. The nymphs did not know where the Golden Apples were, but said that the Old Man of the Sea would know. They explained how to locate the Old Man, said that he must be approached as he slept along the Sea's edge, and that Hercules should be certain to hold onto him regardless of what shape the Old Man took until he got his questioned answered. Hercules thanked the nymphs and set off.

Hercules found the Old Man, whom he knew to be Proteus, asleep by the Sea. He grabbed Proteus and held him as Proteus changed from one vicious being to another. One less stout than Hercules might have needed to bind Proteus in chains of flowers in order to have held him, for Proteus was strong. But Hercules held him and got his question answered.

Hercules walked a long way, then came to the place where he would need to go by water, and on the shore, he saw a golden boat.

"You may borrow my boat," said a voice. "I am Helios, and my boat will take you to the apples you seek." One version: it was Nereus who got for him, Helios' boat.

The ship floated out and took Hercules to the isle where the apples were. Along the way, Hercules came to Atlas. Atlas said that a small man like Hercules could never get those apples, as that dragon was so huge and horrid that he might himself have difficulty getting even one of the apples. But even if he wanted one, he could not get it because he had been given the duty to hold up that corner of the sky, so was stuck there.

Hercules went on and was stopped by nymphs, and these were powerful goddesses. Gaea had given the apple tree to Hera, and Hera had brought a number of goddesses there to guard it. Hercules made his case and was permitted to go on, but was told, the Great Dragon had been given a sacred duty to guard the tree, so would be difficult to deal with. But Helios did send you.

The dragon was huge and Hercules could not grab onto even one of the apples, so went away to rethink his position. As the nymphs had said, Helios must know the apples can be picked, said Hercules. He went to discuss the situation with Atlas.

Hercules looked at the edge of the sky Atlas was holding.

"Look here, why do I not give you a bit of a break from holding the sky, and you, if you can do it, fetch me the three apples?"

Atlas looked down at Hercules, "A small, puny fellow like you hold the sky? That's a laugh. Yes, of course, I could welcome a break, but you hold the sky?"

Hercules climbed up a hill, as Pherecydes tells it.

"Just lower it down on my shoulder," he said.

Hercules took the sky and Atlas went off.

Atlas came back with three apples. He said he reached over, grabbed three apples before the Great Dragon knew what he was up to. Atlas gave Hercules the apples, but said he hoped Hercules was not in a hurry to go someplace; as he, Atlas, intended to enjoy a bit of high life before he again thought about duty and sky and that sort of thing.

Very good, said Hercules, but would Atlas put a hand on the sky a second while he, Hercules, got his position shifted a bit if he was going to be there awhile.

As soon as Atlas' hand touched the sky, Hercules ducked out. Atlas shook stars loose in anger, but that was the worst he could do.

Hercules returned to King Eurystheus with the apples. Good enough, the king had said, but then he wanted Cerberus, the three headed, dog monster goddess who was Guardian of the Underworld. Cerberus was said to look like a mix of dog, pig and nightmare.

Hercules, with the key to the Underworld, took himself to Lerna, entered the gate and walked down the dark way. There he was met by Cerberus. Through quickness and skill, Hercules bound Cerberus up, carried her back to King Eurystheus. Apollodorus noted that Cerberus was defeated without weapons. The king took pleasure in having Cerberus, but it was not long before Cerberus slipped away and returned to the Underworld.

King Eurystheus dismissed Hercules from his service and Hercules began his way back to lands with which he was familiar. On his way, he came upon a giant, the River god, Achelous. Achelous tried to explain the facts of life to Hercules, but the explanations only made Hercules mad and pushing each other around turned into a wrestling match. Achelous, even though larger than Hercules, and very strong, could not match Hercules' angry energy and was forced to surrender.

Hercules went on his way and came to where Anteaus was called the greatest of champions. He challenged Anteaus and the two had angry words before the battle; as Anteaus, as the son of Gaea, thought of himself as being as strong as all Earth. For a while, Anteaus seemed the stronger, for every time he needed extra strength, he touched his mother, Gaea, Earth. But Hercules, seeing this, lifted the giant off the ground, so that his mother's help was out of reach, then slew him.

Hercules got back to familiar lands, and now he was recognized as a mighty champion and marvelous things were expected of him. Diodorus said that Eryx, the son of Aphrodite, was widely recognized as a great champion. He challenged Hercules and Hercules slew him. Hercules went to where there were disputes. He slew the mighty warrior, Busiris.

King Laomedon called for help: someone to rescue his daughter, Hesione, from a seamonster and promised, as a reward, the Horses of Neptune. Hercules went to the rescue, slew the seamonster; then, slew King Laomedon because the king had refused to honour his promise to relinquish the horses.

One land became troubled by a ferocious beast called the Calydonian Boar. A call came for a champion, so Hercules went to where the boar was and slew it.

On his return trip, he met Nereus, a God of the Sea. They wrestled and Hercules defeated Nereus. That was a great feat and Hercules got invited to take part in the Elysian Fields Athletic Contests, or so it was reported. These were games for deities, and it was said, Hercules was the winner at wrestling and at chariot racing. He was given a poplar crown.

When Alcestis gave her life so her husband could live, Hercules went to the Underworld to bring her back to the World of the Living. On the way, he met Mercury and Minerva, and these two went with him. Hercules was advised to wear a poplar crown as a shield against spirit forces. Hercules passed through the gate and was surprised to see two champions: Theseus and Peirthous. Hades would not let Alcestis leave, so Hercules challenged him to wrestle, so if Hercules won, he could leave and take Alcestis out. Hercules won and went out not only with Alcestis, but with Theseus also. Peirthous, however, was so bound by the force of the Underworld that Hercules could not get him out. In the wrestling, Hades was so injured that he had to go to Olympus to get cured.

Hercules returned to familiar lands.

Hercules was lured into taking part in a war. Pluto was aiding the opposing army. Hercules shot an arrow into Pluto's leg and caused that God of Riches much pain. Hercules was a master archer.

Then, back in his own lands, tired of feasting and drinking, Hercules went in search of Prometheus. He came to where that deity was chained, shot the horrid bird which had been ripping at the deities' flesh, then set Prometheus free. He asked Prometheus for suggestions on where he might look, as he was wanting some worthy adventure.

Prometheus said that the West held many savage warriors and that Hercules could find adventures there.

Hercules journeyed to the dangerous western borderland where he was met by a host of savage warriors. According to Dionysius, he marched against the Barbarians. He would have been at a disadvantage, but Jupiter sent a cloud of thunderstones and these, Hercules used to drive off warriors which he did not slay. He had now, a poplar shield with him and with this, deflected many objects which were aimed at him.

In the West, Hercules became known as a champion and through valour, set a good example for men to follow, and this is stated in the histories.

Further west, there was a great dragon and news of it came from there to Hercules. To protect the lands, Hercules set out for the West to find it. In this, many were glad to help.

The dragon was large and although Hercules gave it many injuries, he was caught up at last and swallowed. Finding himself in the dragon, he got out his knife and with it, began trying to make a hole.

A long time, Hercules spent in the dragon; then, one day, he slipped out. The dragon moved away and was gone.

Hercules found himself in a strange land and as he went from place to place, being gifted in many things, he was well received. But always, he was an eating, drinking and fighting man. It was said, Hercules ate more than Lepreus, the Sky Wolf, said Pausanias.

Hercules got to the land of the Centaurs, became a friend of Cheiron and with him, studied music and the art of healing. In that land, he met the beautiful Dejanira and took her for a mate and the two of them, for a time, enjoyed the rowdy, drinking ways of the Centaurs. At one feast, a Centaur, Pholus, gave Hercules the cup of wine which others had wanted. A fight broke out in which Hercules was one of the combatants. A Centaur rushed to find Cheiron, as Cheiron was wise and diplomatic, and it was hoped that he could bring peace; but in the affray, before peace was brought about, Cheiron's knee was injured. Some Centaurs were angry with Hercules, holding him responsible for Cheiron's injury, and there were more hard feelings when Cheiron had to go to the Underworld to get his injured knee healed and was unable to return to the land of the Centaurs. Nessus, one of the Centaurs, often carried persons across waters, but when Dejanira became his passenger, he ran off with her. Hercules gave chase and shot Nassus through the heart. The dying Centaur told Dejanira that she should save some of his blood because it could be used as a love charm. Dejanira, to keep Hercules' attention at home, put the blood on the inside of his shirt. When Hercules put it on, the shirt burned like fire and pulling it off, Hercules tore off skin and flesh. That put Hercules in so much pain that he resolved to die. He directed that his penis, scrotum and head be cut off and, along with his club and bow, put in a boat made of alder and set sailing out to sea. What remained of Hercules was burned on a poplar fire. The Greater Hercules sailed into the night sky, put on a great coat covered with stars.

Hercules continues to represent strength and duty. He continues to instruct. He established oracles to which people could go, could learn of the future. At times he gives knowledge by regulating the throw of dice. Hercules has shrines where people go for instruction and aid. As Hercules is skilled in healing, to some of his shrines people go to be healed. Hercules also protects against nightmares.

Hercules teaches at his shrines. He teaches skills; especially music, archery and athletics. He teaches the importance of knowledge. At the top of a pillar, a temple, Hercules had a crystal globe through which he could look in order to gain knowledge. Hercules teaches shrewdness and diplomacy. He has set examples for diplomacy: the golden horned doe which he chased for a year and captured, was a favourite of Artemis, so it took diplomacy to get back into her good graces.

Hercules teaches the importance of stubborn patience, of endurance, of giving help to the oppressed. He teaches the virtue of justice without vengeance. Most of all, Hercules teaches the importance of strength, of learning the way of gaining strength, of the bold use of strength, bold to the degree of brashness. Victories of Hercules are linked to excess. Hercules teaches the use of action done to excess, and of the value of taking risks.

He is not one for bland caution. If he wants a thing done, he goes for it. Ovidius said that one king, when asleep, was told by Hercules to rise up and found a city.

With Hercules, strength is associated with duty, work and pleasure. One of his strengths and pleasures was in copulation. And there was a strength in his keeping his mind focused on duty and on his work.

Priests at shrines of Hercules wore robes which were not overly masculine, and for weddings at his shrines, there was a custom for both the bride and groom to dress as women. This honoured Hercules' time in which he wore a woman's gown. Van Gennep said that the men might have dressed as women so, with them, Hercules would be better pleased. And for relations with the bride, in the shrine, there would be no competing male.

Hercules instructs men at his shrines. At the shrines, sacrifices are eaten by bare headed men seated, not reclining, and not dressed in the manner of a god, and none of that which is sacrificed is to be taken away from the shrine. It all must be eaten or burned at that place. And there would be meat a plenty. Gluttony is not a word to which Hercules would give much attention. And, said Philostratus the Elder, it is a custom for men to curse while feasting. Hercules approves of cursing. In his rambles, he would come to places where hunters or herds had their cookfires. If he was hungry, he would help himself to food and often in a quantity to make even a generous hunter curse.

"Good to make a noise," Hercules would say. "In a free land, it is good for a man to express himself. I myself, like to curse."

Donar is a god, like Hercules, related to strength. He is the Oak God of Thunder, crude, strong and bad tempered. But he supports justice and hard work. With his hammer, he battles monsters and dragons. From the hammer's strike comes lightning, a force which flashes suddenly down the Tree of Life. It fertilizes the tree and its path, becoming suddenly and shockingly clear, makes basic meanings suddenly understood. Its force can make sudden changes. In an instant, the force connects many points. One might get the big picture.

Omphale represents the wheel, and the force at the center of the wheel. As Rulandus observes, the Spirit of the Gods of Strength would be in nature, as in centrifugal, centripetal and magnetic forces. As Rulandus points out, the Spiritual Force of Hercules would be in magnetic force. Theophrastus showed that forces in stones can work cures.

To the force representing strength, there would be strong counter forces, as strong givers of laws. To counter Hercules, the force would be represented as Juno or Hera. In one encounter which Hercules had, as given by Ridgeway, he needed to go past the Winds which Hera had marshaled against him.

As Hercules, as a magnet, was drawn toward the object he was to destroy; the Winds, the counter force of nature, were trying to blow him away. Then, the destroyed object has force which will be reborn.

Then, Juno, representing the Moon, counters Hercules, representing the Sun. In a way, as Fairbanks said, the two are married.

Strengths of nature are observed in the powers of vegetation. Trees which show strengths, and which relate especially to Hercules, are the Poplar and the Oak.

Relating to strength, the Poplar is a tree of protection. White Poplar is called Hercules' holy plant. He put on a crown of poplar after defeating the malicious giant, Cacus. Poplar is a wood used for shields. Hercules is reported to have used a poplar shield when fighting the Barbarians. When Hercules got bitten by a snake, poplar cured him from it.

The Poplar stands at the Western Gate to the Underworld and serves as a Memorial Tree for Phaeton, a fallen Sun. Near the place where Phaeton fell, poplars stand, shed tears of amber and sing mournful songs to his fall.

As poplar overcomes death, poplar leaves are buried with the dead. And as the Poplar is a tree of hope and sympathy, it is a wood from which coffins are often made and it supplies staffs used in measuring coffins, corpses and graves.

The sacred fires of Jupiter are made with poplar and, to honour Hercules trip to the Underworld, wreaths of poplar are given to the winners at a number of traditional athletic contests. The tops of the poplar leaves were scorched when Hercules wore them into the Underworld, and to honour Hercules, the tops of the leaves remain discoloured. The poplar is a tree of inner reserves of strength. It represents determination to overcome adverse situations.

The poplar gives the power of speech. Poplar leaves, stirred by the Wind, give prophetic knowledge. Father Young said that poplar leaves are put in dream pillows, as they aid prophecy.

The Poplar is a tricky tree. It is not always honest. It is gifted in slight of hand and once stole a golden goblet from Jupiter. It is symbolic of uncertainty. Put in an ointment, poplar gives the ability to fly. It is favoured by Mercury.

Poplar cleans and purifies. Athene had a sacred grove of poplar. Poplar combats snakes and drives worms from the bodies of men and women. It chases the demons of epilepsy. Spence said that to cure scrofula, one would eat mare's milk from a spoon made of poplar.

Poplar tea brings confidence, reduces fevers and treats jaundice and urinary and intestinal ailments. Poplar tonic cures ulcers, and is used to treat rheumatism, kidney ailments and gout. As a lotion, poplar cures sores and inflammations. Poplar potions are used to attract money, bring love and to give feelings of readiness, and to cure many other ailments. Poplar aids eyesight. The Pillars of Hercules are said to honour the Poplar.

Hercules would be symbolized by his oak club, and would have an oak form, so it is dangerous to harm an oak. Apollonius Rhodius gave an example. He said that Peraebius and his family lived in poverty because his father had cut an oak.

The Oak is a tree of strength. It promotes law, stability and balance. In balance, to gain the force of the Oak, a cross is made with oak sticks, and these, bound together with red wool, or red thread. The cross will inspire resolution and balance. From the four directions, the four elements, in equal strengths, meet and balance each other. Campbell said that this meeting could be the door to transcendence. A person might see how he relates to each element, might gain self knowledge, might move toward a balance, toward a balance in his relations to the four quarters and the four elements.

Part of the Oak's strength comes from its relation to duty. Dedication to duty brings strength.

The Oak gives acorns, and these hold many magics. Acorn cups are used for telling fortunes. The acorn has been carried as a charm for finding a lover, and is carried for protection. As swine are fond of acorns, acorns form a link to the Sow Goddess and to the Sun Boar.

Some herbs have special relationships with strength. Valerian, parsley, stonecrop, onion, garlic, basil and saxifrage are some of them. Saxifrage breaks stone. Parsley has an interest in chariot races, as it gives horses health and speed, and it serves as a crown for winners of athletic contests. For athletic contests, the apple, the olive, the laurel, the poplar and the oak also serve as crowns for winners. Parsley is honoured in the Underworld, so it is a custom to curse when sowing its seed. As parsley aids copulation and birthing, pregnant women put it in their bath water. It aids other herbs with their magics and guards other foods from spells. As Venus favours parsley, it grows best where the mistress rules. It is thought, best gathered under the Waxing Moon.

Strength relates to thunder, to Thursday. Birds, it is said, do not build nests on Thursday. It is thought best to avoid moving on Thursday. And it is said, Thursday's Child has far to go.

Hercules erected two great land masses as a gate to the waters of the Far West. A pillar would be on each side of the card and in the center of the card would be Hercules wearing a poplar crown. In his right hand is the oaken club, which is used as the emblem to represent Hercules. In his left hand is a bow and arrows. At the top, from the right, is a limb of poplar. To the right rear is a spinning wheel. In the lower left would be a lion. Lightning would be striking from a dark cloud in the sky, left of center.

XXIII ~ Love

Card twentythree is that of Love. Love is not restricted to Man. It is a general property of Life. It can be so strong a force that it brings the elements into conflict. It inspires, as Eisner has said, the Dionystic Force, which moves toward instant pleasure, happiness and freedom from restriction and worry over problems of the future. It also inspires a conflicting force: protection and care, which conflicts with Dionystic destructiveness. Like the forces of the elements, Love is a force which continues through time. It affects creation and the development of concepts, especially those concerning beauty. Love drives the four elements. Love, with Fire, drives toward birth and toward death. The fire of the wedding torch, said Musaeus, is the same fire that burns on the funeral torch. Fire will cause Love to be held sacred. The flame in the lamp, said Musaeus, serves as witness to secret love. Love as a flame follows life into the grave.

Love drives Life through the force of Water to bring protection, to bring peace, to bring beauty. Water, through the force of Love, brings birth, brings death. According to Marcus Manilius, water signs relate to fertility.

Physical Love, said Bulfinch, is a force sprung out of Chaos and by its shafts is said to create all things. Love, said Case, is the sword at Creation's dawn.

Love is the domain of Venus, the Goddess of Love. Venus holds mysterious, hidden knowledge. She relates to intuition and inspiration. When Apollo, according to Martianus, said an ideal mate could be found by mathematical formula, Venus said she would find that method obnoxious. Love would likely run counter to mathmatics. Rather, it gives the appearance of being unstructured. It can be florid. It can be flamboyant. It can have a wildness, have surprising twists and turns.

The meaning of Venus is Love. Vergilius said Venus was all things which Love embodied: poetry, charity, creativity, justice. Venus forces copulation, birth, generation and regeneration. Venus inspires love and brings lovers together, said Propertius. Venus is called a Goddess of Justice. Venus gives care and protection. She is caring and healing, as with gentle care, Venus will repair problem skin.

Venus gives care and protection to flowers, to fruits, to gardens and homes in general. The Rose is special to Venus. Red roses are flowers of joy and secrecy. They relate to red wine. Red roses and red wine represent the blood of Adonis.

The Violet has been called Venus' emblematic flower. It relates to psychic ability, spirituality and assurance. Violets in gardens bring beauty and loveliness to women and virtue to men, and they give protection, and their aroma stimulates copulation. They are favoured by Priapus and are also favourites of fairies. Violets represent truth and bring love.

Myrtle is associated with Venus. In a bridal bouquet it represents fidelity. Marion Davies said that if myrtle grows on each side of the door it would bring love and peace to the family.

The Apple is associated with Venus. It holds the five point star, which is the symbol for the female human and for mankind. Many philosophers, as Propertius, list Venus as the Evening Star, the brightest star in the evening sky. The Apple is looked to for bringing wisdom.

The Maple has a leaf which holds the sacred five of Venus' Star. The maple is a tree of love. Favoured by Jupiter, it represents law and brings protection. It protects from witchcraft and from other malicious acts. The red of the Maple relates the Maple to the Otherworld, and red is the colour favoured by Venus and Mars. Often, it is the tree selected to be the Maypole, which represents the male aspect of copulation. As maple brings joy, it is often selected as wood for wassail bows. Maple flutes bring in the summer and attract love. The maple is called the emblem of reserve. It is under the maple that King Arthur sits to judge the battle between the Lord of the Unknown and a Guardian of the Underworld for a Goddess of the Sea: a battle which is fought each Mayday.

Plinius emphasized the ability of maple to cure liver ailments.

A sweet honeydew falls from the leaves of the maple and from maple sap comes a delicious, health giving food.

Venus' special tree is the Grape Vine, so would be given special care and protection. And in its name, the Vine pays special tribute to Venus. The Vine takes a person onto the Paths of Love and into the Spirit World and onto the winding paths of this World and into the World of Dream. The Vine is called a gift of Saturn and is associated with riches.

The Vine is honoured with two celebrations and plays a major part with a third. The first celebration, April twentythird, Vinalia Priora, gives special honours to Venus and Jupiter. Ovidius said Venus' alter should be covered with greens and flowers, and he suggested myrtle, mint, rushes and roses. Likely, there would also be violets. One might, said Ovidius, burn incense on Venus' alter and ask for beauty.

At the festival there would be pageantry and music. Often the drama would include the slaying of a dragon. The preceding year's wine would be honoured and libations poured.

The second festival, Vinalia Rustica, August nineteenth, also gave special honours to Venus and Jupiter.

On Valentines' Day, February fourteenth, there is wine, bright red and white decoration and there are candies and pictures of Venus and Cupid. Love would fill songs and dances, and love messages are sent and romantic games played.

Communication with deities is often through the Plant World, and as Venus shares with people the care of gardens, communication would often be through the flowers and fruits which she favours. Basil, black nightshade, rosemary, coriander, cumin, thyme, yarrow, purple orchis and mallow attract Venus' attention and are carried for that reason. And Hyacinth, Bluebell, Valerian and Vervain attract Venus. Balm attracts Venus.

To attract love, the yarrow should be picked, under a Dark Moon, from over a grave.

Albertus said that for attracting love, violets, valerian and coriander should be gathered during the last quarter of the Moon. These are praised for their love producing flowers, flowers which are much favoured by bees.

To appear as a person of great charm, a person, while naked, would go out at night where nightshade grows and while standing on one foot, pick the nightshade and put it in a linen pouch.

Wright said that, to hold love, there are spells in which cumin is used.

Purslain and chicory are used in love charms. One love potion mixes blue iris, clove pink, black nightshade and rowan. Other flowers used in love potions are parsley, marjoram, dill, marigold, periwinkle, enchanters nightshade and laurel. Cornflowers, daisies and roses are used in much love magic. Beyerl tells of a circle of rose petals, a magic temple, built around a couple who were to make mating vows.

For strengthening love bonds, marigolds are planted where a lover's shadow has fallen.

Foxgloves are flowers loved by Venus, as they exhibit a number of aspects of her personality. They are held in high regard by fairies. Juice of foxgloves would be certain to restore any child who had been bewitched by fairies. Foxes, it is said, use foxgloves as an aid in catching chickens. As rabbits favour foxgloves, they are often found growing around rabbit holes. Bees favour foxgloves. Foxgloves cure sores, dropsy, and they stimulate the heart, but it is unwise to take them in the house. Foxgloves are used for communicating with the Underworld and with Venus in her more capricious moods.

To increase beauty and so, to call Venus, women eat saxifrage, or carry, in silence, chicory.

For calling on Venus to aid in the physical aspects of Love, the Bluebell and the Purple Orchis are used, as they inspire copulation. And the strawberry has been called erotic and might be used for attracting Venus' attention. Venus was said to take joy in fields of strawberries.

One love potion contains violets, sweet alyssum for attracting love, bugle for bringing and holding love, asparagus for strengthening lust, Queen Anne's lace for inspiring emotion and for stimulating sensation, hypericum and forgetmenots for opening the way. Put in an applewood bowl, the herbs would be crushed while a spoken charm to Venus is given. Then, to attract Love, the mix should be wrapped in linen and carried.

Another charm combines violet, iris, wood pink, black nightshade, marigold, hawthorn and rowan, and these, put in a maple bowl. Over the herb mix, linseed oil is then poured and the mix, crushed and stirred with an ash pestle while the ash, in a spoken charm, is requested to send love. The bowl, with the mix, is then burned on Venus' alter.

Flowers favoured by Venus might, as love charms, be hidden in a room of the intended object of affection. Flowers selected might be crocus, chard, marjoram, mint, pennyroyal, anemonae, lovage, smallage or any of a number of others.

As Venus has an association with the Moon, as Fiske has said, a number of love charms are done with the aid of the Full Moon. In these charms, iris, daisy, periwinkle or cornflower might be used. Cornflowers give the gift of clairvoyance.

For a charm, Leyel said, people said, "Flower White, Flower White, I wish to see my love tonight."

Beside with flowers, Venus has been communicated with in other ways. A Love charm given by Highet: to secure love, a person would eat a dove's heart; the heart, pointed downward, while the left hand was on the loved one's shoulder.

A charm for bringing love was, a white hen was struck with a black stick; a black hen, with a white stick. From them, blood was taken before death took them; then, the collected blood was hidden in a room of the intended lover.

For banishing melancholy caused by love, a cure is to drink earthworms in wine.

Love charms have been worked with rose quartz, as it is favoured by Venus. Rose quartz brings love. Also, it aids self healing and inspires a person to go with joy to meet challenges. It gives an ability to realize the Spiritual World.

Peridot is carried, said Beyerl, so that it would bring the carrier recognition and love and drive away fears of the dark and the unknown.

Solinus said beryl not only aids the eyes and starts fires, but compels love. Beryl on which a crow is carved has been carried that it might bring copulation. And Leyel said that to return to lust, a man would cover a big toe with honey. And a charm might be made with coral for gaining love, as coral is sacred to Venus. Ovidius said that coral formed from the blood of Medusa and that it attracted copulation. To gain copulation onions have been carried.

For obtaining Venus' aid, at times a darker magic is used, darker energies brought in. One working has black nightshade, snake venom, nail clippings, basil, yarrow, toad stool, a black spider, moss off a human skull, periwinkle, hog dung, a tooth from a hanged man, menstrual blood, ash from a human bone, semen, blood caught in seashell from a toad which had spent three days hanging and three hairs from a woman to be charmed: these, in a cauldron stirred around nine times with a mandrake root.

Another charm is made by combining eggshells, beeswax from candles, balls of hair, crooked pins, small bones, feathers and ashes.

There are also negative communications. A turtle's heart wrapped in a wolf skin is carried in order to keep Venus away.

Venus' influence was said to be strong on Fridays, so it is thought wise to do things on Fridays which would not displease her. Pruning on Fridays is thought to be risky. Under her influence, children born on Friday are said to be loving and giving. Watering the garden's flowers is thought to be generally a good thing, if there would be some need for it. Friday, to sneeze might indicate some sorrow.

Venus has many times been thought of as an ideal form to be loved, and she has, many times, been represented with such a form in mind. Often, from the representation, one would be led to feel that Venus would produce, and care for, births. From ancient times, efforts have been made to represent her as being beautiful; though methods in craftsmanship and approaches in vision have changed to the extent that the representations of one age might seem grotesque to another. However, a person sees Venus as the ideal Love.

Venus is unpredictable. She can come in beauty and bliss, but then be tricky. Venus can play jokes. Reckford said Venus could be very funny, and very cruel. Love has a close tie to death. Musaeus said that for a person to die directly after his or her love's death was pleasing to the deities.

Love has male aspects which complement Venus. The male aspects of Love, which balance as mates to Venus, are not the male representations of Love, but are representing, as male, the love aspects of Fire, when Venus would take the love aspects of Water. But Venus, as complete Love, would have male representations of complete Love as a balance, but not as a mate. Love, as males, would be thought of more as spiritual aspects. The males: Eros, the quiet, spiritual youth, and Cupid, the loving child. Venus would not have been their mother. Pausanias said that Eros was every bit as old as Venus.

Cupid and Eros would often be seen with bows and arrows; the arrow, the shaft of love, being a male tool. Cupid and Eros might resemble young Sun Gods, as shafts of love might have similarities to shafts of light. Both could be dangerous. Cupid is known to be mischievous. Cupid's play with his bow is said sometimes to be displeasing to other deities and that would include Venus.

Cupid and Eros would also be seen with flowers and cups, which would be symbols of the female. In an ancient representation, Eros, on a tomb, is seen making a libation, returning life, or Love, to Mother Earth.

A second Goddess of Love is Aphrodite, and she represents more, the aspects of Love between people. This would include the spiritual aspects of love as well as the physical. Plotinus said Aphrodite was found in the physical love of public ways as well as in the beauty in the heavens. Aphrodite would have much to do with physical love and other relations between male and female. Fiske relates Aphrodite to the Dawn, to Astarte, a shaft of light, as a thing fresh and new, striking the heart. She represents the penis of passion striking beauty. Tacitus said that, in some cases, she was represented by a conical stone. And she is represented rising out of the water on a shell, or half shell.

For Aphrodite, the Mandrake is an important herb. It sits in the middle of her garden. As it sits near the border between the worlds, it relates to forces of darkness, to witchcraft and to hidden knowledge. Mandrakes relate to Medusa. For driving away demons and attracting love, people hang mandrakes in their houses. Mandrake amulets are carried for attracting love.

Tools associated with Venus would be the bow and arrow and the mirror. The mirror relates Venus to Water and the bow and arrow, to Fire.

Venus' bow and arrow would, from shafts of starlight, bring shafts of burning love and these, cause couples to rush fiercely together for mental and physical penetration. The bolts are shot through the hearts, as the whims of Venus move her, of masses of men and women, many of whom are among those who least expect to be hit.

Venus' mirror would be sacred aspects of Water, one of which is a relationship to the Underworld. At times, for communicating love, mirrors are buried with the dead.

The mirror is used in a charm for bringing passion. The image of dogs copulating is caught on the mirror, then, during the copulation, covered with black cloth; then, buried for nine days in a road fork. The mirror, when dug up, would be covered with black cloth until the image would be needed.

Card twentythree would have, in its center, Venus and, except for golden slippers, she would be unclothed. In her right hand she would hold a bow and arrow and in her left, a mirror. In each top corner would be a dove and these, emblematic of love and peace. Associated with clouds, they are sex symbols related to the fertilization of the Earth Goddess. And they are sacred messengers of Venus. And they relate to music.

In each bottom corner is a rabbit. Rabbits can cause love and reproduction. Cupid caught a rabbit as a gift for Venus.

At the top of the card is a branch of the Maple. The maple flute, as it inspires love, has become part of May Day rituals.

At the top, at the bottom and on the sides are four red hearts. Around the card winds a vine. Among the leaves of the vine would be red apples, pears, grapes and strawberries.

Inside the vine circle is a circle of flowers. Flowers relate to love and death. This circle of flowers, red roses, violets and myrtle, holds the chief colours of love and death. Red and green are Underworld colours. Violet is a colour of spirituality. Red inspires passion, courage, energy, force, lust and other deep feelings of love. Love messages have been covered with red hearts; love vows, made and bound with consecrated strands of red wool. Green relates to fertility, preservation, harmony, prosperity, balance, happiness, health, growth and change.

The Mirror and The Golden Sandal are tokens of Venus. The Heart, her symbol. The gold would hold blessings of the Sun, and the Heart, as Chambers has said, reflects the Sea with its virtues.

The song of the doves might be,

"Roses are red, my love. Violets are blue.
With violets and roses, all my love
is given to you."

XXIV ~ Megalith

Card 24 is the place of Chaos. It is the time for sacrifices and for rebirth. As gods who are usually strong in upholding law avoid this time, Saturn is pushed forward to stand in, to provide vague limits to the Chaos. One limit: Saturn has declared a Kings Peace and he can be a dangerous god to cross. In keeping with the declaration, greens are gathered and charms are added to decorations: these to add force to the keeping of peace.

Saturn had been a domineering force. Under Saturn, peoples moved from being savages to forming societies. In those days, bizarre and incredible things occurred. Saturn taught the virtue of having things in common, of sharing with one another. He taught sowing, reaping, fertilization and the care of fruit trees. Under Saturn there was general prosperity and pleasure, simplicity and innocence, so that in those times there was an impression of a perpetual golden glow. Time went on with inertia, with lack of change, so that it was called the Golden Age.

As Saturn is an influence in stability, inertia and stagnation, there were forces building to oppose him, forces demanding change. To keep those forces under controle, Saturn ate other gods until Metis, Goddess of Prudence, gave him a purge, so released the gobbled up gods so that Time could go forward. The released gods overthrew Saturn and Saturn was bound with wool and locked away in a tower.

Saturn, from his Otherworld tower, is still a force. Under his influence, the mood tends to be melancholic. He is said, as under his planet, to be an unhealthy and negative influence. An aspect with Saturn can cause a sign, or another deity, to act in an unfavourable way.

Saturn rules duration. One aspect of Saturn is as Cronus, the Dark Bird who flies toward the West cutting off things as he flies, bringing things to an end; not so much, to give to harvest, but to give to the Well of the Past.

Then Ops, Earth of the Sacred Hearth, who represents the power of the past to make changes on the present; holds what Cronus, Saturn, drops into her pits. She then gives gifts in quite a different way than restricting herself to giving flowers out of fertile ground. Out of Chaos a present is twisted into form, then on past Charon's Crow Landing, Cronus moves on.

As God of Time, Saturn is destructive; so, relates to Death, to the Underworld. With these relationships, he has been a scary god. Where he ruled, he has led societies into destructiveness. He was thought to want human sacrifices. Men of 60 and older, as gifts to Saturn, were thrown into rivers. And at alters outside city limits; as many deities did not want blood sacrifices, so many cities did not permit them; the heads of men were chopped off: the bodies were given to Saturn; the heads, to Hades, another scary deity. The sacrifices reflected savage societies.

Saturn has been considered a most cryptic god, known as the author of secret contemplation, destroying and preserving all things, overturning forces and powers and serving as the keeper of secret things. In societies he ruled, there were priests who were initiated into Saturn's thought, but they weren't permitted to explain to the uninitiated the true nature of it. It has been associated with the furor of melancholia.

The Tree of Saturn is the Pine, called the Flying Torch of Time, which is moving ever on. Gifts to Saturn and to Hades are hung on the Pine. The Pine serves as the funeral torch: it carries the dead to the grave, to the Underworld. It flies with Saturn, with Hecate, to the Land of the Dead.

Hercules questioned about the gifts, said that Saturn and Hades were more interested in spirit than in flesh, that onion heads could very well hold the spirit of human heads and candles, serve for bodies. With this reasoning, dolls, representing bodies, were hung on the tree and masks, representing heads.

At the Time of Chaos, Saturn is needed. From his tower in Tartarus, Saturn sails in on a ship. Saturn is released from the wool with which he had been bound, to serve for the Time of Chaos, to be the King of Capricorn. One sees him, an old man with a sickle which is both a harvest tool and a weapon. It is the weapon with which he cut off the nuts of Uranus. Those, he threw over his left shoulder, into the sea and so, caused the birth of Aphrodite. Cornelius Agrippa sees him bearded.

Saturn in Chaos takes one to the childhood of mankind where one sits in the safe light of a campfire, sheltered from the scary goblins, who include, among them, Black Nick, called Santa, who, in his sack, carries people away to Hades. Chaos is the raw material of creation. A feature of the Chaos: its formlessness. This aspect is seen in unhewn stone. There is a period under Saturn, a dark gap, called the Unhewn Stone Days: a gap of disorder between the 360 days, a day to each degree in a complete circle, and the time for the next circle of days to begin. In the time under Saturn, especially in this dark gap, there is a drift back toward cruder times, toward the Magical Beast; perhaps, toward the Beast that is Magic. Then among the beasts, through the chaos, one is brought to ecstasy. As this is a time for sacrifice and death, it is a time for caring for one another, for enjoying the fruits of harvest, for giving and for receiving and for freely loving. The bond that keeps custom within Saturn's rule is that all tricks, tribulations and sacrifices are accepted, for the most part, as in the spirit of the joy of the season. People are tricked, but they know in advance they are going to be tricked, so they are not, in reality, made fools of.

Relating to disorder and the Unhewn Stone is Ophichus, the Snake Doctor. For disrupting the order of the system, Jupiter threw him out into the stars. Ophichus, by using his skill as a doctor, had eliminated the need for people to go to Hades. From outer space, the stars pulled Ophichus back and gave him a birth in the Zodiac Belt. Ophichus' tail sits near the place which had been given to the Unhewn Stone. The Snake, as is Saturn, is involved in birth and death. The dead are remembered in the Time of Chaos. The Lares, the ghosts, are honoured. Plautus called them guardians of the family.

The Spirit of Saturn would be an influence, the first of December, Poseidon Fest. The fest honours the God of the Sea and the focus is on his prowess, in Horse form, in copulation. Phalluses are carried in procession and community leaders wear phallus topped hats. To honour Poseidon, wine is poured on flat cakes and to promote fertility, there is merrymaking and joking and phallic songs are sung.

December sixth is a feast day which honours Pan and Nick, and these represent the Spirit of the Underworld and Personality in its basic, instinctive natures.

Pan is the Dancing Goat God of ancient times and has been, in some areas, the important god of the people. With the animal gods, the basic needs would be important. The god would be little understood and terrible. Pan was God of Unstructured Nature. Pan, Sylvanus and other extraordinary boundary deities are thought demonic, frightening and rather outside the law. These deities, although somewhat destructive, at times, are quite the reverse, so people attempt to find ways to please them. But they were difficult to harmonize society with. Pausanias said that Pan, by dreams, told leaders how people could be helped to recover from the plague. And Pan gave warnings to war leaders when invaders were coming into the lands. But for each person, to get along well with Pan, he had to work that out for himself. Putnam said that Pine and Holly are the sacred trees of Pan. Hyginus said that to get away from Typhon, the Great Wind Snake, Pan turned himself into a fish. The Goat Fish form appeared on the arms of Augustus Caesar.

The early representations of Nick show him to be much like Pan and certainly, an extraordinary deity. Nick, according to Renterghem, is Nikker, or Nicor, a goblin associated with water. Nick takes persons to the Underworld. He is often shown with a broom, which would be used to purify persons before they would enter the Underworld. Also, as it relates to the male and female sex organs, it is associated with fertility. Porteous said that the Green Man was a Wild Huntsman who took the dead to the Underworld. The Green Man would be Nick. In ancient caves, he could have been seen following deer.

In the time of his rule, Saturn is represented by the Fool King. In keeping with the tradition of Saturn, there is a custom of bringing his stand in, the Fool King, over dry land in a ship. He is sometimes dressed in animal skins, and he has a supreme wisdom which is outside the bounds of reason. Saturn would be welcomed with candle light.

To prepare for the rejoicing, there is a quiet day, Angeronalia, dedicated to the silent Angerona, Goddess of Death. She is said to ease pain and to banish anguish. Her bound mouth is said to conceal her own pain. She points to the fragility of life, its delicate balance.

Saturnalia comes and people shout for joy, "Io Saturnalia". Candles are lit and the Pine is hung with gifts and decorations. Lucius Apuleius suggested that wreaths should be hung on the tree. Then, on Saturnalia, said Tertullianus, it was the custom to bathe at dawn. This would have a connection with rebirth; as dawn, as Macrobius said, comes from the Underworld. And rebirth comes from the Underworld, the Land of the Dead. Then, there is gift giving and, as it has been from the dawn of time, complaint by sedate elders that too much attention is given to gifts and celebration and not enough to honouring the spiritual meaning of the holiday. Libanius said that the importance given to money relaxed and money was put in a more true perspective. Opsopaus called this time, a time of unfettered instinct which encouraged a free expression of personality. In money, there were social customs. If a person was giving a present to another who was richer than himself, it was considered correct to give that person a candle.

At Saturnalia, according to Livius, Saturn was the chief god honoured and sacrifices were made to him. Ops, Hades, Pan, Proserpine, Uranus and Sylvanus were given special recognition.

Saturn is a mysterious god. He is strong and dangerous, Macrobius said that Saturn promoted the unity of populations. He dismantled the social order and taught ways of meeting basic needs. He taught farming and especially, the care of fruit trees, and at his rituals, it was a custom to wear fig crowns. Saturn is a giver of riches. He promotes freedom. Under the influence of Saturn, Corrigan lists stone construction, dealing with bindings and restrictions, actions where time is a factor, teaching and learning. de Givry said that Saturn foretells accidents, violent deaths and disasters, and the line is vague between predicting an event and causing it. Saturn is said to be a protector of the treacherous. A bird Saturn favours is the Owl, a bird of mystery and gloom.

At this time Earth Goddess, Ops, is honoured. She is a generous giver of gifts. And Hades, whom Seymour called the Gate Keeper of Life, is honoured. His realm, that of the dead and the unborn. Sacrifices were given to him. And Bacchus is celebrated at Saturnalia. Bacchus, the God of Wine, has yearly deaths and rebirths. Ovidius said, one of his mothers is said to be Proserpine. Bacchus is usually called the Son of Semele. Hislop said Bacchus is sometimes called the Son of a Snake, the snake being his father. Windle pictured Bacchus with a panther. Iamblichos said that Bacchus serves under Saturn. He adds to the wildness of Saturnalia and adds to its many delights. His wine, said Macrobius, fires a person's intelligence and other powers.

At the celebration, Pan, Sylvanus and Rhea are honoured and often, carnated. Windle pictured Sylvanus on his ass and holding a cup of wine. He would likely be decorated with holly; as holly, said Herodotus, is sacred to donkeys.

At the celebration, there is a custom of serving a Boar, or Boar's head. The Boar, which is considered the carnation of a god, would be decorated and crowned with rosemary, laurel and thyme, and an apple, as a key for reentering this World, would be in its mouth. As the Boar is a distinguished personality, he is paraded into the hall with much ceremony, which might be a burlesque of sedate, official processions. As the Boar is said to be lusty, many of the songs and cheers have to do with fornication. Gubernatis said he is a libidinous animal and so, is sacred to Venus. He is also favoured by Proserpine, Ceres, Ops and Vulcan. However, as he is paraded in, he might be the center of jokes, might be called by humourous names. Giving a deity a humourous name would make the deity a bit less fearsome, would make the powers a little less.

Philyra, with whom Saturn copulated, is also honoured in the celebrations. And Satyrs, some of whom Pausanias believed to have red hair and tails; would, with their flutes, take their places in the celebrations. And elves, whom Porteous said would come in on the greenery, would join in celebrating. The music would be inspired, as it is aided by the craft of Satyrs and Elves and the magic of the deities. At this season, Shakespeare said that witch and fairy have little power to harm. Charms, made of rosemary, thyme and laurel, are given out. There are circle games and other games which provide merriment. The games might relate to the circle of the year. There are games which relate to the Wheel of Fortune. Dice which, many times, have been prohibited, are part of the celebration of Saturnalia. Dice, for some, seem scary and they are often petitioned in loud voices however much the petitioners are told there is nothing frightening about a pair of bone cubes. Said Pausanias, at the Oracle at Bura, dice gave prophecy sent by Hercules. It was said, sometimes dice would show marks beyond what was normally possible. For some, dice are living things. Saturn had an authority over the ground and when the element of earth is used as a table for fortune telling, Saturn is important. Ellis said that for predicting, walnut sticks are often used. Saturn has an interest in fortune.

The sacred fire is a major feature of Saturnalia. The hearth is the sacred alter of Gaea, of Vesta and of Ops. To the Hearth come gifts from the Underworld. The fire would certainly be of oak. Often, libations are made to it, and squint eyed and flat footed and other unworthy people are kept from being in front of it. Shoes and stockings are sometimes left on hearths, not only for collecting blessings from the Goddesses of Earth, but because they protect against witchcraft. The gifts hold magic: a truth young people are aware of.

Saturn's sacred tree would be decorated with sacrifices, gifts, balls and other decorations. The sacrifices would be dolls and masks, and these would hold the spirits of people. At the top of the tree would be a Star. It would represent the Castle of the Dead. Hislop said that the Tree might represent the rebirth of the fallen tree, the burning log, and this would represent the Fallen Sun.

In the season ruled by the Fool King, Saturn inspires great, mad orgies in which all are equal. For those caught up in the orgy, the World is for laughing at, its virtues and troubles lumped together into its mad fabric. The Fool King might be backward to the usual, but he is not the Zero who knows nothing. The Fool King has a relation to the Underworld. In the topsy turvy time, there would have been the cross dressing, men and women dressing as the other sex, as Isidorus said, was done in honouring Janus. Also, there was dressing as animals, said Isidorus, and then dancing, leaping, clapping, stomping, making noise, and men and women bonding together. And there was dramatization, said Isidorus. At Numenia Fest, Polyaenus said cross dressing was done to honour Telesilla, the woman warrior.

Outside, poultry, for its protection, is given extra rations and blessed wheat. Farm animals are given extra rations. Animals, said Spicer, speak on Yule Eve and on Yule Eve, horses and dogs, Armstrong said, are able to see the Otherworld. So, horse trainers are looked to for predictions, as the celebration would continue through the Yule, December twentyfifth.

In one custom, straw clad Ghosts of the Fields go to the fields with shouts and blows to inspire fertility. Libations are poured to fruit trees, toast or cakes are put on tree limbs and trees are asked to bear well. The nut trees, especially, would be swatted with the staff of the Goodman. The rituals are supervised by the Fool King, who represents Saturn. On one tree, a gift of food would be made to the birds.

Inside, the feasting continued as the people enjoyed the blessings given by harvest deities and baked goods, with the blessings of Vesta. Poets, including Horatious, were quick to praise Vesta. And feasting was done in halls highly decorated and bright with candle light and walls were covered with fragrant, protective greenery; including, in doorways, bunches of mistletoe.

In spite of seasonal charms, there are Saturnalia tricks and some of these can be deadly. A Lord Horns might, in a cloud of smoke, carry a person off; or the Wild Hunt might take a person away. But mostly, Saturnalia is safe and happy and no one is injured in the orgies. And the charms work: goblins and demons join the dance. And the Fairy Host appears as time drops into dream time, which is a shadow time linked to ages past and to the Otherworld. There are Otherworld taboos which flood into the season. One: the taboo against giving fire away. Ancient spirits take carnate form, act in accordance with their ancient personalities. Pan and Echo would again embrace.

December twentyfifth and December twentysixth were celebrated as birthdays of the Undefeated Sun, or Solis Invictus.

The coming of the New Year is a door to new life. It is welcomed by the Festival of Janus. Janus is a God of Doors. He is two faced; one face directed toward the past; the other, looking to the future. In time of war, the doors to Janus' temple are kept open.

As Isidorus has said, the New Year's Eve is much like Saturnalia: dancing, noise and cross dressing. Groups of maskers, some in animal skins, wander through the night with chains and pans to bang on to chase away malicious beings or harmful spirits.

As one year moves to another, there is a ringing of bells, so that the air might be cleared of malicious forces.

In spite of the artifacts of civilization, the Spirit of The Past is over the lands. The dark woodlands, the ancient stones, are in peoples thoughts in spite of their noisy gatherings. Ancestors are again seated around fires. Wild woods around them, around the clearing and around the shelters of the ancestors. In the center of the clearing is a great stone. It is decorated with greenery and greenery covers a table which is supplied with food. Some distance away, greenery would cover an alter, which is in a dark grotto, and near the alter would be a pine which would hold sacrifices to Saturn. Hyginus said that the earliest alters were made way back in time by Cyclopses.

Around the fire there would be feasting, drinking and shouts of encouragement for the Undefeated Sun, while in the dark and among the dark trees, ghosts and goblins and terrible gods lurk and beasts call and howl and peek in at the fire, and the wind howls in the trees, and the hounds race through the sky to collect people to take to the Underworld where Proserpine, with her cold face, sits and waits. It was said, some persons were picked up, driven madly, then dumped, battered and bruised, in some strange place.

The stone is the important feature of an area. It is the center from which distances are measured, and, said Gray, stones are thought of in connection with reliability. It is the thing that would always be there. It was said of some stones, if they were moved, they would return to their places. And one man who moved a stone, said Giraldus, came to physical harm because of it. Stones which stand above humans in height would usually be hugely influential and would often be linked, in a major way, to the histories of kings.

Where there is a single large stone, often the name for the community where it is would be taken from the name of the stone, as the stone would have caused people to have settled at that place. Bett tells of an old city which he is certain is at its location because of a boulder of an unusual bluish colour. It drew people to it.

Communities have been in awe of the huge, mysterious stones. The great power which they generate is difficult to characterize. The movement which, in a big way, seems part of their being, gets stated as part of their past, or part of their future. A megalith might be known to have been a lord, and now, as a stone lord, be ready to march down to the city to rule the land. A megalith might be a stone giant who had once, as a giant person, roared through the land and broken heads. And there are stones which dance on the hills when the Moon and stars bring them joy. In joy, the stones might whisper together on the hills.

Some of the stones had, by magic, been turned into stone. A look by Medusa would turn a person into stone. A group of warriors was, by an Elder Woman, turned to stone.

Some stones were said to have the power to block sound. Giraldus located such a stone where those speaking on one side of the stone could not be heard by those on the other side.

Uranus directed attention to the importance of the Stone. Stones represent chaotic, unstructured time; chaos until new birth occurs. Stones are potential new structure, and they have great power. They relate to Uranus, the god who shapes form from the unformed, or unrecognized form. Uranus is honoured in the form of the Unhewn Stone. Great unhewn stones regulate fertility; so by women, they are petitioned for children. Nymphs, satyrs and other beings hold revels with Dancing Stones. Some stones rise up and strike those who have committed impieties against them. One stone was said to have cracked a coffin which was being carried over it.

Megaliths, as they stand, look eternal, but they are ever in the process of change. As Ovidius said, all four elements are ever in a process of change, even from one element to another.

On a hill stood a boulder called the Blowing Stone, and it was said, said E. V. Lucas, to warn of coming invaders and to tell warriors to defend their land.

Stones are thought to have a relationship with the stars, and some are placed so that there would be a harmony with the arrangements of stars, so that people would be attracted to the virtues and teachings of the stars.

Rulandus said, it was thought, some stones held representations of star constellations, and these gave direction and powers.

Stones speak to the rock bottom of our being, said W. G. Gray. A stone, through the ages, would have been building its vortex of power through actions which had fled around it and passed. It had put its influence into judgements. It had been the center from which announcements of great changes had been made. What was said there was trusted. One would not be dishonest near a sacred stone. At the site of the stone, one might find, as Huxley has said, an experience beyond time, a profound stillness, as one established a unity with the sacred area. In the sacred area around the stone, there was the feeling, said Gray, that anything wonderful might happen. One would be in magical space. Space is magical consciousness, said Dave Lee: ecstasy beyond words. Dave Lee quotes W S Burroughs: "You cannot take words with you into space."

Words can be a fence from which one breaks free; perhaps, to feel again hidden joys, terrors, beauties and feelings which one could relate to wisdom.

Coming out of sacred space, a person might be in a different place from where he had been. He might find himself doing things he did not want to do, and his thoughts wandering down strange paths. A person would break out, as Dave Lee has said, of his comfort zone. He might have new thoughts, new abilities.

And in the center of the energy is the stone, Gray said that when a person was still some distance from a circle of megaliths, he could feel their energy. Sylvaticus said that spirits going to the Underworld sometimes leave imprints of their material selves on the great stones.

Westropp said that the big stones might be made into oracles by anointing them with oil, or so it has been believed.

The respected stones are sacred features of landscapes, said Lucius Apuleius, and he said that everyone should have such a stone on his land.

A goddess who dwells in the ancient stone, and whose energy drops downward to darkness, is Proserpine. She is the form who would be there when a person would drop into death, a thin, hard woman with a pale face. On her tall crown she holds the fruit and flowers, which hold the memory of young years spent in sunny fields. She holds the Snake, which holds the memory of copulation. Her pale face is a still, silent mask at the end of dark, winding ways, ways which end in a grey light.

The Wind sighed, the pines swayed in the Wind, a voice, as from a dark cave, whispered, "Not yet – not yet – not yet." An old man with a sickle stood silent in the grey dusk, stood silent.

The chief tree of Saturn is the Pine. The Pine is associated with elements of chaos and has associations with birth and death. It is used in fertility rites. The Pine is Pitys, a goddess slain by Boreas, and she is favoured by that deity. Beside Boreas, she is favoured by Pan, Artemis, Neptune, Bacchus, Venus, Hades, Mars, and Jupiter. Pine serves as a funeral torch. She carries the dead to the grave. She flies with Hekate to the Land of the Dead.

Pine represents uprightness and brings strength and power. Pine is used in ship building, for, as a friend of Neptune, it protects ships. Pine relates to music. The Winds through pines create music and pine is used for making musical instruments. Pine aroma and incense drive away negative forces, freshen and clean and build confidence. Pine aids pulmonary functions and is valued for cleaning and purification. Pillows filled with pine are used to alleviate pain and fatigue and to treat asthma and other respiratory trouble. Pine lotion is used for sores and sore muscles and for treating ailing horses. The magical staff of Bacchus is topped with a pine cone. In pine walls, holes left where knots had been are passage ways for fairies, spirits and demons. Pine boughs drive away demons and malicious forces. Grieve lists pine as a treatment for rheumatism and for kidney and bladder problems. Pitman lists it for reducing fevers. Buchman lists pine as stimulating and calming and, as a lotion, a relief to ailing joints.

Agrippa lists the Juniper Tree, the Owl and the Sickle as three items especially associated with Saturn. Juniper is a tree of the Furies. In ritual use, it will catch thieves. It is burned, as an incense, on the alters of Hades and, to chase demons away, at funerals. Juniper purifies the air, chases away malicious forces and gives protection from demons, witches and dangerous animals. Planted around the house, it attracts love and rids the area of thieves. At funerals it is at times strewed on the ground the way the corpse is to be carried. Juniper is often burnt before battles as an offering to deities. It is looked to as protection from the evil eye. At Saturnalia, it is a welcome addition to the fires. As it chases demons it protects from ailments; especially, palsy and epilepsy. The aroma of juniper is used to balance emotions, strengthen the mind, clear thinking, settle the nerves, aid the circulatory system and to treat neuralgia, arthritis and rheumatism. Dioscorides used juniper in aroma treatment. The aroma uplifts the spirit and brings joy. Juniper berries break the stone, improve memory and eyesight, combat plague, cure dropsy, gout, sciatica, treat kidney and bladder trouble and drive worms out of the body. Juniper is a tree favoured by the Sun. As tea, it cleans the system. It holds onto the Sun's life force.

Holly, said Herodotus, is sacred to Saturn. And Beech and Ivy are said to be sacred to Saturn. Often libations were given to the Beech.

A major figure of the Time of the megalith is the Holly. It is the Tree of the Thirteenth Moon, the Crude Stone. It is the Fool King and, perhaps, the Fool. It is the Tree of Sacrifice. It must be willing to wear the Crown and be willing to die so that the sacred Order of Life's Cycle shall exist. There is a need for him to put on the Crown, because, at that time, he is the only one who can.

The Sun in Oak form has a Club of Oak. In Holly form, the Club is of Holly. The two lords are much alike. The Oak is larger. The Holly relates to the T sound, which is a lighter form of the D sound: the Oak. Holly, as he gives protection, is a wood selected for clubs. The Bard, John Hewitt, said that in ritual, he carried a branch of holly. For the Time of the Crude Stone, the Holly, as Aborrow has pointed out, is in the position of Father. He promotes feasting, pleasure and good health. Cups made of holly cure coughs and bring other blessings.

Holly also represents the Green Man, Robin Goodfellow, who is sacrificed to Winter. In one telling, he agrees to be sacrificed if one representing the Sun would agree to the challenge and make a similar commitment, as both actions have set places on the Wheel of Time. Holly drives away malicious forces. It insists on justice and so, brings balance. Holly remains strong and green throughout hard, cold winters. It is favoured by Saturn, Jupiter, Pan, Sylvanus, Bacchus, Boreas and Mars. To cut down a holly is to invite disaster.

Ivy, a tree sacred especially to Saturn, Bacchus and Selene; is one of the trees which Ovidius listed as being sacred. In the Time of the Crude Stone, the female energy of the Ivy is a balance to the male energy of the Holly. Ivy holds a quality of durability. It symbolizes life moving onward through hard times. It is an emblem of fidelity and so, is often presented to newly married couples. One custom has the newly married couples wearing wreaths of ivy. Ivy wreaths are said to keep the wearers of them sober. And ivywood drinking cups are said to keep people sober and, also, to cure coughs.

As ivy represents birth and creation, wreaths of ivy are given to poets.

Ivy has been related to poetry and poetry has been considered, a thing of great value. Horatious held his gift of being a poet to be greater than having the gift of wealth or the gift of power. Being blind was often the balance for being a great poet. Pausanias said that Thamyris thought himself so great a poet that he was struck blind. Bacchus wears an ivy crown. Bacchus is said to have gone into a frenzy from chewing ivy leaves. The leaves give intoxication.

The Ivy Cup, which provides wine and blessings, would relate to the sacred Well, and to the mystic Cauldron, which brings birth and death among much else.

Ivy, as does Holly, relates to birth and to death. It entwines objects, sucks out the life and crumbles them so that they fade into the Underworld. If the ivy on a house withers, Trevelyan said that it forecasts death for at least one of the inhabitants of the house. As ivy kills worms, it is used as a tonic. Ivy heals ulcers, sores, swollen joints and sore muscles. It takes the pain from stings and bites. Rubbed on the temples, it cures headaches. Gerard said that wet ivy leaves held over sore eyes would bring relief. Birds and bees take pleasure in ivy and especially, in winter. Ivy should not be in the house except at the times of Midsummer and the Yule.

Mistletoe is a force of the Time of the Crude Stone. It is a generating power of the Plant Kingdom and is said to hold unborn life, which would include unborn children. Women wishing to conceive would often, as a charm, carry mistletoe berries, and a good crop of mistletoe berries forecasts a good harvest. Mistletoe is a symbol of fertility.

Mistletoe has the power over birth, life and death. It is the plant which sent the Sun to the Underworld, and it was used by Aeneas for passing through the Gate of Hades. It was a custom, in some areas, to bury mistletoe with the dead, and it has been found in ancient graves.

At the Time of the Crude Stone mistletoe is used to increase joy and to give protection. As it brings fertility, it is a custom to kiss a person who is under mistletoe. Ickis said that a kiss under mistletoe would seal a promise. Mistletoe carried into a haunted house, the ghosts will appear and can be questioned.

Kissing under the mistletoe was a pardon to the Mistletoe for slaying the Sun, and mistletoe was put on the high alter of Eborc, or Hyperion, and in his, the Mistletoe's honour, a general pardon was declared. This was a Yule Eve ritual.

Mistletoe was thought best gathered from an oak on the sixth day of the Moon; then, proper gifts, in compensation, given to the Oak.

Mistletoe is called All Heal; as, with its magic, it can heal every ailment. It counters toxins and witchcraft and chases the demons which cause apoplexy, nerve disorders and epilepsy. It calms delirium, hysteria, convulsions, jitters and spasms. It cures palsy, ulcers and sores. To counter witchcraft, it is hung from the neck. Put in a sty, it protects pigs from illness. When fastened to cows, it calms them. For warding off demons, knives with mistletoe handles are carried. Jupiter favours the Mistletoe. Mistletoe can be deadly.

White Hellebore, Black Hellebore and Plumbago are herbs favoured by Saturn. In gathering the hellebores, as they are protected by Aeschulapius and Apollo, a person should have permission. With the blessings of the deities, with a sword, a circle is drawn sunwise around a selected hellebore. Then, permission is requested to dig. While digging, praises to the deities are sung; otherwise, the guardian eagle of the hellebore might slay the digger.

Black hellebore is used in casting spells, in working malicious magic, in making binding spells and in shape shifting. It is used in blessing and protecting animals and, especially, in blessing cattle. Black or white hellebore might be used for blessing cattle. A hole is put in an ailing cow's ear, the hellebore is put in; then, removed the next day at the same hour of the day. Gerard said that bits of black hellebore were inserted in the dewlaps of cattle and horses as a protection from respiratory ailments. Black hellebore is carried so that a person can move from place to place without being noticed, as the person carrying it would become shadowy. The powdered root is used to cloud the air so that the one using it can not be seen. So that she might not be seen, a witch might sow black hellebore seeds in front of her. As a purge, black hellebore is given to cure sluggishness, dullness and madness. Given to sane people, it might cause them to become mad. Apuleius Platonicus said that the prophet, Melampus, used hellebore to purge lunacy out of the daughters of King Proetus of Argos. Black hellebore smoke is used for purifications and in rituals for Mars. The root is used in treating sciatica, jaundice, falling sickness, gout and ague. It chases melancholy. For provoking their terms, women put it in their vaginas. For flying, black hellebore is mixed with soot and bats blood.

White hellebore, said Gerard, powdered, is put up the nose to purge the brain of gross humours. It is used in treating epilepsy and gout and in bringing health to animals. It is put on weapons so that the weapons would have more power.

Black and White hellebore are taken into houses for blessings and for protection from malicious spirits. The hellebore might be carried through the house while hymns are being sung. With hellebore, malicious spells are drawn away from animals. Paracelsus used black and white hellebore for the rejuvenation of humans and chickens. He said that hellebores should be gathered when the Moon is in a sign of conservation and dried in the East Wind.

On each hellebore there will be a leaf which holds malicious power.

The black hellebore is a cousin of the monkshood: the white, a cousin of the onion.

Plumbago, or Leadwort, is favoured by Saturn. Associated with lead, it draws out toxins. It is found useful for toothaches and the itch. It inspires action done from instinct, so would often go against laws. In this, it might cause small problems, but help to solve larger problems.

Dock is favoured by Saturn. From its roots a black dye might be obtained.

Apple, Pear, Ash, Yew, Walnut, Chestnut and Oak all relate to the Megalith. Eating acorns was said to give inspiration. Trees can predict weddings. Fruit trees prolonging their blooming season indicate an increase in births. Fruit trees blooming out of season forecast disasters. There is a saying, "Untimely fruits, untimely news."

The bells at the New Year ring out the chaos of the Megalith, the disorder of the unhewn stone, but the influence of Saturn would continue to be a major factor through the Time of the Horned Piper.

Saturday, the day at the end of the week, represents the Time of the Crude Stone. By its name it honours Saturn. The days of the week are the seven steps to another cycle: a death and a birth. At the border to a new cycle, the danger is there of a step into the Underworld. With this danger, it is thought, Saturday would not be a good time for getting married. There is a saying, "Married on Saturday, death within a year."

There is a saying, said Trevelyan, "Born on Saturday, late to marry."

And it is said, "Saturday's child works hard for a living."

A sneeze on Saturday is said to foretell a coming love. Saturday is said to be a correct time for judgements, a good time for official business. It is said to be a good time for moving into a new house. Matthews said that it is thought, a good time for buying and selling and especially so, for meat and dairy products. Saturday, if a woman wove or spun, it was thought, she would walk after death, and if she had not her distaff cleared by Saturday night, her threads would never again bleach out to white.

Putnam said that in some areas travel on Saturdays was prohibited. Saturday, as the completion of a cycle, had its dangers. Saturday night ended not only a week, but also a day. Gomme said, it was thought, if a baby was born in the hour after midnight, he would be able to see ghosts.

On Card Twentyfour there is a feeling of chaos. There is disorder. A crude, standing stone, perhaps, ominous, is to the rear and right of a fire between stones. On flat rocks is a roast boar, an apple in its mouth, and fruit and nuts and around them, holly, ivy and other greens. To the right front, a pair of dice show a seven: a four and a three. On the lower left is a small juniper and below that, a snake in the darkness under stones. Near the fire would be a dark cauldron. To the rear, on the card, is a dark forest, and, to the left, in front of the forest is a pine: the pine, hung with heads and on its top, a star. Along the top of the card would be holly, and from its center would hang mistletoe. Along the bottom of the card would be ivy. At the top left on the card sits an owl; at the top right, a skull. At the bottom right is an evergreens wreath. In the darkness in front of the trees, dancing goblins and Pan with a flute. Pausanias said that Pan showed men how they could recover from the plague. Aristophanes said Pan causes men to lust. Holly and Pine are trees favoured by Pan.

The Forest would be the enchanted Forest of No Return; which, as Zimmer has said, would be equated with death.

The Snake, a symbol of death and rebirth, is associated with Proserpine, and with Gaea. Said to have a Snake form, Proserpine has been pictured holding a snake and Ingersoll said that snakes were worshipped in caverns underground. The Snake God would be Ophiuchus who, in human form, was the healer, Aesculapius. And he would be a form of the ancient Snake God, Ophion. As Ophiuchus, he healed so many that he was upsetting the balance between the Underworld and the World of the Living. As no one was dying, Hades went up from the Underworld and complained to Jupiter. Jupiter saw the problem and threw Ophiuchus away out into the dark sky. But little by little, Ophiuchus crept back until he was able to stick his tail in among the twelve groups along the path of the Sun.

Gaea is great meandering Earth. In early times, she taught the use of tokens, made of the ground, in reading the future and this, to show Apollo that she could give away what he made such a big deal of. This, from Ovidius.

Ophiuchus would be wrapped seven times around the World Egg.

Left of the rocks holding dinner is Saturn, much as Agrippa saw him, dressed in a ragged robe, holding a sickle, a slender old man with a white beard. Saturn relates to the Land of Dream. It is said, "Friday's dream on Saturday told would be likely to come true."

From a cord around Saturn's waist hangs an hour glass. Saturn is not in a hurry. His influence is toward strength and endurance. He gives a feeling of coldness. He rules time, gives wisdom through age and brings dullness. He brings intelligence, brings ignorance, brings goods. Those born under Saturn might well be melancholic, perfidious and ignorant.

The Pine is the Candle of Saturn and it flies with Hekate to the Land of the Dead. And Saturn, like Hekate, flies toward the West and cuts off things as he flies and most, he gives to the Well of the Past. Then Gaea, then Ops, deities of the Sacred Hearth, as power of the past, make changes on the present. They give birth to more than flowers, give gifts from what Saturn drops in their pits. Out of Chaos, a present will be twisted into form. And on past Charon's dock, Crow Landing, Saturn will move on: the Pine, the flying torch of Time, a Flying Star, moving ever on.

The Megalith stands tall, strangely shaped oddly textured, a couple of crows near its base. There is a suggestion of movement, of shapes taking forms relating to life. Saturn holds the potential of the return of spirit to physical form.

One might hear a spirit voice:
"I am the mask, bare to the bone,
That peeks unhewn from the standing stone.
I am the tear above the tower.
I am the wonder within the flower.
I am the blaze upon the hill.
I am the water that turns the mill.
I am the spear that roars for blood.
I am the breaker that brings the flood.
I am the hangman, I am the rope.
I am the tomb of every hope."

This suggested by Graves' translation.

Like a bolt of lightning, Chaos might take form, might show meaning, so that ever after, thought and study of the card would come on the foundation of that first flash.

Card Twentyfour is a card of darkness, of shape shifting, of binding.

Saturn stands gaunt and cadaverous. He empowers ancient tools. It is said, he is a protector of the treacherous.

Then, coming out of the forest, a sheet like a ghost with a hooded horse's skull.

And the mood of the card is the Spirit of Darkness. It wakes the demonic spirit of Onyx, which walks at night, causes terror. In the darkness is a lostness, a confusion, but in the darkness there is freedom.

Bibliography

Aborrow, Yvonne
    The Sacred Grove
    Capall Bann Publishing, 1994
Aeschylus
    Complete Plays
    Allen and Unwin, 1952
Agrippa, Cornelius
    Fourth Book of Occult Philosophy Tr. – Turner, R.
    Kessinger Publishing Co., 1992
Albertus Magnus
    Book of Secrets
    Oxford University Press, 1973
Allcroft, Arthur Hadrian
    Downland Pathways
    Houghton Mifflin Co., 1924
    The Circle and The Cross
    MacMillan and Co., 1927
Ammianus Marcellinus
    History Tr. – Rolf, J. C.
    William Heinemann Ltd., 1935
Antoninus Marcus Aurelius
    Meditations Tr. – Farquharson, A. S. L.
    Alfred A Knopf Inc., 1992
Apollodorus
    The Library Tr. – Frazer, J. G.
    William Heinemann Ltd., 1976
Apollonius Rhodius
    The Argonautika Tr. – Green, P.
    University of California Press, 1997
Apuleius Barbarus Platonicus
    Herbarium
    Longman, Green, Longman, Roberts, and Green, 1864

Apuleius Lucius
>	*Works*
>	George Bell and Sons, 1893
>	*Metamorphoses* Tr. – Hanson, J. A.
>	Harvard University Press, 1989

Aratus of Athenodorus
>	*Phaenomena* Tr. – Mair, G. R.
>	William Heinemann Ltd., 1977

Aristophanes Acharnenses
>	*Comedies*
>	Rarity Press Inc., 1931

Armstrong, Edward Allworth
>	*Folklore of The Birds*
>	Dover Publicatons, 1970

Ausonius Decimus Magnus
>	Book I and II Tr. – White, H. G. E.
>	William Heinemann Ltd, 1919

Bach, Edward
>	*Heal Thyself*
>	C. W. Daniel Company, 1931

Bach, Marcus
>	*The Unity Way of Life*
>	Unity Books, 1972

Barnes, L. K.
>	Necromicon
>	Avon Books, 1980

Bartram, Thomas
>	*Bartrams Encyclopedia of Herbal Medicine*
>	Grace Publishers, 1995

Bett, Henry
>	*English Myths and Legends*
>	Dorset Press, 1991

Beyerl, Paul
>	*A Wiccan Bardo*
>	Prism Press, 1989

Blackstone, Harry Jr
>	*There's One Born Every Minute*
>	J. P. Tarcher, 1976

Blair, Nancy
- *Amulets of The Goddess*
- Wingbow Press, 1993

Blamires, Stephen
- *The Irish Celtic Magical Tradition*
- Harper Collins Publishers, 1992

Boethius Anicius Manlius Severinus
- *Consolation of Philosophy*   Tr. – Walsh, P. G.
- Regnery Gateway, 1981

Bozwa, Jura
- *Six Lessons in Crystal Gazing*
- Alla Rageh Publishing Co., 1926

Bringsvaerd, Tor Age
- *Phantoms and Fairies*
- Johan Grundt Tanum Forlag, 1969

Buchman, Dian Dincin
- *Herbal Medicine*
- Gramercy Publishing Co., 1980

Buckland, Raymond
- *Doors to Other Worlds*
- Llewellyn Publications, 1994
- *Scottish Witchcraft*
- Llewellyn Publications, 1991

Bulfinch, Thomas
- *Age of Fable*
- J. M. Dent Co., 1908

Butler, Eliza Marian
- *The Tyranny of Greece Over Germany*
- Beacon Press, 1958
- *The Myth of The Magus*
- Cambridge University Press, 1948

Butler, William E.
- *Magic: Its Ritual Power and Purpose*
- Samuel Weiser, 1971
- *How To Read An Aura*
- Aquarian Press, 1979

Callimachus of Battus
    Fragments Tr. – Trypanis, C. A.
    William Heinemann Ltd., 1975
Callistratus
    Descriptions Tr. – Fairbanks, A.
    G. P. Putnams Sons, 1931
Campbell, Joseph
    Inner Reaches of Outer Space
    Harper and Row Publishers, 1988
    Hero With a Thousand Faces
    Princeton University Press, 1968
Case, Paul Foster
    Book of Tokens
    Builders of The Adytum, 1983
Cassiodorus Magnus Aurelius
    Institutions of Divine and Secular Learning Tr. – Mynors, R.
    Clarendon Press, 1937
Catullus Gaius Valerius
    Poetry
    Onion Press, 1967
Cavendish, Richard
    The Black Arts
    Capricorn Books, 1968
Ceram, C. W.
    Gods Graves and Scholars
    Vintage Books Random House, 1986
Chadwick, Hector Munro
    The Origin of The English Nation
    Cambridge University Press, 1907
Chambers, Robert
    Book of Days
    R. and W. Chambers, 1863
Clodd, Edward
    Tom Tit Tot
    Singing Tree Press, 1968
Coleridge, Samuel Taylor
    Complete Poetical Works
    Clarendon Press, 1912

Collingwood, R. G.
    Roman Britain
    Oxford University Press, 1923
Cooper, Gordon
    Festivals of Europe
    Percival Marshall Co., 1961
Corrigan, Ian
    Book of The Dragon
    Jefferey L. Wyndham, 1983
    Sacred Fire Holy Well
    Tredara Hearth Publishing, 2006
Cremonensis, Gerard
    Of Astronomical Geomancy
    Kessinger Publishing Co., 1992
Crow, W. B.
    Witchcraft Magic and Occultism
    Wilshire Book Co., 1979
    Precious Stones
    Samuel Weiser Co., 1968
Culpeper, Nicholas
    Complete Herbal and English Physician
    Meyerbooks, 1990
Curtius, Ernst Robert Tr. – Trask, W. R.
    European Literature in The Latin Middle Ages
    Harper and Row Publishers, 1953
Dalyell, Sir John Graham
    Musical Memories of Scotland
    Thomas G. Stevenson Co., 1849
    Darker Superstitions of Scotland
    Waugh and Innes, 1834
Davies, Edward
    Mythology and Rites of The British Druids
    Booth, 1809
Davies, Marion
    The Magical Lore of Herbs
    Capall Bann Publishing, 1994

Decker, R. and Depaulis, T. and Demmett, M.
> *A Wicked Pack of Cards*
> St. Martins Press, 1996

Diodorus Siculus
> *The First Century*
> William Heinemann Ltd., 1933

Dionysius of Halicarnassus
> *The Roman Antiquities Vol. 1* Tr. – Spelman, T.
> Booksellers of London and Westminster, 1758

Dioscorides Pedanius
> *Greek Herbal* Tr. – Goodyer, J.
> Hafner Publishing Co., 1959

Dodonaeus, Rembert
> *A New Herbal* Tr. – Lyte, H.
> E. Griffin, 1619

Durdin Robertson, Lawrence Lord Ruadh
> *Juno Covella*
> Cesara Publications, 1982

Eiseley, Loren
> *The Invisible Pyramid*
> Charles Scribners Sons, 1970
> *The Star Thrower*
> Charles Scribners Sons, 1971
> *The Immense Journey*
> Random House, 1957
> *Notes of an Alchemist*
> Charles Scribners Sons, 1972

Eisner, Robert
> *The Road to Daulis*
> Syracuse University Press, 1987

Ellis, Hilda R.
> *The Road To Hel*
> Cambridge University Press, 1943

Davidson, H. R. Ellis
> *Myths and Symbols of Ancient Europe*
> Syracuse University Press, 1988

Epictetus
    Works   Tr. – Higginson, T. W.
    Little Brown and Company, 1890
Eugenius Philalethes
    Magical Writings
    George Redway Co., 1888
Euripides
    Iphigenia In Tauris   Tr. – Murray, G.
    George Allen and Unwin, 1910
    Bacchae
    Oxford University Press, 1944
Evans Wentz, W. Y.
    Fairy Faith in Celtic Countries
    Henry Frowde, 1911
Fairbanks, Sir Arthur
    Mythology of Greece and Rome
    D. Appleton and Co., 1907
Ferguson, Diana
    The Magical Year
    B. T. Batsford, 1996
Fernie, William Thomas
    Herbal Simples
    Boericke and Tafel, 1897
    Meals Medicinal
    John Wright and Co., 1905
    Occult and Curative Powers of Precious Stones
    Harper and Row Publishers, 1973
Figulus, Benedictus
    A Golden and Blessed Casket
    Kessinger Publishing Co., 1992
Firmicus Maternus Julius
    The Error of The Pagan Religions
    Newman Press, 1970
Fiske, John
    Myths and Myth Makers
    James A Osgood Co., 1873

Flanagan, G. P.
>   *Beyond Pyramid Power*
>   Devorss and Company, 1976

Flowers, Stephen Edred
>   *Fire and Ice*
>   Llewellyn Publications, 1990

Thorsson, E.
>   *Northern Magic*
>   Llewellyn Publications, 1998

Fox, Frances Margaret
>   *Flowers and Their Travels*
>   Bobbs Merrill Company, 1936

Frazer, Sir James George
>   *The Golden Bough*
>   Macmillan Company, 1950

Frobenius, Leo
>   *Prehistoric Rock Pictures of Europe and Africa*
>   Museum of Modern Art, 1937
>   *The Childhood of Man*
>   J. B. Lippincott Co., 1909

Galienus of Pergamum
>   *On Antecedent Causes*   Tr. – Hankinson, R J
>   Cambridge University Press, 1998

Gaufridus Arturus
>   *History of The Kings of Britain*
>   J. M. Dent and Sons, 1912

Gennep, Arnold Van
>   *Rites of Passage*   Tr. – Vizedom, M. B.
>   Phoenix Books, 1961

Gerard, John
>   *Gerards Herball*
>   Houghton Mifflin Co., 1928

Giraldus Cambrensis
>   *Itinerary Through Wales*   Tr. – Hoare, R. C.
>   J. M. Dent And Sons, 1909

Givry, Grillot de
>   *Witchcraft Magic and Alchemy*   Tr. – Lucke, J. C.
>   Dover Publications, 1971

Gladstar, Rosemary
    Herbal Healing For Women
    Simon and Schuster, 1993

Gomme, George Laurence
    Folklore Relics of Early Village Life
    Elliot Stock Co., 1883
    Ethnology of Folklore
    D. Appleton and Company, 1892

Graves, Robert
    The White Goddess
    Noonday Press, 1966
    Greek Myths
    George Braziller Inc., 1959

Gray, William Gordon
    By Standing Stone and Elder Tree
    Llewellyn Publications, 1990

Grieve, Maude
    A Modern Herbal – Vol. I and II
    Harcourt Brace and Company, 1931

Grimm, Jacob
    Teutonic Mythology
    James S. Stallybrass Co., 1882

Gubernatis, Angelo De
    Zoological Mythology
    Singing Tree Press, 1968

Halliday, W. R.
    Greek Divination
    Argonaut Publishers, 1967
    Greek and Roman Folklore
    Longmans Green and Co., 1927
    Lectures on The History of Roman Religion
    University Press of Liverpool Ltd., 1922

Harrison, Michael
    The Roots of Witchcraft
    Frederick Muller, 1973
    The Story of Christmas
    Odhams Press Ltd, 1952

Hartmann, Franz
> *Alchemy*
> Sure Fire Press, 1984

Hawthorne, Nathaniel
> *A Wonderbook For Girls and Boys*
> Houghton Mifflin Co., 1879
> *Septimius Felton*
> James A. Osgood Co., 1872

Herodotus Halicarnassus
> *Histories*
> Heritage Press, 1958

Heselton, Philip
> *Secret Places of The Goddess*
> Capall Bann Publishing, 1995

Highet, Gilbert
> *Poets In A Landscape*
> Alfred A. Knopf Inc., 1957

Hislop, Alexander
> *Two Babylons*
> Loizeaux Brothers, 1959

Hocart, A M
> *The Life Giving Myth*
> Methuen and Company, 1952
> *The Progress of Man*
> Methuen and Company, 1933

Hodson, Geoffrey
> *Fairies at Work and Play*
> Theosophical Publishing House Ltd., 1925

Hole, Christina
> *British Folk Customs*
> Hutchinson and Co., 1976
> *Christmas and Its Customs*
> M. Barrows and Co., 1958
> *Haunted England*
> B. T. Batsford Ltd., 1941

Holzer, Hans
> *The Alchemist*
> Stein and Day, 1974

  Patterns of Destiny
  Nash Publishing, 1974
Horatious Flaccus Quintas
  Complete Odes and Epodes
  Penguin Books, 1983
Howard, Michael
  The Sacred Ring
  Capall Bann Publishing, 1995
Hulme, T. E.
  Speculations
  Routledge and Kegan Paul Ltd., 1936
Huxley, Aldous
  Do What You Will
  Doubleday Doran and Company Inc., 1929
  Heaven and Hell
  Harper and Brothers, 1956
Hyginus
  The Myths Tr. – Grant, M. A.
  University of Kansas Press, 1960
Iamblichos
  Theurgia
  Metaphysical Publishing Co., 1911
Ickis, Marguerite
  Book of Festival Holidays
  Dodd Mead and Company, 1964
Ingersoll, Ernest
  Dragons and Dragon Lore
  Payson and Clarke Ltd., 1928
Isidorus Hispalensis
  Medical Writings Tr. – Sharpe, W. D.
  American Philosophical Society, 1964
Jackson, Nigel Aldcroft
  The Call of The Horned Piper
  Capall Bann Publishing, 1994
  Masks of Misrule
  Capall Bann Publishing, 1996

James, Edwin Oliver
> *Seasonal Feasts and Festivals*
> Barnes and Noble, 1963
> *From Cave to Cathedral*
> Frederick A. Praeger, 1965

Jung, Carl Gustav
> *Psychology of Transference*   Tr. – Hull, R. F. C.
> Princeton University Press, 1969
> *Psychology and Alchemy*
> Princeton University Press, 1968

Junius, Manfred M.
> *Practical Handbook of Plant Alchemy*
> Inner Traditions International, 1985

Keightley, Thomas
> *The Fairy Mythology*
> H. G. Bohn Ltd., 1850

Kepler, Hohannes
> *Somnium*
> Faber and Faber Ltd., 1942

Kightly, Charles
> *Customs and Ceremonies of Britain*
> Thames and Hudson Ltd., 1986

Kittredge, George Lyman
> *Witchcraft in Old and New England*
> Russell and Russell Ltd., 1958

Kloss, Jethro
> *Back To Eden*
> Lotus Press, 1946

Kunz, George Frederick
> *Mystical Lore of Precious Stones Vol. I and II*
> Newcastle Publishing Co., 1986

Lactantius Firmianus
> *Divine Institutes*   Tr. – Mcdonald, M. F.
> Catholic University of America Press, 1964

Layamon
> *The Brut*
> F Madden Co., 1847

Leadbeater, Charles
>	*Man, Visible and Invisible*
>	Theosophical Publishing House Ltd., 1971

Ledwidge, Francis
>	*Songs of The Fields*
>	Duffield and Company, 1916

Lee, David
>	*Chaotopia*
>	Attractor, 1997

Leland, Charles Godfrey
>	*Aradia*
>	Phoenix Publishing, 1990
>	*The Mystic Will*
>	Yogi Publication Society, 1907

Lethbridge, T. C.
>	*Witches*
>	Citadel Press, 1962
>	*Painted Men*
>	Philosophical Library, 1954

Leyel, Hilda
>	*The Magic of Herbs*
>	Harcourt Brace and Company, 1926

Libanius
>	*Selected Works*
>	William Heinemann Ltd, 1987
>	*Autobiography and Selected Letters*
>	Harvard University Press, 1992

Lindholm, Lars
>	*Pilgrims of The Night*
>	Llewellyn Publishing, 1993

Linnaeus, Carolus
>	*Travels*
>	Charles Scribners Sons, 1979

Livius Titus
>	*History of Rome Vol III*
>	T. Cadell and Davies on The Strand Ltd., 1814

Loomis, Roger Sherman
    The Grail
    Princeton University Press, 1991

Lucanus Marcus Annaeus
    Pharsalia   Tr. – Graves, R.
    Penguin Books, 1957
    Belli Civilis
    Harvard University Press, 1926

Lucas, Edward Verrall
    Travellers Luck
    J. B. Lippincott Co., 1931
    Phanton Journal
    Methuen and Company, 1919

Lucas, Richard Melvin
    Miracle Medicine Herbs
    Reward, 1991
    Nature's Medicines
    Parker Publishing Co., 1966

Lucretius Carus Titus
    De Rerum Natura   Tr. – Munro, H. A. J.
    Deighton Bell and Co., 1886

Lyndoe, Edward
    Astrology For Everyone
    E. P. Dutton and Company, 1970

Macaulay, Thomas Babington
    The Lays of Ancient Rome
    D. C. Heath and Company, 1910

Maccana, Proinsias
    Celtic Mythology
    Hamlyn House, 1970

Macmanus, Seumas
    The Story of The Irish Race
    Devin Adair Co, 1944

Macrobius Ambrosius Aurelius
    Saturnalia   Tr. – Davies, P.
    Columbia University Press, 1969

Magnusson, Magnus
    The Hammer of The North
    G. P. Putnams Sons, 1976

Maltwood, Katharine
    Enchantments of Britain
    Attic Press, 1982

Manas, John H.
    Divination Ancient and Modern
    Pathagorean Society, 1947

Manilius Marcus
    Astronomica   Tr. – Goold, G. P.
    William Heinemann Ltd., 1977

Maple, Eric
    The Dark World of Witches
    Robert Hale, 1962
    The Ancient Art of Healing
    Samuel Weiser Inc., 1974

Martianus Minneius Capella
    De Nuptiis Philologiae Et Mercurii   Tr. – Willis, J.
    Bodlein Library, 1983

Matthews, John
    The Celtic Shaman
    Element Books Ltd., 1991

Meyer, Joseph
    The Herbalist
    Meyerbooks, 1918

Meyer, Robert
    Festivals of Europe
    Ives Washburn Co., 1954

Minucius Felix
    Octavius   Tr. – Rendall, G. H.
    William Heinemann Ltd., 1966

Monaghan, Patricia
    O Mother Sun
    The Crossing Press, 1994
    The Book of Goddesses and Heroines
    Llewellyn Publications, 1993

Murray, Margaret
>   *The Witch Cult in Western Europe*
>   Clarendon Press, 1921
>   *The God of The Witches*
>   Oxford University Press, 1952

Musaeus Grammaticus
>   *Hero And Leander*   Tr. – Whitman, C.
>   William Heinemann Ltd., 1975

Nagy, Gregory
>   *The Best of The Achaeans*
>   Johns Hopkins University Press, 1979
>   *Greek Mythology and Poetics*
>   Cornell University Press, 1990

Nennius
>   *History of The Britons*
>   J. M. Dent and Sons, 1912

Nettleship, Henry
>   *The Ancient Lives of Vergil*
>   Macmillan and Co., 1879

Nevius, John Livingstone
>   *Demons, Possession, and Allied Themes*
>   Kregel Publications, 1968

Nomolos, Yaj
>   *The Witches Broomstick Manual*
>   Cosmic Vision Press, 1983

Nutt, Alfred
>   *The Happy Otherworld*
>   David Nutt In The Strand, 1895

Ogilvie, Robert
>   *The Romans and Their Gods*
>   W. W. Norton and Company, 1969

Opsopaus, John
>   *Pathagorean Tarot*
>   Llewellyn Publications, 2001

Ordericus Vitalis
>   *Ecclesiastical History of England and Normandy*
>   Henry G. Bohn Ltd., 1853

Ottewell, Guy
    Astronomical Companion
    Furman University, 1981
Ouseley, S. G. J.
    Colour Meditations
    L. N. Fowler and Company Ltd., 1949
Ovidius Naso Publius
    Metamorphoses   Tr. – Miller, F. J.
    G. P. Putnams Sons, 1929
Paracelsus Theophrasius Bombasius
    Selected Writings
    Princeton University Press, 1951
Pater, Walter
    Marius The Epicurian
    Boni and Liveright, 1918
Pausanias Magnesia
    Description of Greece, Books I - VI
    George Bell and Sons, 1886
Pennick, Nigel
    Pagan Book of Days
    Inner Traditions International, 1992
Petronius Gaius
    The Satyricon   Tr. – Firebaugh, W. C.
    Liveright Publishing Co., 1943
Philostratus Nervianus
    Life of Apollonius of Tyana   Tr. – Conybeare, F.
    G. P. Putnams Sons, 1931
Philostratus The Younger
    Imagines   Tr. – Fairbanks, A.
    G. P. Putnams Sons, 1931
Pitman, Vicki
    Berbal Medicine
    Element Books Ltd., 1994
Placitus Sextus
    Medicina De Quadropedibus
    Longman, Green, Longman, Roberts, and Green, 1864

Plinius Secundus Gaius
> *Natural History Vol I – III*
> William Heinemann, Ltd, 1942

Plotinus
> *Enneads*   Tr. – Mackenna, S.
> Faber And Faber, 1962

Polybius
> *History*   Tr. – Shuckburgh, E. S.
> Macmillan and Company, 1889

Porteous Alexander
> *Forest Folklore Mythology and Romance*
> Macmillan and Company, 1928

Plinius Secundus Gaius
> *Natural History Vol. 1, II, III*
> William Heinemann Ltd., 1942

Plotinus
> *Enneads*   Tr. – Mackenna, S.
> Faber and Faber, 1962

Polybius
> *History*   Tr. – Shuckburgh, E. S.
> Macmillan and Company, 1889

Porteous Alexander
> *Forest Folklore Mythology and Romance*
> Macmillan and Company, 1928

Procopius Caesarea
> *The Secret History*
> Cox and Wyman, 1966

Propertius Sextus Aurelius
> *Poems*
> Bobbs Merrill Co., 1972

Putnam, Michael
> *Tibullus: A Commentary*
> University of Oklahoma Press, 1973

Rago, Linda Ours
> *Herbal Almanac*
> Fulcrum, 1984

  Mugworts In May
  Quarrier Press, 1995
Reckford, Kenneth
  Horace
  Twayne Publishers Inc., 1969
Remigius Autissiodorensis
  Commentium In Martianum Capellam
  E. J. Brill, 1962
Remigius Nicholas II
  Daemonolatria
  John Rodker Co., 1930
Renterghem, Tony Van
  When Santa Was a Shaman
  Llewellyn Publications, 1995
Rhys, Sir John
  Celtic Britain
  E. and J. B. Young and Company, 1884
  Lectures on The Origin and Growth of Religion
  Williams and Norgate, 1888
Ridgeway, Sir William
  The Early Age of Greece
  Cambridge University Press, 1901
Robbins, Rossell
  Encyclopedia of Witchcraft and Demonology
  Crown Publishers, 1959
Rose, Jeanne
  Herbs and Things
  G. P. Putnam, 1972
  Herbal Guide to Inner Health
  Grosset and Dunlap, 1979
Rudhyar, Dane
  The Lunation Cycle
  Shambhala, 1971
Rulandus Martinus
  A Lexicon of Alchemy   Tr. – Waite, A. E.
  John M. Watkins, 1964

Rutherford, Ward
    Celtic Mythology
    Harper Collins Publishers, 1995
    The Druids and Their Heritage
    Gordon and Cremonesi, 1978

Seymour, Thomas
    Life In The Homeric Age
    Bilbo and Tannew, 1963

Shakespeare, William
    Complete Plays
    Methuen and Company, 1982

Simms, Maria Kay
    Circle of The Cosmic Muse
    Llewellyn Publicatons, 1994

Simplicius of Cilicia
    Corollaries on Place and Time   Tr. – Urmson, J. O.
    Cornell University Press, 1992

Sitwell, Sacheverell
    The Gothic North
    Houghton Mifflin Co., 1929
    Monks, Nuns, and Monasteries
    Holt, Rinehart, and Winston, 1965

Skelton, Robin
    Spell Craft
    Phoenix Publishing, 1978

Skene, William F.
    The Four Ancient Books of Wales
    Edmonston and Douglas, 1868
    Celtic Scotland
    Edmonston and Douglas, 1876

Skinner, Charles
    Myths and Legends of Flowers, Trees, and Plants
    J. B. Lippincott Co., 1911

Snell, Bruno
    Poetry and Society
    Indiana University Press, 1961

    The Discovery of The Mind
    Harvard University Press, 1953
Spence, Lewis
    History and Origins of Druidism
    Samuel Weiser Inc., 1971
    Mysteries of Britain
    Samuel Weiser Inc., 1970
    Magic Arts In Celtic Britain
    Aquarian Press, 1970
Spicer, Dorothy
    Festivals of Western Europe
    Woman's Press, 1937
    Thirteen Goblins
    Coward Mccann, 1969
Stacy, Barbara
    Ancient Roman Holidays
    Witches Almanac, 1998
Steiner, Rudolf
    Occult Signs and Symbols   Tr. – Kurland, S.
    Anthroposophic Press, 1972
Suetonius Tranquilius Caius
    Lives of Illustrious Men
    William Heinemann Ltd., 1914
Summers, Montague
    The History of Witchcraft and Demonology
    Castle Books, 1992
Tacitus Cornelius
    Historiarum
    William Heinemann Ltd., 1937
    Germania
    Eldredge Co., 1885
Talbot, Thomas
    Greece and The Greeks
    Sampson, Low, Marston, Searle, and Rivington, 1881
Tertullianus Quintus Septimius
    Apology   Tr. – Glover, T. R.
    William Heinemann Ltd., 1966

Theocritus of Syracuse
    Idylliums   Tr. – Fawkes, F.
    Drydon Leach, 1767
Theophrastus of Lesbos
    Enquiry Into Plants   Tr. – Hort, Sir A.
    William Heinemann Ltd., 1916
Tibullus Albius
    Elegies
    American Book Co., 1913
Trent, Christopher
    Festivals and Events In Britain
    Phoenix House, 1966
Trevelyan, Marie
    Folk Lore and Folk Stories of Wales
    Elliot Stock Co., 1909
Ure, Peter
    Toward A Mythology
    Greenwood Press, 1986
Ussher, Arland
    Journey Through Dread
    Devin Adair Co., 1955
    Twentytwo Keys of The Tarot
    Dolmen Press, 1970
Valentinus Basilius
    Triumphal Chariot of Antimony
    Vincent Stuart Ltd., 1962
Valerius Flaccus Gaius
    Argonauticon
    William Heinemann Ltd., 1934
Vergilius Maro Publius
    Ecologues
    Penguin Books, 1980
    Aeneid   Tr. – Beresford, J.
    J. Johnson, 1794
Villinganus Georg Pictorius
    Isagoge
    Kessinger Publishing, 1992

Vitruvius Marcus Pollio
    Architecture
    Lockwood and Co., 1874
Waite, Arthur Edward
    Pictorial Key to The Tarot
    U. S. Games Systems, 1982
    The Holy Grail
    University Books, 1961
Wallace, C. H.
    Witchcraft in The World Today
    Award Books, 1967
Wendell, Leilah
    Necromantic Ritual Book
    Westgate Press, 1991
Westropp, Hodder
    Primitive Symbolism as Illustrated in Phallic Worship
    George Redway Co., 1885
Whewell, William
    Astronomy and General Physics
    Carey, Lea, and Blanchard, 1833
    History of Inductive Sciences
    John W. Parker and Son, 1857
Windle, Bertram
    Life In Early Britain
    D. Nutt Co., 1897
Worthen, T. D.
    The Myth of Replacement
    University of Arizona Press, 1991
Wright, Elbee
    Book of Legendary Spells
    Marlar Publishing, 1974
Yarrell, William
    The History of British Fishes
    John Van Voorst, 1859
Young, Andrew
    A Prospect of Flowers
    Viking Penguin Inc., 1985

Zacharias, Gerhard P.
>   *The Satanic Cult*
>   Allen and Unwin, 1980

Zimmer, Heinrich
>   *The King and The Corpse*
>   Princeton University Press, 1971

>> Thank you Lloyd Library and Museum
>> for permitting me to read books in
>> the museum's collection.
>>
>> – Owen

www.ingramcontent.com/pod-product-compliance
Lightning Source LLC
Chambersburg PA
CBHW032122160426
43197CB00008B/483